Java 8 in Action

Java 8 in Action

Lambdas, streams, and functional-style programming

RAOUL-GABRIEL URMA
MARIO FUSCO
ALAN MYCROFT

MANNING

Published by:

dreamtech PRESS

This edition has been published by arrangement with the **Manning Publications Co., USA.** and published in India by **Dreamtech Press, 19-A, Ansari Road, Daryaganj, New Delhi-110002.**

ISBN: 978-93-5119-743-0

Reprint: 2025

Printed at: Nisha Enterprises

To our parents

brief contents

contents

preface

Back in 1998 when I was eight years old, I picked up my first book on computing—on JavaScript and HTML. Little did I know that opening that book would transform my life by exposing me to programming languages and the amazing things I could do with them. I was hooked. Every so often I still find a new programming language feature that revives this excitement because it enables me to write clearer, more concise code in half the time. I hope that the new ideas in Java 8, incorporated from functional programming and explored in this book, inspire you in the same way.

So, you may wonder, how did this book come about?

Well, back in 2011, Brian Goetz (the Java Language Architect at Oracle) was sharing various proposals to add lambda expressions to Java, with the aim of getting the community involved. These rekindled my excitement, and I started to evangelize the ideas, organizing Java 8 workshops at various developer conferences and giving lectures to students at the University of Cambridge.

By April 2013, word had spread, and our publisher at Manning emailed asking whether I was interested in writing a book about lambdas in Java 8. At the time I was a "humble" second-year PhD candidate, and that seemed to be a bad idea because it would interfere with my thesis submission schedule. On the other hand, *carpe diem*; I thought writing a short book shouldn't be too much work, right? (It was only later that I realized I was utterly wrong!) So I sought advice from my PhD supervisor, Professor Alan Mycroft, who, it turned out, was ready to support me in this adventure (even offering to help in such non-PhD work—I'm forever in his debt). A few days later we met fellow Java 8 evangelist Mario Fusco, who had vast professional experience and had become well known for his talks on functional programming at major developer conferences.

We quickly realized that by combining our energy and diverse backgrounds we could deliver, not just a short book on Java 8 lambdas, but instead a book that, we hope, the Java community will still be reading in five or ten years. We had a unique opportunity to discuss in depth many topics that will benefit Java programmers and open doors to a new universe of ideas: functional programming.

Now—July 2014, 15 months later, after many long nights, endless edits, and an unforgettable experience—you have our work in your hands and we hope you will enjoy it!

RAOUL-GABRIEL URMA
UNIVERSITY OF CAMBRIDGE

acknowledgments

This book would not have been possible without the support of many amazing people:

- Personal friends and people who provided valuable reviews and suggestions on a volunteer basis: Richard Walker, Jan Saganowski, Brian Goetz, Stuart Marks, Cem Redif, Paul Sandoz, Stephen Colebourne, Íñigo Mediavilla, Allahbaksh Asadullah, Tomasz Nurkiewicz, and Michael Müller
- Our Manning Early Access Program (MEAP) readers who posted comments in the Author Online forum
- The reviewers from the development process who provided helpful feedback: Antonio Magnaghi, Brent Stains, Franziska Meyer, Furkan Kamachi, Jason Lee, Jörn Dinkla, Lochana Menikarachchi, Mayur Patil, Nikolaos Kaintantzis, Simone Bordet, Steve Rogers, Will Hayworth, and William Wheeler
- Susan Conant, our development editor at Manning, who was very patient in answering all our questions and concerns, provided detailed feedback for each of our draft chapters, and supported us in all possible ways
- Ivan Todorović and Jean-François Morin, who provided a thorough technical proofread of the manuscript shortly before it went to production; and Al Scherer, who provided technical expertise during development

RAOUL-GABRIEL URMA

First and foremost, I'd like to thank my parents for their endless love and support in my life. This little dream of writing a book has now come true! Next, I would like to express my eternal gratitude to Alan Mycroft, my PhD supervisor and coauthor, for his trust and support. I'd also like to thank my coauthor Mario Fusco for sharing this fun journey. Finally, I'd like to thank friends who have provided mentorship, useful advice, and encouragement in my life: Sophia Drossopoulou, Aidan Roche, Warris Bokhari, Alex Buckley, Martijn Verburg, Tomas Petricek, and Tian Zhao. You guys rock!

MARIO FUSCO
I'd like to especially thank my wife, Marilena, whose boundless patience allowed me to stay focused on the book, and our daughter, Sofia, because the infinite chaos she can produce allowed me to get creatively distracted from the book. As you'll discover reading the book, Sofia also taught us, like only a two-year-old baby girl can, the difference between internal and external iteration. I'd like to also thank Raoul-Gabriel Urma and Alan Mycroft, with whom I shared the (big) joys and the (small) pains of this writing experience.

ALAN MYCROFT
I'd like to thank my wife, Hilary, and the rest of my family for enduring the many hours that "just a bit more work to do on the book" consumed. I also thank my colleagues and students over the years for teaching me how to teach, Mario and Raoul for being such efficient coauthors, and particularly Raoul for his skill at being so pleasantly demanding when requiring "the next bit of text by Friday."

about this book

Put simply, the new features in Java 8 are the biggest change to Java in the 18 years since Java 1.0 was released. Nothing has been taken away, so all your existing Java code continues to work—but the new features provide powerful new idioms and design patterns to help you write clearer, more concise code. At first you might think (as with all new features), "Why are they changing my language again?" But then, after a bit of practice, comes the revelation that you've just used the features to write shorter, clearer code in half the time you expected—and you realize you could never go back to "old Java" again.

This book, *Java 8 in Action: Lambdas, streams, and functional-style programming*, is written to get you over that initial hump of "sounds good in principle, but it's all a bit new and unfamiliar" and into coding like a native.

"Perhaps," you might think, "but lambdas, functional programming—aren't those the sort of things that bearded sandal-wearing academics talk about in their ivory towers?" They might, but Java 8 has incorporated just the right balance of ideas into Java to gain many of their advantages in a way that's comprehensible to ordinary Java programmers. And this book tells the story from the ordinary-programmer viewpoint, with an occasional "how this arose" for perspective.

"Lambdas—that sounds Greek to me!" Yes, it might, but it's a great idea for enabling you to write concise Java programs. Many of you are familiar with event handlers and callbacks, where you register an object containing a method to be used when some event happens. Lambdas make this sort of idea much more widely usable in Java. Put simply, lambdas, and their friends, method references, provide the ability to concisely pass code or methods as arguments to be executed in the middle of doing something else. You'll see in this book how this idea occurs more frequently than you might think: from simply parameterizing a sort method with code to do the comparison to expressing complex queries on collections of data using the new Streams API.

"Streams—what are they?" They're a great new Java 8 addition. They behave like collections but have several advantages that enable new styles of programming. First, if you've ever programmed using a database query language such as SQL, you'll recognize that it enables queries to be written in a few lines that would take many lines in Java. Java 8 streams support this concise database-queries style of programming—but with Java syntax and none of the need to know about databases! Second, streams are designed so that not all their data needs to be in memory (or even computed) at once. Thus you can process streams that are too big to fit in your computer memory. But Java 8 can optimize operations on streams in a way that Java can't do for collections—for example, it can group together several operations on the same stream, so that the data is traversed only once instead of expensively traversing it multiple times. Even better, Java can automatically parallelize stream operations for you (unlike collections).

"And functional-style programming, what's that?" It's another style of programming, just like object-oriented programming, but centered on using functions as values, just as we mentioned previously when discussing lambdas.

What's great about Java 8 is that it incorporates many of the best ideas from functional programming into the familiar Java syntax. The fine design choices enable you to see functional-style programming in Java 8 as an additional set of design patterns and idioms to enable you to write clearer, more concise code in less time. Think of it as having a wider range of weapons in your programming armory.

Oh yes, in addition to these features that lean on big conceptual additions to Java, we also explain the many other useful Java 8 features and updates such as default methods, the new `Optional` class, `CompletableFuture`, and the new Date and Time API.

But hey, this is an overview, and it's time now for us to leave you to read the book.

Roadmap

Java 8 in Action is divided into four parts: "Fundamentals," "Functional-style data processing," "Effective Java 8 programming," and "Beyond Java 8." We strongly recommend that you read the chapters in order because many of the concepts presented build on previous chapters. Most chapters include several quizzes to help you work through the material.

The first part of the book contains three chapters that aim to get you started with Java 8. By the end of this first part you'll have a full understanding of what lambda expressions are, and you'll be able to write code that's both concise and flexible enough to easily adapt to changing requirements:

- In chapter 1, we summarize the main changes to Java (lambda expressions, method references, streams, and default methods) and set the scene for the book.
- In chapter 2, you'll learn about behavior parameterization, a software development pattern that Java 8 heavily relies on and is the motivation for lambda expressions.

- Chapter 3 gives a full explanation, with code examples and quizzes at every step, of the concepts of lambda expressions and method references.

The second part takes a close look at the new Streams API. By the end of it you'll have a full understanding of what streams are and how you can use them in your Java applications to process a collection of data concisely and efficiently:

- Chapter 4 introduces the concept of streams and explains how they compare with collections.
- Chapter 5 investigates in detail the stream operations available to express sophisticated data processing queries. We'll look at many patterns such as filtering, slicing, finding, matching, mapping, and reducing.
- Chapter 6 covers collectors—a feature of the Streams API that lets you express even more complex data processing queries.
- In chapter 7, you'll learn about how streams can automatically run in parallel and leverage your multicore architectures. In addition, you'll learn about various pitfalls to avoid in order to use parallel streams correctly and effectively.

The third part of this book explores various Java 8 topics that will make you more effective at using Java 8 and enhance your codebase with modern idioms:

- Chapter 8 explores how you can improve your existing code using new Java 8 features and a few recipes. In addition, it explores vital software development techniques such as design patterns, refactoring, testing, and debugging.
- In chapter 9, you'll learn what default methods are, how you can evolve APIs in a compatible way using them, some practical usage patterns, and rules for using default methods effectively.
- Chapter 10 covers the new `java.util.Optional` class, which allows you to both design better APIs and reduce `null` pointer exceptions.
- Chapter 11 explores `CompletableFuture`, which lets you express complex asynchronous computations in a declarative way—paralleling the design of the Streams API.
- Chapter 12 explores the new Date and Time API, which greatly improves on the previous error-prone APIs for working with dates and time.

In the final part of this book, we draw back a little with a tutorial introduction to writing effective functional-style programs in Java, and we offer a comparison of Java 8 features with those of Scala:

- Chapter 13 gives a full tutorial to functional programming, introduces some of its terminology, and explains how to write functional-style programs in Java 8.
- Chapter 14 covers more-advanced functional programming techniques including higher-order functions, currying, persistent data structures, lazy lists, and pattern matching. You can view this chapter as a mix of practical techniques to apply in your codebase as well as academic information that will make you a more knowledgeable programmer.

- Chapter 15 follows by discussing how Java 8 features compare to features in the Scala language—a language that, like Java, is implemented on top of the JVM and that has evolved quickly to threaten some aspects of Java's niche in the programming language ecosystem.
- In chapter 16, we review the journey of learning about Java 8 and the gentle push toward functional-style programming. In addition, we speculate on what future enhancements and great new features may be in Java's pipeline beyond Java 8.

Finally, there are four appendixes, which cover a number of other topics related to Java 8. Appendix A summarizes other minor Java 8 language features that we didn't discuss in the book. Appendix B gives an overview of other main additions to the Java library that you may find useful. Appendix C is a continuation of part 2 and looks at advanced uses of streams. Appendix D explores how the Java compiler implements lambda expressions behind the scenes.

Code conventions and downloads

All source code in listings or in text is in a `fixed-width font like this` to separate it from ordinary text. Code annotations accompany many of the listings, highlighting important concepts.

Source code for all the working examples in the book and instructions to run them are available at https://github.com/java8/Java8InAction. You will also find a zip file with all of the examples in the book available for download from the publisher's website at www.manning.com/Java8inAction.

Author Online

Purchase of *Java 8 in Action* includes free access to a private web forum run by Manning Publications where you can make comments about the book, ask technical questions, and receive help from the authors and other users. To access the Author Online forum and subscribe to it, point your web browser to www.manning.com/Java8inAction. This page provides information on how to get on the forum once you're registered, what kind of help is available, and the rules of conduct on the forum.

Manning's commitment to our readers is to provide a venue where a meaningful dialog among individual readers and between readers and the authors can take place. It's not a commitment to any specific amount of participation on the part of the authors, whose contribution to the forum remains voluntary (and unpaid). We suggest you try asking the authors some challenging questions, lest their interest stray!

The Author Online forum and the archives of previous discussions will be accessible from the publisher's website as long as the book is in print.

about the authors

RAOUL-GABRIEL URMA is a PhD candidate in Computer Science at the University of Cambridge. He holds a MEng degree in Computer Science from Imperial College London and graduated with first-class honors, having won several prizes for technical innovation. He has collaborated with large companies such as Google, eBay, Oracle, and Goldman Sachs, as well as worked on several startup projects. In addition, Raoul has authored over 10 peer-reviewed technical articles and given over 20 talks at international developer conferences.

MARIO FUSCO is a senior software engineer at Red Hat working on the core development of Drools, the JBoss rule engine. He has vast experience as a Java developer, having been involved in (and often leading) many enterprise-level projects in several industries ranging from media companies to the financial sector. Among his interests are functional programming and domain-specific languages. By leveraging these two passions he created the open source library lambdaj with the goal of providing an internal Java DSL for manipulating collections and allowing a bit of functional programming in Java.

ALAN MYCROFT is Professor of Computing in the Computer Laboratory of Cambridge University, where he has been a faculty member since 1984. He's also a fellow at Robinson College, a cofounder of the European Association for Programming Languages and Systems, and a cofounder and trustee of the Raspberry Pi Foundation. He has degrees in Mathematics (Cambridge) and Computer Science (Edinburgh). He's the author of around 100 research papers and has supervised more than 20 PhD theses. His research centers on programming languages and their semantics, optimization, and implementation. He maintains strong industrial links, having worked at AT&T Laboratories and Intel Research during academic leave, as well as spinning out Codemist Ltd., which built the original ARM C compiler under the Norcroft name.

about the cover illustration

The figure on the cover of *Java 8 in Action* is captioned "Habit of a Mandarin of War in Chinese Tartary in 1700." The Mandarin's habit is ornately decorated and he is carrying a sword and a bow and quiver on his back. And if you look carefully at his belt, you will find a lambda buckle (added by our designer as a wink at one of the topics of this book). The illustration is taken from Thomas Jefferys' *A Collection of the Dresses of Different Nations, Ancient and Modern*, London, published between 1757 and 1772. The title page states that these are hand-colored copperplate engravings, heightened with gum arabic. Thomas Jefferys (1719–1771) was called "Geographer to King George III." He was an English cartographer who was the leading map supplier of his day. He engraved and printed maps for government and other official bodies and produced a wide range of commercial maps and atlases, especially of North America. His work as a map maker sparked an interest in local dress customs of the lands he surveyed and mapped; they are brilliantly displayed in this four-volume collection.

Fascination with faraway lands and travel for pleasure were relatively new phenomena in the eighteenth century, and collections such as this one were popular, introducing both the tourist as well as the armchair traveler to the inhabitants of other countries. The diversity of the drawings in Jefferys' volumes speaks vividly of the uniqueness and individuality of the world's nations centuries ago. Dress codes have changed, and the diversity by region and country, so rich at one time, has faded away. It is now often hard to tell the inhabitant of one continent from another. Perhaps, trying to view it optimistically, we have traded a cultural and visual diversity for a more varied personal life—or a more varied and interesting intellectual and technical life.

At a time when it is hard to tell one computer book from another, Manning celebrates the inventiveness and initiative of the computer business with book covers based on the rich diversity of national costumes three centuries ago, brought back to life by Jefferys' pictures.

Part 1

Fundamentals

This first part of the book provides the fundamentals to help you get started with Java 8. By the end of this first part, you'll have a full understanding of what lambda expressions are, and you'll be able to write code that's both concise and flexible enough to easily adapt to changing requirements.

In chapter 1, we summarize the main changes to Java (lambda expressions, method references, streams, and default methods) and set the scene for the book.

In chapter 2, you'll learn about behavior parameterization, a software development pattern that Java 8 relies heavily on and is the motivation for lambda expressions.

Chapter 3 gives a full explanation, with code examples and quizzes at every step, of the concepts of lambda expressions and method references.

1 Java 8: why should you care?

This chapter covers

- Why Java is changing again
- Changing computing background: multicore and processing large datasets (big data)
- Pressure to evolve: new architectures favor functional style over imperative
- Introducing core new features of Java 8: lambdas, streams, default methods

Since the release of JDK 1.0 (Java 1.0) in 1996, Java has won a large following of students, project managers, and programmers who are active users. It's an expressive language and continues to be used for projects both large and small. Its evolution (via the addition of new features) from Java 1.1 (1997) to Java 7 (2011) has been well managed. Java 8 was released in March 2014. So the question is this: why should you care about Java 8?

We argue that the changes to Java 8 are in many ways more profound than any other changes to Java in its history. The good news is that the changes enable you to write programs more easily—instead of writing verbose code like the following (to sort a list of apples in `inventory` based on their weight),

```
Collections.sort(inventory, new Comparator<Apple>() {
    public int compare(Apple a1, Apple a2){
        return a1.getWeight().compareTo(a2.getWeight());
    }
});
```

in Java 8 you can write more concise code that reads a lot closer to the problem statement:

```
inventory.sort(comparing(Apple::getWeight));
```

The first Java 8 code of the book!

It reads "sort inventory comparing apple weight." Don't worry about this code for now. This book will explain what it does and how you can write similar code!

There's also a hardware influence: commodity CPUs have become multicore—the processor in your laptop or desktop machine probably has four or more CPU cores within it. But the vast majority of existing Java programs use only one of these cores and leave the other three idle (or spend a small fraction of their processing power running part of the operating system or a virus checker).

Prior to Java 8, experts might tell you that you have to use threads to use these cores. The problem is that working with threads is difficult and error prone. Java has followed an evolutionary path of continually trying to make concurrency easier and less error prone. Java 1.0 had threads and locks and even a memory model—the best practice at the time—but these primitives proved too difficult to use reliably in nonspecialist project teams. Java 5 added industrial-strength building blocks like thread pools and concurrent collections. Java 7 added the fork/join framework, making parallelism more practical but still difficult. Java 8 has a new, simpler way of thinking about parallelism. But you still have to follow some rules, which you'll learn in this book!

From these two examples (more concise code and simpler use of multicore processors) springs the whole consistent edifice that is Java 8. We start by giving you a quick taste of these ideas (hopefully enough to intrigue you, but short enough to summarize them):

- The Streams API
- Techniques for passing code to methods
- Default methods in interfaces

Java 8 provides a new API (called Streams) that supports many parallel operations to process data and resembles the way you might think in database query languages—you express what you want in a higher-level manner, and the implementation (here the Streams library) chooses the best low-level execution mechanism. As a result, it avoids the need for you to write code that uses `synchronized`, which is not only highly error prone but is also more expensive than you may realize on multicore CPUs.[1]

From a slightly revisionist viewpoint, the addition of `Streams` in Java 8 can be seen as a direct cause of the two other additions to Java 8: *concise techniques to pass code to methods* (method references, lambdas) and *default methods* in interfaces.

---

[1] Multicore CPUs have separate caches (fast memory) attached to each processor core. Locking requires these to be synchronized, requiring relatively slow cache-coherency-protocol intercore communication.

But thinking of passing code to methods as a mere consequence of `Streams` downplays its range of uses within Java 8. It gives you a new concise way to express *behavior parameterization.* Suppose you want to write two methods that differ in only a few lines of code; you can now just pass the code of the parts that differ as an argument (this programming technique is shorter, clearer, and less error prone than the common tendency to use copy and paste). Experts will here note that behavior parameterization could, prior to Java 8, be encoded using anonymous classes—but we'll let the example on the first page of this chapter, which shows increased code conciseness with Java 8, speak for itself in terms of clarity!

The Java 8 feature of passing code to methods (and also being able to return it and incorporate it into data structures) also provides access to a whole range of additional techniques that are commonly referred to as *functional-style programming.* In a nutshell, such code, called *functions* in the functional programming community, can be passed around and combined in a way to produce powerful programming idioms that you'll see in Java 8 guise throughout this book.

The meat of this chapter begins with a high-level discussion on why languages evolve, continues with sections on the core features of Java 8, and then introduces the ideas of functional-style programming that the new features simplify using and that new computer architectures favor. In essence, section 1.1 discusses the evolution process and the concepts, which Java was previously lacking, to exploit multicore parallelism in an easy way. Section 1.2 explains why passing code to methods in Java 8 is such a powerful new programming idiom, and section 1.3 does the same for `Streams`—the new Java 8 way of representing sequenced data and flexibly indicating whether these can be processed in parallel. Section 1.4 explains how the new Java 8 feature of default methods enables interfaces and their libraries to evolve with less fuss and less recompilation. Finally, section 1.5 looks ahead at the ideas of functional-style programming in Java and other languages sharing the JVM. In summary, this chapter introduces ideas that are successively elaborated in the rest of the book. Enjoy the ride!

1.1 Why is Java still changing?

With the 1960s came the quest for the perfect programming language. Peter Landin, famous computer scientist of his day, noted in 1966 in a landmark article[2] that there had *already* been 700 programming languages and speculated on what the next 700 would be like—including arguments for functional-style programming similar to that in Java 8.

Many thousands of programming languages later, academics have concluded that programming languages behave like an ecosystem: new languages appear and old languages are supplanted unless they evolve. We all hope for a perfect universal language, but in reality certain languages are better fitted for certain niches. For example, C and C++ remain popular for building operating systems and various other embedded systems because of their small run-time footprint and in spite of their lack

---

[2] P. J. Landin, "The Next 700 Programming Languages," *CACM* 9(3):157–65, March 1966.

of programming safety. This lack of safety can lead to programs crashing unpredictably and exposing security holes for viruses and the like; indeed, type-safe languages such as Java and C# have supplanted C and C++ in various applications when the additional run-time footprint is acceptable.

Prior occupancy of a niche tends to discourage competitors. Changing to a new language and tool chain is often too painful for just a single feature, but newcomers will eventually displace existing languages, unless they evolve fast enough to keep up (older readers are often able to quote a range of such languages in which they've previously coded but whose popularity has since waned—Ada, Algol, COBOL, Pascal, Delphi, and SNOBOL, to name but a few).

You're a Java programmer, and Java has been successful at colonizing (and displacing competitor languages in) a large ecosystem niche of programming tasks for the last 15 years. Let's examine some reasons for that.

1.1.1 *Java's place in the programming language ecosystem*

Java started well. Right from the start, it was a well-designed object-oriented language with many useful libraries. It also supported small-scale concurrency from day one, with its integrated support for threads and locks (and with its early prescient acknowledgement, in the form of a hardware-neutral memory model, that concurrent threads on multicore processors can have unexpected behaviors in addition to those that happen on single-core processors). Also, the decision to compile Java to JVM bytecode (a virtual machine code that soon every browser supported) meant that it became the language of choice for internet applet programs (do you remember applets?). Indeed, there's a danger that the Java virtual machine (JVM) and its bytecode will be seen as more important than the Java language itself and that, for certain applications, Java might be replaced by one of its competing languages such as Scala or Groovy, which also run on the JVM. Various recent updates to the JVM (for example, the new `invokedynamic` bytecode in JDK7) aim to help such competitor languages run smoothly on the JVM—and to interoperate with Java. Java has also been successful at colonizing various aspects of embedded computing (everything from smartcards, toasters, and set-top boxes to car braking systems).

How did Java get into a general programming niche?

Object orientation became fashionable in the 1990s for two reasons: its encapsulation discipline resulted in fewer software engineering issues than those of C; and as a mental model it easily captured the WIMP programming model of Windows 95 and up. This can be summarized as follows: everything is an object; and a mouse click sends an event message to a handler (invokes the `Clicked` method in a `Mouse` object). The write-once run-anywhere model of Java and the ability of early browsers to (safely) execute Java code applets gave it a niche in universities, whose graduates then populated industry. There was initial resistance to the additional run cost of Java over C/C++, but machines got faster and programmer time became more and more important. Microsoft's C# further validated the Java-style object-oriented model.

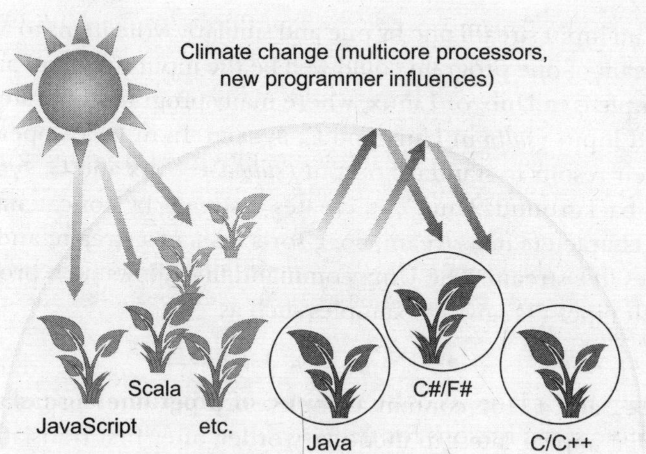

Figure 1.1 Programming languages ecosystem and climate change

But the climate is changing for the programming language ecosystem; programmers are increasingly dealing with so-called *big data* (datasets of terabytes and up) and wishing to exploit multicore computers or computing clusters effectively to process it. And this means using parallel processing—something Java wasn't previously friendly to.

You may have come across programming ideas from other programming niches (for example, Google's map-reduce or the relative ease of data manipulation using database query languages such as SQL) that help you work with large volumes of data and multicore CPUs. Figure 1.1 summarizes the language ecosystem pictorially: think of the landscape as the space of programming problems and the dominant vegetation for a particular bit of ground as the favorite language for that program. Climate change is the idea that new hardware or new programming influences (for example, "Why can't I program in SQL-like style?") mean that different languages become the language of choice for new projects, just like increasing regional temperatures mean grapes now thrive in higher latitudes. But of course there's hysteresis—many an old farmer will keep raising traditional crops. In summary, new languages are appearing and becoming increasingly popular because they've adapted quickly to the climate change.

The main benefit of Java 8 to a programmer is that it provides more programming tools and concepts to solve new or existing programming problems more quickly or, more importantly, in a more concise, more easily maintainable way. Although the concepts are new to Java, they've proved powerful in niche research-like languages. We highlight and develop the ideas behind three such programming concepts that have driven the development of the Java 8 features to exploit parallelism and write more concise code in general. We introduce them in a slightly different order from the rest of the book to enable a Unix-based analogy and to expose the "need *this* because of *that*" dependencies in Java 8's new parallelism for multicore.

1.1.2 Stream processing

The first programming concept is *stream processing*. For introductory purposes, a *stream* is a sequence of data items that are conceptually produced one at a time—a program might read items from an input stream one by one and similarly write items to an output stream. The output stream of one program could well be the input stream of another.

One practical example is in Unix or Linux, where many programs operate by reading data from standard input (*stdin* in Unix and C, `System.in` in Java), operating on it, and then writing their results to standard output (*stdout* in Unix and C, `System.out` in Java). First, a little background: Unix `cat` creates a stream by concatenating two files, `tr` translates the characters in a stream, `sort` sorts lines in a stream, and `tail -3` gives the last three lines in a stream. The Unix command line allows such programs to be linked together with pipes (|), giving examples such as

```
cat file1 file2  |  tr "[A-Z]"  "[a-z]"  |  sort  |  tail -3
```

which (supposing `file1` and `file2` contain a single word per line) prints the three words from the files that appear latest in dictionary order, after first translating them to lowercase. We say that `sort` takes a *stream* of lines[3] as input and produces another stream of lines as output (the latter being sorted), as illustrated in figure 1.2. Note that in Unix the commands (`cat`, `tr`, `sort`, and `tail`) are executed concurrently, so that `sort` can be processing the first few lines before `cat` or `tr` has finished. A more mechanical analogy is a car-manufacturing assembly line where a stream of cars is queued between processing stations that each take a car, modify it, and pass it on to the next station for further processing; processing at separate stations is typically concurrent even though the assembly line is physically a sequence.

Java 8 adds a Streams API (note the uppercase *S*) in `java.util.stream` based on this idea; `Stream<T>` is a sequence of items of type `T`. You can think of it as a fancy iterator for now. The Streams API has many methods that can be chained to form a complex pipeline just like Unix commands were chained in the previous example.

The key motivation for this is that you can now program in Java 8 at a higher level of abstraction, structuring your thoughts of turning a stream of this into a stream of that (similarly to how you think when writing database queries) rather than one item at a time. Another advantage is that Java 8 can transparently run your pipeline of `Stream` operations on several CPU cores on disjoint parts of the input—this is parallelism *almost for free* instead of hard work using `Threads`. We cover the Java 8 Streams API in detail in chapters 4–7.

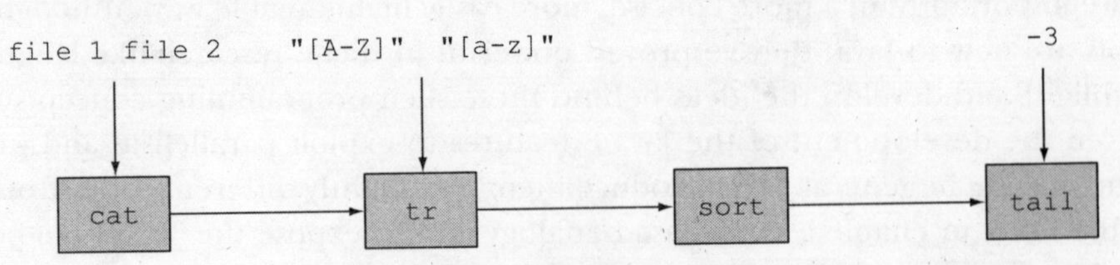

Figure 1.2 Unix commands operating on streams

[3] Purists will say a "stream of characters," but it's conceptually simpler to think that `sort` reorders *lines*.

1.1.3 Passing code to methods with behavior parameterization

The second programming concept added to Java 8 is the ability to pass a piece of code to an API. This sounds awfully abstract. In the Unix example, you might want to tell the `sort` command to use a custom ordering. Although the `sort` command supports command-line parameters to perform various predefined kinds of sorting such as reverse order, these are limited.

For example, let's say you have a collection of invoice IDs with format similar to 2013UK0001, 2014US0002, ... The first four digits represent the year, the next two letters a country code, and last four digits the ID of a client. You may want to sort these invoice IDs by year or perhaps using the customer ID or even the country code. What you really want is the ability to tell the `sort` command to take as an argument an ordering defined by the user: a separate piece of code passed to the `sort` command.

Now, as a direct parallel in Java, you want to tell a `sort` method to compare using a customized order. You could write a method `compareUsingCustomerId` to compare two invoice IDs but, prior to Java 8, you couldn't pass this method to another method! You could create a `Comparator` object to pass to the `sort` method as we showed at the start of this chapter, but this is verbose and obfuscates the idea of simply reusing an existing piece of behavior. Java 8 adds the ability to pass methods (your code) as arguments to other methods. Figure 1.3, based on figure 1.2, illustrates this idea. We also refer to this conceptually as *behavior parameterization.* Why is this important? The Streams API is built on the idea of passing code to parameterize the behavior of its operations, just as you passed `compareUsingCustomerId` to parameterize the behavior of `sort`.

We summarize how this works in section 1.2 of this chapter but leave full details to chapters 2 and 3. Chapters 13 and 14 look at more advanced things you can do using this feature, with techniques from the *functional programming* community.

1.1.4 Parallelism and shared mutable data

The third programming concept is rather more implicit and arises from the phrase "parallelism almost for free" in our previous discussion on stream processing. What do you have to give up? You may have to make some small changes in the way you code the behavior passed to stream methods. At first, these changes might feel a little uncomfortable, but once you get used to them, you'll love them. You must provide behavior that *is safe to execute* concurrently on different pieces of the input. Typically

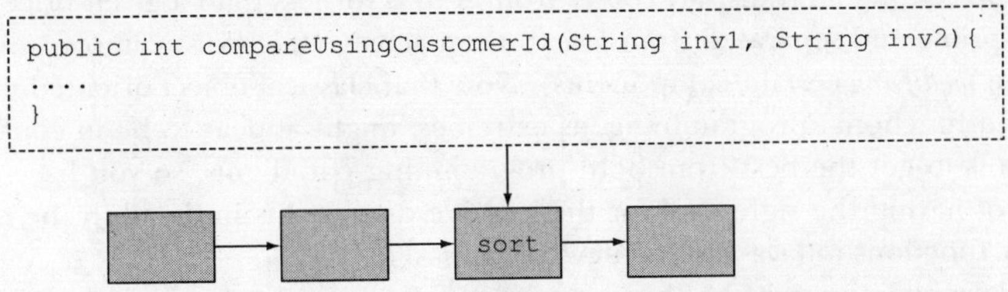

Figure 1.3 Passing method `compareUsingCustomerId` as an argument to `sort`

this means writing code that doesn't access shared mutable data to do its job. Sometimes these are referred to as pure functions or side-effect-free functions or stateless functions, and we'll discuss these in detail in chapters 7 and 13. The previous parallelism arises only by assuming that multiple copies of your piece of code can work independently. If there's a shared variable or object, which is written to, then things no longer work: what if two processes want to modify the shared variable at the same time? (Section 1.3 gives a more detailed explanation with a diagram.) You'll find more about this style throughout the book.

Java 8 streams exploit parallelism more easily than Java's existing Threads API, so although it's *possible* to use `synchronized` to break the no-shared-mutable-data rule, it's fighting the system in that it's abusing an abstraction optimized around that rule. Using `synchronized` across multiple processing cores is often far more expensive than you expect, because synchronization forces code to execute sequentially, which works against the goal of parallelism.

Two of these points (no shared mutable data and the ability to pass methods and functions—code—to other methods) are the cornerstones of what's generally described as the paradigm of *functional programming,* which you'll see in detail in chapters 13 and 14. In contrast, in the *imperative programming* paradigm you typically describe a program in terms of a sequence of statements that mutate state. The no-shared-mutable-data requirement means that a method is perfectly described solely by the way it transforms arguments to results; in other words, it behaves as a mathematical function and has no (visible) side effects.

1.1.5 Java needs to evolve

You've seen evolution in Java before. For example, the introduction of generics and using `List<String>` instead of just `List` may initially have been irritating. But you're now familiar with this style and the benefits it brings (catching more errors at compile time and making code easier to read, because you now know what something is a list of).

Other changes have made common things easier to express, for example, using a `for-each` loop instead of exposing the boilerplate use of an `Iterator`. The main changes in Java 8 reflect a move away from classical object orientation, which often focuses on mutating existing values, and toward the functional-style programming spectrum in which *what* you want to do in broad-brush terms (for example, *create a value* representing all transport routes from A to B for less than a given price) is considered prime and separated from *how* you can achieve this (for example, *scan* a data structure *modifying* certain components). Note that classical object-oriented programming and functional programming, as extremes, might appear to be in conflict. But the idea is to get the best from both programming paradigms, so you have a better chance of having the right tool for the job! We discuss this in detail in the next two sections: functions in Java and the new Streams API.

A takeaway line might be this: languages need to evolve to track changing hardware or programmer expectations (if you need convincing, then consider that COBOL was once one of the most important languages commercially). To endure, Java has to evolve by adding new features. This evolution will be pointless unless the new features are used, so in using Java 8 you're protecting your way of life as a Java programmer. On top of that, we have a feeling you'll love using Java 8's new features. Ask anyone who's used Java 8 whether they're willing to go back! Additionally, the new Java 8 features might, in the ecosystem analogy, enable Java to conquer programming-task territory currently occupied by other languages, so Java 8 programmers will be even more in demand.

We now introduce the new concepts in Java 8, one by one—pointing out on the way the chapters that cover these concepts in more detail.

1.2 Functions in Java

The word *function* in programming languages is commonly used as a synonym for *method*, particularly a static method; this is in addition to it being used for *mathematical function*, one without side effects. Fortunately, as you'll see, when Java 8 refers to functions these usages very nearly coincide.

Java 8 adds functions as new forms of value. These facilitate the use of `Streams`, covered in section 1.3, which Java 8 provides to exploit parallel programming on multicore processors. We start by showing that functions as values are useful in themselves.

Think about the possible values manipulated by Java programs. First, there are primitive values such as 42 (of type `int`) and 3.14 (of type `double`). Second, values can be objects (more strictly, references to objects). The only way to get one of these is by using `new`, perhaps via a factory method or a library function; object references point to *instances* of a class. Examples include `"abc"` (of type `String`), `new Integer(1111)` (of type `Integer`), and the result `new HashMap<Integer, String>(100)` of explicitly calling a constructor for `HashMap`. Even arrays are objects. So what's the problem?

To help answer this, we'll note that the whole point of a programming language is to manipulate values, which, following historical programming-language tradition, are therefore called first-class values (or citizens, in the terminology borrowed from the 1960s civil rights movement in the United States). Other structures in our programming languages, which perhaps help us express the structure of values but which can't be passed around during program execution, are second-class citizens. Values as listed previously are first-class Java citizens, but various other Java concepts, such as methods and classes, exemplifv second-class citizens. Methods are fine when used to define classes, which in turn may be instantiated to produce values, but neither are values themselves. So does this matter? Yes, it turns out that being able to pass methods around at run-time, and hence making them first-class citizens, is very useful in programming, and so the Java 8 designers added this ability to Java. Incidentally, you might wonder whether making other second-class citizens such as classes into first-class-citizen values might also be a good idea. Various languages such as Smalltalk and JavaScript have explored this route.

1.2.1 Methods and lambdas as first-class citizens

Experiments in other languages such as Scala and Groovy have determined that allowing concepts like methods to be used as first-class values made programming easier by adding to the toolset available to programmers. And once programmers become familiar with a powerful feature, they become reluctant to use languages without it! So the designers of Java 8 decided to allow methods to be values—to make it easier for you to program. Moreover, the Java 8 feature of methods as values forms the basis of various other Java 8 features (such as `Streams`).

The first new Java 8 feature we introduce is that of *method references*. Suppose you want to filter all the hidden files in a directory. You need to start writing a method that given a `File` will tell you whether it's hidden or not. Thankfully there's such a method inside the `File` class called `isHidden`. It can be viewed as a function that takes a `File` and returns a `boolean`. But to use it for filtering you need to wrap it into a `FileFilter` object that you then pass to the `File.listFiles` method, as follows:

```
File[] hiddenFiles = new File(".").listFiles(new FileFilter() {
    public boolean accept(File file) {
        return file.isHidden();          <-- Filtering
    }                                        hidden files!
});
```

Yuck! That's horrible! Although it's only three lines, it's three opaque lines—we all remember saying "Do I really have to do it this way?" on first encounter. You already have a method `isHidden` that you could use. Why do you have to wrap it up in a verbose `FileFilter` class and then instantiate it? Because that's what you had to do prior to Java 8!

Now, in Java 8 you can rewrite that code as follows:

```
File[] hiddenFiles = new File(".").listFiles(File::isHidden);
```

Wow! Isn't that cool? You already have the function `isHidden` available, so you just pass it to the `listFiles` method using the Java 8 *method reference* :: syntax (meaning "use this method as a value"); note that we've also slipped into using the word *function* for methods. We'll explain later how the mechanics work. One advantage is that your code now reads closer to the problem statement. Here's a taste of what's coming: methods are no longer second-class values. Analogously to using an *object reference* when you pass an object around (and object references are created by `new`), in Java 8 when you write `File::isHidden` you create a *method reference*, which can similarly be passed around. This concept is discussed in detail in chapter 3. Given that methods contain code (the executable body of a method), then using method references enables passing code around as in figure 1.3. Figure 1.4 illustrates the concept. You'll also see a concrete example (selecting apples from an inventory) in the next section.

LAMBDAS—ANONYMOUS FUNCTIONS

As well as allowing (named) methods to be first-class values, Java 8 allows a richer idea of *functions as values*, including *lambdas*[4] (or anonymous functions). For example, you

---

[4] Originally named after the Greek letter λ (lambda). Although the symbol isn't used in Java, its name lives on.

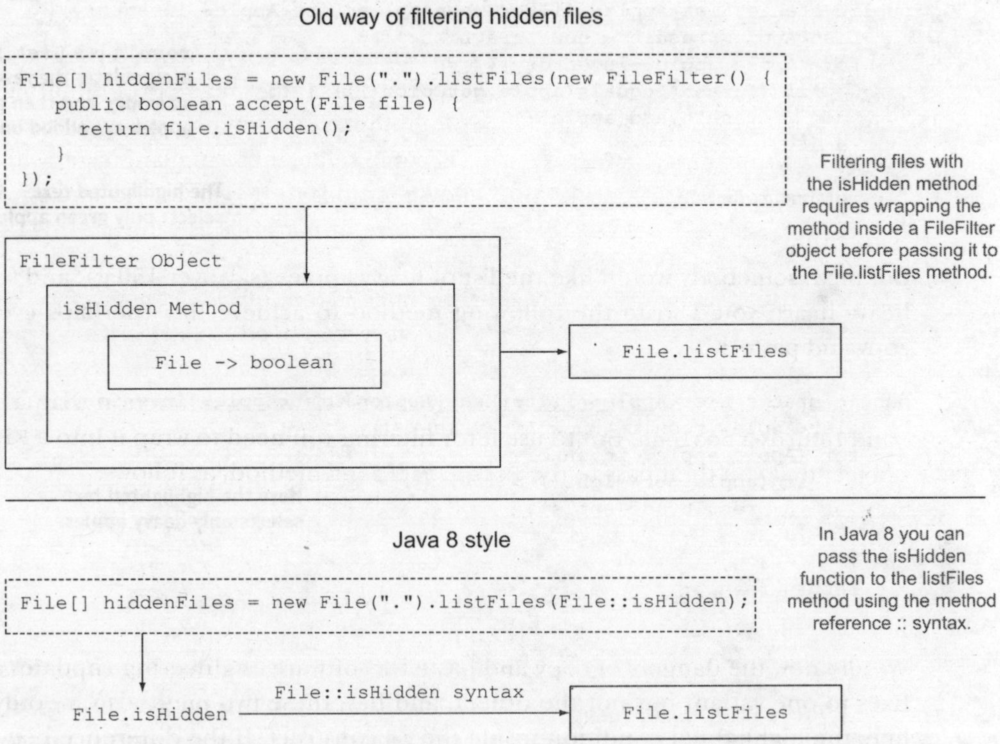

Figure 1.4 Passing the method reference `File::isHidden` to the method `listFiles`

can now write `(int x) -> x + 1` to mean "the function that, when called with argument x, returns the value x + 1." You might wonder why this is necessary because you could define a method `add1` inside a class `MyMathsUtils` and then write `MyMaths-Utils::add1`! Yes, you could, but the new lambda syntax is more concise for cases where you don't have a convenient method and class available. Chapter 3 explores lambdas in detail. Programs using these concepts are said to be written in functional-programming style—this phrase means "writing programs that pass functions around as first-class values."

1.2.2 Passing code: an example

Let's look at an example (discussed in more detail in chapter 2, "Passing code with behavior parameterization") of how this helps you write programs. All the code for the examples is available on the book's GitHub page (https://github.com/java8/). Suppose you have a class `Apple` with a method `getColor` and a variable `inventory` holding a list of `Apples`; then you might wish to select all the green apples and return them in a list. The word *filter* is commonly used to express this concept. Before Java 8, you thus might write a method `filterGreenApples`:

```
public static List<Apple> filterGreenApples(List<Apple> inventory){
    List<Apple> result = new ArrayList<>();
    for (Apple apple: inventory){
        if ("green".equals(apple.getColor())) {
            result.add(apple);
        }
    }
    return result;
}
```

`result` is a `List`, which accumulates the result; it starts as empty, and then green apples are added one by one.

The highlighted text selects only green apples.

But next, somebody would like the list of heavy apples (say over 150 g), and so, with a heavy heart, you'd write the following method to achieve this (perhaps even using copy and paste):

```
public static List<Apple> filterHeavyApples(List<Apple> inventory) {
    List<Apple> result = new ArrayList<>();
    for (Apple apple: inventory){
        if (apple.getWeight() > 150) {
            result.add(apple);
        }
    }
    return result;
}
```

Here the highlighted text selects only heavy apples.

We all know the dangers of copy and paste for software engineering (updates and bug fixes to one variant but not the other), and hey, these two methods vary only in one line: the highlighted condition inside the `if` construct. If the difference between the two method calls in the highlighted code had been simply as to what weight range was acceptable, then you could have just passed lower and upper acceptable weights as arguments to `filter`—perhaps `(150, 1000)` to select heavy apples (over 150 g) or `(0, 80)` to select light apples (under 80 g).

But as we mentioned previously, Java 8 makes it possible to pass the code of the condition as an argument, thus avoiding code duplication of the `filter` method. You can now write this:

```
public static boolean isGreenApple(Apple apple) {
    return "green".equals(apple.getColor());
}
public static boolean isHeavyApple(Apple apple) {
    return apple.getWeight() > 150;
}
public interface Predicate<T>{
    boolean test(T t);
}
static List<Apple> filterApples(List<Apple> inventory,
                                Predicate<Apple> p) {
    List<Apple> result = new ArrayList<>();
    for (Apple apple: inventory){
        if (p.test(apple)) {
            result.add(apple);
        }
    }
```

Included for clarity (normally simply imported from `java.util.function`).

A method is passed as a `Predicate` parameter named `p` (see the sidebar "What's a Predicate?").

Does the apple match the condition represented by `p`?

```
    return result;
}
```

And to use this, you call either

```
filterApples(inventory, Apple::isGreenApple);
```

or

```
filterApples(inventory, Apple::isHeavyApple);
```

We explain how this works in detail in the next two chapters. The key idea to take away for now is that you can pass around a method in Java 8!

> **What's a Predicate?**
>
> The previous code passed a method `Apple::isGreenApple` (which takes an `Apple` for argument and returns a `boolean`) to `filterApples`, which expected a `Predicate<Apple>` parameter. The word *predicate* is often used in mathematics to mean something function-like that takes a value for an argument and returns `true` or `false`. As you'll see later, Java 8 would also allow you to write `Function<Apple,Boolean>`—more familiar to readers who learned about functions but not predicates at school—but using `Predicate<Apple>` is more standard (and slightly more efficient because it avoids boxing a `boolean` into a `Boolean`).

1.2.3 From passing methods to lambdas

Passing methods as values is clearly useful, but it's a bit annoying having to write a definition for short methods such as `isHeavyApple` and `isGreenApple` when they're used perhaps only once or twice. But Java 8 has solved this too. It introduces a new notation (anonymous functions, or lambdas) that enables you to write just

```
filterApples(inventory, (Apple a) -> "green".equals(a.getColor()) );
```

or

```
filterApples(inventory, (Apple a) -> a.getWeight() > 150 );
```

or even

```
filterApples(inventory, (Apple a) -> a.getWeight() < 80 ||
                                     "brown".equals(a.getColor()) );
```

So you don't even need to write a method definition that's used only once; the code is crisper and clearer because you don't need to search to find the code you're passing. But if such a lambda exceeds a few lines in length (so that its behavior isn't instantly clear), then you should instead use a method reference to a method with a descriptive name instead of using an anonymous lambda. Code clarity should be your guide.

The Java 8 designers could almost have stopped here, and perhaps they would have done so before multicore CPUs! Functional-style programming as presented so far turns out to be powerful, as you'll see. Java might then have been rounded off by adding `filter` and a few friends as generic library methods, such as

```
static <T> Collection<T> filter(Collection<T> c, Predicate<T> p);
```

So you wouldn't even have to write methods like `filterApples` because, for example, the previous call

```
filterApples(inventory, (Apple a) -> a.getWeight() > 150 );
```

could simply be written as a call to the library method `filter`:

```
filter(inventory, (Apple a) -> a.getWeight() > 150 );
```

But, for reasons centered on better exploiting parallelism, the designers didn't do this. Java 8 instead contains a whole new Collections-like API called Streams, containing a comprehensive set of operations similar to `filter` that functional programmers may be familiar with (for example, `map`, `reduce`), along with methods to convert between `Collections` and `Streams`, which we now investigate.

1.3 Streams

Nearly every Java application *makes* and *processes* collections. But working with collections isn't always ideal. For example, let's say you need to filter expensive transactions from a list and then group them by currency. You'd need to write a lot of boilerplate code to implement this data processing query, as shown here:

```
Map<Currency, List<Transaction>> transactionsByCurrencies =
    new HashMap<>();
for (Transaction transaction : transactions) {
    if(transaction.getPrice() > 1000){
        Currency currency = transaction.getCurrency();
        List<Transaction> transactionsForCurrency =
            transactionsByCurrencies.get(currency);
        if (transactionsForCurrency == null) {
            transactionsForCurrency = new ArrayList<>();
            transactionsByCurrencies.put(currency,
                                         transactionsForCurrency);
        }
        transactionsForCurrency.add(transaction);
    }
}
```

Create the `Map` where the grouped transaction will be accumulated.

Iterate the `List` of transactions.

Filter expensive transactions.

Extract the transaction's currency.

If there isn't any entry in the grouping `Map` for this currency, create it.

Add the currently traversed transaction to the `List` of transactions with the same currency.

In addition, it's difficult to understand at a glance what the code does because of the multiple nested control-flow statements.

Using the Streams API, you can solve this problem as follows:

```
import static java.util.stream.Collectors.toList;
Map<Currency, List<Transaction>> transactionsByCurrencies =
    transactions.stream()
                .filter((Transaction t) -> t.getPrice() > 1000)
                .collect(groupingBy(Transaction::getCurrency));
```

Filter expensive transactions.

Group them by currency.

Don't worry about this code for now because it may look like a bit of magic. Chapters 4–7 are dedicated to explaining how to make sense of the Streams API. For now it's worth noticing that the Streams API provides a very different way to process data in comparison to the Collections API. Using a collection, you're managing the iteration process yourself. You need to iterate through each element one by one using a `for-each` loop and then process the elements. We call this way of iterating over data *external iteration.* In contrast, using the Streams API, you don't need to think in terms of loops at all. The data processing happens internally inside the library. We call this idea *internal iteration.* We come back to these ideas in chapter 4.

As a second pain point of working with collections, think for a second about how you would process the list of transactions if you had a vast number of them; how can you process this huge list? A single CPU wouldn't be able to process this large amount of data, but you probably have a multicore computer on your desk. Ideally, you'd like to share the work among the different CPU cores available on your machine to reduce the processing time. In theory, if you have eight cores, they should be able to process your data eight times as fast as using one core because they work in parallel.

Multicore

All new desktop and laptop computers are multicore computers. Instead of a single CPU, they have four or eight or more CPUs (usually called cores[5]). The problem is that a classic Java program uses just a single one of these cores, and the power of the others is wasted. Similarly, many companies use *computing clusters* (computers connected together with fast networks) to be able to process vast amounts of data efficiently. Java 8 facilitates new programming styles to better exploit such computers.

Google's search engine is an example of a piece of code that's too big to run on a single computer. It reads every page on the internet and creates an index, mapping every word appearing on any internet page back to every URL containing that word. Then, when you do a Google search involving several words, software can quickly use this index to give you a set of web pages containing those words. Try to imagine how you might code this algorithm in Java (even for a smaller index than Google's you'd need to exploit all the cores in your computer).

1.3.1 Multithreading is difficult

The problem is that exploiting parallelism by writing *multithreaded* code (using the Threads API from previous versions of Java) is difficult. You have to think differently: threads can access and update shared variables at the same time. As a result, data could change unexpectedly if not coordinated[6] properly. This model is harder to

---

5 This naming is unfortunate in some ways. Each of the cores in a multicore chip is a full-fledged CPU. But the phrase "multicore CPU" has become common, so *core* is used to refer to the individual CPUs.

6 Traditionally via the keyword `synchronized`, but many subtle bugs arise from its misplacement. Java 8's `Stream`-based parallelism encourages a functional programming style where `synchronized` is rarely used; it focuses on partitioning the data rather than coordinating access to it.

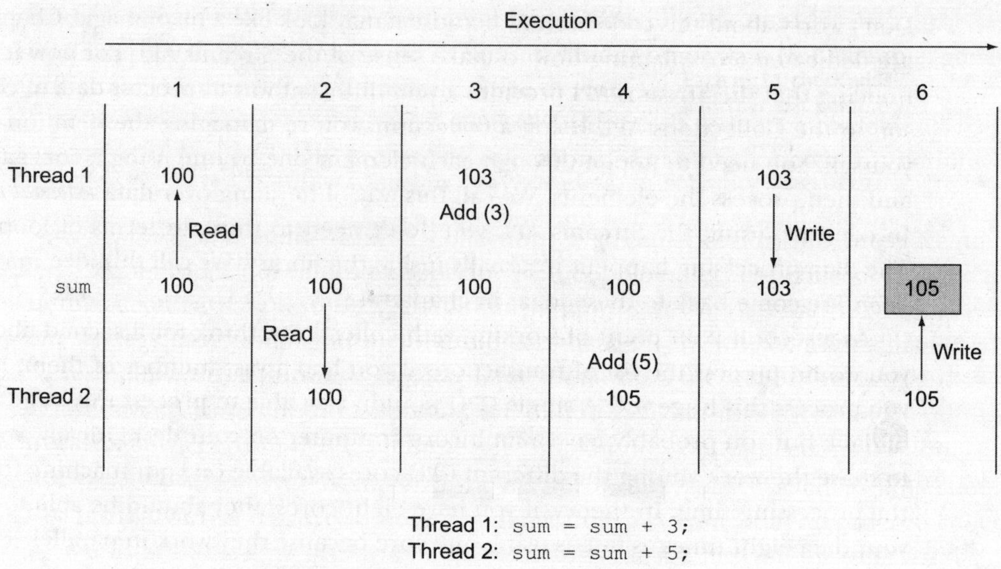

Figure 1.5 A possible problem with two threads trying to add to a shared `sum` variable. The result is 105 instead of an expected result of 108.

think about[7] than a step-by-step sequential model. For example, figure 1.5 shows a possible problem with two `Threads` trying to add a number to a shared variable `sum` if they're not synchronized properly.

Java 8 also addresses both problems (boilerplate and obscurity involving processing collections and difficulty leveraging multicore) with the Streams API (`java.util.stream`). The first design motivator is that there are many data processing patterns (similar to `filterApples` in the previous section, or operations familiar from database query languages such as SQL) that occur over and over again and that would benefit from forming part of a library: *filtering* data based on a criterion (for example, heavy apples), *extracting* data (for example, extracting the weight field from each apple in a list), or *grouping* data (for example, grouping a list of numbers into separate lists of even and odd numbers), and so on. The second motivator is that such operations can often be parallelized. For instance, as illustrated in figure 1.6, filtering a list on two CPUs could be done by asking one CPU to process the first half of a list and the second CPU to process the other half of the list (this is called the *forking step* (1)). The CPUs then filter their respective half-lists (2). Finally (3), one CPU would join the two results (this is closely related to how Google searches work so quickly, of course using many more than two processors).

For now, we'll just say that the new Streams API behaves very similarly to Java's existing Collections API: both provide access to sequences of data items. But it's useful for now to keep in mind that Collections is mostly about storing and accessing data,

---

7 Aha—a source of pressure for the language to evolve!

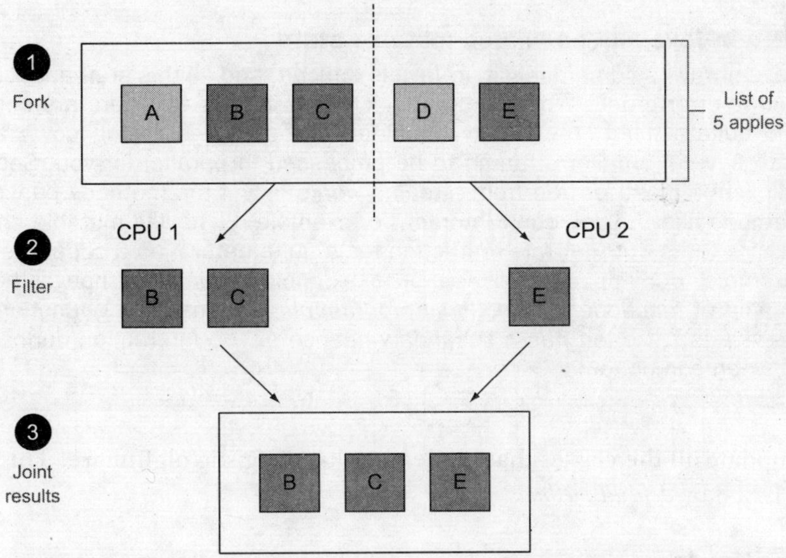

Figure 1.6 Forking `filter` onto two CPUs and joining the result

whereas `Streams` is mostly about describing computations on data. The key point here is that `Streams` allows and encourages the elements within a `Stream` to be processed in parallel. Although it may seem odd at first, often the fastest way to filter a `Collection` (using `filterApples` on a `List` in the previous section) is to convert it to a `Stream`, process it in parallel, and then convert it back to a `List`, as exemplified here for both the serial and parallel cases. Again we'll just say "parallelism almost for free" and provide a taste of how you can filter heavy apples from a list sequentially or in parallel using `Streams` and a lambda expression:

Sequential processing:

```
import static java.util.stream.Collectors.toList;
List<Apple> heavyApples =
    inventory.stream().filter((Apple a) -> a.getWeight() > 150)
                      .collect(toList());
```

Parallel processing:

```
import static java.util.stream.Collectors.toList;
List<Apple> heavyApples =
    inventory.parallelStream().filter((Apple a) -> a.getWeight() > 150)
                              .collect(toList());
```

Chapter 7 explores parallel data processing in Java 8 and its performance in more detail. One of the practical issues the Java 8 developers found in evolving Java with all these new goodies was that of evolving existing interfaces. For example, the method `Collections.sort` really belongs to the `List` interface but was never included. Ideally, you'd like to do `list.sort(comparator)` instead of `Collections.sort(list, comparator)`. This may seem trivial but, prior to Java 8, you can update an interface

Parallelism in Java and no shared mutable state

People have always said parallelism in Java is difficult, and all this stuff about `synchronized` is error prone. Where's the magic bullet in Java 8? There are actually two magic bullets. First, the library handles partitioning—breaking down a big stream into several smaller streams to be processed in parallel for you. Second, this parallelism almost for free from streams works only if the methods passed to library methods like `filter` don't interact, for example, by having mutable shared objects. But it turns out that this restriction feels quite natural as a coder (see, by way of example, our `Apple::isGreenApple` example). Indeed, although the primary meaning of *functional* in *functional programming* means "using functions as first class values," it often has a secondary nuance of "no interaction during execution between components."

only if you update all the classes that implement it—a logistic nightmare! This issue is resolved in Java 8 by *default methods.*

1.4 Default methods

Default methods are added to Java 8 largely to support library designers by enabling them to write *more evolvable* interfaces. We cover them in detail in chapter 9. They're important because you'll increasingly encounter them in interfaces, but because relatively few programmers will need to write default methods themselves and because they facilitate program evolution rather than helping write any particular program, we keep the explanation here short and example-based:

In section 1.3, we gave the following example Java 8 code:

```
List<Apple> heavyApples1 =
    inventory.stream().filter((Apple a) -> a.getWeight() > 150)
                      .collect(toList());
List<Apple> heavyApples2 =
    inventory.parallelStream().filter((Apple a) -> a.getWeight() > 150)
                              .collect(toList());
```

But there's a problem here: a `List<T>` prior to Java 8 doesn't have `stream` or `parallelStream` methods—and neither does the `Collection<T>` interface that it implements—because these methods hadn't been conceived of! And without these methods this code won't compile. The simplest solution, which you might employ for your own interfaces, would have been for the Java 8 designers simply to add the `stream` method to the `Collection` interface and add the implementation in the `ArrayList` class.

But doing this would have been a nightmare for users. There are many alternative collection frameworks that implement interfaces from the Collections API. Adding a new method to an interface means all concrete classes must provide an implementation for it. Language designers have no control on all existing implementations of `Collections`, so you have a bit of a dilemma: how can you evolve published interfaces without disrupting existing implementations?

The Java 8 solution is to break the last link—an interface can now contain method signatures for which an implementing class doesn't provide an implementation! So who implements them? The missing method bodies are given as part of the interface (hence default implementations) rather than in the implementing class.

This provides a way for an interface designer to enlarge an interface beyond those methods that were originally planned—without breaking existing code. Java 8 uses the new `default` keyword in the interface specification to achieve this.

For example, in Java 8 you can now call the `sort` method directly on a `List`. This is made possible with the following default method in the Java 8 `List` interface, which calls the static method `Collections.sort`:

```
default void sort(Comparator<? super E> c) {
    Collections.sort(this, c);
}
```

This means any concrete classes of `List` don't have to explicitly implement `sort`, whereas in previous Java versions such concrete classes would fail to recompile unless they provided an implementation for `sort`.

But wait a second—a single class can implement multiple interfaces, right? So if you have multiple default implementations in several interfaces, does that mean you have a form of multiple inheritance in Java? Yes, to some extent! We show in chapter 9 that there are some restrictions that prevent issues such as the infamous *diamond inheritance problem* in C++.

1.5 Other good ideas from functional programming

The previous sections introduced two core ideas from functional programming that are now part of Java: using methods and lambdas as first-class values, and the idea that calls to functions or methods can be efficiently and safely executed in parallel in the absence of mutable shared state. Both of these ideas are exploited by the new Streams API we described earlier.

Common functional languages (SML, OCaml, Haskell) also provide further constructs to help programmers. One of these is avoiding `null` by explicit use of more descriptive data types. Indeed, Tony Hoare, one of the giants of computer science, said in a presentation at QCon London 2009:

> I call it my billion-dollar mistake. It was the invention of the null reference in 1965.... I couldn't resist the temptation to put in a null reference, simply because it was so easy to implement.

In Java 8 there's an `Optional<T>` class that, if used consistently, can help you avoid `NullPointer` exceptions. It's a container object that may or not contain a value. `Optional<T>` includes methods to explicitly deal with the case where a value is absent, and as a result you can avoid `NullPointer` exceptions. In other words, it uses the type system to allow you to indicate when a variable is anticipated to potentially have a missing value. We discuss `Optional<T>` in detail in chapter 10.

A second idea is that of *(structural) pattern matching*.[8] This is used in mathematics, for example:

```
f(0) = 1
f(n) = n*f(n-1) otherwise
```

In Java you would here write an `if-then-else` or a `switch` statement. Other languages have shown that, for more complex data types, pattern matching can express programming ideas more concisely compared to using `if-then-else`. For such data types, you might also use polymorphism and method overriding as an alternative to `if-then-else`, but there's still language-design discussion as to which is more appropriate.[9] We'd say that both are useful tools and you should have both in your armory. Unfortunately, Java 8 doesn't have full support for pattern matching, although we show how it can be expressed in chapter 14. In the meantime, we illustrate with an example expressed in the Scala programming language (another Java-like language using the JVM that has inspired some aspects of Java evolution; see chapter 15). Suppose you want to write a program that does basic simplifications on a tree representing an arithmetic expression. Given a data type `Expr` representing such expressions, in Scala you can write the following code to decompose an `Expr` into its parts and then return another `Expr`:

```
def simplifyExpression(expr: Expr): Expr = expr match {
    case BinOp("+", e, Number(0)) => e      // Adding zero
    case BinOp("*", e, Number(1)) => e      // Multiplying by one
    case BinOp("/", e, Number(1)) => e      // Dividing by one
    case _ => expr                          // Can't simplify expr
}
```

Here Scala's syntax `expr match` corresponds to Java's `switch (expr)`; don't worry about this code for now—you'll read more on pattern matching in chapter 14. For now, you can think of pattern matching as an extended form of `switch` that can decompose a data type into its components at the same time.

Why should the `switch` statement in Java be limited to primitive values and `Strings`? Functional languages tend to allow `switch` to be used on many more data types, including allowing pattern matching (in the Scala code, this is achieved using a `match` operation). In object-oriented design, the visitor pattern is a common pattern used to walk through a family of classes (such as the different components of a car: wheel, engine, chassis, and so on) and apply an operation to each object visited. One advantage of pattern matching is that a compiler can report common errors such as "Class `Brakes` is part of the family of classes used to represent components of class `Car`. You forgot to explicitly deal with it."

---

[8] There are two uses of this phrase. Here we mean the one familiar from mathematics and functional programming whereby a function is defined by cases, rather than using `if-then-else`. The other meaning concerns phrases like "find all files of the form 'IMG*.JPG' in a given directory" associated with so-called regular expressions.

[9] The Wikipedia article on "expression problem" (a term coined by Phil Wadler) provides an entry to the discussion.

Chapters 13 and 14 give a full tutorial introduction to functional programming and how to write functional-style programs in Java 8—including the toolkit of functions provided in its library. Chapter 15 follows by discussing how Java 8 features compare to features in Scala—a language that, like Java, is implemented on top of the JVM and that has evolved quickly to threaten some aspects of Java's niche in the programming language ecosystem. This material is positioned toward the end of the book to provide additional insight into why the new Java 8 features were added.

1.6 Summary

Following are the key concepts you should take away from this chapter:

- Keep in mind the idea of language ecosystem and the consequent evolve-or-wither pressure on languages. Although Java may be supremely healthy at the moment, you can recall other healthy languages such as COBOL that failed to evolve.
- The core additions to Java 8 provide exciting new concepts and functionality to ease the writing of programs that are both effective and concise.
- Multicore processors aren't fully served by existing Java programming practice.
- Functions are first-class values; remember how methods can be passed as functional values and how anonymous functions (lambdas) are written.
- The Java 8 concept of `Streams` generalizes many aspects of `Collections` but both enables more readable code and allows elements of a stream to be processed in parallel.
- You can use a default method in an interface to provide a method body if an implementing class chooses not to do so.
- Other interesting ideas from functional programming include dealing with `null` and using pattern matching.

2 Passing code with behavior parameterization

This chapter covers

- Coping with changing requirements
- Behavior parameterization
- Anonymous classes
- Preview of lambda expressions
- Real-world examples: `Comparator`, `Runnable`, and GUI

A well-known problem in software engineering is that no matter what you do, user requirements will change. For example, imagine an application to help a farmer understand his inventory. The farmer might want a functionality to find all green apples in his inventory. But the next day he might tell you, "Actually I also want to find all apples heavier than 150 g." Two days later, the farmer comes back and adds, "It would be really nice if I could find all apples that are green *and* heavier than 150 g." How can you cope with these changing requirements? Ideally you'd like to minimize your engineering effort. In addition, similar new functionalities ought to be straightforward to implement and maintainable in the long term.

Behavior parameterization is a software development pattern that lets you handle frequent requirement changes. In a nutshell, it means taking a block of code and making it available without executing it. This block of code can be called later by other parts of your programs, which means that you can defer the execution of that block of code. For instance, you could pass the block of code as an argument to another method that will execute it later. As a result, the method's behavior is parameterized based on that block of code. For example, if you process a collection, you may want to write a method that

- Can do "something" for every element of a list
- Can do "something else" when you finish processing the list
- Can do "yet something else" if you encounter an error

This is what *behavior parameterization* refers to. Here's an analogy: your roommate knows how to drive to the supermarket and back home. So you can tell him to buy a list of things such as bread, cheese, and wine. This is equivalent to calling a method `goAndBuy` with a list of products as argument. But one day you're at the office and you need him to do something he's never done before: pick up a package from the post office. You now need to pass him a list of instructions: go to the post office, use this reference number, talk to the manager, and pick up the parcel. You could pass him the list of instructions by email, and when he receives it, he can go ahead and follow the instructions. You've now done something a bit more advanced that's equivalent to a method: `go`, which can take different new behaviors as arguments and execute them.

We start the chapter by walking you through an example of how you can evolve your code to be more flexible for changing requirements. Building on this knowledge, we show how to use behavior parameterization for several real-world examples. For example, you may have already used the behavior parameterization pattern using existing classes and interfaces in the Java API to sort a `List`, to filter names of files, or to tell a `Thread` to execute a block of code or even perform GUI event handling. You'll soon realize that using this pattern is verbose in Java at the moment. Lambda expressions in Java 8 tackle the problem of verbosity. We show in chapter 3 how to construct lambda expressions, where to use them, and how you can make your code more concise by adopting them.

2.1 Coping with changing requirements

Writing code that can cope with changing requirements is difficult. Let's walk through an example that we'll gradually improve, showing some best practices for making your code more flexible. In the context of a farm-inventory application, you have to implement a functionality to filter *green* apples from a list. Sounds easy, right?

2.1.1 First attempt: filtering green apples

A first solution might be as follows:

```
public static List<Apple> filterGreenApples(List<Apple> inventory) {
    List<Apple> result = new ArrayList<>();          <-- An accumulator
    for(Apple apple: inventory){                         list for apples.
```

```
        if( "green".equals(apple.getColor() ) {      <-- Select only
            result.add(apple);                            green apples.
        }
    }
    return result;
}
```

The highlighted line shows the condition required to select green apples. But now the farmer changes his mind and wants to also filter *red* apples. What can you do? A naïve solution would be to duplicate your method, rename it as `filterRedApples`, and change the `if` condition to match red apples. Nonetheless, this approach doesn't cope well with changes if the farmer wants multiple colors: light green, dark red, yellow, and so on. A good principle is this: after writing similar code, try to abstract.

2.1.2 Second attempt: parameterizing the color

What you could do is add a parameter to your method to parameterize the color and be more flexible to such changes:

```
public static List<Apple> filterApplesByColor(List<Apple> inventory,
                                              String color) {
    List<Apple> result = new ArrayList<>();
    for (Apple apple: inventory){
        if ( apple.getColor().equals(color) ) {
            result.add(apple);
        }
    }
    return result;
}
```

You can now make the farmer happy and call your method as follows:

```
List<Apple> greenApples = filterApplesByColor(inventory, "green");
List<Apple> redApples = filterApplesByColor(inventory, "red");
…
```

Too easy, right? Let's complicate the example a bit. The farmer comes back to you and says, "It would be really cool to differentiate between light apples and heavy apples. Heavy apples typically have a weight greater than 150 g."

Wearing your software engineering hat, you realize in advance that the farmer may want to vary the weight, so you create the following method to cope with various weights through an additional parameter:

```
public static List<Apple> filterApplesByWeight(List<Apple> inventory,
                                               int weight) {
    List<Apple> result = new ArrayList<>();
    For (Apple apple: inventory){
        if ( apple.getWeight() > weight ){
            result.add(apple);
        }
    }
    return result;
}
```

This is a good solution, but notice how you have to duplicate most of the implementation for traversing the inventory and applying the filtering criteria on each apple. This is somewhat disappointing because it breaks the DRY (don't repeat yourself) principle of software engineering. What if you want to alter the filter traversing to enhance performance? You now have to modify the implementation of *all* of your methods instead of a single one. This is expensive from an engineering effort perspective.

You could combine the color and weight into one method called `filter`. But then you'd still need a way to differentiate what attribute you want to filter on. You could add a flag to differentiate between color and weight queries. (But never do this! We'll explain why shortly.)

2.1.3 Third attempt: filtering with every attribute you can think of

Our ugly attempt of merging all attributes appears as follows:

```
public static List<Apple> filterApples(List<Apple> inventory, String color,
                                       int weight, boolean flag) {
    List<Apple> result = new ArrayList<>();
    for (Apple apple: inventory){
        if ( (flag && apple.getColor().equals(color)) ||
             (!flag && apple.getWeight() > weight) ){      <- A really ugly
            result.add(apple);                                way to select
        }                                                     color or weight
    }
    return result;
}
```

You could use it as follows (but it's really ugly):

```
List<Apple> greenApples = filterApples(inventory, "green", 0, true);
List<Apple> heavyApples = filterApples(inventory, "", 150, false);
...
```

This solution is extremely bad. First, the client code looks terrible. What do `true` and `false` mean? In addition, this solution doesn't cope well with changing requirements. What if the farmer asks you to filter with different attributes of an apple, for example, its size, its shape, its origin, and so on? Furthermore, what if the farmer asks you for more complicated queries that combine attributes, such as green apples that are also heavy? You'd either have multiple duplicated `filter` methods or one giant, very complex method. So far you've parameterized the `filterApples` method *with values* such as a `String`, an `Integer`, or a `boolean`. This can be fine for certain well-defined problems. But in this case what you need is a better way to tell your `filterApples` method the selection criteria for apples. In the next section we describe how to make use of *behavior parameterization* to attain that flexibility.

2.2 Behavior parameterization

You saw in the previous section that you need a better way than adding lots of parameters to cope with changing requirements. Let's step back and find a better level of abstraction. One possible solution is to model your selection criteria: you're working with apples and returning a boolean based on some attributes of Apple (for example, is it green? is it heavier than 150 g?). We call this a *predicate* (that is, a function that returns a boolean). Let's therefore define an interface *to model the selection criteria*:

```
public interface ApplePredicate{
    boolean test (Apple apple);
}
```

You can now declare multiple implementations of ApplePredicate to represent different selection criteria, for example (and illustrated in figure 2.1):

```
public class AppleHeavyWeightPredicate implements ApplePredicate{    <-- Select only heavy apples.
    public boolean test(Apple apple){
        return apple.getWeight() > 150;
    }
}
public class AppleGreenColorPredicate implements ApplePredicate{    <-- Select only green apples.
    public boolean test(Apple apple){
        return "green".equals(apple.getColor());
    }
}
```

You can see these criteria as different behaviors for the filter method. What you just did is related to the strategy design pattern,[1] which lets you define a family of algorithms, encapsulate each algorithm (called a strategy), and select an algorithm at run-time. In this case the family of algorithms is ApplePredicate and the different strategies are AppleHeavyWeightPredicate and AppleGreenColorPredicate.

But how can you make use of the different implementations of ApplePredicate? You need your filterApples method to accept ApplePredicate objects to test a condition on an Apple. This is what *behavior parameterization* means: the ability to tell a method to *take* multiple behaviors (or strategies) as parameters and use them internally to *accomplish* different behaviors.

To achieve this in the running example, you add a parameter to the filterApples method to take an ApplePredicate object. This has a great software engineering benefit: you can now separate the logic of iterating the collection inside the filterApples

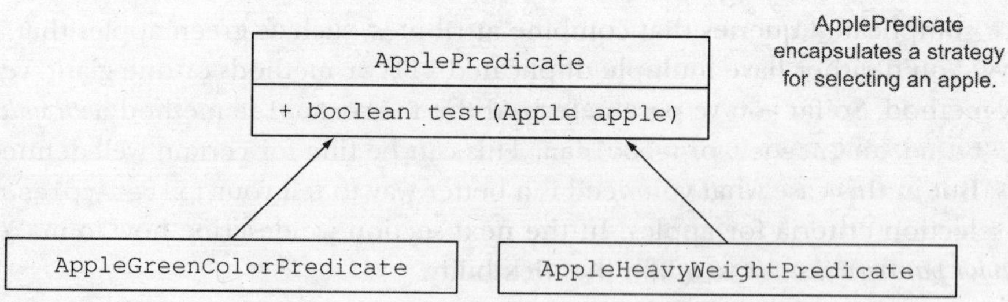

Figure 2.1 Different strategies for selecting an Apple

---

1 See http://en.wikipedia.org/wiki/Strategy_pattern.

method with the behavior you want to apply to each element of the collection (in this case a predicate).

2.2.1 Fourth attempt: filtering by abstract criteria

Our modified `filter` method, which uses an `ApplePredicate`, looks like this:

```
public static List<Apple> filterApples(List<Apple> inventory,
                                       ApplePredicate p){
    List<Apple> result = new ArrayList<>();
    for(Apple apple: inventory){
        if(p.test(apple)){          <-- The predicate object
            result.add(apple);          encapsulates the condition
        }                               to test on an apple.
    }
    return result;
}
```

PASSING CODE/BEHAVIOR

It's worth pausing for a moment for a small celebration. This code is much more flexible than our first attempt, while at the same time it's easy to read and to use! You can now create different `ApplePredicate` objects and pass them to the `filterApples` method. Free flexibility! For example, if the farmer asks you to find all red apples that are heavier than 150 g, all you need to do is create a class that implements the `ApplePredicate` accordingly. Your code is now flexible enough for any change of requirements involving the attributes of `Apple`:

```
public class AppleRedAndHeavyPredicate implements ApplePredicate{
    public boolean test(Apple apple){
        return "red".equals(apple.getColor())
               && apple.getWeight() > 150;
    }
}

List<Apple> redAndHeavyApples =
    filter(inventory, new AppleRedAndHeavyPredicate());
```

You've achieved something really cool: the behavior of the `filterApples` method depends on the *code you pass* to it via the `ApplePredicate` object. In other words, you've parameterized the behavior of the `filterApples` method!

Note that in the previous example, the only code that really matters is the implementation of the `test` method, as illustrated in figure 2.2; this is what defines the new behaviors for the `filterApples` method. Unfortunately, because the `filterApples` method can only take objects, you have to wrap that code inside an `ApplePredicate` object. What you're doing is similar to "passing code" inline, because you're passing a boolean expression through an object that implements the `test` method. You'll see in section 2.3 (and in more detail in chapter 3) that by using lambdas, you'll be able to directly pass the expression `"red".equals(apple.getColor()) && apple.getWeight() > 150` to the `filterApples` method without having to define multiple `ApplePredicate` classes and thus removing unnecessary verbosity.

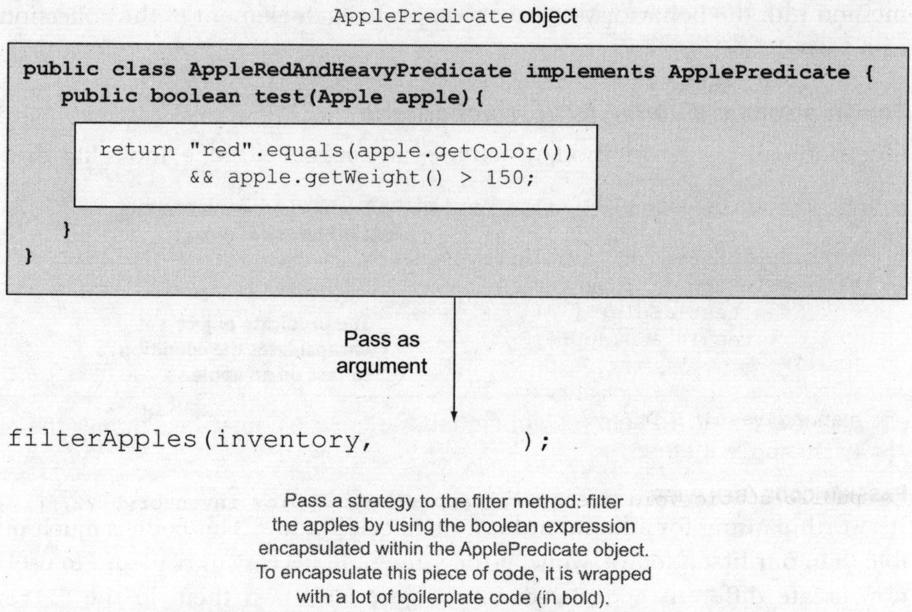

Figure 2.2 Parameterizing the behavior of `filterApples` and passing different filter strategies

MULTIPLE BEHAVIORS, ONE PARAMETER

As we explained earlier, behavior parameterization is great because it enables you to separate the logic of iterating the collection to filter and the behavior to apply on each element of that collection. As a consequence, you can reuse the same method and give it different behaviors to achieve different things, as illustrated in figure 2.3.

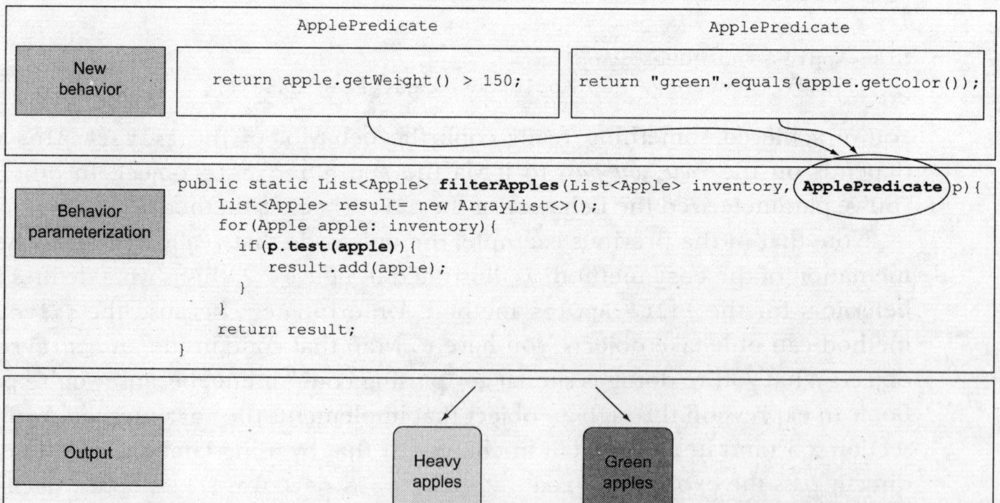

Figure 2.3 Parameterizing the behavior of `filterApples` and passing different filter strategies

This is why *behavior parameterization* is a useful concept you should have in your toolset for creating flexible APIs.

To make sure you feel comfortable with the idea of behavior parameterization, have a go at Quiz 2.1!

Quiz 2.1: Write a flexible prettyPrintApple method

Write a `prettyPrintApple` method that takes a `List` of `Apple`s and that can be parameterized with multiple ways to generate a `String` output from an apple (a bit like multiple customized `toString` methods). For example, you could tell your `prettyPrintApple` method to print only the weight of each apple. In addition, you could tell your `prettyPrintApple` method to print each apple individually and mention whether it's heavy or light. The solution is similar to the filtering examples we've explored so far. To help you get started, we provide a rough skeleton of the `prettyPrintApple` method:

```
public static void prettyPrintApple(List<Apple> inventory, ???){
    for(Apple apple: inventory) {
        String output = ???.???(apple);
        System.out.println(output);
    }
}
```

Answer:

First, you need a way to represent a behavior that takes an `Apple` and returns a formatted `String` result. You did something similar when you created an `ApplePredicate` interface:

```
public interface AppleFormatter{
    String accept(Apple a);
}
```

You can now represent multiple formatting behaviors by implementing the `AppleFormatter` interface:

```
public class AppleFancyFormatter implements AppleFormatter{
    public String accept(Apple apple){
        String characteristic = apple.getWeight() > 150 ? "heavy" :
            "light";
        return "A " + characteristic +
               " " + apple.getColor() +" apple";
    }
}
public class AppleSimpleFormatter implements AppleFormatter{
    public String accept(Apple apple){
        return "An apple of " + apple.getWeight() + "g";
    }
}
```

Finally, you need to tell your `prettyPrintApple` method to take `AppleFormatter` objects and use them internally. You can do this by adding a parameter to `prettyPrintApple`:

(continued)

```
public static void prettyPrintApple(List<Apple> inventory,
                                    AppleFormatter formatter){
  for(Apple apple: inventory){
    String output = formatter.accept(apple);
    System.out.println(output);
  }
}
```

Bingo! You're now able to pass multiple behaviors to your `prettyPrintApple` method. You do this by instantiating implementations of `AppleFormatter` and giving them as arguments to `prettyPrintApple`:

```
prettyPrintApple(inventory, new AppleFancyFormatter());
```

This will produce an output along the lines of

```
A light green apple
A heavy red apple
…
```

Or try this:

```
prettyPrintApple(inventory, new AppleSimpleFormatter());
```

This will produce an output along the lines of

```
An apple of 80g
An apple of 155g
…
```

You've seen that you can abstract over behavior and make your code adapt to requirement changes, but the process is verbose because you need to declare multiple classes that you instantiate only once. Let's see how to improve that.

2.3 Tackling verbosity

We all know that a feature or concept that's cumbersome to use will be avoided. At the moment, when you want to pass new behavior to your `filterApples` method, you're forced to declare several classes that implement the `ApplePredicate` interface and then instantiate several `ApplePredicate` objects that you allocate only once, as shown in the following listing that summarizes what you've seen so far. There's a lot of verbosity involved and it's a time-consuming process!

Listing 2.1 Behavior parameterization: filtering apples with predicates

```
public class AppleHeavyWeightPredicate implements ApplePredicate{
    public boolean test(Apple apple){
        return apple.getWeight() > 150;
    }
}
```

A predicate to select heavy apples.

```
public class AppleGreenColorPredicate implements ApplePredicate{
    public boolean test(Apple apple){
        return "green".equals(apple.getColor());
    }
}

public class FilteringApples{

    public static void main(String...args){
        List<Apple> inventory = Arrays.asList(new Apple(80,"green"),
                                              new Apple(155, "green"),
                                              new Apple(120, "red"));

        List<Apple> heavyApples =
            filterApples(inventory, new AppleHeavyWeightPredicate());
        List<Apple> greenApples =
            filterApples(inventory, new AppleGreenColorPredicate());

    }
    public static List<Apple> filterApples(List<Apple> inventory,
                                           ApplePredicate p) {
        List<Apple> result = new ArrayList<>();
        for (Apple apple : inventory){
            if (p.test(apple)){
                result.add(apple);
            }
        }
        return result;
    }
}
```

A predicate to select green apples.

The result will be a `List` containing one `Apple` of 155 g.

The result will be a `List` containing two green `Apples`.

This is unnecessary overhead; can you do better? Java has a mechanism called *anonymous classes*, which let you declare and instantiate a class at the same time. They enable you to improve your code one step further by making it a little more concise. But they're not entirely satisfactory. Section 2.3.3 shows a short preview of how lambda expressions can make your code more readable before we discuss them in detail in the next chapter.

2.3.1 Anonymous classes

Anonymous classes are like the local classes (a class defined in a block) that you're already familiar with in Java. But anonymous classes don't have a name. They allow you to declare and instantiate a class at the same time. In other words, they allow you to create ad hoc implementations.

2.3.2 Fifth attempt: using an anonymous class

The following code shows how to rewrite the filtering example by creating an object that implements `ApplePredicate` using an anonymous class:

```
List<Apple> redApples = filterApples(inventory, new ApplePredicate() {
    public boolean test(Apple apple){
        return "red".equals(apple.getColor());
    }
});
```

Parameterizing the behavior of the method `filterApples` directly inline!

Anonymous classes are often used in the context of GUI applications to create event-handler objects (here using the JavaFX API, a modern UI platform for Java):

```
button.setOnAction(new EventHandler<ActionEvent>() {
    public void handle(ActionEvent event) {
        System.out.println("Woooo a click!!");
    }
});
```

But anonymous classes are still not good enough. First, they tend to be very bulky because they take a lot of space, as shown in the highlighted code here using the same two examples used previously:

```
List<Apple> redApples = filterApples(inventory, new ApplePredicate() {
    public boolean test(Apple a){
        return "red".equals(a.getColor());
    }
});
button.setOnAction(new EventHandler<ActionEvent>() {
    public void handle(ActionEvent event) {
        System.out.println("Woooo a click!!");
    }
});
```

Lots of boilerplate code

Second, many programmers find them confusing to use. For example, Quiz 2.2 shows a classic Java puzzler that catches most programmers off guard! Try your hand at it.

Quiz 2.2: Anonymous class puzzler

What will the output be when this code is executed: `4`, `5`, `6`, or `42`?

```
public class MeaningOfThis
{
    public final int value = 4;
    public void doIt()
    {
        int value = 6;
        Runnable r = new Runnable(){
                public final int value = 5;
                public void run(){
                    int value = 10;
                    System.out.println(this.value);
                }
            };
            r.run();
    }
    public static void main(String...args)
    {
        MeaningOfThis m = new MeaningOfThis();
        m.doIt();
    }
}
```

What's the output of this line?

(continued)

Answer:

The answer is `5`, because `this` refers to the enclosing `Runnable`, not the enclosing class `MeaningOfThis`.

Verbosity in general is bad; it discourages the use of a language feature because it takes a long time to write and maintain verbose code, and it's not pleasant to read! Good code should be easy to comprehend at a glance. Even though anonymous classes somewhat tackle the verbosity associated with declaring multiple concrete classes for an interface, they're still unsatisfactory. In the context of passing a simple piece of code (for example, a `boolean` expression representing a selection criterion), you still have to create an object and explicitly implement a method to define a new behavior (for example, the method `test` for `Predicate` or the method `handle` for `EventHandler`).

Ideally we'd like to encourage programmers to use the behavior parameterization pattern, because as you've just seen, it makes your code more adaptive to requirement changes. In chapter 3 you'll see that the Java 8 language designers solved this problem by introducing lambda expressions, a more concise way to pass code. Enough suspense; here's a short preview of how lambda expressions can help you in your quest for clean code.

2.3.3 *Sixth attempt: using a lambda expression*

The previous code can be rewritten as follows in Java 8 using a lambda expression:

```
List<Apple> result =
  filterApples(inventory, (Apple apple) -> "red".equals(apple.getColor()));
```

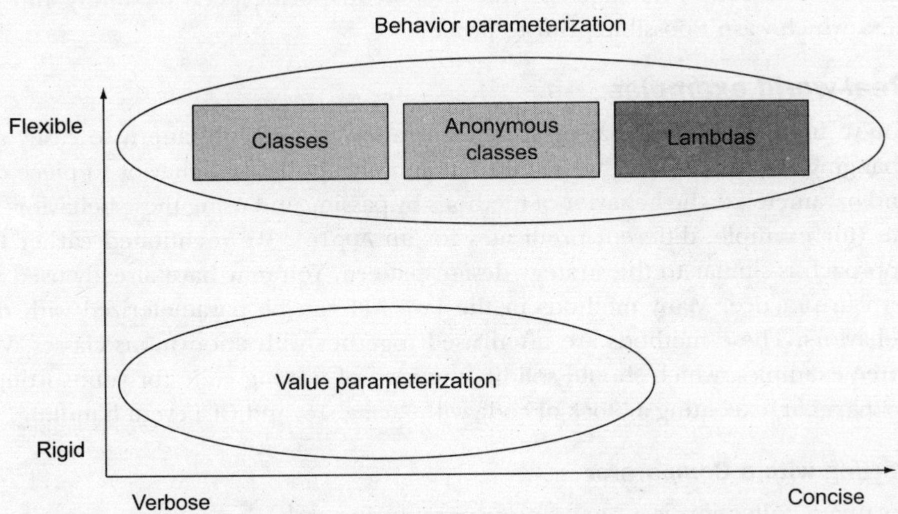

Figure 2.4 Behavior parameterization vs. value parameterization

You have to admit this code looks a lot cleaner than our previous attempts! It's great because it's starting to look a lot closer to the problem statement. We've now tackled the verbosity issue. Figure 2.4 summarizes our journey so far.

2.3.4 Seventh attempt: abstracting over List type

There's one more step that you can do in your journey toward abstraction. At the moment, the `filterApples` method works only for `Apple`. But you can also abstract on the `List` type to go beyond the problem domain you're thinking of right now:

```
public interface Predicate<T>{
    boolean test(T t);
}
public static <T> List<T> filter(List<T> list, Predicate<T> p){     <-- Introducing a type parameter T
    List<T> result = new ArrayList<>();
    for(T e: list){
        if(p.test(e)){
            result.add(e);
        }
    }
    return result;
}
```

You can now use the method `filter` with a `List` of bananas, oranges, `Integer`s, or `String`s! Here's an example, using lambda expressions:

```
List<Apple> redApples =
  filter(inventory, (Apple apple) -> "red".equals(apple.getColor()));
List<String> evenNumbers =
  filter(numbers, (Integer i) -> i % 2 == 0);
```

Isn't it cool? You've managed to find the sweet spot between flexibility and conciseness, which wasn't possible prior to Java 8!

2.4 Real-world examples

You've now seen that behavior parameterization is a useful pattern to easily adapt to changing requirements. This pattern lets you encapsulate a behavior (a piece of code) and parameterize the behavior of methods by passing and using these behaviors you create (for example, different predicates for an `Apple`). We mentioned earlier that this approach is similar to the strategy design pattern. You may have already used this pattern in practice. Many methods in the Java API can be parameterized with different behaviors. These methods are often used together with anonymous classes. We show three examples, which should solidify the idea of passing code for you: sorting with a `Comparator`, executing a block of code with `Runnable`, and GUI event handling.

2.4.1 Sorting with a Comparator

Sorting a collection is a recurring programming task. For example, say your farmer wants you to sort the inventory of apples based on their weight. Or perhaps he changes his mind and wants you to sort the apples by color. Sound familiar? Yes, you need a way to represent and use different sorting behaviors to easily adapt to changing requirements.

In Java 8, a `List` comes with a `sort` method (you could also use `Collections.sort`). The behavior of `sort` can be parameterized using a `java.util.Comparator` object, which has the following interface:

```
// java.util.Comparator
public interface Comparator<T> {
    public int compare(T o1, T o2);
}
```

You can therefore create different behaviors for the `sort` method by creating an ad hoc implementation of `Comparator`. For example, you can use it to sort the inventory by increasing weight using an anonymous class:

```
inventory.sort(new Comparator<Apple>() {
        public int compare(Apple a1, Apple a2){
            return a1.getWeight().compareTo(a2.getWeight());
        }
});
```

If the farmer changes his mind about how to sort apples, you can create an ad hoc `Comparator` to match the new requirement and pass it to the `sort` method! The internal details of how to sort are abstracted away. With a lambda expression it would look like this:

```
inventory.sort(
  (Apple a1, Apple a2) -> a1.getWeight().compareTo(a2.getWeight()));
```

Again, don't worry about this new syntax for now; the next chapter covers in detail how to write and use lambda expressions.

2.4.2 Executing a block of code with Runnable

Threads are like a lightweight process: they execute a block of code on their own. But how can you tell a thread what block of code to run? Several threads may run different code. What you need is a way to represent a piece of code to be executed later. In Java, you can use the `Runnable` interface to represent a block of code to be executed; note that the code will return no result (that is, `void`):

```
// java.lang.Runnable
public interface Runnable{
    public void run();
}
```

You can use this interface to create threads with different behaviors as follows:

```
Thread t = new Thread(new Runnable() {
    public void run(){
        System.out.println("Hello world");
    }
});
```

With a lambda expression it would look like this:

```
Thread t = new Thread(() -> System.out.println("Hello world"));
```

2.4.3 GUI event handling

A typical pattern in GUI programming is to perform an action in response to a certain event such as clicking or hovering over text. For example, if the user clicks the Send button, you may wish to display a popup or perhaps log the action in a file. Again, you need a way to cope with changes; you should be able to perform any response. In JavaFX you can use an `EventHandler` to represent a response to an event by passing it to `setOnAction`:

```
Button button = new Button("Send");
button.setOnAction(new EventHandler<ActionEvent>() {
    public void handle(ActionEvent event) {
        label.setText("Sent!!");
    }
});
```

Here, the behavior of the `setOnAction` method is parameterized with `EventHandler` objects. With a lambda expression it would look like this:

```
button.setOnAction((ActionEvent event) -> label.setText("Sent!!"));
```

2.5 Summary

Following are the key concepts you should take away from this chapter:

- Behavior parameterization is the ability for a method to *take* multiple different behaviors as parameters and use them internally to *accomplish* different behaviors.
- Behavior parameterization lets you make your code more adaptive to changing requirements and saves on engineering efforts in the future.
- Passing code is a way to give new behaviors as arguments to a method. But it's verbose prior to Java 8. Anonymous classes helped a bit before Java 8 to get rid of the verbosity associated with declaring multiple concrete classes for an interface that are needed only once.
- The Java API contains many methods that can be parameterized with different behaviors, which include sorting, threads, and GUI handling.

Lambda expressions

This chapter covers

- Lambdas in a nutshell
- Where and how to use lambdas
- The execute around pattern
- Functional interfaces, type inference
- Method references
- Composing lambdas

In the previous chapter, you saw that passing code with behavior parameterization is useful for coping with frequent requirement changes in your code. It lets you define a block of code that represents a behavior and then pass it around. You can decide to run that block of code when a certain event happens (for example, a click on a button) or at certain points in an algorithm (for example, a predicate such as "only apples heavier than 150 g" in the filtering algorithm or the customized comparison operation in sorting). In general, using this concept you can write code that's more flexible and reusable.

But you saw that using anonymous classes to represent different behaviors is unsatisfying: it's verbose, which doesn't encourage programmers to use behavior parameterization in practice. In this chapter, we teach you about a new feature in

Java 8 that tackles this problem: lambda expressions, which let you represent a behavior or pass code in a concise way. For now you can think of lambda expressions as anonymous functions, basically methods without declared names, but which can also be passed as arguments to a method as you can with an anonymous class.

We show how to construct them, where to use them, and how you can make your code more concise by using them. We also explain some new goodies such as type inference and new important interfaces available in the Java 8 API. Finally, we introduce method references, a useful new feature that goes hand in hand with lambda expressions.

This chapter is organized in such a way as to teach you step by step how to write more concise and flexible code. At the end of this chapter, we bring together all the concepts taught into a concrete example: we take the sorting example shown in chapter 2 and gradually improve it using lambda expressions and method references to make it more concise and readable. This chapter is important in itself and also because you'll use lambdas extensively throughout the book.

3.1 Lambdas in a nutshell

A *lambda expression* can be understood as a concise representation of an anonymous function that can be passed around: it doesn't have a name, but it has a list of parameters, a body, a return type, and also possibly a list of exceptions that can be thrown. That's one big definition; let's break it down:

- *Anonymous*—We say *anonymous* because it doesn't have an explicit name like a method would normally have: less to write and think about!
- *Function*—We say *function* because a lambda isn't associated with a particular class like a method is. But like a method, a lambda has a list of parameters, a body, a return type, and a possible list of exceptions that can be thrown.
- *Passed around*—A lambda expression can be passed as argument to a method or stored in a variable.
- *Concise*—You don't need to write a lot of boilerplate like you do for anonymous classes.

If you're wondering where the term *lambda* comes from, it originates from a system developed in academia called *lambda calculus*, which is used to describe computations.

Why should you care about lambda expressions? You saw in the previous chapter that passing code is currently tedious and verbose in Java. Well, good news! Lambdas fix this problem: they let you pass code in a concise way. Lambdas technically don't let you do anything that you couldn't do prior to Java 8. But you no longer have to write clumsy code using anonymous classes to benefit from behavior parameterization! Lambda expressions will encourage you to adopt the style of behavior parameterization that we described in the previous chapter. The net result is that your code will be clearer and more flexible. For example, using a lambda expression you can create a custom `Comparator` object in a more concise way.

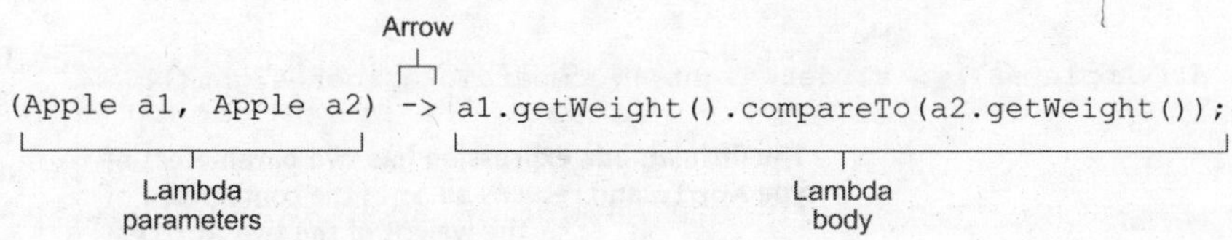

Figure 3.1 A lambda expression is composed of parameters, an arrow, and a body.

Before:

```
Comparator<Apple> byWeight = new Comparator<Apple>() {
    public int compare(Apple a1, Apple a2){
        return a1.getWeight().compareTo(a2.getWeight());
    }
};
```

After (with lambda expressions):

```
Comparator<Apple> byWeight =
     (Apple a1, Apple a2) -> a1.getWeight().compareTo(a2.getWeight());
```

You must admit that the code looks clearer! Don't worry if all the parts of the lambda expression don't make sense yet; we explain all the pieces soon. For now, note that you're literally passing only the code that's really needed to compare two apples using their weight. It looks like you're just passing the body of the method `compare`. You'll learn soon that you can simplify your code even more. We explain in the next section exactly where and how you can use lambda expressions.

The lambda we just showed you has three parts, as shown in figure 3.1:

- *A list of parameters*—In this case it mirrors the parameters of the `compare` method of a `Comparator`—two `Apple`s.
- *An arrow*—The arrow -> separates the list of parameters from the body of the lambda.
- *The body of the lambda*—Compare two `Apple`s using their weights. The expression is considered the lambda's return value.

To illustrate further, the following listing shows five examples of valid lambda expressions in Java 8.

Listing 3.1 Valid lambda expressions in Java 8

```
(String s) -> s.length()
(Apple a) -> a.getWeight() > 150
(int x, int y) -> {
    System.out.println("Result:");
    System.out.println(x+y);
}
```

The first lambda expression has one parameter of type `String` and returns an `int`. The lambda doesn't have a `return` statement here because the `return` is implied.

second lambda sion has ameter `Apple` turns a olean her the heavier 150 g).

The third lambda expression has two parameters of type `int` with no return (`void` return). Note that lambda expressions can contain multiple statements, in this case two.

```
() -> 42
(Apple a1, Apple a2) -> a1.getWeight().compareTo(a2.getWeight())
```

The fourth lambda expression has no parameter and returns an `int`.

The fifth lambda expression has two parameters of type `Apple` and returns an `int`: the comparison of the weight of the two `Apples`.

This syntax was chosen by the Java language designers because it was well received in other languages such as C# and Scala, which have a similar feature. The basic syntax of a lambda is either

```
(parameters) -> expression
```

or (note the curly braces for statements)

```
(parameters) -> { statements; }
```

As you can see, lambda expressions follow a simple syntax. Working through Quiz 3.1 should let you know if you understand the pattern.

Quiz 3.1: Lambda syntax

Based on the syntax rules just shown, which of the following are not valid lambda expressions?

1. `() -> {}`
2. `() -> "Raoul"`
3. `() -> {return "Mario";}`
4. `(Integer i) -> return "Alan" + i;`
5. `(String s) -> {"Iron Man";}`

Answer:

Only 4 and 5 are invalid lambdas.

1. This lambda has no parameters and returns `void`. It's similar to a method with an empty body: `public void run() { }`.
2. This lambda has no parameters and returns a `String` as an expression.
3. This lambda has no parameters and returns a `String` (using an explicit return statement).
4. `return` is a control-flow statement. To make this lambda valid, curly braces are required as follows: `(Integer i) -> {return "Alan" + i;}`.
5. "Iron Man" is an expression, not a statement. To make this lambda valid, you can remove the curly braces and semicolon as follows: `(String s) -> "Iron Man"`. Or if you prefer, you can use an explicit return statement as follows: `(String s) -> {return "Iron Man";}`.

Table 3.1 provides a list of example lambdas with examples of use cases.

Table 3.1 Examples of lambdas

Use case	Examples of lambdas
A boolean expression	`(List<String> list) -> list.isEmpty()`
Creating objects	`() -> new Apple(10)`
Consuming from an object	`(Apple a) -> { System.out.println(a.getWeight()); }`
Select/extract from an object	`(String s) -> s.length()`
Combine two values	`(int a, int b) -> a * b`
Compare two objects	`(Apple a1, Apple a2) -> a1.getWeight().compareTo(a2.getWeight())`

3.2 *Where and how to use lambdas*

You may now be wondering where you're allowed to use lambda expressions. In the previous example, you assigned a lambda to a variable of type `Comparator<Apple>`. You could also use another lambda with the `filter` method you implemented in the previous chapter:

```
List<Apple> greenApples =
        filter(inventory, (Apple a) -> "green".equals(a.getColor()));
```

So where exactly can you use lambdas? You can use a lambda expression in the context of a functional interface. In the code shown here, you can pass a lambda as second argument to the method `filter` because it expects a `Predicate<T>`, which is a functional interface. Don't worry if this sounds abstract; we now explain in detail what this means and what a functional interface is.

3.2.1 *Functional interface*

Remember the interface `Predicate<T>` you created in chapter 2 so you could parameterize the behavior of the `filter` method? It's a functional interface! Why? Because `Predicate` specifies only one abstract method:

```
public interface Predicate<T>{
    boolean test (T t);
}
```

In a nutshell, a *functional interface* is an interface that specifies exactly one abstract method. You already know several other functional interfaces in the Java API such as `Comparator` and `Runnable`, which we explored in chapter 2:

```
public interface Comparator<T> {          <-- java.util.Comparator
    int compare(T o1, T o2);
}
```

```
public interface Runnable{            <-- java.lang.Runnable
    void run();
}

public interface ActionListener extends EventListener{      <--
    void actionPerformed(ActionEvent e);
}                                       java.awt.event.ActionListener

public interface Callable<V>{         <-- java.util.concurrent.Callable
    V call();
}

public interface PrivilegedAction<V>{    <-- java.security.PrivilegedAction
    T run();
}
```

> **NOTE** You'll see in chapter 9 that interfaces can now also have *default methods* (that is, a method with a body that provides some default implementation for a method in case it isn't implemented by a class). An interface is still a functional interface if it has many default methods as long as it specifies *only one abstract method.*

To check your understanding, Quiz 3.2 should let you know if you grasp the concept of a functional interface.

Quiz 3.2: Functional interface

Which of these interfaces are functional interfaces?

```
public interface Adder{
    int add(int a, int b);
}
public interface SmartAdder extends Adder{
    int add(double a, double b);
}
public interface Nothing{
}
```

Answer:

Only `Adder` is a functional interface.

`SmartAdder` isn't a functional interface because it specifies two abstract methods called `add` (one is inherited from `Adder`).

`Nothing` isn't a functional interface because it declares no abstract method at all.

What can you do with functional interfaces? Lambda expressions let you provide the implementation of the abstract method of a functional interface directly inline and *treat the whole expression as an instance of a functional interface* (more technically speaking, an instance of a *concrete implementation* of the functional interface). You can achieve the same thing with an anonymous inner class, although it's clumsier: you provide an implementation and instantiate it directly inline. The following code is valid because `Runnable` is a functional interface defining only one abstract method, `run`:

```
Runnable r1 = () -> System.out.println("Hello World 1");        <-- Using a lambda

Runnable r2 = new Runnable(){                                    <-- Using an
    public void run(){                                               anonymous class
        System.out.println("Hello World 2");
    }
};

public static void process(Runnable r){
    r.run();
}
process(r1);                                                     <-- Prints "Hello World 1"
process(r2);                                                     <-- Prints "Hello World 2"
process(() -> System.out.println("Hello World 3"));              <-- Prints "Hello World 3" with a lambda passed directly
```

3.2.2 Function descriptor

The signature of the abstract method of the functional interface essentially describes the signature of the lambda expression. We call this abstract method a *function descriptor*. For example, the `Runnable` interface can be viewed as the signature of a function that accepts nothing and returns nothing (`void`) because it has only one abstract method called `run`, which accepts nothing and returns nothing (`void`).[1]

We use a special notation throughout the chapter to describe the signatures of lambdas and functional interfaces. The notation `() -> void` represents a function with an empty list of parameters returning `void`. This is exactly what the `Runnable` interface represents. As another example, `(Apple, Apple) -> int` denotes a function taking two `Apple`s as parameters and returning an `int`. We'll provide more information about function descriptors in section 3.4 and table 3.2 later in the chapter.

You may already be wondering how lambda expressions are type checked. We detail how the compiler checks whether a lambda is valid in a given context in section 3.5. For now, it suffices to understand that a lambda expression can be assigned to a variable or passed to a method expecting a functional interface as argument, provided the lambda expression has the same signature as the abstract method of the functional interface. For instance, in our earlier example, you could pass a lambda directly to the `process` method as follows:

---

[1] Some languages such as Scala provide explicit type annotations in their type system to describe the type of a function (called function types). Java reuses existing nominal types provided by functional interfaces and maps them into a form of function types behind the scenes.

```
public void process(Runnable r){
  r.run();
}

process(() -> System.out.println("This is awesome!!"));
```

This code when executed will print "This is awesome!!" The lambda expression `() -> System.out.println("This is awesome!!")` takes no parameters and returns `void`. This is exactly the signature of the `run` method defined in the `Runnable` interface.

You may be wondering, "Why can we pass a lambda only where a functional interface is expected?" The language designers considered alternative approaches such as adding function types (a bit like the special notation we introduced to describe the signature of lambda expressions—we revisit this topic in chapters 15 and 16) to Java. But they chose this way because it fits naturally without increasing the complexity of the language. In addition, most Java programmers are already familiar with the idea of an interface with a single abstract method (for example, with event handling). Try Quiz 3.3 to test your knowledge of where lambdas can be used.

Quiz 3.3: Where can you use lambdas?

Which of the following are valid uses of lambda expressions?

1
```
execute(() -> {});
public void execute(Runnable r){
  r.run();
}
```

2
```
public Callable<String> fetch() {
  return () -> "Tricky example ;-)";
}
```

3
```
Predicate<Apple> p = (Apple a) -> a.getWeight();
```

Answer:

Only 1 and 2 are valid.

The first example is valid because the lambda `() -> {}` has the signature `() -> void`, which matches the signature of the abstract method `run` defined in `Runnable`. Note that running this code will do nothing because the body of the lambda is empty!

The second example is also valid. Indeed, the return type of the method `fetch` is `Callable<String>`. `Callable<String>` essentially defines a method with the signature `() -> String` when `T` is replaced with `String`. Because the lambda `() -> "Tricky example ;-)"` has the signature `() -> String`, the lambda can be used in this context.

The third example is invalid because the lambda expression `(Apple a) -> a.getWeight()` has the signature `(Apple) -> Integer`, which is different than the signature of the method `test` defined in `Predicate<Apple>: (Apple) -> boolean`.

> **What about @FunctionalInterface?**
>
> If you explore the new Java API, you'll notice that functional interfaces are annotated with `@FunctionalInterface` (we show an extensive list in section 3.4, where we explore functional interfaces in depth). This annotation is used to indicate that the interface is intended to be a functional interface. The compiler will return a meaningful error if you define an interface using the `@FunctionalInterface` annotation and it isn't a functional interface. For example, an error message could be "Multiple non-overriding abstract methods found in interface Foo" to indicate that more than one abstract method is available. Note that the `@FunctionalInterface` annotation isn't mandatory, but it's good practice to use it when an interface is designed for that purpose. You can think of it like the `@Override` notation to indicate that a method is overridden.

3.3 Putting lambdas into practice: the execute around pattern

Let's look at an example of how lambdas, together with behavior parameterization, can be used in practice to make your code more flexible and concise. A recurrent pattern in resource processing (for example, dealing with files or databases) is to open a resource, do some processing on it, and then close the resource. The setup and cleanup phases are always similar and surround the important code doing the processing. This is called the *execute around* pattern, as illustrated in figure 3.2. For example, in the following code, the highlighted lines show the boilerplate code required to read one line from a file (note also that you use Java 7's try-with-resources statement, which already simplifies the code, because you don't have to close the resource explicitly):

```
public static String processFile() throws IOException {
    try (BufferedReader br =
            new BufferedReader(new FileReader("data.txt"))) {
        return br.readLine();
    }
}
```

This is the line that does useful work.

3.3.1 Step 1: Remember behavior parameterization

This current code is limited. You can read only the first line of the file. What if you'd like to return the first two lines instead or even the word used most frequently? Ideally, you'd like to reuse the code doing setup and cleanup and tell the `processFile`

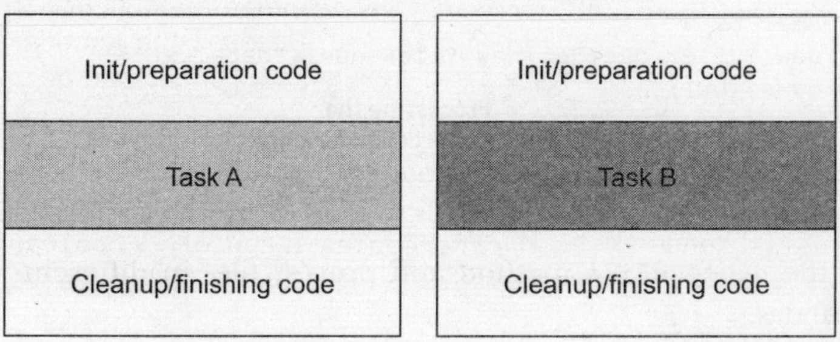

Figure 3.2 Tasks A and B are surrounded by the same redundant code responsible for preparation/cleanup.

method to perform different actions on the file. Does this sound familiar? Yes, you need to parameterize the behavior of `processFile`. You need a way to pass behavior to `processFile` so it can execute different behaviors using a `BufferedReader`.

Passing behavior is exactly what lambdas are for. So what should the new `processFile` method look like if you wanted to read two lines at once? You basically need a lambda that takes a `BufferedReader` and returns a `String`. For example, here's how to print two lines of a `BufferedReader`:

```
String result = processFile((BufferedReader br) ->
                                br.readLine() + br.readLine());
```

3.3.2 *Step 2: Use a functional interface to pass behaviors*

We explained earlier that lambdas can be used only in the context of a functional interface. You need to create one that matches the signature `BufferedReader -> String` and that may throw an `IOException`. Let's call this interface `BufferedReaderProcessor`:

```
@FunctionalInterface
public interface BufferedReaderProcessor {
    String process(BufferedReader b) throws IOException;
}
```

You can now use this interface as the argument to your new `processFile` method:

```
public static String processFile(BufferedReaderProcessor p) throws
    IOException {
    …
}
```

3.3.3 *Step 3: Execute a behavior!*

Any lambdas of the form `BufferedReader -> String` can be passed as arguments, because they match the signature of the `process` method defined in the `BufferedReaderProcessor` interface. You now need only a way to execute the code represented by the lambda inside the body of `processFile`. Remember, lambda expressions let you provide the implementation of the abstract method of a functional interface directly inline, and they *treat the whole expression as an instance of a functional interface.* You can therefore call the method `process` on the resulting `BufferedReaderProcessor` object inside the `processFile` body to perform the processing:

```
public static String processFile(BufferedReaderProcessor p) throws
     IOException {
    try (BufferedReader br =
                   new BufferedReader(new FileReader("data.txt"))) {
        return p.process(br);          <-- Processing the
    }                                      BufferedReader object
}
```

3.3.4 *Step 4: Pass lambdas*

You can now reuse the `processFile` method and process files in different ways by passing different lambdas.

Processing one line:

```
String oneLine =
  processFile((BufferedReader br) -> br.readLine());
```

Processing two lines:

```
String twoLines =
  processFile((BufferedReader br) -> br.readLine() + br.readLine());
```

Figure 3.3 summarizes the four steps taken to make the `processFile` method more flexible.

So far, we've showed how you can make use of functional interfaces to pass lambdas. But you had to define your own interfaces. In the next section we explore new interfaces that were added to Java 8 that you can reuse to pass multiple different lambdas.

```
1
public static String processFile() throws IOException {
    try (BufferedReader br =
              new BufferedReader(new FileReader("data.txt"))){
        return br.readLine();
    }
}
```

```
2
public interface BufferedReaderProcessor {
  String process(BufferedReader b) throws IOException;
}

public static String processFile(BufferedReaderProcessor p) throws
IOException {
   …
}
```

```
3
public static String processFile(BufferedReaderProcessor p)
throws IOException {
   try (BufferedReader br =
             new BufferedReader(new FileReader("data.txt"))){
       return p.process(br);
   }
}
```

```
4
String oneLine = processFile((BufferedReader br) ->
                                   br.readLine());

String twoLines = processFile((BufferedReader br) ->
                                   br.readLine()) + br.readLine());

..
```

Figure 3.3 Four-step process to apply the execute around pattern

3.4 Using functional interfaces

As you learned in section 3.2.1, a functional interface specifies exactly one abstract method. Functional interfaces are useful because the signature of the abstract method can describe the signature of a lambda expression. The signature of the abstract method of a functional interface is called a *function descriptor*. So in order to use different lambda expressions, you need a set of functional interfaces that can describe common function descriptors. There are several functional interfaces already available in the Java API such as `Comparable`, `Runnable`, and `Callable`, which you saw in section 3.2.

The Java library designers for Java 8 have helped you by introducing several new functional interfaces inside the `java.util.function` package. We describe the interfaces `Predicate`, `Consumer`, and `Function` next, and a more complete list is available in table 3.2 at the end of this section.

3.4.1 Predicate

The `java.util.function.Predicate<T>` interface defines an abstract method named `test` that accepts an object of generic type `T` and returns a `boolean`. It's exactly the same one that you created earlier, but is available out of the box! You might want to use this interface when you need to represent a boolean expression that uses an object of type `T`. For example, you can define a lambda that accepts `String` objects, as shown in the following listing.

Listing 3.2 Working with a `Predicate`

```
@FunctionalInterface
public interface Predicate<T>{
    boolean test(T t);
}

public static <T> List<T> filter(List<T> list, Predicate<T> p) {
    List<T> results = new ArrayList<>();
    for(T s: list){
        if(p.test(s)){
            results.add(s);
        }
    }
    return results;
}

Predicate<String> nonEmptyStringPredicate = (String s) -> !s.isEmpty();
List<String> nonEmpty = filter(listOfStrings, nonEmptyStringPredicate);
```

If you look up the Javadoc specification of the `Predicate` interface, you may notice additional methods such as `and` and `or`. Don't worry about them for now. We come back to these in section 3.8.

3.4.2 Consumer

The `java.util.function.Consumer<T>` interface defines an abstract method named `accept` that takes an object of generic type `T` and returns no result (`void`). You might use this interface when you need to access an object of type T and perform some operations on it. For example, you can use it to create a method forEach, which takes a list of Integers and applies an operation on each element of that list. In the following listing you use this forEach method combined with a lambda to print all the elements of the list.

Listing 3.3 Working with a Consumer

```
@FunctionalInterface
public interface Consumer<T>{
    void accept(T t);
}
public static <T> void forEach(List<T> list, Consumer<T> c){
    for(T i: list){
        c.accept(i);
    }
}
forEach(
         Arrays.asList(1,2,3,4,5),
        (Integer i) -> System.out.println(i)
       );
```

The lambda is the implementation of the accept method from Consumer.

3.4.3 *Function*

The java.util.function.Function<T, R> interface defines an abstract method named apply that takes an object of generic type T as input and returns an object of generic type R. You might use this interface when you need to define a lambda that maps information from an input object to an output (for example, extracting the weight of an apple or mapping a string to its length). In the listing that follows we show how you can use it to create a method map to transform a list of Strings into a list of Integers containing the length of each String.

Listing 3.4 Working with a Function

```
@FunctionalInterface
public interface Function<T, R>{
    R apply(T t);
}
public static <T, R> List<R> map(List<T> list,
                                 Function<T, R> f) {
    List<R> result = new ArrayList<>();
    for(T s: list){
        result.add(f.apply(s));
    }
    return result;
}
// [7, 2, 6]
List<Integer> l = map(
                       Arrays.asList("lambdas","in","action"),
                       (String s) -> s.length()
               );
```

The lambda is the implementation for the apply method of Function.

PRIMITIVE SPECIALIZATIONS

We described three functional interfaces that are generic: `Predicate<T>`, `Consumer<T>`, and `Function<T, R>`. There are also functional interfaces that are specialized with certain types.

To refresh a little: every Java type is either a reference type (for example, `Byte`, `Integer`, `Object`, `List`) or a primitive type (for example, `int`, `double`, `byte`, `char`). But generic parameters (for example, the `T` in `Consumer<T>`) can be bound only to reference types. This is due to how generics are internally implemented.[2] As a result, in Java there's a mechanism to convert a primitive type into a corresponding reference type. This mechanism is called *boxing*. The opposite approach (that is, converting a reference type into a corresponding primitive type) is called *unboxing*. Java also has an *autoboxing* mechanism to facilitate the task for programmers: boxing and unboxing operations are done automatically. For example, this is why the following code is valid (an `int` gets boxed to an `Integer`):

```
List<Integer> list = new ArrayList<>();
for (int i = 300; i < 400; i++){
    list.add(i);
}
```

But this comes with a performance cost. Boxed values are essentially a wrapper around primitive types and are stored on the heap. Therefore, boxed values use more memory and require additional memory lookups to fetch the wrapped primitive value.

Java 8 brings a specialized version of the functional interfaces we described earlier in order to avoid autoboxing operations when the inputs or outputs are primitives. For example, in the following code, using an `IntPredicate` avoids a boxing operation of the value `1000`, whereas using a `Predicate<Integer>` would box the argument `1000` to an `Integer` object:

```
public interface IntPredicate{
    boolean test(int t);
}

IntPredicate evenNumbers = (int i) -> i % 2 == 0;
evenNumbers.test(1000);                              <-- true (no boxing)

Predicate<Integer> oddNumbers = (Integer i) -> i % 2 == 1;
oddNumbers.test(1000);                               <-- false (boxing)
```

In general, the names of functional interfaces that have a specialization for the input type parameter are preceded by the appropriate primitive type, for example, `DoublePredicate`, `IntConsumer`, `LongBinaryOperator`, `IntFunction`, and so on. The `Function` interface has also variants for the output type parameter: `ToIntFunction<T>`, `IntToDoubleFunction`, and so on.

---

2 Some other languages such as C# don't have this restriction. Other languages such as Scala have only reference types. We revisit this issue in chapter 16.

Table 3.2 gives a summary of the most commonly used functional interfaces available in the Java API and their function descriptors. Keep in mind that they're only a starter kit. You can always make your own if needed! Remember, the notation `(T, U) -> R` shows how to think about a function descriptor. The left side of the table is a list representing the types of the arguments. In this case it represents a function with two arguments of respectively generic type `T` and `U` and that has a return type of `R`.

Table 3.2 Common functional interfaces in Java 8

Functional interface	Function descriptor	Primitive specializations
`Predicate<T>`	`T -> boolean`	`IntPredicate, LongPredicate, DoublePredicate`
`Consumer<T>`	`T -> void`	`IntConsumer, LongConsumer, DoubleConsumer`
`Function<T, R>`	`T -> R`	`IntFunction<R>, IntToDoubleFunction, IntToLongFunction, LongFunction<R>, LongToDoubleFunction, LongToIntFunction, DoubleFunction<R>, ToIntFunction<T>, ToDoubleFunction<T>, ToLongFunction<T>`
`Supplier<T>`	`() -> T`	`BooleanSupplier, IntSupplier, LongSupplier, DoubleSupplier`
`UnaryOperator<T>`	`T -> T`	`IntUnaryOperator, LongUnaryOperator, DoubleUnaryOperator`
`BinaryOperator<T>`	`(T, T) -> T`	`IntBinaryOperator, LongBinaryOperator, DoubleBinaryOperator`
`BiPredicate<L, R>`	`(L, R) -> boolean`	
`BiConsumer<T, U>`	`(T, U) -> void`	`ObjIntConsumer<T>, ObjLongConsumer<T>, ObjDoubleConsumer<T>`
`BiFunction<T, U, R>`	`(T, U) -> R`	`ToIntBiFunction<T, U>, ToLongBiFunction<T, U>, ToDoubleBiFunction<T, U>`

You've now seen a lot of functional interfaces that can be used to describe the signature of various lambda expressions. To check your understanding so far, have a go at Quiz 3.4.

Quiz 3.4: Functional interfaces

What functional interfaces would you use for the following function descriptors (that is, signatures of a lambda expression)? You'll find most of the answers in table 3.2. As a further exercise, come up with valid lambda expressions that you can use with these functional interfaces.

1. `T -> R`
2. `(int, int) -> int`
3. `T -> void`
4. `() -> T`
5. `(T, U) -> R`

Answers:

1. `Function<T, R>` is a good candidate. It's typically used for converting an object of type `T` into an object of type `R` (for example, `Function<Apple, Integer>` to extract the weight of an apple).
2. `IntBinaryOperator` has a single abstract method called `applyAsInt` representing a function descriptor `(int, int) -> int`.
3. `Consumer<T>` has a single abstract method called `accept` representing a function descriptor `T -> void`.
4. `Supplier<T>` has a single abstract method called `get` representing a function descriptor `() -> T`. Alternatively, `Callable<T>` also has a single abstract method called `call` representing a function descriptor `() -> T`.
5. `BiFunction<T, U, R>` has a single abstract method called `apply` representing a function descriptor `(T, U) -> R`.

To summarize the discussion about functional interfaces and lambdas, table 3.3 provides a summary of use cases, examples of lambdas, and functional interfaces that can be used.

Table 3.3 Examples of lambdas with functional interfaces

Use case	Example of lambda	Matching functional interface
A boolean expression	`(List<String> list) -> list.isEmpty()`	`Predicate<List<String>>`
Creating objects	`() -> new Apple(10)`	`Supplier<Apple>`
Consuming from an object	`(Apple a) -> System.out.println(a.getWeight())`	`Consumer<Apple>`
Select/extract from an object	`(String s) -> s.length()`	`Function<String, Integer>` or `ToIntFunction<String>`
Combine two values	`(int a, int b) -> a * b`	`IntBinaryOperator`

Table 3.3 Examples of lambdas with functional interfaces *(continued)*

Use case	Example of lambda	Matching functional interface
Compare two objects	`(Apple a1, Apple a2) -> a1.getWeight().compareTo (a2.getWeight())`	`Comparator<Apple>` or `BiFunction<Apple, Apple, Integer>` or `ToIntBiFunction<Apple, Apple>`

What about exceptions, lambdas, and functional interfaces?

Note that none of the functional interfaces allow for a checked exception to be thrown. You have two options if you need a lambda expression to throw an exception: define your own functional interface that declares the checked exception, or wrap the lambda with a `try/catch` block.

For example, in section 3.3 we introduced a new functional interface `BufferedReaderProcessor` that explicitly declared an `IOException`:

```
@FunctionalInterface
public interface BufferedReaderProcessor {
    String process(BufferedReader b) throws IOException;
}
BufferedReaderProcessor p = (BufferedReader br) -> br.readLine();
```

But you may be using an API that expects a functional interface such as `Function<T, R>` and there's no option to create your own (you'll see in the next chapter that the Streams API makes heavy use of the functional interfaces from table 3.2). In this case you can explicitly catch the checked exception:

```
Function<BufferedReader, String> f =
  (BufferedReader b) -> {
    try {
      return b.readLine();
    }
    catch(IOException e) {
      throw new RuntimeException(e);
    }
  };
```

You've now seen how to create lambdas and where and how to use them. Next, we explain some more advanced details: how lambdas are type checked by the compiler and rules you should be aware of, such as lambdas referencing local variables inside their body and void-compatible lambdas. There's no need to fully understand the next section right away, and you may wish to come back to it later and move on to section 3.6 about method references.

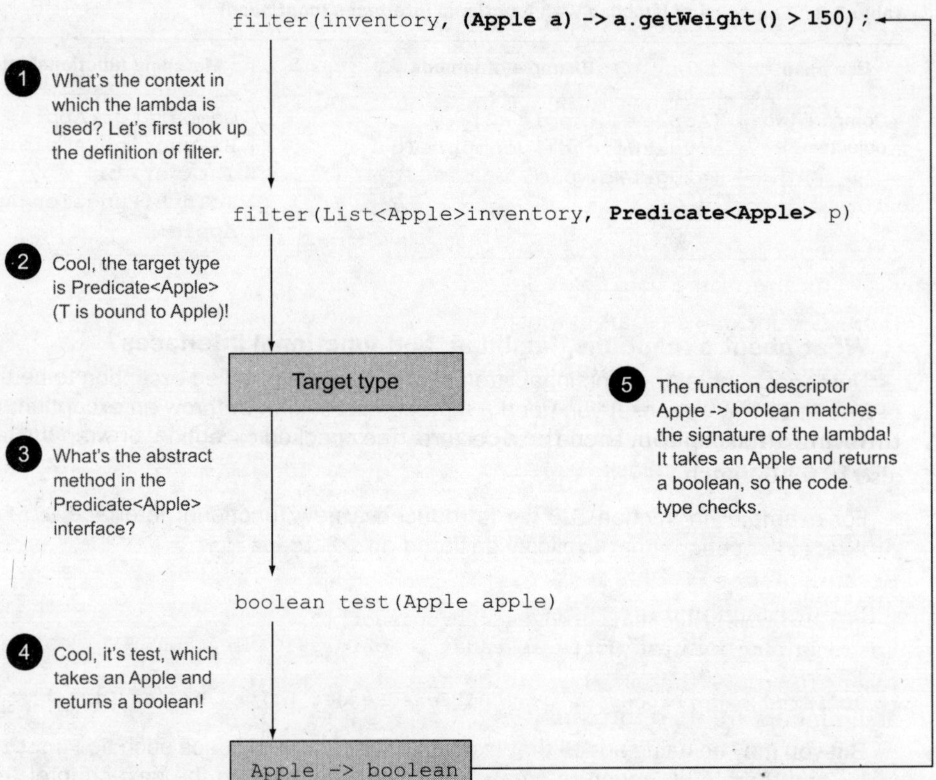

Figure 3.4 Deconstructing the type-checking process of a lambda expression

3.5 Type checking, type inference, and restrictions

When we first mentioned lambda expressions, we said that they let you generate an instance of a functional interface. Nonetheless, a lambda expression itself doesn't contain the information about which functional interface it's implementing. In order to have a more formal understanding of lambda expressions, you should know what the actual type of a lambda is.

3.5.1 Type checking

The type of a lambda is deduced from the context in which the lambda is used. The type expected for the lambda expression inside the context (for example, a method parameter that it's passed to or a local variable that it's assigned to) is called the *target type*. Let's look at an example to see what happens behind the scenes when you use a lambda expression. Figure 3.4 summarizes the type-checking process for the following code:

```
List<Apple> heavierThan150g =
        filter(inventory, (Apple a) -> a.getWeight() > 150);
```

The type-checking process is deconstructed as follows:

- First, you look up the declaration of the filter method.
- Second, it expects as the second formal parameter an object of type Predicate<Apple> (the target type).
- Third, Predicate<Apple> is a functional interface defining a single abstract method called test.
- Fourth, the method test describes a function descriptor that accepts an Apple and returns a boolean.
- Finally, any actual argument to the filter method needs to match this requirement.

The code is valid because the lambda expression that we're passing also takes an Apple as parameter and returns a boolean. Note that if the lambda expression were throwing an exception, then the declared throws clause of the abstract method would also have to match.

3.5.2 Same lambda, different functional interfaces

Because of the idea of *target typing*, the same lambda expression can be associated with different functional interfaces if they have a compatible abstract method signature. For example, both interfaces Callable and PrivilegedAction described earlier represent functions that accept nothing and return a generic type T. The following two assignments are therefore valid:

```
Callable<Integer> c = () -> 42;
PrivilegedAction<Integer> p = () -> 42;
```

In this case the first assignment has target type Callable<Integer> and the second assignment has target type PrivilegedAction<Integer>.

In table 3.3 we showed a similar example; the same lambda can be used with multiple different functional interfaces:

```
Comparator<Apple> c1 =
    (Apple a1, Apple a2) -> a1.getWeight().compareTo(a2.getWeight());
ToIntBiFunction<Apple, Apple> c2 =
    (Apple a1, Apple a2) -> a1.getWeight().compareTo(a2.getWeight());
BiFunction<Apple, Apple, Integer> c3 =
    (Apple a1, Apple a2) -> a1.getWeight().compareTo(a2.getWeight());
```

Diamond operator

Those of you who are familiar with Java's evolution will recall that Java 7 had already introduced the idea of types being inferred from context with generic inference using the diamond operator (<>) (this idea can be found even earlier with generic methods). A given class instance expression can appear in two or more different contexts, and the appropriate type argument will be inferred as exemplified here:

```
List<String> listOfStrings = new ArrayList<>();
List<Integer> listOfIntegers = new ArrayList<>();
```

Special void-compatibility rule

If a lambda has a statement expression as its body, it's compatible with a function descriptor that returns `void` (provided the parameter list is compatible too). For example, both of the following lines are legal even though the method `add` of a `List` returns a `boolean` and not `void` as expected in the `Consumer` context (`T -> void`):

```
// Predicate has a boolean return
Predicate<String> p = s -> list.add(s);
// Consumer has a void return
Consumer<String> b = s -> list.add(s);
```

By now you should have a good understanding of when and where you're allowed to use lambda expressions. They can get their target type from an assignment context, method invocation context (parameters and return), and a cast context. To check your knowledge, try Quiz 3.5.

Quiz 3.5: Type checking–why won't the following code compile?

How could you fix the problem?

```
Object o = () -> {System.out.println("Tricky example"); };
```

Answer:

The context of the lambda expression is `Object` (the target type). But `Object` isn't a functional interface. To fix this you can change the target type to `Runnable`, which represents a function descriptor `() -> void`:

```
Runnable r = () -> {System.out.println("Tricky example"); };
```

You've seen how the target type can be used to check whether a lambda can be used in a particular context. It can also be used to do something slightly different: infer the types of the parameters of a lambda.

3.5.3 *Type inference*

You can simplify your code one step further. The Java compiler deduces what functional interface to associate with a lambda expression from its surrounding context (the target type), meaning it can also deduce an appropriate signature for the lambda because the function descriptor is available through the target type. The benefit is that the compiler has access to the types of the parameters of a lambda expression, and they can be omitted in the lambda syntax. In other words, the Java compiler infers the types of the parameters of a lambda as shown here:[3]

[3] Note that when a lambda has just one parameter whose type is inferred, the parentheses surrounding the parameter name can also be omitted.

```
List<Apple> greenApples =
        filter(inventory, a -> "green".equals(a.getColor()));   <-- No explicit type on the parameter a
```

The benefits of code readability are more noticeable with lambda expressions that have several parameters. For example, here's how to create a `Comparator` object:

```
Comparator<Apple> c =
  (Apple a1, Apple a2) -> a1.getWeight().compareTo(a2.getWeight());   <-- Without type inference
Comparator<Apple> c =
  (a1, a2) -> a1.getWeight().compareTo(a2.getWeight());   <-- With type inference
```

Note that sometimes it's more readable to include the types explicitly and sometimes more readable to exclude them. There's no rule for which way is better; developers must make their own choices about what makes their code more readable.

3.5.4 Using local variables

All the lambda expressions we've shown so far used only their arguments inside their body. But lambda expressions are also allowed to use *free variables* (variables that aren't the parameters and defined in an outer scope) just like anonymous classes can. They're called *capturing lambdas*. For example, the following lambda captures the variable `portNumber`:

```
int portNumber = 1337;
Runnable r = () -> System.out.println(portNumber);
```

Nonetheless, there's a small twist: there are some restrictions on what you can do with these variables. Lambdas are allowed to capture (that is, to reference in their bodies) instance variables and static variables without restrictions. But local variables have to be explicitly declared `final` or are effectively `final`. In other words, lambda expressions can capture local variables that are assigned to them only once. (Note: capturing an instance variable can be seen as capturing the final local variable `this`.) For example, the following code doesn't compile because the variable `portNumber` is assigned to twice:

```
int portNumber = 1337;
Runnable r = () -> System.out.println(portNumber);   <-- Error: local variables referenced from a lambda expression must be final or effectively final.
portNumber = 31337;
```

RESTRICTIONS ON LOCAL VARIABLES

You may be asking yourself why local variables have these restrictions. First, there's a key difference in how instance and local variables are implemented behind the scenes. Instance variables are stored on the heap, whereas local variables live on the stack. If a lambda could access the local variable directly and the lambda were used in a thread, then the thread using the lambda could try to access the variable after the thread that allocated the variable had deallocated it. Hence, Java implements access to a free local variable as access to a copy of it rather than access to the original variable. This makes no difference if the local variable is assigned to only once—hence the restriction.

Second, this restriction also discourages typical imperative programming patterns (which, as we explain in later chapters, prevent easy parallelization) that mutate an outer variable.

> **Closure**
>
> You may have heard of the term *closure* and may be wondering whether lambdas meet the definition of a closure (not to be confused with the Clojure programming language). To put it scientifically, a *closure* is an instance of a function that can reference nonlocal variables of that function with no restrictions. For example, a closure could be passed as argument to another function. It could also *access and modify* variables defined outside its scope. Now Java 8 lambdas and anonymous classes do something similar to closures: they can be passed as argument to methods and can access variables outside their scope. But they have a restriction: they can't modify the content of local variables of a method in which the lambda is defined. Those variables have to be implicitly final. It helps to think that lambdas close over *values* rather than *variables*. As explained previously, this restriction exists because local variables live on the stack and are implicitly confined to the thread they're in. Allowing capture of mutable local variables opens new thread-unsafe possibilities, which are undesirable (instance variables are fine because they live on the heap, which is shared across threads).

We now describe another feature that you'll see in Java 8 code: *method references.* Think of them as shorthand versions of certain lambdas.

3.6 Method references

Method references let you reuse existing method definitions and pass them just like lambdas. In some cases they appear more readable and feel more natural than using lambda expressions. Here's our sorting example written with a method reference and a bit of help from the updated Java 8 API (we explore this example in more detail in section 3.7):

Before:

```
inventory.sort((Apple a1, Apple a2)
                -> a1.getWeight().compareTo(a2.getWeight()));
```

After (using a method reference and `java.util.Comparator.comparing`):

```
inventory.sort(comparing(Apple::getWeight));
```

Your first method reference!

3.6.1 In a nutshell

Why should you care about method references? Method references can be seen as shorthand for lambdas calling only a specific method. The basic idea is that if a lambda represents "call this method directly," it's best to refer to the method by name rather than by a description of how to call it. Indeed, a method reference lets you create a lambda expression from an existing method implementation. But by referring to a method name explicitly, your code *can gain better readability*. How does it work? When you need a method reference, the target reference is placed before the delimiter `::` and the name of the method is provided after it. For example, `Apple::getWeight` is a method reference to the method `getWeight` defined in the `Apple` class. Remember that no brackets are needed because you're not actually calling the method. The method reference is shorthand for the lambda expression `(Apple a) -> a.getWeight()`. Table 3.4 gives a couple more examples of possible method references in Java 8.

Table 3.4 Examples of lambdas and method reference equivalents

Lambda	Method reference equivalent
`(Apple a) -> a.getWeight()`	`Apple::getWeight`
`() -> Thread.currentThread().dumpStack()`	`Thread.currentThread()::dumpStack`
`(str, i) -> str.substring(i)`	`String::substring`
`(String s) -> System.out.println(s)`	`System.out::println`

You can think of method references as syntactic sugar for lambdas that refer only to a single method because you write less to express the same thing.

RECIPE FOR CONSTRUCTING METHOD REFERENCES

There are three main kinds of method references:

1. A method reference to a *static method* (for example, the method `parseInt` of `Integer`, written `Integer::parseInt`)
2. A method reference to an *instance method of an arbitrary type* (for example, the method `length` of a `String`, written `String::length`)
3. A method reference to an *instance method of an existing object* (for example, suppose you have a local variable `expensiveTransaction` that holds an object of type `Transaction`, which supports an instance method `getValue`; you can write `expensiveTransaction::getValue`)

The second and third kinds of method references may be a bit overwhelming at first. The idea with the second kind of method references such as `String::length` is that you're referring to a method to an object that will be supplied as one of the parameters of the lambda. For example, the lambda expression `(String s) -> s.toUpperCase()` can be rewritten as `String::toUpperCase`. But the third kind of method references refers to a situation when you're calling a method in a lambda to an external object that already exists. For example, the lambda expression `() -> expensiveTransaction.getValue()` can be rewritten as `expensiveTransaction::getValue`.

The shorthand rules to refactor a lambda expression to an equivalent method reference follow simple recipes, shown in figure 3.5.

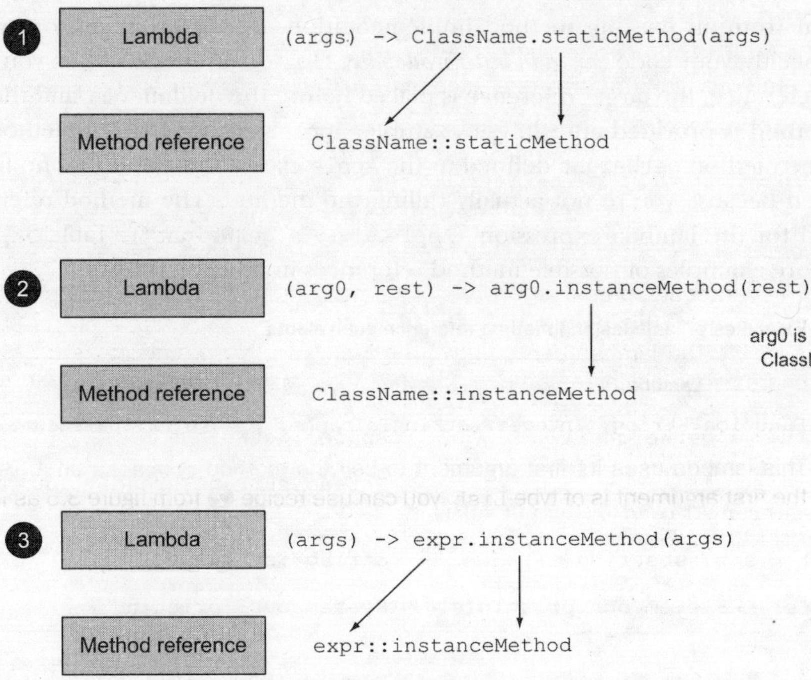

Figure 3.5 Recipes for constructing method references for three different types of lambda expressions

Note that there are also special forms of method references for constructors, array constructors, and super-calls. Let's apply method references in a concrete example. Say you'd like to sort a `List` of strings, ignoring case differences. The `sort` method on a `List` expects a `Comparator` as parameter. You saw earlier that `Comparator` describes a function descriptor with the signature `(T, T) -> int`. You can define a lambda expression that leverages the method `compareToIgnoreCase` in the `String` class as follows (note that `compareToIgnoreCase` is predefined in the `String` class):

```
List<String> str = Arrays.asList("a","b","A","B");
str.sort((s1, s2) -> s1.compareToIgnoreCase(s2));
```

The lambda expression has a signature compatible with the function descriptor of `Comparator`. Using the recipes described previously, the example can also be written using a method reference as follows:

```
List<String> str = Arrays.asList("a","b","A","B");
str.sort(String::compareToIgnoreCase);
```

Note that the compiler goes through a similar type-checking process as for lambda expressions to figure out whether a method reference is valid with a given functional interface: the signature of the method reference has to match the type of the context.

To check your understanding of method references, have a go at Quiz 3.6!

Quiz 3.6: Method references

What are equivalent method references for the following lambda expressions?

```
1 Function<String, Integer> stringToInteger =
                    (String s) -> Integer.parseInt(s);
2 BiPredicate<List<String>, String> contains =
                    (list, element) -> list.contains(element);
```

Answers:

1. This lambda expression forwards its argument to the static method `parseInt` of `Integer`. This method takes a `String` to parse and returns an `Integer`. As a result, the lambda can be rewritten using recipe ❶ from figure 3.5 (lambda expressions calling a static method) as follows:

   ```
   Function<String, Integer> stringToInteger = Integer::parseInt;
   ```

2. This lambda uses its first argument to call the method `contains` on it. Because the first argument is of type `List`, you can use recipe ❷ from figure 3.5 as follows:

   ```
   BiPredicate<List<String>, String> contains = List::contains;
   ```

This is because the target type describes a function descriptor `(List<String>, String) -> boolean`, and `List::contains` can be unpacked to that function descriptor.

So far we showed only how to reuse existing method implementations and create method references. But you can do something similar with constructors of a class.

3.6.2 Constructor references

You can create a reference to an existing constructor using its name and the keyword `new` as follows: `ClassName::new`. It works similarly to a reference to a static method. For example, suppose there's a zero-argument constructor. This fits the signature `() -> Apple` of `Supplier`; you can do the following,

```
Supplier<Apple> c1 = Apple::new;      // A constructor reference to the default Apple() constructor.
Apple a1 = c1.get();                  // Calling Supplier's get method will produce a new Apple.
```

which is equivalent to

```
Supplier<Apple> c1 = () -> new Apple();   // A lambda expression creating an Apple with the default constructor.
Apple a1 = c1.get();                      // Calling Supplier's get method will produce a new Apple.
```

If you have a constructor with signature `Apple(Integer weight)`, it fits the signature of the `Function` interface, so you can do this,

```
Function<Integer, Apple> c2 = Apple::new;   // A constructor reference to Apple(Integer weight).
Apple a2 = c2.apply(110);                   // Calling the Function's apply method with the requested weight will produce an Apple.
```

which is equivalent to

```
Function<Integer, Apple> c2 = (weight) -> new Apple(weight);
Apple a2 = c2.apply(110);
```

A lambda expression creating an `Apple` with a requested weight.

Calling the `Function`'s `apply` method with the requested weight will produce a new `Apple` object.

In the following code, each element of a `List` of `Integers` is passed to the constructor of `Apple` using a similar `map` method we defined earlier, resulting in a `List` of apples with different weights:

```
List<Integer> weights = Arrays.asList(7, 3, 4, 10);
List<Apple> apples = map(weights, Apple::new);

public static List<Apple> map(List<Integer> list,
                              Function<Integer, Apple> f){
    List<Apple> result = new ArrayList<>();
    for(Integer e: list){
        result.add(f.apply(e));
    }
    return result;
}
```

Passing a constructor reference to the `map` method

If you have a two-argument constructor, `Apple(String color, Integer weight)`, it fits the signature of the `BiFunction` interface, so you can do this,

```
BiFunction<String, Integer, Apple> c3 = Apple::new;
Apple c3 = c3.apply("green", 110);
```

A constructor reference to `Apple(String color, Integer weight)`.

Calling the `BiFunction`'s `apply` method with the requested color and weight will produce a new `Apple` object.

which is equivalent to

```
BiFunction<String, Integer, Apple> c3 =
    (color, weight) -> new Apple(color, weight);
Apple c3 = c3.apply("green", 110);
```

A lambda expression creating an `Apple` with a requested color and weight.

Calling the `BiFunction`'s `apply` method with the requested color and weight will produce a new `Apple` object.

The capability of referring to a constructor without instantiating it enables interesting applications. For example, you can use a `Map` to associate constructors with a string value. You can then create a method `giveMeFruit` that, given a `String` and an `Integer`, can create different types of fruits with different weights:

```
static Map<String, Function<Integer, Fruit>> map = new HashMap<>();
static {
    map.put("apple", Apple::new);
    map.put("orange", Orange::new);
    // etc...
}
```

```
public static Fruit giveMeFruit(String fruit, Integer weight){
    return map.get(fruit.toLowerCase())
              .apply(weight);
}
```

You get a `Function<Integer, Fruit>` from the map.

Calling the `Function`'s `apply()` method with an `Integer` `weight` parameter will provide the requested `Fruit`.

To check your understanding of method and constructor references, try out Quiz 3.7.

> **Quiz 3.7: Constructor references**
>
> You saw how to transform zero-, one-, and two-argument constructors into constructor references. What would you need to do in order to use a constructor reference for a three-argument constructor such as `Color(int, int, int)`?
>
> Answer:
>
> You saw that the syntax for a constructor reference is `ClassName::new`, so in this case it's `Color::new`. But you need a functional interface that will match the signature of that constructor reference. Because there isn't one in the functional interface starter set, you can create your own:
>
> ```
> public interface TriFunction<T, U, V, R>{
>     R apply(T t, U u, V v);
> }
> ```
>
> And you can now use the constructor reference as follows:
>
> ```
> TriFunction<Integer, Integer, Integer, Color> colorFactory = Color::new;
> ```

We've gone through a lot of new information: lambdas, functional interfaces, and method references. We put it all into practice in the next section!

3.7 Putting lambdas and method references into practice!

To wrap up this chapter and all we've discussed on lambdas, we continue with our initial problem of sorting a list of `Apples` with different ordering strategies and show how you can progressively evolve a naïve solution into a concise solution, using all the concepts and features explained so far in the book: behavior parameterization, anonymous classes, lambda expressions, and method references. The final solution we work toward is this (note that all source code is available on the book's web page):

```
inventory.sort(comparing(Apple::getWeight));
```

3.7.1 Step 1: Pass code

You're lucky; the Java 8 API already provides you with a `sort` method available on `List` so you don't have to implement it. So the hard part is done! But how can you pass an ordering strategy to the `sort` method? Well, the `sort` method has the following signature:

```
void sort(Comparator<? super E> c)
```

It expects a `Comparator` object as argument to compare two `Apple`s! This is how you can pass different strategies in Java: they have to be wrapped in an object. We say that the *behavior* of `sort` is *parameterized*: its behavior will be different based on different ordering strategies passed to it.

Your first solution looks like this:

```
public class AppleComparator implements Comparator<Apple> {
        public int compare(Apple a1, Apple a2){
                return a1.getWeight().compareTo(a2.getWeight());
        }
}
inventory.sort(new AppleComparator());
```

3.7.2 Step 2: Use an anonymous class

Rather than implementing `Comparator` for the purpose of instantiating it once, you saw that you could use an *anonymous class* to improve your solution:

```
inventory.sort(new Comparator<Apple>() {
    public int compare(Apple a1, Apple a2){
        return a1.getWeight().compareTo(a2.getWeight());
    }
});
```

3.7.3 Step 3: Use lambda expressions

But your current solution is still verbose. Java 8 introduces lambda expressions, which provide a lightweight syntax to achieve the same goal: *passing code*. You saw that a lambda expression can be used where a *functional interface* is expected. As a reminder, a functional interface is an interface defining only one abstract method. The signature of the abstract method (called *function descriptor*) can describe the signature of a lambda expression. In this case, the `Comparator` represents a function descriptor `(T, T) -> int`. Because you're using apples, it represents more specifically `(Apple, Apple) -> int`. Your new improved solution looks therefore as follows:

```
inventory.sort((Apple a1, Apple a2)
                -> a1.getWeight().compareTo(a2.getWeight())
);
```

We explained that the Java compiler could *infer the types* of the parameters of a lambda expression by using the context in which the lambda appears. So you can rewrite your solution like this:

```
inventory.sort((a1, a2) -> a1.getWeight().compareTo(a2.getWeight()));
```

Can you make your code even more readable? `Comparator` has a static helper method called `comparing` that takes a `Function` extracting a `Comparable` key and produces a `Comparator` object (we explain why interfaces can have static methods in chapter 9). It can be used as follows (note that you now pass a lambda with only one argument: the lambda specifies how to extract the key to compare with from an apple):

```
Comparator<Apple> c = Comparator.comparing((Apple a) -> a.getWeight());
```

You can now rewrite your solution in a slightly more compact form:

```
import static java.util.Comparator.comparing;
inventory.sort(comparing((a) -> a.getWeight()));
```

3.7.4 Step 4: Use method references

We explained that method references are syntactic sugar for lambda expressions that forwards their arguments. You can use a method reference to make your code slightly less verbose (assuming a static import of `java.util.Comparator.comparing`):

```
inventory.sort(comparing(Apple::getWeight));
```

Congratulations, this is your final solution! Why is this better than code prior to Java 8? It's not just because it's shorter; it's also obvious what it means, and the code reads like the problem statement "sort inventory comparing the weight of the apples."

3.8 Useful methods to compose lambda expressions

Several functional interfaces in the Java 8 API contain convenient methods. Specifically, many functional interfaces such as `Comparator`, `Function`, and `Predicate` that are used to pass lambda expressions provide methods that allow composition. What does this mean? In practice it means you can combine several simple lambda expressions to build more complicated ones. For example, you can combine two predicates into a larger predicate that performs an `or` operation between the two predicates. Moreover, you can also compose functions such that the result of one becomes the input of another function. You may wonder how it's possible that there are additional methods in a functional interface. (After all, this goes against the definition of a functional interface!) The trick is that the methods that we'll introduce are called *default methods* (that is, they're not abstract methods). We explain them in detail in chapter 9. For now, just trust us and read chapter 9 later when you want to find out more about default methods and what you can do with them.

3.8.1 Composing Comparators

You've seen that you can use the static method `Comparator.comparing` to return a `Comparator` based on a `Function` that extracts a key for comparison as follows:

```
Comparator<Apple> c = Comparator.comparing(Apple::getWeight);
```

REVERSED ORDER

What if you wanted to sort the apples by decreasing weight? There's no need to create a different instance of a `Comparator`. The interface includes a default method `reverse` that imposes the reverse ordering of a given comparator. So you can simply modify the previous example to sort the apples by decreasing weight by reusing the initial `Comparator`:

```
inventory.sort(comparing(Apple::getWeight).reversed());   <-- Sorting by decreasing weight
```

CHAINING COMPARATORS

This is all nice, but what if you find two apples that have the same weight? Which apple should have priority in the sorted list? You may want to provide a second `Comparator` to further refine the comparison. For example, after two apples are compared based on their weight, you may want to sort them by country of origin. The `thenComparing` method allows you to do just that. It takes a function as parameter (just like the method `comparing`) and provides a second `Comparator` if two objects are considered equal using the initial `Comparator`. You can solve the problem elegantly again:

```
inventory.sort(comparing(Apple::getWeight)
        .reversed()
        .thenComparing(Apple::getCountry));
```

Sorting by decreasing weight

Sorting further by country when two apples have same weight

3.8.2 Composing Predicates

The `Predicate` interface includes three methods that let you reuse an existing `Predicate` to create more complicated ones: `negate`, `and`, and `or`. For example, you can use the method `negate` to return the negation of a `Predicate`, such as an apple that is not red:

```
Predicate<Apple> notRedApple = redApple.negate();
```

Produces the negation of the existing `Predicate` object `redApple`

You may want to combine two lambdas to say that an apple is both red and heavy with the and method:

```
Predicate<Apple> redAndHeavyApple =
    redApple.and(a -> a.getWeight() > 150);
```

Chaining two predicates to produce another `Predicate` object

You can combine the resulting predicate one step further to express apples that are red and heavy (above 150 g) or just green apples:

```
Predicate<Apple> redAndHeavyAppleOrGreen =
    redApple.and(a -> a.getWeight() > 150)
            .or(a -> "green".equals(a.getColor()));
```

Chaining `Predicate's` methods to construct a more complex `Predicate` object

Why is this great? From simpler lambda expressions you can represent more complicated lambda expressions that still read like the problem statement! Note that the precedence of methods `and` and `or` is managed from left to right using their positions in the chain. So `a.or(b).and(c)` can be seen as `(a || b) && c`.

3.8.3 Composing Functions

Finally, you can also compose lambda expressions represented by the `Function` interface. The `Function` interface comes with two default methods for this, andThen and `compose`, which both return an instance of `Function`.

The method andThen returns a function that first applies a given function to an input and then applies another function to the result of that application. For example, given a function f that increments a number (x -> x + 1) and another function g that multiplies a number by 2, you can combine them to create a function h that first increments a number and then multiplies the result by 2:

```
Function<Integer, Integer> f = x -> x + 1;
Function<Integer, Integer> g = x -> x * 2;
Function<Integer, Integer> h = f.andThen(g);
int result = h.apply(1);
```

In math you'd write g(f(x)) or (g o f)(x).

This returns 4.

You can also use the method compose similarly to first apply the function given as argument to compose and then apply the function to the result. For example, in the previous example using compose, it would mean f(g(x)) instead of g(f(x)) using andThen:

```
Function<Integer, Integer> f = x -> x + 1;
Function<Integer, Integer> g = x -> x * 2;
Function<Integer, Integer> h = f.compose(g);
int result = h.apply(1);
```

In math you'd write f(g(x)) or (f o g)(x).

This returns 3.

Figure 3.6 illustrates the difference between andThen and compose.

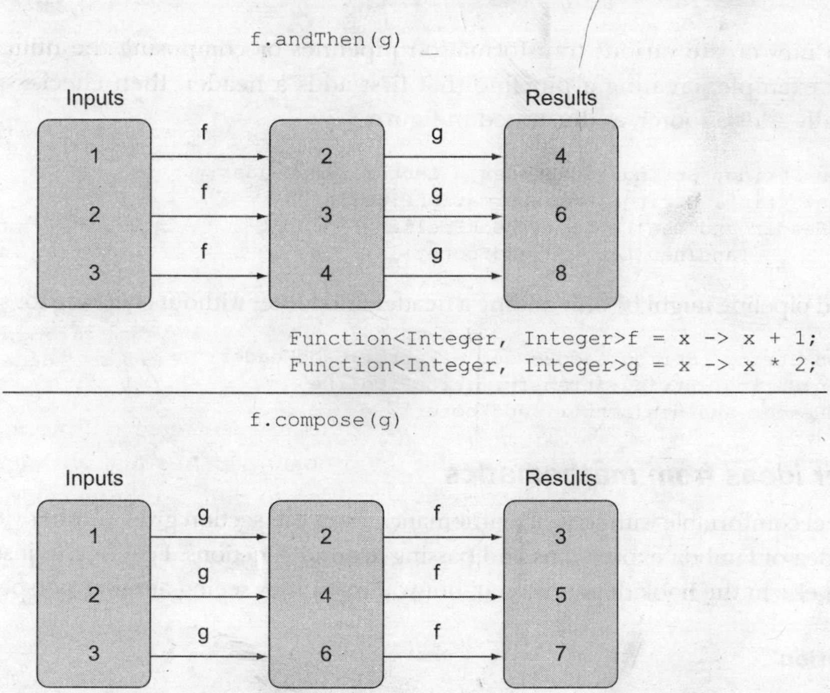

Figure 3.6 Using andThen vs. compose

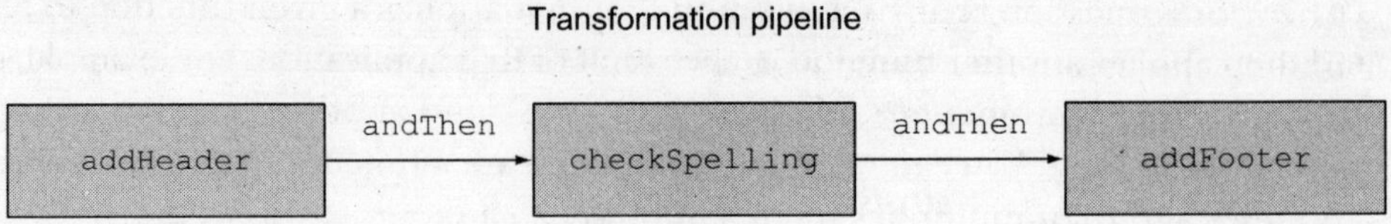

Figure 3.7 A transformation pipeline using `andThen`

This all sounds a bit too abstract. How can you use these in practice? Let's say you have various utility methods that do text transformation on a letter represented as a `String`:

```
public class Letter{
    public static String addHeader(String text){
        return "From Raoul, Mario and Alan: " + text;
    }

    public static String addFooter(String text){
        return text + " Kind regards";
    }

    public static String checkSpelling(String text){
        return text.replaceAll("labda", "lambda");
    }
}
```

You can now create various transformation pipelines by composing the utility methods, for example, creating a pipeline that first adds a header, then checks spelling, and finally adds a footer, as illustrated in figure 3.7:

```
Function<String, String> addHeader = Letter::addHeader;
Function<String, String> transformationPipeline
  = addHeader.andThen(Letter::checkSpelling)
             .andThen(Letter::addFooter);
```

A second pipeline might be only adding a header and footer without checking for spelling:

```
Function<String, String> addHeader = Letter::addHeader;
Function<String, String> transformationPipeline
  = addHeader.andThen(Letter::addFooter);
```

3.9 Similar ideas from mathematics

If you feel comfortable with school mathematics, then this section gives another viewpoint of the idea of lambda expressions and passing around functions. Feel free to just skip it; nothing else in the book depends on it, but you may enjoy seeing another perspective.

3.9.1 Integration

Suppose you have a (mathematical, not Java) function `f`, perhaps defined by

$f(x) = x + 10$

Then, one question that's often asked (at school, in engineering degrees) is that of finding the area beneath the function when drawn on paper (counting the x-axis as the zero line). For example, you write

$$\int_3^7 f(x)\,dx \quad \text{or} \quad \int_3^7 (x+10)\,dx$$

for the area shown in figure 3.8.

In this example, the function `f` is a straight line, and so you can easily work out this area by the trapezium method (essentially drawing triangles) to discover the solution:

$$1/2 \times ((3+10) + (7+10)) \times (7-3) = 60$$

Now, how might you express this in Java? Your first problem is reconciling the strange notation like the integration symbol or `dy/dx` with familiar programming language notation.

Indeed, thinking from first principles you need a method, perhaps called `integrate`, that takes three arguments: one is `f`, and the others are the limits (3.0 and 7.0 here). Thus, you want to write in Java something that looks like this, where the function `f` is just passed around:

```
integrate(f, 3, 7)
```

Note that you can't write something as simple as

```
integrate(x+10, 3, 7)
```

for two reasons. First, the scope of `x` is unclear, and second, this would pass a value of `x+10` to integrate instead of passing the function `f`.

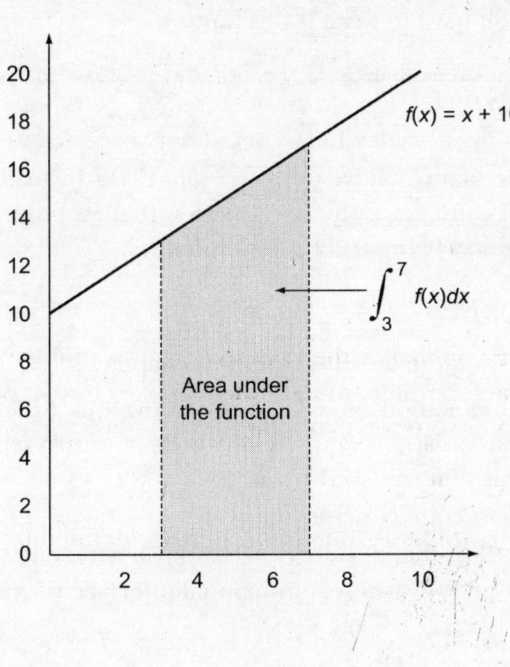

Figure 3.8 Area under the function `f(x) = x + 10` for x from 3 to 7

Indeed, the secret role of dx in mathematics is to say "that function taking argument x whose result is x+10."

3.9.2 Connecting to Java 8 lambdas

Now, as we mentioned earlier, Java 8 uses the notation (double x) -> x+10 (a lambda expression) for exactly this purpose; hence you can write

```
integrate((double x) -> x + 10, 3, 7)
```

or

```
integrate((double x) -> f(x), 3, 7)
```

or, using a method reference as mentioned earlier, simply

```
integrate(C::f, 3, 7)
```

if C is a class containing f as a static method. The idea is that you're passing the code for f to the method integrate.

You may now wonder how you'd write the method integrate itself. Continue to suppose that f is a linear function (straight line). You'd probably like to write in a form similar to mathematics:

```
public double integrate((double -> double)f, double a, double b) {
      return (f(a)+f(b))*(b-a)/2.0
}
```

Incorrect Java code! (You can't write functions as you do in mathematics.)

But because lambda expressions can be used only in a context expecting a functional interface (in this case, Function), you have to write it this way:

```
public double integrate(DoubleFunction<Double> f, double a, double b) {
      return (f.apply(a) + f.apply(b)) * (b-a) / 2.0;
}
```

As a side remark, it's a bit of a shame that you have to write f.apply(a) instead of just f(a) as in mathematics, but Java just can't get away from the view that everything is an object—instead of the idea of a function being truly independent!

3.10 Summary

Following are the key concepts you should take away from this chapter:

- A *lambda expression* can be understood as a kind of anonymous function: it doesn't have a name, but it has a list of parameters, a body, a return type, and also possibly a list of exceptions that can be thrown.
- Lambda expressions let you pass code concisely.
- A *functional interface* is an interface that declares exactly one abstract method.
- Lambda expressions can be used only where a functional interface is expected.

- Lambda expressions let you provide the implementation of the abstract method of a functional interface directly inline and *treat the whole expression as an instance of a functional interface.*
- Java 8 comes with a list of common functional interfaces in the `java.util.function` package, which includes `Predicate<T>`, `Function<T, R>`, `Supplier<T>`, `Consumer<T>`, and `BinaryOperator<T>`, described in table 3.2.
- There are primitive specializations of common generic functional interfaces such as `Predicate<T>` and `Function<T, R>` that can be used to avoid boxing operations: `IntPredicate`, `IntToLongFunction`, and so on.
- The execute around pattern (that is, you need to execute a bit of behavior in the middle of code that's always required in a method, for example, resource allocation and cleanup) can be used with lambdas to gain additional flexibility and reusability.
- The type expected for a lambda expression is called the *target* type.
- Method references let you reuse an existing method implementation and pass it around directly.
- Functional interfaces such as `Comparator`, `Predicate`, and `Function` have several default methods that can be used to combine lambda expressions.

Part 2

Functional-style data processing

The second part of this book is a deep exploration of the new Streams API, which lets you write powerful code that processes a collection of data in a declarative way. By the end of this second part, you'll have a full understanding of what streams are and how you can use them in your codebase to process a collection of data concisely and efficiently.

Chapter 4 introduces the concept of a stream and explains how it compares with a collection.

Chapter 5 investigates in detail the stream operations available to express sophisticated data processing queries. You'll look at many patterns such as filtering, slicing, finding, matching, mapping, and reducing.

Chapter 6 covers collectors—a feature of the Streams API that lets you express even more complex data processing queries.

In chapter 7, you'll learn about how streams can automatically run in parallel and leverage your multicore architectures. In addition, you'll learn about various pitfalls to avoid when using parallel streams correctly and effectively.

4 Introducing streams

This chapter covers

- What is a stream?
- Collections vs. streams
- Internal vs. external iteration
- Intermediate vs. terminal operations

Collections is the most heavily used API in Java. What would you do without collections? Nearly every Java application *makes* and *processes* collections. Collections are fundamental to many programming tasks: they let you group and process data. To illustrate collections in action, imagine you want to create a collection of dishes to represent a menu and then iterate through it to sum the calories of each dish. You may want to process the collection to select only low-calorie dishes for a special healthy menu. But despite collections being necessary for almost any Java application, manipulating collections is far from perfect:

- Much business logic entails database-like operations such as *grouping* a list of dishes by category (for example, all vegetarian dishes) or *finding* the most expensive dish. How many times do you find yourself reimplementing these operations using iterators? Most databases let you specify such operations declaratively. For example, the following SQL query lets you select the names of dishes that are low in calories: `SELECT name FROM dishes WHERE calorie < 400`. As you can see, you don't need to implement how to filter using the attributes of a dish (for example, using an iterator and an accumulator). Instead, you express only what you expect. This basic idea means that you worry less about how to explicitly implement such queries—it's handled for you! Why can't you do something similar with collections?

- How would you process a large collection of elements? To gain performance you'd need to process it in parallel and leverage multicore architectures. But writing parallel code is complicated in comparison to working with iterators. In addition, it's no fun to debug!

So what could the Java language designers do to save your precious time and make your life easier as programmers? You may have guessed: the answer is *streams*.

4.1 What are streams?

Streams are an update to the Java API that lets you manipulate collections of data in a declarative way (you express a query rather than code an ad hoc implementation for it). For now you can think of them as fancy iterators over a collection of data. In addition, streams can be processed in parallel *transparently*, without you having to write any multithreaded code! We explain in detail in chapter 7 how streams and parallelization work. Here's a taste of the benefits of using streams: compare the following code to return the names of dishes that are low in calories, sorted by number of calories, first in Java 7 and then in Java 8 using streams. Don't worry about the Java 8 code too much; we explain it in detail in the next sections!

Before (Java 7):

```
List<Dish> lowCaloricDishes = new ArrayList<>();
for(Dish d: menu){
    if(d.getCalories() < 400){                       <-- Filter the elements using an accumulator.
        lowCaloricDishes.add(d);
    }
}
Collections.sort(lowCaloricDishes, new Comparator<Dish>() {   <-- Sort the dishes with an anonymous class.
    public int compare(Dish d1, Dish d2){
        return Integer.compare(d1.getCalories(), d2.getCalories());
    }
});
List<String> lowCaloricDishesName = new ArrayList<>();
for(Dish d: lowCaloricDishes){
    lowCaloricDishesName.add(d.getName());           <-- Process the sorted list to select the names of dishes.
}
```

In this code you use a "garbage variable," `lowCaloricDishes`. Its only purpose is to act as an intermediate throwaway container. In Java 8, this implementation detail is pushed into the library where it belongs.

After (Java 8):

```
import static java.util.Comparator.comparing;
import static java.util.stream.Collectors.toList;
```

```
List<String> lowCaloricDishesName =
            menu.stream()
                .filter(d -> d.getCalories() < 400)
                .sorted(comparing(Dish::getCalories))
                .map(Dish::getName)
                .collect(toList());
```

Select dishes that are below 400 calories.

Sort them by calories.

Extract the names of these dishes.

Store all the names in a `List`.

To exploit a multicore architecture and execute this code in parallel, you need only change `stream()` to `parallelStream()`:

```
List<String> lowCaloricDishesName =
            menu.parallelStream()
                .filter(d -> d.getCalories() < 400)
                .sorted(comparing(Dishes::getCalories))
                .map(Dish::getName)
                .collect(toList());
```

You may be wondering what exactly happens when you call the method `parallelStream`. How many threads are being used? What are the performance benefits? Chapter 7 covers these questions in detail. For now, you can see that the new approach offers several immediate benefits from a software engineering point of view:

- The code is written in a *declarative way*: you specify *what* you want to achieve (that is, *filter* dishes that are *low* in calories) as opposed to specifying *how* to implement an operation (using control-flow blocks such as loops and `if` conditions). As you saw in the previous chapter, this approach, together with behavior parameterization, enables you to cope with changing requirements: you could easily create an additional version of your code to filter high-calorie dishes using a lambda expression, without having to copy and paste code.
- You chain together several building-block operations to express a complicated data processing pipeline (you chain the `filter` by linking `sorted`, `map`, and `collect` operations, as illustrated in figure 4.1) while keeping your code readable and its intent clear. The result of the `filter` is passed to the `sorted` method, which is then passed to the `map` method and then to the `collect` method.

Because operations such as `filter` (or `sorted`, `map`, and `collect`) are available as *high-level building blocks* that don't depend on a specific threading model, their internal implementation could be single-threaded or potentially maximize your multicore architecture transparently! In practice, this means you no longer have to worry about threads and locks to figure out how to parallelize certain data processing tasks: the Streams API does it for you!

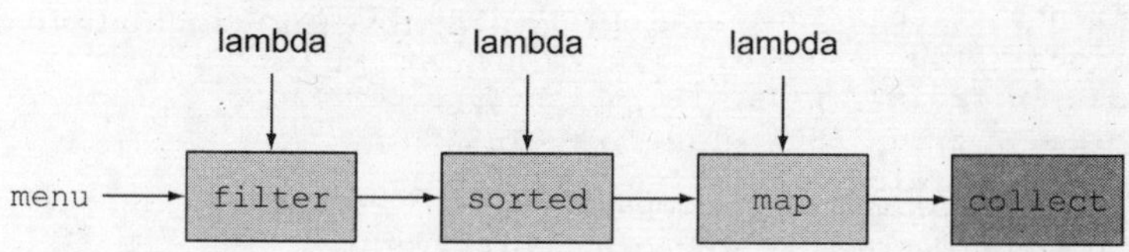

Figure 4.1 Chaining stream operations forming a stream pipeline

The new Streams API is very expressive. For example, after reading this chapter and chapters 5 and 6, you'll be able to write code like this:

```
Map<Dish.Type, List<Dish>> dishesByType =
    menu.stream().collect(groupingBy(Dish::getType));
```

This particular example is explained in detail in chapter 6, "Collecting data with streams." It basically groups dishes by their types inside a `Map`. For example, the `Map` may contain the following result:

```
{FISH=[prawns, salmon],
 OTHER=[french fries, rice, season fruit, pizza],
 MEAT=[pork, beef, chicken]}
```

Now try to think how you'd implement this with the typical imperative programming approach using loops. Don't waste too much of your time. Embrace the power of streams in this and the following chapters!

> **Other libraries: Guava, Apache, and lambdaj**
>
> There have been many attempts at providing Java programmers with better libraries to manipulate collections. For example, Guava is a popular library created by Google. It provides additional container classes such as multimaps and multisets. The Apache Commons Collections library provides similar features. Finally, lambdaj, written by Mario Fusco, coauthor of this book, provides many utilities to manipulate collections in a declarative manner, inspired by functional programming.
>
> Now Java 8 comes with its own official library for manipulating collections in a more declarative style.

To summarize, the Streams API in Java 8 lets you write code that's

- *Declarative*—More concise and readable
- *Composable*—Greater flexibility
- *Parallelizable*—Better performance

For the remainder of this chapter and the next, we'll use the following domain for our examples: a `menu` that's nothing more than a list of dishes

```
List<Dish> menu = Arrays.asList(
    new Dish("pork", false, 800, Dish.Type.MEAT),
    new Dish("beef", false, 700, Dish.Type.MEAT),
    new Dish("chicken", false, 400, Dish.Type.MEAT),
    new Dish("french fries", true, 530, Dish.Type.OTHER),
    new Dish("rice", true, 350, Dish.Type.OTHER),
    new Dish("season fruit", true, 120, Dish.Type.OTHER),
    new Dish("pizza", true, 550, Dish.Type.OTHER),
    new Dish("prawns", false, 300, Dish.Type.FISH),
    new Dish("salmon", false, 450, Dish.Type.FISH) );
```

where a Dish is an immutable class defined as

```
public class Dish {
    private final String name;
    private final boolean vegetarian;
    private final int calories;
    private final Type type;

    public Dish(String name, boolean vegetarian, int calories, Type type) {
        this.name = name;
        this.vegetarian = vegetarian;
        this.calories = calories;
        this.type = type;
    }

    public String getName() {
        return name;
    }

    public boolean isVegetarian() {
        return vegetarian;
    }

    public int getCalories() {
        return calories;
    }
    public Type getType() {
        return type;
    }

    @Override
    public String toString() {
        return name;
    }

    public enum Type { MEAT, FISH, OTHER }
}
```

We'll now explore how you can use the Streams API in more detail. We'll compare streams to collections and provide some background. In the next chapter, we'll investigate in detail the stream operations available to express sophisticated data processing queries. We'll look at many patterns such as filtering, slicing, finding, matching, mapping, and reducing. There will be many quizzes and exercises to try to solidify your understanding.

Next, we'll discuss how you can create and manipulate numeric streams, for example, to generate a stream of even numbers or Pythagorean triples! Finally, we'll discuss how you can create streams from different sources such as from a file. We'll also discuss how to generate streams with an infinite number of elements—something you definitely can't do with collections!

4.2 Getting started with streams

We start our discussion of streams with collections, because that's the simplest way to begin working with streams. Collections in Java 8 support a new `stream` method that returns a stream (the interface definition is available in `java.util.stream.Stream`). You'll later see that you can also get streams in various other ways (for example, generating stream elements from a numeric range or from I/O resources).

So first, what exactly is a *stream*? A short definition is "a sequence of elements from a source that supports data processing operations." Let's break down this definition step by step:

- *Sequence of elements*—Like a collection, a stream provides an interface to a sequenced set of values of a specific element type. Because collections are data structures, they're mostly about storing and accessing elements with specific time/space complexities (for example, an `ArrayList` vs. a `LinkedList`). But streams are about expressing computations such as `filter`, `sorted`, and `map` that you saw earlier. Collections are about data; streams are about computations. We explain this idea in greater detail in the coming sections.
- *Source*—Streams consume from a data-providing source such as collections, arrays, or I/O resources. Note that generating a stream from an ordered collection preserves the ordering. The elements of a stream coming from a list will have the same order as the list.
- *Data processing operations*—Streams support database-like operations and common operations from functional programming languages to manipulate data, such as `filter`, `map`, `reduce`, `find`, `match`, `sort`, and so on. Stream operations can be executed either sequentially or in parallel.

In addition, stream operations have two important characteristics:

- *Pipelining*—Many stream operations return a stream themselves, allowing operations to be chained and form a larger pipeline. This enables certain optimizations that we explain in the next chapter, such as *laziness* and *short-circuiting*. A pipeline of operations can be viewed as a database-like query on the data source.
- *Internal iteration*—In contrast to collections, which are iterated explicitly using an iterator, stream operations do the iteration behind the scenes for you. We briefly mentioned this idea in chapter 1 and return to it later in the next section.

Let's look at a code example to explain all of these ideas:

```
import static java.util.stream.Collectors.toList;
List<String> threeHighCaloricDishNames =
  menu.stream()
      .filter(d -> d.getCalories() > 300)
      .map(Dish::getName)
      .limit(3)
      .collect(toList());
System.out.println(threeHighCaloricDishNames);
```

Get a stream from `menu` (the list of dishes).

Create a pipeline of operations: first filter high-calorie dishes.

Get the names of the dishes.

Select only the first three.

Store the results in another `List`.

The result is [pork, beef, chicken].

In this example, you first get a stream from the list of dishes by calling the `stream` method on `menu`. The *data source* is the list of dishes (the menu) and it provides *a*

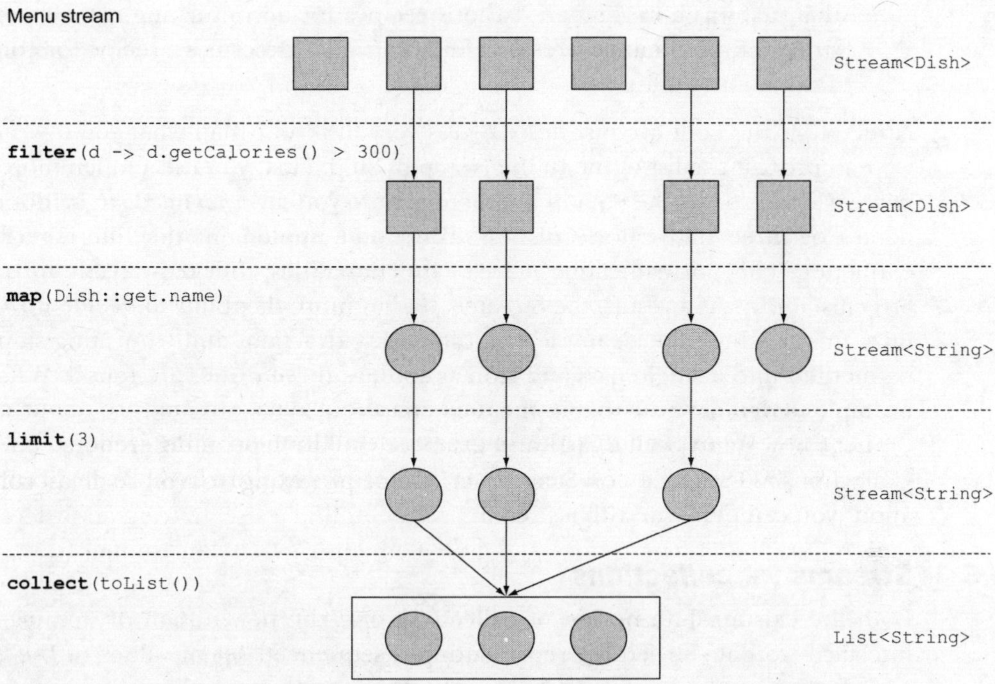

Figure 4.2 Filtering a menu using a stream to find out three high-calorie dish names

sequence of elements to the stream. Next, you apply a series of *data processing operations* on the stream: `filter`, `map`, `limit`, and `collect`. All these operations except `collect` return another stream so they can be connected to form a *pipeline*, which can be viewed as a query on the source. Finally, the `collect` operation starts processing the pipeline to return a result (it's different because it returns something other than a stream—here, a `List`). No result is produced, and indeed no element from `menu` is even selected, until `collect` is invoked. You can think of it as if the method invocations in the chain are queued up until `collect` is called. Figure 4.2 shows the sequence of stream operations: `filter`, `map`, `limit`, and `collect`, each of which is briefly described here:

- `filter`—Takes a lambda to exclude certain elements from the stream. In this case, you select dishes that have more than 300 calories by passing the lambda `d -> d.getCalories() > 300`.
- `map`—Takes a lambda to transform an element into another one or to extract information. In this case, you extract the name for each dish by passing the method reference `Dish::getName`, which is equivalent to the lambda `d -> d.getName()`.
- `limit`—Truncates a stream to contain no more than a given number of elements.
- `collect`—Converts a stream into another form. In this case you convert the stream into a list. It looks like a bit of magic; we describe how `collect` works in more detail in chapter 6. At the moment, you can see `collect` as an operation

that takes as an argument various recipes for accumulating the elements of a stream into a summary result. Here, `toList()` describes a recipe for converting a stream into a list.

Notice how the code we just described is very different than what you'd write if you were to process the list of menu items step by step. First, you use a much more declarative style to process the data in the menu where you say *what* needs to be done: "Find names of three high-calorie dishes." You don't implement the filtering (`filter`), extracting (`map`), or truncating (`limit`) functionalities; they're available through the Streams library. As a result, the Streams API has more flexibility to decide how to optimize this pipeline. For example, the filtering, extracting, and truncating steps could be merged into a single pass and stop as soon as three dishes are found. We show an example to demonstrate that in the next chapter.

Let's now stand back a little and examine the conceptual differences between the Collections API and the new Streams API, before we explore in more detail what operations you can perform with a stream.

4.3 Streams vs. collections

Both the existing Java notion of collections and the new notion of streams provide interfaces to data structures representing a sequenced set of values of the element type. By *sequenced*, we mean that we commonly step through the values in turn rather than randomly accessing them in any order. So what's the difference?

We'll start with a visual metaphor. Consider a movie stored on a DVD. This is a collection (perhaps of bytes or of frames—we don't care which here) because it contains the whole data structure. Now consider watching the same video when it's being *streamed* over the internet. This is now a stream (of bytes or frames). The streaming video player needs to have downloaded only a few frames in advance of where the user is watching, so you can start displaying values from the beginning of the stream before most of the values in the stream have even been computed (consider streaming a live football game). Note particularly that the video player may lack the memory to buffer the whole stream in memory as a collection—and the startup time would be appalling if you had to wait for the final frame to appear before you could start showing the video. You might choose for video-player implementation reasons to *buffer* a part of a stream into a collection, but this is distinct from the conceptual difference.

In coarsest terms, the difference between collections and streams has to do with *when* things are computed. A collection is an in-memory data structure that holds *all* the values the data structure currently has—every element in the collection has to be computed before it can be added to the collection. (You can add things to, and remove them from, the collection, but at each moment in time, every element in the collection is stored in memory; elements have to be computed before becoming part of the collection.)

By contrast, a stream is a conceptually fixed data structure (you can't add or remove elements from it) whose elements are *computed on demand*. This gives rise to significant programming benefits. In chapter 6 we show how simple it is to construct a stream containing all the prime numbers (2,3,5,7,11,...) even though there are an infinite number of them. The idea is that a user will extract only the values they require from a stream, and these elements are produced—invisibly to the user—only *as* and *when* required. This is a form of a producer-consumer relationship. Another view is that a stream is like a lazily constructed collection: values are computed when they're solicited by a consumer (in management speak this is demand-driven, or even just-in-time, manufacturing).

In contrast, a collection is eagerly constructed (supplier-driven: fill your warehouse before you start selling, like a Christmas novelty that has a limited life). Applying this to the primes example, attempting to construct a collection of all prime numbers would result in a program loop that forever computes a new prime, adding it to the collection, but of course could never finish making the collection, so the consumer would never get to see it.

Figure 4.3 illustrates the difference between a stream and a collection applied to our DVD vs. internet streaming example.

Another example is a browser internet search. Suppose you search for a phrase with many matches in Google or in an e-commerce online shop. Instead of waiting for the whole collection of results along with their photographs to be downloaded, you get a stream whose elements are the best 10 or 20 matches, along with a button to click for the next 10 or 20. When you, the consumer, click for the next 10, the supplier computes these on demand, before returning them to your browser for display.

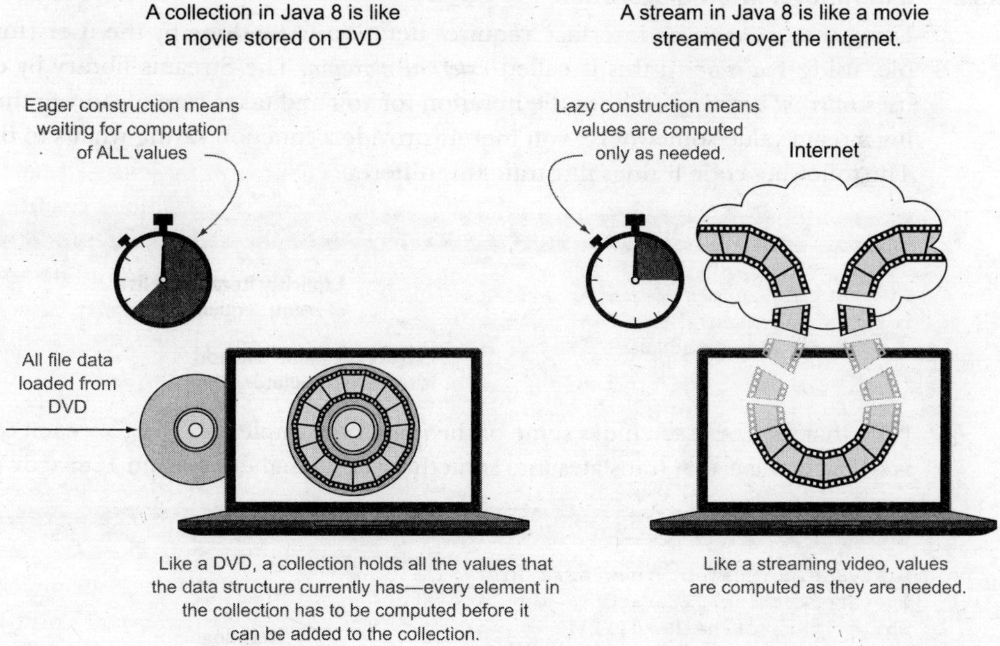

Figure 4.3 Streams vs. collections

4.3.1 Traversable only once

Note that, similarly to iterators, a stream can be traversed only once. After that a stream is said to be consumed. You can get a new stream from the initial data source to traverse it again just like for an iterator (assuming it's a repeatable source like a collection; if it's an I/O channel, you're out of luck). For example, the following code would throw an exception indicating the stream has been consumed:

```
List<String> title = Arrays.asList("Java8", "In", "Action");
Stream<String> s = title.stream();
s.forEach(System.out::println);
s.forEach(System.out::println);
```

Prints each word in the title.

java.lang.IllegalStateException: stream has already been operated upon or closed.

So keep in mind that you can consume a stream only once!

> **Streams and collections philosophically**
>
> For readers who like philosophical viewpoints, you can see a stream as a set of values spread out in time. In contrast, a collection is a set of values spread out in space (here, computer memory), which all exist at a single point in time—and which you access using an iterator to access members inside a `for-each` loop.

Another key difference between collections and streams is how they manage the iteration over data.

4.3.2 External vs. internal iteration

Using the `Collection` interface requires iteration to be done by the user (for example, using `for-each`); this is called *external iteration*. The Streams library by contrast uses *internal iteration*—it does the iteration for you and takes care of storing the resulting stream value somewhere; you merely provide a function saying what's to be done. The following code listings illustrate this difference.

Listing 4.1 Collections: external iteration with a `for-each` loop

```
List<String> names = new ArrayList<>();
for(Dish d: menu){
    names.add(d.getName());
}
```

Explicitly iterate the list of menu sequentially.

Extract the name and add it to an accumulator.

Note that the `for-each` hides some of the iteration complexity. The `for-each` construct is syntactic sugar that translates into something much uglier using an `Iterator` object.

Listing 4.2 Collections: external iteration using an iterator behind the scenes

```
List<String> names = new ArrayList<>();
Iterator<String> iterator = menu.iterator();
while(iterator.hasNext()) {
    Dish d = iterator.next();
    names.add(d.getName());
}
```

Iterating explicitly

Listing 4.3 Streams: internal iteration

```
List<String> names = menu.stream()
                         .map(Dish::getName)
                         .collect(toList());
```

Start executing the pipeline of operations; no iteration! (annotation for `.collect(toList())`)

Parameterize map with the getName method to extract the name of a dish. (annotation for `.map(Dish::getName)`)

Let's use an analogy to understand the differences and benefits of internal iteration. Let's say you're talking to your two-year-old daughter, Sofia, and want her to put her toys away:

> You: "Sofia, let's put the toys away. Is there a toy on the ground?"
> Sofia: "Yes, the ball."
> You: "Okay, put the ball in the box. Is there something else?"
> Sofia: "Yes, there's my doll."
> You: "Okay, put the doll in the box. Is there something else?"
> Sofia: "Yes, there's my book."
> You: "Okay, put the book in the box. Is there something else?"
> Sofia: "No, nothing else."
> You: "Fine, we're finished."

This is exactly what you do every day with your Java collections. You iterate a collection *externally*, explicitly pulling out and processing the items one by one. It would be far better if you could just tell Sofia, "Put all the toys that are on the floor inside the box." There are two other reasons why an internal iteration is preferable: first, Sofia could choose to take at the same time the doll with one hand and the ball with the other, and second, she could decide to take the objects closest to the box first and then the others. In the same way, using an internal iteration, the processing of items could be transparently done in parallel or in a different order that may be more optimized. These optimizations are difficult if you iterate the collection externally as you're used to doing in Java. This may seem like nit-picking, but it's much of the raison-d'être of Java 8's introduction of streams—the internal iteration in the Streams library can automatically choose a data representation and implementation of parallelism to match your hardware. By contrast, once you've chosen external iteration by writing `for-each`, then you've essentially committed to self-manage any parallelism. (*Self-managing* in practice means either "one fine day we'll parallelize this" or "starting the long and arduous battle involving tasks and `synchronized`".) Java 8 needed an interface like `Collection` but without iterators, ergo `Stream`! Figure 4.4 illustrates the difference between a stream (internal iteration) and a collection (external iteration).

We've described the conceptual differences between collections and streams. Specifically, streams make use of internal iteration: iteration is taken care of for you. But this is useful only if you have a list of predefined operations to work with (for example, `filter` or `map`) that hide the iteration. Most of these operations take lambda expressions as arguments so you can parameterize their behavior as we showed in the previous chapter. The Java language designers shipped the Streams API with an extensive

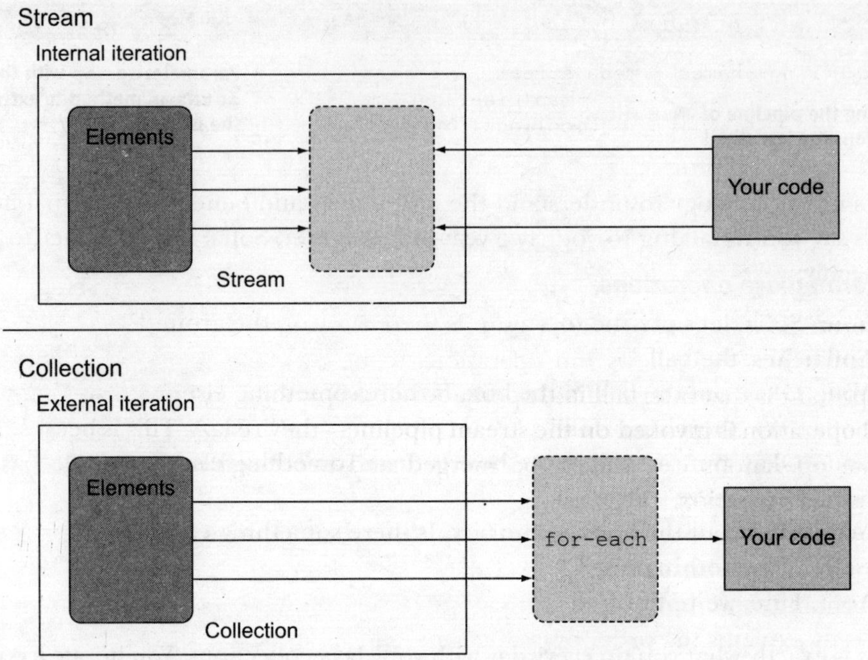

Figure 4.4 Internal vs. external iteration

list of operations you can use to express complicated data processing queries. We'll briefly look at this list of operations now and explore them in more detail with examples in the next chapter.

4.4 Stream operations

The `Stream` interface in `java.util.stream.Stream` defines many operations. They can be classified into two categories. Let's look at our previous example once again:

```
List<String> names = menu.stream()
                         .filter(d -> d.getCalories() > 300)
                         .map(Dish::getName)
                         .limit(3)
                         .collect(toList());
```

Get a stream from the list of dishes. (`menu.stream()`)

Intermediate operation. (`filter`)

Intermediate operation. (`map`)

Intermediate operation. (`limit`)

Converts the `Stream` into a `List`. (`collect`)

You can see two groups of operations:

- `filter`, `map`, and `limit` can be connected together to form a pipeline.
- `collect` causes the pipeline to be executed and closes it.

Stream operations that can be connected are called *intermediate operations*, and operations that close a stream are called *terminal operations*. Figure 4.5 highlights these two groups. So why is the distinction important?

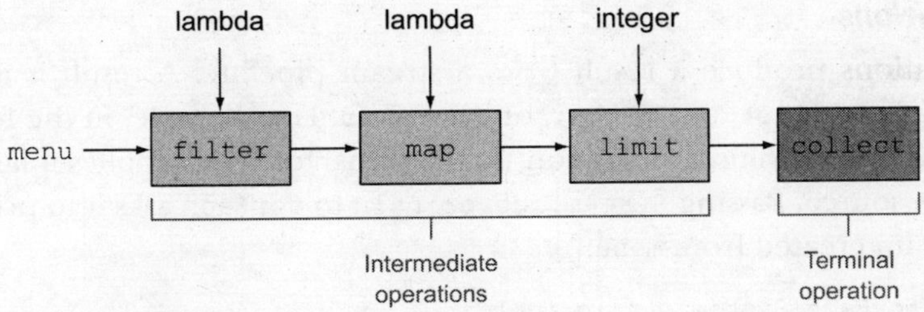

Figure 4.5 Intermediate vs. terminal operations

4.4.1 *Intermediate operations*

Intermediate operations such as `filter` or `sorted` return another stream as the return type. This allows the operations to be connected to form a query. What's important is that intermediate operations don't perform any processing until a terminal operation is invoked on the stream pipeline—they're lazy. This is because intermediate operations can usually be merged and processed into a single pass by the terminal operation.

To understand what's happening in the stream pipeline, modify the code so each lambda also prints the current dish it's processing (like many demonstration and debugging techniques, this is appalling programming style for production code but directly explains the order of evaluation when you're learning):

```
List<String> names =
    menu.stream()
        .filter(d -> {
                        System.out.println("filtering" + d.getName());
                        return d.getCalories() > 300;
                    })
        .map(d -> {
                      System.out.println("mapping" + d.getName());
                      return d.getName();
                  })
        .limit(3)
        .collect(toList());
System.out.println(names);
```

Printing the dishes as they're filtered

Printing the dishes as you extract their names

This code when executed will print the following:

```
filtering pork
mapping pork
filtering beef
mapping beef
filtering chicken
mapping chicken
[pork, beef, chicken]
```

You can notice several optimizations due to the lazy nature of streams. First, despite the fact that many dishes have more than 300 calories, only the first three are selected! This is because of the `limit` operation and a technique called *short-circuiting*, as we'll explain in the next chapter. Second, despite the fact that `filter` and `map` are two separate operations, they were merged into the same pass (we call this technique *loop fusion*).

4.4.2 *Terminal operations*

Terminal operations produce a result from a stream pipeline. A result is any non-stream value such as a `List`, an `Integer`, or even `void`. For example, in the following pipeline, `forEach` is a terminal operation that returns `void` and applies a lambda to each dish in the source. Passing `System.out.println` to `forEach` asks it to print every `Dish` in the stream created from `menu`:

```
menu.stream().forEach(System.out::println);
```

To check your understanding of intermediate versus terminal operations, try out Quiz 4.1.

> **Quiz 4.1: Intermediate vs. terminal operations**
>
> In the stream pipeline that follows, can you identify the intermediate and terminal operations?
>
> ```
> long count = menu.stream()
>                  .filter(d -> d.getCalories() > 300)
>                  .distinct()
>                  .limit(3)
>                  .count();
> ```
>
> Answer:
>
> The last operation in the stream pipeline `count` returns a `long`, which is a non-`Stream` value. It's therefore a *terminal operation*. All previous operations, `filter`, `distinct`, `limit`, are connected and return a `Stream`. They are therefore *intermediate operations*.

4.4.3 *Working with streams*

To summarize, working with streams in general involves three items:

- A *data source* (such as a collection) to perform a query on
- A chain of *intermediate operations* that form a stream pipeline
- A *terminal operation* that executes the stream pipeline and produces a result

The idea behind a stream pipeline is similar to the builder pattern.[1] In the builder pattern, there's a chain of calls to set up a configuration (for streams this is a chain of intermediate operations), followed by a call to a `build` method (for streams this is a terminal operation).

For convenience, tables 4.1 and 4.2 summarize the intermediate and terminal stream operations you've seen in the code examples so far. Note that this is an incomplete list of operations provided by the Streams API; you'll see several more in the next chapter!

---

[1] See http://en.wikipedia.org/wiki/Builder_pattern.

Table 4.1 Intermediate operations

Operation	Type	Return type	Argument of the operation	Function descriptor
`filter`	Intermediate	`Stream<T>`	`Predicate<T>`	`T -> boolean`
`map`	Intermediate	`Stream<R>`	`Function<T, R>`	`T -> R`
`limit`	Intermediate	`Stream<T>`		
`sorted`	Intermediate	`Stream<T>`	`Comparator<T>`	`(T, T) -> int`
`distinct`	Intermediate	`Stream<T>`		

Table 4.2 Terminal operations

Operation	Type	Purpose
`forEach`	Terminal	Consumes each element from a stream and applies a lambda to each of them. The operation returns `void`.
`count`	Terminal	Returns the number of elements in a stream. The operation returns a `long`.
`collect`	Terminal	Reduces the stream to create a collection such as a `List`, a `Map`, or even an `Integer`. See chapter 6 for more detail.

In the next chapter, we detail the available stream operations with use cases so you can see what kinds of queries you can express with them. We look at many patterns such as filtering, slicing, finding, matching, mapping, and reducing, which can be used to express sophisticated data processing queries.

Because chapter 6 deals with collectors in great detail, the only use this chapter and the next one make of the `collect()` terminal operation on streams is the special case of `collect(toList())`, which creates a `List` whose elements are the same as those of the stream it's applied to.

4.5 Summary

Here are some key concepts to take away from this chapter:

- A stream is a sequence of elements from a source that supports data processing operations.
- Streams make use of internal iteration: the iteration is abstracted away through operations such as `filter`, `map`, and `sorted`.
- There are two types of stream operations: intermediate and terminal operations.
- Intermediate operations such as `filter` and `map` return a stream and can be chained together. They're used to set up a pipeline of operations but don't produce any result.
- Terminal operations such as `forEach` and `count` return a nonstream value and process a stream pipeline to return a result.
- The elements of a stream are computed on demand.

5 Working with streams

This chapter covers

- Filtering, slicing, and matching
- Finding, matching, and reducing
- Using numeric streams such as ranges of numbers
- Creating streams from multiple sources
- Infinite streams

In the previous chapter, you saw that streams let you move from *external iteration* to *internal iteration*. Instead of writing code as follows where you explicitly manage the iteration over a collection of data (external iteration),

```
List<Dish> vegetarianDishes = new ArrayList<>();
for(Dish d: menu){
    if(d.isVegetarian()){
        vegetarianDishes.add(d);
    }
}
```

you can use the Streams API (internal iteration), which supports the `filter` and `collect` operations, to manage the iteration over the collection of data for you. All you need to do is pass the filtering behavior as argument to the `filter` method:

```
import static java.util.stream.Collectors.toList;
List<Dish> vegetarianDishes =
    menu.stream()
        .filter(Dish::isVegetarian)
        .collect(toList());
```

This different way of working with data is useful because you let the Streams API manage how to process the data. As a consequence, the Streams API can work out several optimizations behind the scenes. In addition, using internal iteration, the Streams API can decide to run your code in parallel. Using external iteration, this isn't possible because you're committed to a single-threaded step-by-step sequential iteration.

In this chapter, you'll have an extensive look at the various operations supported by the Streams API. These operations will let you express complex data processing queries such as filtering, slicing, mapping, finding, matching, and reducing. Next, we'll explore special cases of streams: numeric streams, streams built from multiple sources such as files and arrays, and finally infinite streams.

5.1 Filtering and slicing

In this section, we look at how to select elements of a stream: filtering with a predicate, filtering only unique elements, ignoring the first few elements of a stream, or truncating a stream to a given size.

5.1.1 Filtering with a predicate

The `Streams` interface supports a `filter` method (which you should be familiar with by now). This operation takes as argument a *predicate* (a function returning a `boolean`) and returns a stream including all elements that match the predicate. For example, you can create a vegetarian menu by filtering all vegetarian dishes as follows and as illustrated in figure 5.1:

```
List<Dish> vegetarianMenu = menu.stream()
                                .filter(Dish::isVegetarian)   <-- A method reference to check if a dish is vegetarian friendly
                                .collect(toList());
```

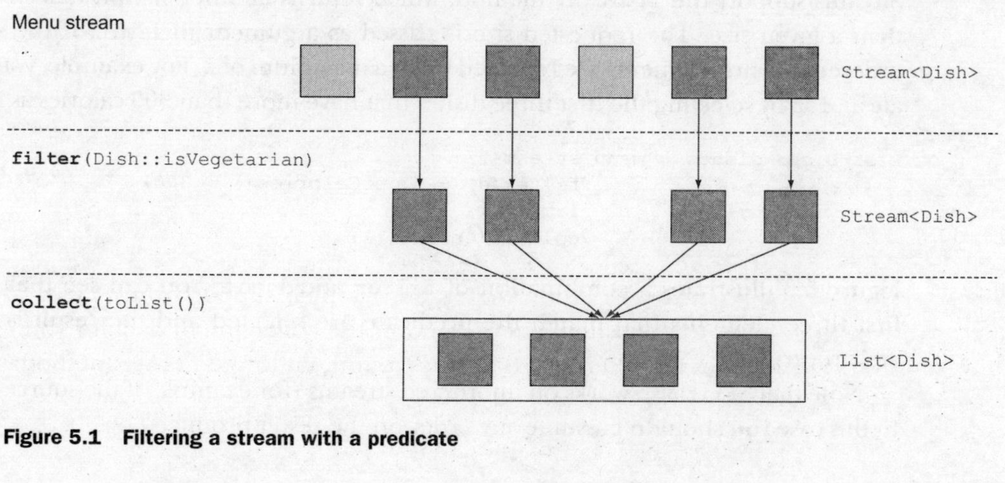

Figure 5.1 Filtering a stream with a predicate

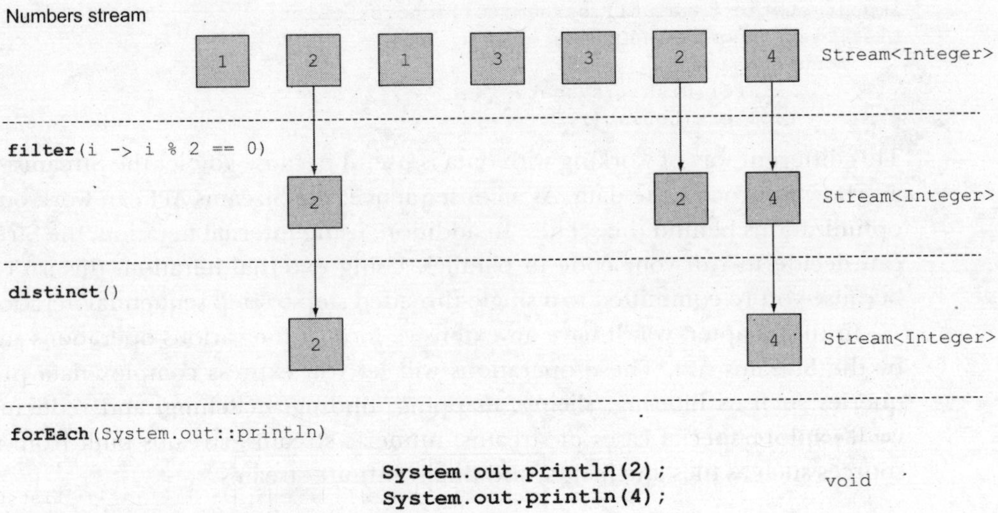

Figure 5.2 Filtering unique elements in a stream

5.1.2 *Filtering unique elements*

Streams also support a method called `distinct` that returns a stream with unique elements (according to the implementation of the `hashCode` and `equals` methods of the objects produced by the stream). For example, the following code filters all even numbers from a list and makes sure that there are no duplicates. Figure 5.2 shows this visually:

```
List<Integer> numbers = Arrays.asList(1, 2, 1, 3, 3, 2, 4);
numbers.stream()
       .filter(i -> i % 2 == 0)
       .distinct()
       .forEach(System.out::println);
```

5.1.3 *Truncating a stream*

Streams support the `limit(n)` method, which returns another stream that's no longer than a given size. The requested size is passed as argument to `limit`. If the stream is ordered, the first elements are returned up to a maximum of `n`. For example, you can create a `List` by selecting the first three dishes that have more than 300 calories as follows:

```
List<Dish> dishes = menu.stream()
                        .filter(d -> d.getCalories() > 300)
                        .limit(3)
                        .collect(toList());
```

Figure 5.3 illustrates a combination of `filter` and `limit`. You can see that only the first three elements that match the predicate are selected and the result is immediately returned.

Note that `limit` also works on unordered streams (for example, if the source is a `Set`). In this case you shouldn't assume any order on the result produced by `limit`.

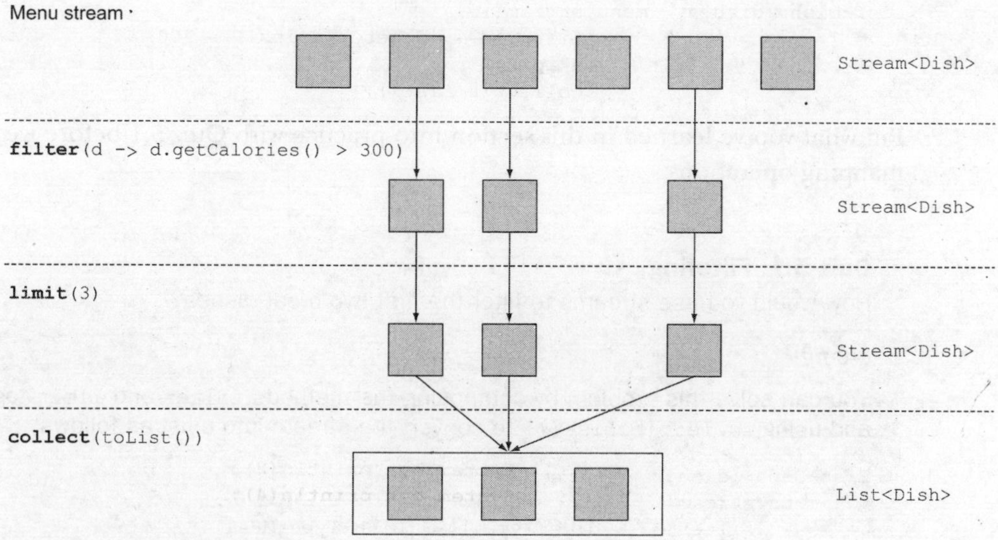

Figure 5.3 Truncating a stream

5.1.4 *Skipping elements*

Streams support the `skip(n)` method to return a stream that discards the first `n` elements. If the stream has fewer elements than `n`, then an empty stream is returned. Note that `limit(n)` and `skip(n)` are complementary! For example, the following code skips the first two dishes that have more than 300 calories and returns the rest. Figure 5.4 illustrates this query:

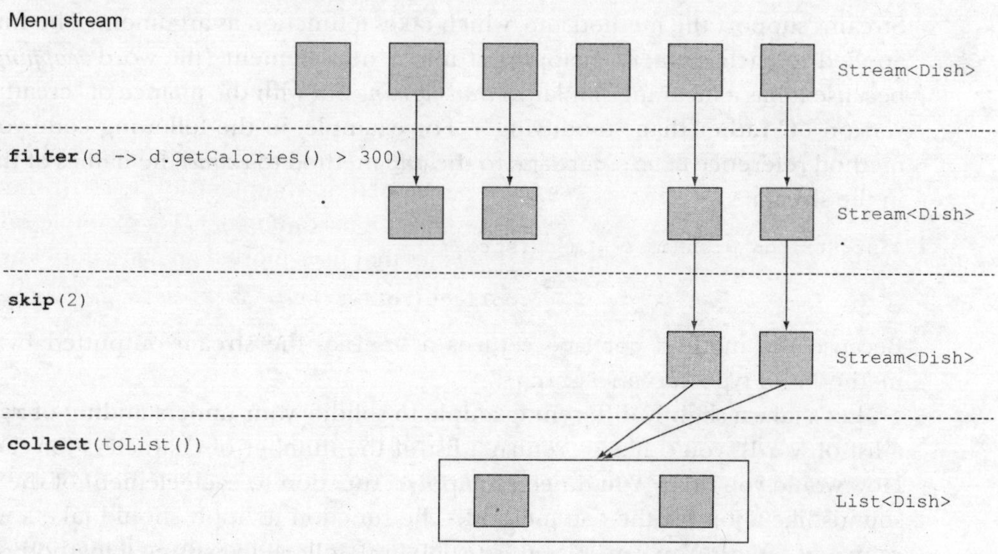

Figure 5.4 Skipping elements in a stream

```
List<Dish> dishes = menu.stream()
                        .filter(d -> d.getCalories() > 300)
                        .skip(2)
                        .collect(toList());
```

Put what you've learned in this section into practice with Quiz 5.1 before we move to mapping operations.

Quiz 5.1: Filtering

How would you use streams to filter the first two meat dishes?

Answer:

You can solve this problem by composing the methods `filter` and `limit` together and using `collect(toList())` to convert the stream into a list as follows:

```
List<Dish> dishes =
    menu.stream()
        .filter(d -> d.getType() == Dish.Type.MEAT)
        .limit(2)
        .collect(toList());
```

5.2 *Mapping*

A very common data processing idiom is to select information from certain objects. For example, in SQL you can select a particular column from a table. The Streams API provides similar facilities through the `map` and `flatMap` methods.

5.2.1 *Applying a function to each element of a stream*

Streams support the method `map`, which takes a function as argument. The function is applied to each element, mapping it into a new element (the word *mapping* is used because it has a meaning similar to *transforming* but with the nuance of "creating a new version of" rather than "modifying"). For example, in the following code you pass a method reference `Dish::getName` to the `map` method to *extract* the names of the dishes in the stream:

```
List<String> dishNames = menu.stream()
                             .map(Dish::getName)
                             .collect(toList());
```

Because the method `getName` returns a `String`, the stream outputted by the `map` method is of type `Stream<String>`.

Let's take a slightly different example to solidify your understanding of `map`. Given a list of words, you'd like to return a list of the number of characters for each word. How would you do it? You'd need to apply a function to each element of the list. This sounds like a job for the `map` method! The function to apply should take a word and return its length. You can solve this problem as follows by passing a method reference `String::length` to `map`:

```
List<String> words = Arrays.asList("Java8", "Lambdas", "In", "Action");
List<Integer> wordLengths = words.stream()
                                 .map(String::length)
                                 .collect(toList());
```

Let's now return to the example where you extracted the name of each dish. What if you wanted to find out the length of the name of each dish? You could do this by chaining another `map` as follows:

```
List<Integer> dishNameLengths = menu.stream()
                                    .map(Dish::getName)
                                    .map(String::length)
                                    .collect(toList());
```

5.2.2 *Flattening streams*

You saw how to return the length for each word in a list using the method `map`. Let's extend this idea a bit further: how could you return a list of all the *unique characters* for a list of words? For example, given the list of words `["Hello", "World"]` you'd like to return the list `["H", "e", "l", "o", "W", "r", "d"]`.

You might think that this is easy, that you can just map each word into a list of characters and then call `distinct` to filter duplicate characters. A first go could be like this:

```
words.stream()
     .map(word -> word.split(""))
     .distinct()
     .collect(toList());
```

The problem with this approach is that the lambda passed to the `map` method returns a `String[]` (an array of `String`) for each word. So the stream returned by the `map` method is actually of type `Stream<String[]>`. What you really want is `Stream<String>` to represent a stream of characters. Figure 5.5 illustrates the problem.

Luckily there's a solution to this problem using the method `flatMap`! Let's see step by step how to solve it.

ATTEMPT USING MAP AND ARRAYS.STREAM

First, you need a stream of characters instead of a stream of arrays. There's a method called `Arrays.stream()` that takes an array and produces a stream, for example:

```
String[] arrayOfWords = {"Goodbye", "World"};
Stream<String> streamOfwords = Arrays.stream(arrayOfWords);
```

Use it in the previous pipeline to see what happens:

```
words.stream()
     .map(word -> word.split(""))      <-- Converts each word into an array of its individual letters
     .map(Arrays::stream)              <-- Makes each array into a separate stream
     .distinct()
     .collect(toList());
```

The current solution still doesn't work! This is because you now end up with a list of streams (more precisely, `Stream<Stream<String>>`)! Indeed, you first convert

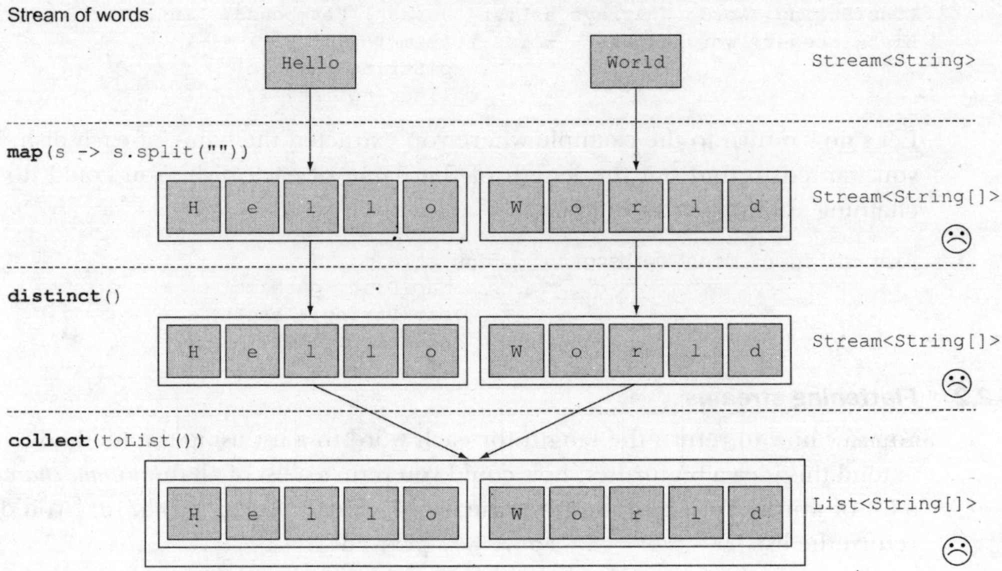

Figure 5.5 Incorrect use of `map` to find unique characters from a list of words

each word into an array of its individual letters and then make each array into a separate stream.

USING FLATMAP

You can fix this problem by using `flatMap` as follows:

```
List<String> uniqueCharacters =
  words.stream()
       .map(w -> w.split(""))
       .flatMap(Arrays::stream)
       .distinct()
       .collect(Collectors.toList());
```

Converts each word into an array of its individual letters

Flattens each generated stream into a single stream

Using the `flatMap` method has the effect of mapping each array not with a stream but *with the contents of that stream.* All the separate streams that were generated when using `map(Arrays::stream)` get amalgamated—flattened into a single stream. Figure 5.6 illustrates the effect of using the `flatMap` method. Compare it with what `map` does in figure 5.5.

In a nutshell, the `flatMap` method lets you replace each value of a stream with another stream and then concatenates all the generated streams into a single stream.

We come back to `flatMap` in chapter 10 when we discuss more advanced Java 8 patterns such as using the new library class `Optional` for `null` checking. To solidify your understanding of `map` and `flatMap`, try out Quiz 5.2.

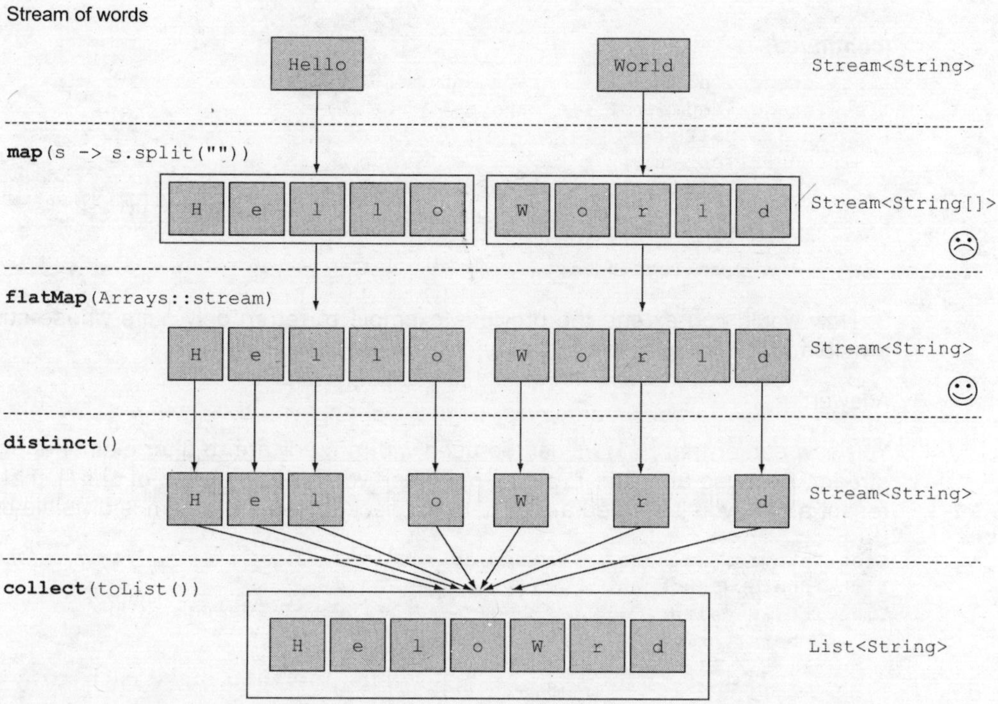

Figure 5.6 Using `flatMap` to find the unique characters from a list of words

Quiz 5.2: Mapping

1. Given a list of numbers, how would you return a list of the square of each number? For example, given [1, 2, 3, 4, 5] you should return [1, 4, 9, 16, 25].

Answer:

You can solve this problem by using `map` with a lambda that takes a number and returns the square of the number:

```
List<Integer> numbers = Arrays.asList(1, 2, 3, 4, 5);
List<Integer> squares =
    numbers.stream()
           .map(n -> n * n)
           .collect(toList());
```

2. Given two lists of numbers, how would you return all pairs of numbers? For example, given a list [1, 2, 3] and a list [3, 4] you should return [(1, 3), (1, 4), (2, 3), (2, 4), (3, 3), (3, 4)]. For simplicity, you can represent a pair as an array with two elements.

Answer:

You could use two `maps` to iterate on the two lists and generate the pairs. But this would return a `Stream<Stream<Integer[]>>`. What you need to do is flatten the generated streams to result in a `Stream<Integer[]>`. This is what `flatMap` is for:

(continued)

```
List<Integer> numbers1 = Arrays.asList(1, 2, 3);
List<Integer> numbers2 = Arrays.asList(3, 4);
List<int[]> pairs =
    numbers1.stream()
            .flatMap(i -> numbers2.stream()
                                  .map(j -> new int[]{i, j})
                    )
            .collect(toList());
```

3. How would you extend the previous example to return only pairs whose sum is divisible by 3? For example, (2, 4) and (3, 3) are valid.

Answer:

You saw earlier that `filter` can be used with a predicate to filter elements from a stream. Because after the `flatMap` operation you have a stream of `int[]` that represent a pair, you just need a predicate to check to see if the sum is divisible by 3:

```
List<Integer> numbers1 = Arrays.asList(1, 2, 3);
List<Integer> numbers2 = Arrays.asList(3, 4);
List<int[]> pairs =
    numbers1.stream()
            .flatMap(i ->
                       numbers2.stream()
                               .filter(j -> (i + j) % 3 == 0)
                               .map(j -> new int[]{i, j})
                    )
            .collect(toList());
```

The result is [(2, 4), (3, 3)].

5.3 Finding and matching

Another common data processing idiom is finding whether some elements in a set of data match a given property. The Streams API provides such facilities through the `allMatch`, `anyMatch`, `noneMatch`, `findFirst`, and `findAny` methods of a stream.

5.3.1 Checking to see if a predicate matches at least one element

The `anyMatch` method can be used to answer the question "Is there an element in the stream matching the given predicate?" For example, you can use it to find out whether the menu has a vegetarian option:

```
if(menu.stream().anyMatch(Dish::isVegetarian)){
    System.out.println("The menu is (somewhat) vegetarian friendly!!");
}
```

The `anyMatch` method returns a `boolean` and is therefore a terminal operation.

5.3.2 *Checking to see if a predicate matches all elements*

The `allMatch` method works similarly to `anyMatch` but will check to see if all the elements of the stream match the given predicate. For example, you can use it to find out whether the menu is healthy (that is, all dishes are below 1000 calories):

```
boolean isHealthy = menu.stream()
                        .allMatch(d -> d.getCalories() < 1000);
```

NONEMATCH

The opposite of `allMatch` is `noneMatch`. It ensures that no elements in the stream match the given predicate. For example, you could rewrite the previous example as follows using `noneMatch`:

```
boolean isHealthy = menu.stream()
                        .noneMatch(d -> d.getCalories() >= 1000);
```

These three operations, `anyMatch`, `allMatch`, and `noneMatch`, make use of what we call *short-circuiting*, a stream version of the familiar Java short-circuiting `&&` and `||` operators.

> **Short-circuiting evaluation**
>
> Some operations don't need to process the whole stream to produce a result. For example, say you need to evaluate a large boolean expression chained with and operators. You need only find out that one expression is `false` to deduce that the whole expression will return `false`, no matter how long the expression is; there's no need to evaluate the entire expression. This is what *short-circuiting* refers to.
>
> In relation to streams, certain operations such as `allMatch`, `noneMatch`, `findFirst`, and `findAny` don't need to process the whole stream to produce a result. As soon as an element is found, a result can be produced. Similarly, `limit` is also a short-circuiting operation: the operation only needs to create a stream of a given size without processing all the elements in the stream. Such operations are useful, for example, when you need to deal with streams of infinite size, because they can turn an infinite stream into a stream of finite size. We show examples of infinite streams in section 5.7.

5.3.3 *Finding an element*

The `findAny` method returns an arbitrary element of the current stream. It can be used in conjunction with other stream operations. For example, you may wish to find a dish that's vegetarian. You can combine the `filter` method and `findAny` to express this query:

```
Optional<Dish> dish =
  menu.stream()
      .filter(Dish::isVegetarian)
      .findAny();
```

The stream pipeline will be optimized behind the scenes to perform a single pass and finish as soon as a result is found by using short-circuiting. But wait a minute; what's this `Optional` thing in the code?

OPTIONAL IN A NUTSHELL

The Optional<T> class (java.util.Optional) is a container class to represent the existence or absence of a value. In the previous code, it's possible that findAny doesn't find any element. Instead of returning null, which is well known for being error prone, the Java 8 library designers introduced Optional<T>. We won't go into the details of Optional here, because we show in detail in chapter 10 how your code can benefit from using Optional to avoid bugs related to null checking. But for now, it's good to know that there are a few methods available in Optional that force you to explicitly check for the presence of a value or deal with the absence of a value:

- isPresent() returns true if Optional contains a value, false otherwise.
- ifPresent(Consumer<T> block) executes the given block if a value is present. We introduced the Consumer functional interface in chapter 3; it lets you pass a lambda that takes an argument of type T and returns void.
- T get() returns the value if present; otherwise it throws a NoSuchElement-Exception.
- T orElse(T other) returns the value if present; otherwise it returns a default value.

For example, in the previous code you'd need to explicitly check for the presence of a dish in the Optional object to access its name:

```
menu.stream()
    .filter(Dish::isVegetarian)
    .findAny()                                      <-- Returns an Optional<Dish>.
    .ifPresent(d -> System.out.println(d.getName());   <-- If a value is contained, it's printed; otherwise nothing happens.
```

5.3.4 Finding the first element

Some streams have an *encounter order* that specifies the order in which items logically appear in the stream (for example, a stream generated from a List or from a sorted sequence of data). For such streams you may wish to find the first element. There's the findFirst method for this, which works similarly to findAny. For example, the code that follows, given a list of numbers, finds the first square that's divisible by 3:

```
List<Integer> someNumbers = Arrays.asList(1, 2, 3, 4, 5);
Optional<Integer> firstSquareDivisibleByThree =
  someNumbers.stream()
             .map(x -> x * x)
             .filter(x -> x % 3 == 0)
             .findFirst(); // 9
```

When to use findFirst and findAny

You may wonder why we have both findFirst and findAny. The answer is parallelism. Finding the first element is more constraining in parallel. If you don't care about which element is returned, use findAny because it's less constraining when using parallel streams.

5.4 Reducing

So far, the terminal operations you've seen return a `boolean` (`allMatch` and so on), `void` (`forEach`), or an `Optional` object (`findAny` and so on). You've also been using `collect` to combine all elements in a stream into a `List`.

In this section, you'll see how you can combine elements of a stream to express more complicated queries such as "Calculate the sum of all calories in the menu," or "What is the highest calorie dish in the menu?" using the `reduce` operation. Such queries combine all the elements in the stream repeatedly to produce a single value such as an `Integer`. These queries can be classified as *reduction operations* (a stream is reduced to a value). In functional programming-language jargon, this is referred to as a *fold* because you can view this operation as repeatedly folding a long piece of paper (your stream) until it forms a small square, which is the result of the fold operation.

5.4.1 Summing the elements

Before we investigate how to use the `reduce` method, it helps to first see how you'd sum the elements of a list of numbers using a `for-each` loop:

```
int sum = 0;
for (int x : numbers) {
    sum += x;
}
```

Each element of `numbers` is combined iteratively with the addition operator to form a result. You *reduce* the list of numbers into one number by repeatedly using addition. There are two parameters in this code:

- The initial value of the sum variable, in this case `0`
- The operation to combine all the elements of the list, in this case `+`

Wouldn't it be great if you could also multiply all the numbers without having to repeatedly copy and paste this code? This is where the `reduce` operation, which abstracts over this pattern of repeated application, can help. You can sum all the elements of a stream as follows:

```
int sum = numbers.stream().reduce(0, (a, b) -> a + b);
```

`reduce` takes two arguments:

- An initial value, here `0`.
- A `BinaryOperator<T>` to combine two elements and produce a new value; here you use the lambda `(a, b) -> a + b`.

You could just as easily multiply all the elements by passing a different lambda, `(a, b) -> a * b`, to the `reduce` operation:

```
int product = numbers.stream().reduce(1, (a, b) -> a * b);
```

Figure 5.7 illustrates how the `reduce` operation works on a stream: the lambda combines each element repeatedly until the stream is reduced to a single value.

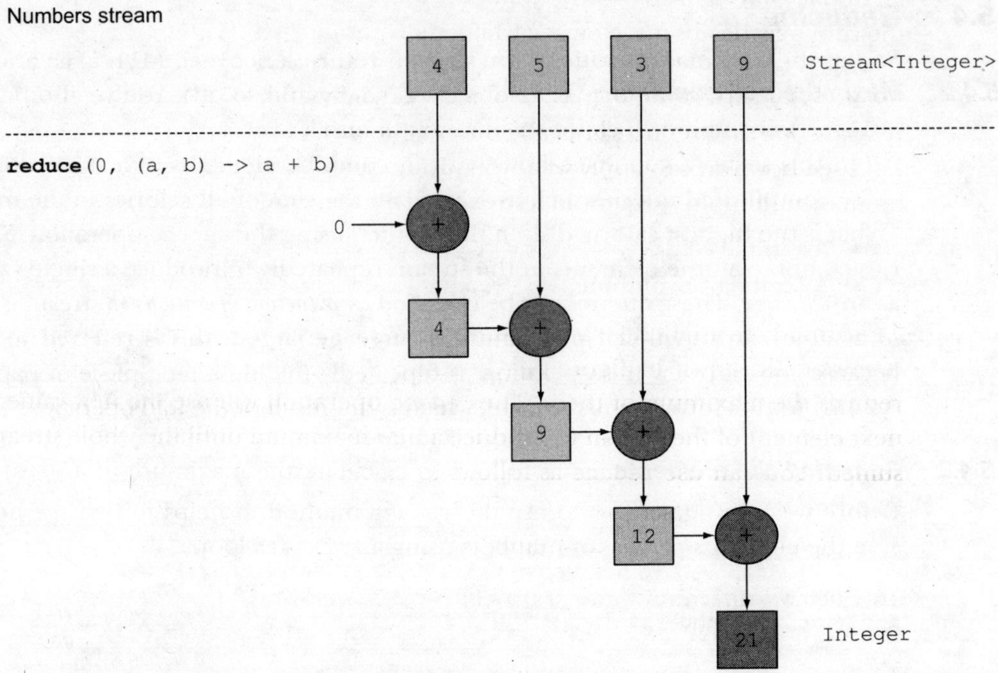

Figure 5.7 Using `reduce` to sum the numbers in a stream

Let's take an in-depth look into how the `reduce` operation happens to sum a stream of numbers. First, `0` is used as the first parameter of the lambda (`a`), and `4` is consumed from the stream and used as the second parameter (`b`). `0 + 4` produces `4`, and it becomes the new accumulated value. Then the lambda is called again with the accumulated value and the next element of the stream, `5`, which produces the new accumulated value, `9`. Moving forward, the lambda is called again with the accumulated value and the next element, `3`, which produces `12`. Finally, the lambda is called with `12` and the last element of the stream, `9`, which produces the final value, `21`.

You can make this code more concise by using a method reference. In Java 8 the `Integer` class now comes with a static `sum` method to add two numbers, which is just what you want instead of repeatedly writing out the same code as lambda:

```
int sum = numbers.stream().reduce(0, Integer::sum);
```

NO INITIAL VALUE

There's also an overloaded variant of `reduce` that doesn't take an initial value, but it returns an `Optional` object:

```
Optional<Integer> sum = numbers.stream().reduce((a, b) -> (a + b));
```

Why does it return an `Optional<Integer>`? Consider the case when the stream contains no elements. The `reduce` operation can't return a sum because it doesn't have an initial value. This is why the result is wrapped in an `Optional` object to indicate that the sum may be absent. Now see what else you can do with `reduce`.

5.4.2 Maximum and minimum

It turns out that reduction is all you need to compute maxima and minima as well! Let's see how you can apply what you just learned about `reduce` to calculate the maximum or minimum element in a stream. As you saw, `reduce` takes two parameters:

- An initial value
- A lambda to combine two stream elements and produce a new value

The lambda is applied step by step to each element of the stream with the addition operator, as shown in figure 5.7. So you need a lambda that, given two elements, returns the maximum of them. The `reduce` operation will use the new value with the next element of the stream to produce a new maximum until the whole stream is consumed! You can use `reduce` as follows to calculate the maximum in a stream; this is illustrated in figure 5.8:

```
Optional<Integer> max = numbers.stream().reduce(Integer::max);
```

To calculate the minimum, you need to pass `Integer.min` to the `reduce` operation instead of `Integer.max`:

```
Optional<Integer> min = numbers.stream().reduce(Integer::min);
```

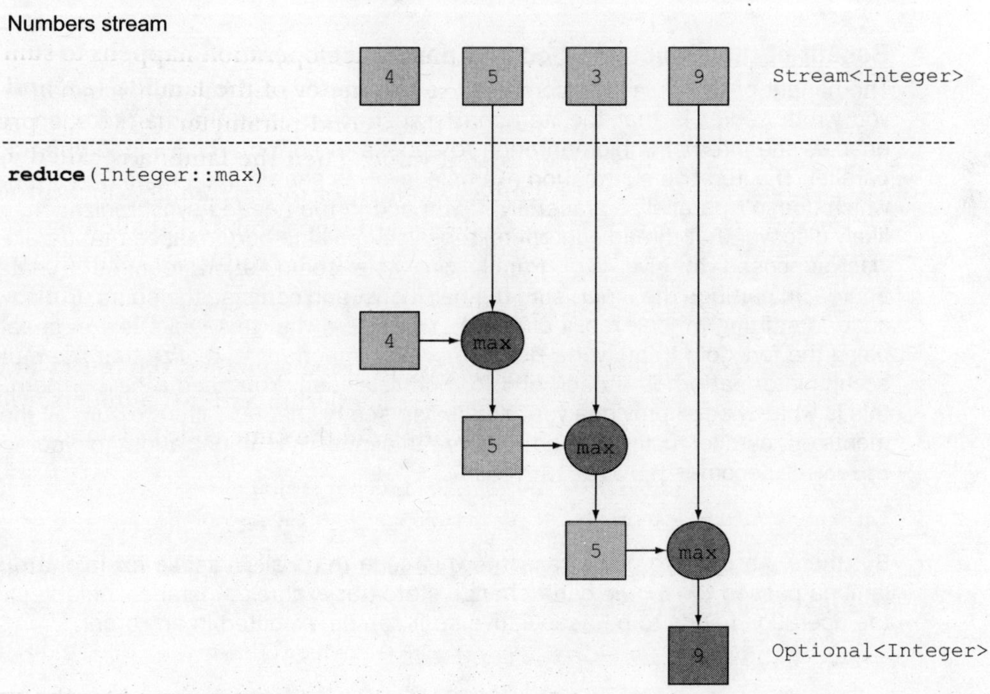

Figure 5.8 A reduce operation—calculating the maximum

You could have equally well used the lambda `(x,y)->x<y?x:y` instead of `Integer::min`, but the latter is easier to read.

To test your understanding of the `reduce` operation, have a go at Quiz 5.3.

Quiz 5.3: Reducing

How would you count the number of dishes in a stream using the `map` and `reduce` methods?

Answer:

You can solve this problem by mapping each element of a stream into the number 1 and then summing them using `reduce`! This is equivalent to counting in order the number of elements in the stream.

```
int count = menu.stream()
                .map(d -> 1)
                .reduce(0, (a, b) -> a + b);
```

A chain of `map` and `reduce` is commonly known as the map-reduce pattern, made famous by Google's use of it for web searching because it can be easily parallelized. Note that in chapter 4 you saw the built-in method `count` to count the number of elements in the stream:

```
long count = menu.stream().count();
```

Benefit of the reduce method and parallelism

The benefit of using `reduce` compared to the step-by-step iteration summation that you wrote earlier is that the iteration is abstracted using internal iteration, which enables the internal implementation to choose to perform the `reduce` operation in parallel. The iterative summation example involves shared updates to a `sum` variable, which doesn't parallelize gracefully. If you add in the needed synchronization, you'll likely discover that thread contention robs you of all the performance that parallelism was supposed to give you! Parallelizing this computation requires a different approach: partition the input, sum the partitions, and combine the sums. But now the code is starting to look really different. You'll see what this looks like in chapter 7 using the fork/join framework. But for now it's important to realize that the mutable accumulator pattern is a dead end for parallelization. You need a new pattern, and this is what `reduce` provides you. You'll also see in chapter 7 that to sum all the elements in parallel using streams, there's almost no modification to your code: `stream()` becomes `parallelStream()`:

```
int sum = numbers.parallelStream().reduce(0, Integer::sum);
```

But there's a price to pay to execute this code in parallel, as we explain later: the lambda passed to `reduce` can't change state (for example, instance variables), and the operation needs to be associative so it can be executed in any order.

So far you saw reduction examples that produced an `Integer`: the sum of a stream, the maximum of a stream, or the number of elements in a stream. You'll see in section 5.6 that built-in methods such as `sum` and `max` are available as well to help you write slightly more concise code for common reduction patterns. We investigate a more complex form of reductions using the `collect` method in the next chapter. For example, instead of reducing a stream into an `Integer`, you can also reduce it into a `Map` if you want to group dishes by types.

> **Stream operations: stateless vs. stateful**
>
> You've seen a lot of stream operations. An initial presentation can make them seem a panacea; everything just works, and you get parallelism for free when you use `parallelStream` instead of `stream` to get a stream from a collection.
>
> Certainly for many applications this is the case, as you've seen in the previous examples. You can turn a list of dishes into a stream, `filter` to select various dishes of a certain type, then `map` down the resulting stream to add on the number of calories, and then `reduce` to produce the total number of calories of the menu. You can even do such stream calculations in parallel. But these operations have different characteristics. There are issues about what internal state they need to operate.
>
> Operations like `map` and `filter` take *each* element from the input stream and produce *zero or one* result in the output stream. These operations are thus in general *stateless*: they don't have an internal state (assuming the user-supplied lambda or method reference has no internal mutable state).
>
> But operations like `reduce`, `sum`, and `max` need to have internal state to accumulate the result. In this case the internal state is small. In our example it consisted of an `int` or `double`. The internal state is of *bounded size* no matter how many elements are in the stream being processed.
>
> By contrast, some operations such as `sorted` or `distinct` seem at first to behave like `filter` or `map`—all take a stream and produce another stream (an intermediate operation), but there's a crucial difference. Both sorting and removing duplicates from a stream require knowing the previous history to do their job. For example, sorting requires *all the elements to be buffered* before a single item can be added to the output stream; the storage requirement of the operation is *unbounded*. This can be problematic if the data stream is large or infinite. (What should reversing the stream of all prime numbers do? It should return the largest prime number, which mathematics tells us doesn't exist.) We call these operations *stateful operations*.

You've now seen a lot of stream operations that you can use to express sophisticated data processing queries! Table 5.1 summarizes the operations seen so far. You get to practice them in the next section through an exercise.

Table 5.1 Intermediate and terminal operations

Operation	Type	Return type	Type/functional interface used	Function descriptor
filter	Intermediate	Stream<T>	Predicate<T>	T -> boolean
distinct	Intermediate (stateful-unbounded)	Stream<T>		
skip	Intermediate (stateful-bounded)	Stream<T>	long	
limit	Intermediate (stateful-bounded)	Stream<T>	long	
map	Intermediate	Stream<R>	Function<T, R>	T -> R
flatMap	Intermediate	Stream<R>	Function<T, Stream<R>>	T -> Stream<R>
sorted	Intermediate (stateful-unbounded)	Stream<T>	Comparator<T>	(T, T) -> int
anyMatch	Terminal	boolean	Predicate<T>	T -> boolean
noneMatch	Terminal	boolean	Predicate<T>	T -> boolean
allMatch	Terminal	boolean	Predicate<T>	T -> boolean
findAny	Terminal	Optional<T>		
findFirst	Terminal	Optional<T>		
forEach	Terminal	void	Consumer<T>	T -> void
collect	terminal	R	Collector<T, A, R>	
reduce	Terminal (stateful-bounded)	Optional<T>	BinaryOperator<T>	(T, T) -> T
count	Terminal	long		

5.5 *Putting it all into practice*

In this section, you get to practice what you've learned about streams so far. We give a different domain: traders executing transactions. You're asked by your manager to find answers to eight queries. Can you do it? We give the solutions in section 5.5.2, but you should try them yourself first to get some practice.

1. Find all transactions in the year 2011 and sort them by value (small to high).
2. What are all the unique cities where the traders work?
3. Find all traders from Cambridge and sort them by name.
4. Return a string of all traders' names sorted alphabetically.
5. Are any traders based in Milan?
6. Print all transactions' values from the traders living in Cambridge.

7 What's the highest value of all the transactions?

8 Find the transaction with the smallest value.

5.5.1 The domain: Traders and Transactions

Here's the domain you'll be working with, a list of `Traders` and `Transactions`:

```
Trader raoul = new Trader("Raoul", "Cambridge");
Trader mario = new Trader("Mario","Milan");
Trader alan = new Trader("Alan","Cambridge");
Trader brian = new Trader("Brian","Cambridge");

List<Transaction> transactions = Arrays.asList(
    new Transaction(brian, 2011, 300),
    new Transaction(raoul, 2012, 1000),
    new Transaction(raoul, 2011, 400),
    new Transaction(mario, 2012, 710),
    new Transaction(mario, 2012, 700),
    new Transaction(alan, 2012, 950)
);
```

`Trader` and `Transaction` are classes defined as follows:

```
public class Trader{

    private final String name;
    private final String city;

    public Trader(String n, String c){
        this.name = n;
        this.city = c;
    }

    public String getName(){
        return this.name;
    }

    public String getCity(){
        return this.city;
    }

    public String toString(){
        return "Trader:"+this.name + " in " + this.city;
    }
}
public class Transaction{

    private final Trader trader;
    private final int year;
    private final int value;

    public Transaction(Trader trader, int year, int value){
        this.trader = trader;
        this.year = year;
        this.value = value;
    }

    public Trader getTrader(){
        return this.trader;
    }
```

```
    public int getYear(){
        return this.year;
    }

    public int getValue(){
        return this.value;
    }

    public String toString(){
        return "{" + this.trader + ", " +
               "year: "+this.year+", " +
               "value:" + this.value +"}";
    }
}
```

5.5.2 *Solutions*

We now provide the solutions in the following code listings, so you can verify your understanding of what you've learned so far. Well done!

Listing 5.1 Find all transactions in 2011 and sort by value (small to high)

```
List<Transaction> tr2011 =
    transactions.stream()
                .filter(transaction -> transaction.getYear() == 2011)
                .sorted(comparing(Transaction::getValue))
                .collect(toList());
```

- Pass a predicate to `filter` to select transactions in year 2011. (`.filter(...)`)
- Sort them by using the value of the transaction. (`.sorted(...)`)
- Collect all the elements of the resulting `Stream` into a `List`. (`.collect(...)`)

Listing 5.2 What are all the unique cities where the traders work?

```
List<String> cities =
    transactions.stream()
                .map(transaction -> transaction.getTrader().getCity())
                .distinct()
                .collect(toList());
```

- Extract the city from each trader associated with the transaction. (`.map(...)`)
- Select only unique cities. (`.distinct()`)

You haven't seen this yet, but you could also drop `distinct()` and use `toSet()` instead, which would convert the stream into a set. You'll learn more about it in chapter 6.

```
Set<String> cities =
    transactions.stream()
                .map(transaction -> transaction.getTrader().getCity())
                .collect(toSet());
```

Listing 5.3 Find all traders from Cambridge and sort them by name

```
List<Trader> traders =
    transactions.stream()
                .map(Transaction::getTrader)
                .filter(trader -> trader.getCity().equals("Cambridge"))
                .distinct()
                .sorted(comparing(Trader::getName))
                .collect(toList());
```

- Extract all traders from the transactions. (`.map(...)`)
- Select only the traders from Cambridge. (`.filter(...)`)
- Make sure you don't have any duplicates. (`.distinct()`)
- Sort the resulting stream of traders by their names. (`.sorted(...)`)

Listing 5.4 Return a string of all traders' names sorted alphabetically

```
String traderStr =
    transactions.stream()
                .map(transaction -> transaction.getTrader().getName())
                .distinct()
                .sorted()
                .reduce("", (n1, n2) -> n1 + n2);
```

Select only the unique names. Extract all the names of the traders as a Stream of Strings. Sort the names alphabetically. Combine each name one by one to form a String that concatenates all the names.

Note that this solution isn't very efficient (all Strings are repeatedly concatenated, which creates a new String object at each iteration). In the next chapter, you'll see a more efficient solution that uses joining() as follows (which internally makes use of a StringBuilder):

```
String traderStr =
    transactions.stream()
                .map(transaction -> transaction.getTrader().getName())
                .distinct()
                .sorted()
                .collect(joining());
```

Listing 5.5 Are any traders based in Milan?

```
boolean milanBased =
    transactions.stream()
                .anyMatch(transaction -> transaction.getTrader()
                                                    .getCity()
                                                    .equals("Milan"));
```

Pass a predicate to anyMatch to check if there's a trader from Milan.

Listing 5.6 Print all transactions' values from the traders living in Cambridge

```
transactions.stream()
            .filter(t -> "Cambridge".equals(t.getTrader().getCity()))
            .map(Transaction::getValue)
            .forEach(System.out::println);
```

Select the transactions where the traders live in Cambridge. Extract the values of these trades. Print each value.

Listing 5.7 What's the highest value of all the transactions?

```
Optional<Integer> highestValue =
    transactions.stream()
                .map(Transaction::getValue)
                .reduce(Integer::max);
```

Extract the value of each transaction. Calculate the max of the resulting stream.

Listing 5.8 Find the transaction with the smallest value

```
Optional<Transaction> smallestTransaction =
  transactions.stream()
              .reduce((t1, t2) ->
                       t1.getValue() < t2.getValue() ? t1 : t2);
```

Find the smallest transaction by repeatedly comparing the values of each transaction.

You can do better. A stream supports the methods `min` and `max` that take a `Comparator` as argument to specify which key to compare with when calculating the minimum or maximum:

```
Optional<Transaction> smallestTransaction =
  transactions.stream()
              .min(comparing(Transaction::getValue));
```

5.6 Numeric streams

You saw earlier that you could use the `reduce` method to calculate the sum of the elements of a stream. For example, you can calculate the number of calories in the menu as follows:

```
int calories = menu.stream()
                   .map(Dish::getCalories)
                   .reduce(0, Integer::sum);
```

The problem with this code is that there's an insidious boxing cost. Behind the scenes each `Integer` needs to be unboxed to a primitive before performing the summation. In addition, wouldn't it be nicer if you could call a `sum` method directly as follows?

```
int calories = menu.stream()
                   .map(Dish::getCalories)
                   .sum();
```

But this isn't possible. The problem is that the method `map` generates a `Stream<T>`. Even though the elements of the stream are of type `Integer`, the `Streams` interface doesn't define a `sum` method. Why not? Say you had only a `Stream<Dish>` like the `menu`; it wouldn't make any sense to be able to sum dishes. But don't worry; the Streams API also supplies *primitive stream specializations* that support specialized methods to work with streams of numbers.

5.6.1 Primitive stream specializations

Java 8 introduces three primitive specialized stream interfaces to tackle this issue, `IntStream`, `DoubleStream`, and `LongStream`, that respectively specialize the elements of a stream to be `int`, `long`, and `double`—and thereby avoid hidden boxing costs. Each of these interfaces brings new methods to perform common numeric reductions such as `sum` to calculate the sum of a numeric stream and `max` to find the maximum element. In addition, they have methods to convert back to a stream of objects when necessary. The thing to remember is that these specializations aren't more complexity about streams but instead more complexity caused by boxing—the (efficiency-based) difference between `int` and `Integer` and so on.

MAPPING TO A NUMERIC STREAM

The most common methods you'll use to convert a stream to a specialized version are `mapToInt`, `mapToDouble`, and `mapToLong`. These methods work exactly like the method `map` that you saw earlier but return a specialized stream instead of a `Stream<T>`. For example, you can use `mapToInt` as follows to calculate the sum of calories in the `menu`:

```
int calories = menu.stream()                          <-- Returns a Stream<Dish>
                .mapToInt(Dish::getCalories)          <-- Returns an IntStream
                .sum();
```

Here, the method `mapToInt` extracts all the calories from each dish (represented as an `Integer`) and returns an `IntStream` as the result (rather than a `Stream<Integer>`). You can then call the `sum` method defined on the `IntStream` interface to calculate the sum of calories! Note that if the stream were empty, `sum` would return `0` by default. `IntStream` also supports other convenience methods such as `max`, `min`, and `average`.

CONVERTING BACK TO A STREAM OF OBJECTS

Similarly, once you have a numeric stream, you may be interested in converting it back to a nonspecialized stream. For example, the operations of an `IntStream` are restricted to produce primitive integers: the `map` operation of an `IntStream` takes a lambda that takes an `int` and produces an `int` (an `IntUnaryOperator`). But you may want to produce a different value such as a `Dish`. For this you need to access the operations defined in the `Streams` interface that are more general. To convert from a primitive stream to a general stream (each `int` will be boxed to an `Integer`) you can use the method `boxed` as follows:

```
IntStream intStream = menu.stream().mapToInt(Dish::getCalories);   <-- Converting a Stream to a numeric stream
Stream<Integer> stream = intStream.boxed();   <-- Converting the numeric stream to a Stream
```

You'll learn in the next section that `boxed` is particularly useful when you deal with numeric ranges that need to be boxed into a general stream.

DEFAULT VALUES: OPTIONALINT

The sum example was convenient because it has a default value: `0`. But if you want to calculate the maximum element in an `IntStream`, you need something different because `0` is a wrong result. How can you differentiate that the stream has no element and that the real maximum is `0`? Earlier we introduced the `Optional` class, which is a container that indicates the presence or absence of a value. `Optional` can be parameterized with reference types such as `Integer`, `String`, and so on. There's a primitive specialized version of `Optional` as well for the three primitive stream specializations: `OptionalInt`, `OptionalDouble`, and `OptionalLong`.

For example, you can find the maximal element of an `IntStream` by calling the `max` method, which returns an `OptionalInt`:

```
OptionalInt maxCalories = menu.stream()
                              .mapToInt(Dish::getCalories)
                              .max();
```

You can now process the `OptionalInt` explicitly to define a default value if there's no maximum:

```
int max = maxCalories.orElse(1);     <-- Provide an explicit default maximum if there's no value.
```

5.6.2 *Numeric ranges*

A common use case when dealing with numbers is working with ranges of numeric values. For example, suppose you'd like to generate all numbers between 1 and 100. Java 8 introduces two static methods available on `IntStream` and `LongStream` to help generate such ranges: `range` and `rangeClosed`. Both methods take the starting value of the range as the first parameter and the end value of the range as the second parameter. But `range` is exclusive, whereas `rangeClosed` is inclusive. Let's look at an example:

```
IntStream evenNumbers = IntStream.rangeClosed(1, 100)
                                 .filter(n -> n % 2 == 0);

System.out.println(evenNumbers.count());
```

Represents the range [1, 100].

A stream of even numbers from 1 to 100.

There are 50 even numbers from 1 to 100.

Here you use the `rangeClosed` method to generate a range of all numbers from 1 to 100. It produces a stream so you can chain the `filter` method to select only even numbers. At this stage no computation has been done. Finally, you call `count` on the resulting stream. Because `count` is a terminal operation, it will process the stream and return the result `50`, which is the number of even numbers from 1 to 100, inclusive. Note that by comparison, if you were using `IntStream.range(1, 100)` instead, the result would be `49` even numbers because `range` is exclusive.

5.6.3 *Putting numerical streams into practice: Pythagorean triples*

We now look at a more difficult example so you can solidify what you've learned about numeric streams and all the stream operations you've learned so far. Your mission, if you choose to accept it, is to create a stream of Pythagorean triples.

PYTHAGOREAN TRIPLE

So what's a Pythagorean triple? We have to go back a few years in the past. In one of your exciting math classes, you learned that the famous Greek mathematician Pythagoras discovered that certain triples of numbers `(a, b, c)` satisfy the formula `a * a + b * b = c * c` where `a`, `b`, and `c` are integers. For example, (3, 4, 5) is a valid Pythagorean triple because 3 * 3 + 4 * 4 = 5 * 5 or 9 + 16 = 25. There are an infinite number of such triples. For example, (5, 12, 13), (6, 8, 10), and (7, 24, 25) are all valid Pythagorean triples. Such triples are useful because they describe the three side lengths of a right-angled triangle, as illustrated in figure 5.9.

REPRESENTING A TRIPLE

So where do you start? The first step is to define a triple. Instead of (more properly) defining a new class to represent a triple, you can use an array of `int` with three elements, for example, `new int[]{3, 4, 5}` to represent the tuple (3, 4, 5). You can now access each individual component of the tuple using array indexing.

FILTERING GOOD COMBINATIONS

Let's assume someone provides you with the first two numbers of the triple: `a` and `b`. How do you know whether that will form a good combination? You need to test

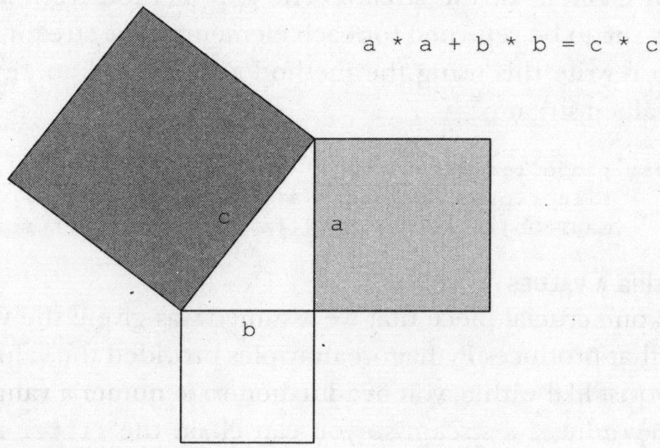

Figure 5.9 The Pythagorean theorem

whether the square root of `a * a + b * b` is an integer number; that is, it has no fractional part, which in Java can be expressed using `expr % 1.0`. If it's not an integer, that means `c` is not an integer. You can express this requirement as a `filter` operation (you'll see how to connect it later to form valid code):

```
filter(b -> Math.sqrt(a*a + b*b) % 1 == 0)
```

Assuming that surrounding code has given a value for `a` and assuming `stream` provides possible values for `b`, `filter` will select only those values for `b` that can form a Pythagorean triple with `a`. You may be wondering what the line `Math.sqrt(a*a + b*b) % 1 == 0` is about. It's basically a way to test whether `Math.sqrt(a*a + b*b)` returns an integer result. The condition will fail if the result of the square root produces a number with a decimal such as 9.1 (9.0 is valid).

GENERATING TUPLES

Following the filter, you know that both `a` and `b` can form a correct combination. You now need to create a triple. You can use the `map` operation to transform each element into a Pythagorean triple as follows:

```
stream.filter(b -> Math.sqrt(a*a + b*b) % 1 == 0)
      .map(b -> new int[]{a, b, (int) Math.sqrt(a * a + b * b)});
```

GENERATING B VALUES

You're getting closer! You now need to generate values for `b`. You saw that `Stream.rangeClosed` allows you to generate a stream of numbers in a given interval. You can use it to provide numeric values for `b`, here 1 to 100:

```
IntStream.rangeClosed(1, 100)
         .filter(b -> Math.sqrt(a*a + b*b) % 1 == 0)
         .boxed()
         .map(b -> new int[]{a, b, (int) Math.sqrt(a * a + b * b)});
```

Note that you call boxed after the filter to generate a Stream<Integer> from the IntStream returned by rangeClosed. This is because your map returns an array of int for each element of the stream. The map method from an IntStream expects only another int to be returned for each element of the stream, which isn't what you want! You can rewrite this using the method mapToObj of an IntStream, which returns an object-valued stream:

```
IntStream.rangeClosed(1, 100)
         .filter(b -> Math.sqrt(a*a + b*b) % 1 == 0)
         .mapToObj(b -> new int[]{a, b, (int) Math.sqrt(a * a + b * b)});
```

GENERATING A VALUES

There's one crucial piece that we assumed was given: the value for a. You now have a stream that produces Pythagorean triples provided the value a is known. How can you fix this? Just like with b, you need to generate numeric values for a! The final solution is as follows:

```
Stream<int[]> pythagoreanTriples =
    IntStream.rangeClosed(1, 100).boxed()
             .flatMap(a ->
                IntStream.rangeClosed(a, 100)
                         .filter(b -> Math.sqrt(a*a + b*b) % 1 == 0)
                         .mapToObj(b ->
                            new int[]{a, b, (int)Math.sqrt(a * a + b * b)})
             );
```

Okay, what's the flatMap about? First, you create a numeric range from 1 to 100 to generate values for a. For each given value of a you're creating a stream of triples. Mapping a value of a to a stream of triples would result in a stream of streams! The flatMap method does the mapping and also flattens all the generated streams of triples into a single stream. As a result you produce a stream of triples. Note also that you change the range of b to be a to 100. There's no need to start the range at the value 1 because this would create duplicate triples (for example, (3, 4, 5) and (4, 3, 5)).

RUNNING THE CODE

You can now run your solution and select explicitly how many triples you'd like to return from the generated stream using the limit operation that you saw earlier:

```
pythagoreanTriples.limit(5)
                  .forEach(t ->
                     System.out.println(t[0] + ", " + t[1] + ", " + t[2]));
```

This will print

```
3, 4, 5
5, 12, 13
6, 8, 10
7, 24, 25
8, 15, 17
```

CAN YOU DO BETTER?

The current solution isn't optimal because you calculate the square root twice. One possible way to make your code more compact is to generate all triples of the form (a*a, b*b, a*a+b*b) and then filter the ones that match your criteria:

```
Stream<double[]> pythagoreanTriples2 =
  IntStream.rangeClosed(1, 100).boxed()
           .flatMap(a ->
              IntStream.rangeClosed(a, 100)
                 .mapToObj(
                    b -> new double[]{a, b, Math.sqrt(a*a + b*b)})   <-- Produce triples.
                 .filter(t -> t[2] % 1 == 0));   <-- The third element of the tuple must be an integer.
```

5.7 Building streams

Hopefully by now you're convinced that streams are very powerful and useful to express data processing queries. So far, you were able to get a stream from a collection using the stream method. In addition, we showed you how to create numerical streams from a range of numbers. But you can create streams in many more ways! This section shows how you can create a stream from a sequence of values, from an array, from a file, and even from a generative function to create infinite streams!

5.7.1 Streams from values

You can create a stream with explicit values by using the static method Stream.of, which can take any number of parameters. For example, in the following code you create a stream of strings directly using Stream.of. You then convert the strings to uppercase before printing them one by one:

```
Stream<String> stream = Stream.of("Java 8 ", "Lambdas ", "In ", "Action");
stream.map(String::toUpperCase).forEach(System.out::println);
```

You can get an empty stream using the empty method as follows:

```
Stream<String> emptyStream = Stream.empty();
```

5.7.2 Streams from arrays

You can create a stream from an array using the static method Arrays.stream, which takes an array as parameter. For example, you can convert an array of primitive ints into an IntStream as follows:

```
int[] numbers = {2, 3, 5, 7, 11, 13};
int sum = Arrays.stream(numbers).sum();   <-- The sum is 41.
```

5.7.3 Streams from files

Java's NIO API (non-blocking I/O), which is used for I/O operations such as processing a file, has been updated to take advantage of the Streams API. Many static methods in java.nio.file.Files return a stream. For example, a useful method is Files.lines, which returns a stream of lines as strings from a given file. Using what you've learned so far, you could use this method to find out the number of unique words in a file as follows:

```
long uniqueWords = 0;
try(Stream<String> lines =
        Files.lines(Paths.get("data.txt"), Charset.defaultCharset())){
uniqueWords = lines.flatMap(line -> Arrays.stream(line.split(" ")))
                   .distinct()
                   .count();
}
catch(IOException e){

}
```

Streams are autoclosable.
Generate a stream of words.
Remove duplicates.
Count the number of unique words.
Deal with the exception if one occurs when opening the file.

You use `Files.lines` to return a stream where each element is a line in the given file. You then split each line into words by calling the `split` method on `line`. Notice how you use `flatMap` to produce one flattened stream of words instead of multiple streams of words for each line. Finally, you count each distinct word in the stream by chaining the methods `distinct` and `count`.

5.7.4 Streams from functions: creating infinite streams!

The Streams API provides two static methods to generate a stream from a function: `Stream.iterate` and `Stream.generate`. These two operations let you create what we call an *infinite stream*: a stream that doesn't have a fixed size like when you create a stream from a fixed collection. Streams produced by `iterate` and `generate` create values on demand given a function and can therefore calculate values forever! It's generally sensible to use `limit(n)` on such streams to avoid printing an infinite number of values.

ITERATE

Let's look at a simple example of how to use `iterate` before we explain it:

```
Stream.iterate(0, n -> n + 2)
      .limit(10)
      .forEach(System.out::println);
```

The `iterate` method takes an initial value, here `0`, and a lambda (of type `UnaryOperator<T>`) to apply successively on each new value produced. Here you return the previous element added with `2` using the lambda `n -> n + 2`. As a result, the `iterate` method produces a stream of all even numbers: the first element of the stream is the initial value `0`. Then it adds `2` to produce the new value `2`; it adds `2` again to produce the new value `4` and so on. This `iterate` operation is fundamentally sequential because the result depends on the previous application. Note that this operation produces an *infinite stream*—the stream doesn't have an end because values are computed on demand and can be computed forever. We say the stream is *unbounded*. As we discussed earlier, this is a key difference between a stream and a collection. You're using the `limit` method to explicitly limit the size of the stream. Here you select only the first 10 even numbers. You then call the `forEach` terminal operation to consume the stream and print each element individually.

In general, you should use `iterate` when you need to produce a sequence of successive values, for example, a date followed by its next date: January 31, February 1, and so on. To see a more difficult example of how you can apply `iterate`, try out Quiz 5.4.

Quiz 5.4: Fibonacci tuples series

The Fibonacci series is famous as a classic programming exercise. The numbers in the following sequence are part of the Fibonacci series: 0, 1, 1, 2, 3, 5, 8, 13, 21, 34, 55.... The first two numbers of the series are 0 and 1, and each subsequent number is the sum of the previous two.

The series of Fibonacci tuples is similar; you have a sequence of a number and its successor in the series: (0, 1), (1, 1), (1, 2), (2, 3), (3, 5), (5, 8), (8, 13), (13, 21)....

Your task is to generate the first 20 elements of the series of Fibonacci tuples using the `iterate` method!

Let us help you get started. The first problem is that the `iterate` method takes a `UnaryOperator<T>` as argument and you need a stream of tuples such as (0, 1). You can, again rather sloppily, use an array of two elements to represent a tuple. For example, `new int[]{0, 1}` represents the first element of the Fibonacci series (0, 1). This will be the initial value of the `iterate` method:

```
Stream.iterate(new int[]{0, 1}, ???)
      .limit(20)
      .forEach(t -> System.out.println("(" + t[0] + "," + t[1] +")"));
```

In this quiz, you need to figure out the highlighted code with the `???`. Remember that `iterate` will apply the given lambda successively.

Answer:

```
Stream.iterate(new int[]{0, 1},
               t -> new int[]{t[1], t[0]+t[1]})
      .limit(20)
      .forEach(t -> System.out.println("(" + t[0] + "," + t[1] +")"));
```

How does it work? `iterate` needs a lambda to specify the successor element. In the case of the tuple (3, 5) the successor is (5, 3+5) = (5, 8). The next one is (8, 5+8). Can you see the pattern? Given a tuple, the successor is (t[1], t[0] + t[1]). This is what the following lambda specifies: `t -> new int[]{t[1],t[0] + t[1]}`. By running this code you'll get the series (0, 1), (1, 1), (1, 2), (2, 3), (3, 5), (5, 8), (8, 13), (13, 21).... Note that if you just wanted to print the normal Fibonacci series, you could use a `map` to extract only the first element of each tuple:

```
Stream.iterate(new int[]{0, 1},
               t -> new int[]{t[1],t[0] + t[1]})
      .limit(10)
      .map(t -> t[0])
      .forEach(System.out::println);
```

This code will produce the Fibonacci series: 0, 1, 1, 2, 3, 5, 8, 13, 21, 34....

GENERATE

Similarly to the method `iterate`, the method `generate` lets you produce an infinite stream of values computed on demand. But `generate` doesn't apply successively a function on each new produced value. It takes a lambda of type `Supplier<T>` to provide new values. Let's look at an example of how to use it:

```
Stream.generate(Math::random)
      .limit(5)
      .forEach(System.out::println);
```

This code will generate a stream of five random double numbers from 0 to 1. For example, one run gives the following:

```
0.9410810294106129
0.6586270755634592
0.9592859117266873
0.13743396659487006
0.3942776037651241
```

The static method `Math.random` is used as a generator for new values. Again you limit the size of the stream explicitly using the `limit` method; otherwise the stream would be unbounded!

You may be wondering if there's anything else useful you can do using the method `generate`. The supplier we used (a method reference to `Math.random`) was stateless: it wasn't recording any values somewhere that can be used in later computations. But a supplier doesn't have to be stateless. You can create a supplier that stores state that it can modify and use when generating the next value of the stream. As an example, we show how you can also create the Fibonacci series from Quiz 5.4 using `generate` so you can compare it with the approach using the `iterate` method! But it's important to note that a supplier that's stateful isn't safe to use in parallel code. So what follows is shown just for completeness but should be avoided! We discuss the problem of operations with side effects and parallel streams further in chapter 7.

We'll use an `IntStream` in our example to illustrate code that's designed to avoid boxing operations. The `generate` method on `IntStream` takes an `IntSupplier` instead of a `Supplier<T>`. For example, here's how to generate an infinite stream of ones:

```
IntStream ones = IntStream.generate(() -> 1);
```

You saw in the chapter 3 that lambdas let you create an instance of a functional interface by providing the implementation of the method directly inline. You can also pass an explicit object as follows by implementing the `getAsInt` method defined in the `IntSupplier` interface (although this seems gratuitously long-winded, please bear with us):

```
IntStream twos = IntStream.generate(new IntSupplier(){
            public int getAsInt(){
                return 2;
            }
        });
```

The `generate` method will use the given supplier and repeatedly call the `getAsInt` method, which always returns 2. But the difference between the anonymous class used here and a lambda is that the anonymous class can define state via fields, which the `getAsInt` method can modify. This is an example of a side effect. All lambdas you've seen so far were side-effect free; they didn't change any state.

To come back to our Fibonacci tasks, what you need to do now is create an `IntSupplier` that maintains in its state the previous value in the series, so `getAsInt` can use it to calculate the next element. In addition, it can update the state of the `IntSupplier` for the next time it's called. The following code shows how to create an `IntSupplier` that will return the next Fibonacci element when it's called:

```
IntSupplier fib = new IntSupplier(){
    private int previous = 0;
    private int current = 1;
    public int getAsInt(){
        int oldPrevious = this.previous;
        int nextValue = this.previous + this.current;
        this.previous = this.current;
        this.current = nextValue;
        return oldPrevious;
    }
};
IntStream.generate(fib).limit(10).forEach(System.out::println);
```

In the preceding code you create an instance of `IntSupplier`. This object has *mutable* state: it tracks the previous Fibonacci element and the current Fibonacci element in two instance variables. The `getAsInt` method changes the state of the object when it's called so that it produces new values on each call. In comparison, our approach using `iterate` was purely *immutable*: you didn't modify existing state but were creating new tuples at each iteration. You'll learn in chapter 7 that you should always prefer an *immutable approach* in order to process a stream in parallel and expect a correct result.

Note that because you're dealing with a stream of infinite size, you have to limit its size explicitly using the operation `limit`; otherwise, the terminal operation (in this case `forEach`) will compute forever. Similarly, you can't sort or reduce an infinite stream because all elements need to be processed, but this would take forever because the stream is infinite!

5.8 Summary

It's been a long but rewarding chapter! You can now process collections more effectively. Indeed, streams let you express sophisticated data processing queries concisely. In addition, streams can be parallelized transparently. Here are some key concepts to take away from this chapter:

- The Streams API lets you express complex data processing queries. Common stream operations are summarized in table 5.1.
- You can filter and slice a stream using the `filter`, `distinct`, `skip`, and `limit` methods.

- You can extract or transform elements of a stream using the `map` and `flatMap` methods.
- You can find elements in a stream using the `findFirst` and `findAny` methods. You can match a given predicate in a stream using the `allMatch`, `noneMatch`, and `anyMatch` methods.
- These methods make use of short-circuiting: a computation stops as soon as a result is found; there's no need to process the whole stream.
- You can combine all elements of a stream iteratively to produce a result using the `reduce` method, for example, to calculate the sum or find the maximum of a stream.
- Some operations such as `filter` and `map` are stateless; they don't store any state. Some operations such as `reduce` store state to calculate a value. Some operations such as `sorted` and `distinct` also store state because they need to buffer all the elements of a stream before returning a new stream. Such operations are called *stateful operations*.
- There are three primitive specializations of streams: `IntStream`, `DoubleStream`, and `LongStream`. Their operations are also specialized accordingly.
- Streams can be created not only from a collection but also from values, arrays, files, and specific methods such as `iterate` and `generate`.
- An infinite stream is a stream that has no fixed size.

Collecting data with streams

This chapter covers

- Creating and using a collector with the `Collectors` class
- Reducing streams of data to a single value
- Summarization as a special case of reduction
- Grouping and partitioning data
- Developing your own custom collectors

You learned in the previous chapter that streams help you process collections with database-like operations. You can view Java 8 streams as fancy lazy iterators of sets of data. They support two types of operations: intermediate operations such as `filter` or `map` and terminal operations such as `count`, `findFirst`, `forEach`, and `reduce`. Intermediate operations can be chained to convert a stream into another stream. These operations don't consume from a stream; their purpose is to set up a pipeline of streams. By contrast, terminal operations *do* consume from a stream—to produce a final result (for example, returning the largest element in a stream). They can often shorten computations by optimizing the pipeline of a stream.

We already used the `collect` terminal operation on streams in chapters 4 and 5, but we employed it there mainly to combine all the elements of a `Stream` into a

`List`. In this chapter, you'll discover that `collect` is a reduction operation, just like `reduce`, that takes as argument various recipes for accumulating the elements of a stream into a summary result. These recipes are defined by a new `Collector` interface, so it's important to distinguish `Collection`, `Collector`, and `collect`!

Here are some example queries of what you'll be able to do using `collect` and collectors:

- Group a list of transactions by currency to obtain the sum of the values of all transactions with that currency (returning a `Map<Currency, Integer>`)
- Partition a list of transactions into two groups: expensive and not expensive (returning a `Map<Boolean, List<Transaction>>`)
- Create multilevel groupings such as grouping transactions by cities and then further categorizing by whether they're expensive or not (returning a `Map<String, Map<Boolean, List<Transaction>>>`)

Excited? Great, let's start by exploring an example that benefits from collectors. Imagine a scenario where you have a `List` of `Transaction`s, and you want to group them based on their nominal currency. In pre-lambda Java, even a simple use case like this is cumbersome to implement, as shown in the following listing.

Listing 6.1 Grouping transactions by currency in imperative style

```
Map<Currency, List<Transaction>> transactionsByCurrencies =
                                               new HashMap<>();
for (Transaction transaction : transactions) {
    Currency currency = transaction.getCurrency();
    List<Transaction> transactionsForCurrency =
                                   transactionsByCurrencies.get(currency);
    if (transactionsForCurrency == null) {
        transactionsForCurrency = new ArrayList<>();
        transactionsByCurrencies
                            .put(currency, transactionsForCurrency);
    }
    transactionsForCurrency.add(transaction);
}
```

Create the `Map` where the grouped transaction will be accumulated.

Iterate the `List` of `Transaction`

Extract the `Transaction`'s currency.

If there's no entry in the grouping `Map` for this currency, create it.

Add the currently traversed `Transaction` to the `List` of `Transactions` with the same currency.

If you're an experienced Java developer, you'll probably feel comfortable writing something like this, but you have to admit that it's a lot of code for such a simple task. Even worse, this is probably harder to read than to write! The purpose of the code isn't immediately evident at first glance, even though it can be expressed in a straightforward manner in plain English: "Group a list of transactions by their currency." As you'll learn in this chapter, you can achieve exactly the same result with a single statement by using a more general `Collector` parameter to the `collect` method on `Stream` rather than the `toList` special case used in the previous chapter:

```
Map<Currency, List<Transaction>> transactionsByCurrencies =
        transactions.stream().collect(groupingBy(Transaction::getCurrency));
```

The comparison is quite embarrassing, isn't it?

6.1 Collectors in a nutshell

The previous example clearly shows one of the main advantages of functional-style programming over an imperative approach: you just have to formulate the result you want to obtain the "what" and not the steps you need to perform to obtain it—the "how." In the previous example, the argument passed to the `collect` method is an implementation of the `Collector` interface, which is a recipe for how to build a summary of the elements in the `Stream`. In the previous chapter, the `toList` recipe just said "Make a list of each element in turn"; in this example, the `groupingBy` recipe says "Make a `Map` whose keys are (currency) buckets and whose values are a list of elements in those buckets."

The difference between the imperative and functional versions of this example is even more pronounced if you perform multilevel groupings: in this case the imperative code quickly becomes harder to read, maintain, and modify due to the number of deeply nested loops and conditions required. In comparison, the functional-style version, as you'll discover in section 6.3, can be easily enhanced with an additional collector.

6.1.1 Collectors as advanced reductions

This last observation brings up another typical benefit of a well-designed functional API: its higher degree of composability and reusability. Collectors are extremely useful because they provide a concise yet flexible way to define the criteria that `collect` uses to produce the resulting collection. More specifically, invoking the `collect` method on a stream triggers a reduction operation (parameterized by a `Collector`) on the elements of the stream itself. This *reduction operation*, illustrated in figure 6.1, internally does for you what you had to code imperatively in listing 6.1. It traverses each element of the stream and lets the `Collector` process them.

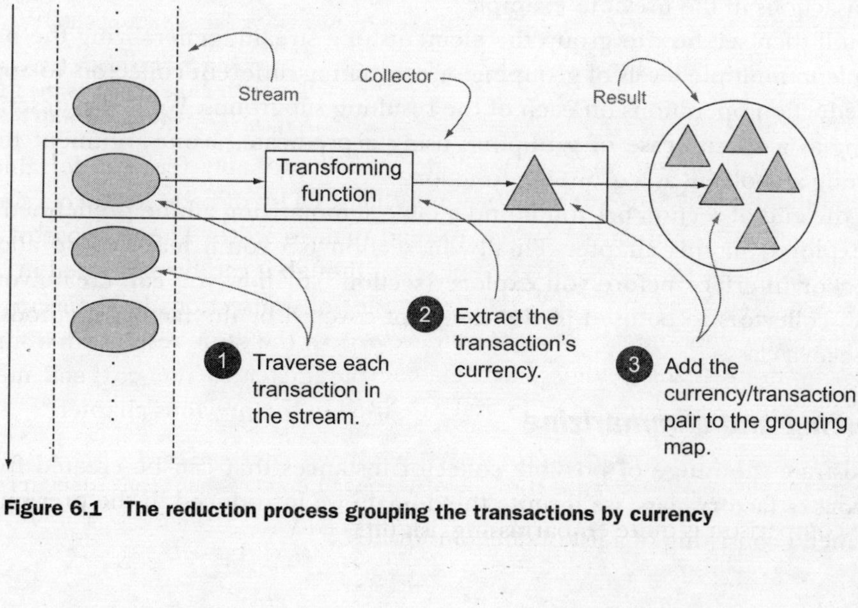

Figure 6.1 The reduction process grouping the transactions by currency

Typically, the `Collector` applies a transforming function to the element (quite often this is the identity transformation, which has no effect, for example, as in `toList`), and accumulates the result in a data structure that forms the final output of this process. For instance, in our transaction-grouping example shown previously, the transformation function extracts the currency from each transaction, and subsequently the transaction itself is accumulated in the resulting `Map`, using the currency as key.

The implementation of the methods of the `Collector` interface defines how to perform a reduction operation on a stream, such as the one in our currency example. We investigate how to create customized collectors in sections 6.5 and 6.6. But the `Collectors` utility class provides lots of static factory methods to conveniently create an instance of the most common collectors that are ready to use. The most straightforward and frequently used collector is the `toList` static method, which gathers all the elements of a stream into a `List`:

```
List<Transaction> transactions =
    transactionStream.collect(Collectors.toList());
```

6.1.2 *Predefined collectors*

In the rest of this chapter, we mainly explore the features of the predefined collectors, those that can be created from the factory methods (such as `groupingBy`) provided by the `Collectors` class. These offer three main functionalities:

- Reducing and summarizing stream elements to a single value
- Grouping elements
- Partitioning elements

We start with collectors that allow you to reduce and summarize. These are handy in a variety of use cases such as finding the total amount of the transacted values in the list of transactions in the previous example.

You'll then see how to group the elements of a stream, generalizing the previous example to multiple levels of grouping or combining different collectors to apply further reduction operations on each of the resulting subgroups. We'll also describe *partitioning* as a special case of grouping, using a predicate, a one-argument function returning a boolean, as a grouping function.

At the end of section 6.4 you'll find a table summarizing all the predefined collectors explored in this chapter. Finally, in section 6.5 you'll learn more about the `Collector` interface before you explore (section 6.6) how you can create your own custom collectors to be used in the cases not covered by the factory methods of the `Collectors` class.

6.2 *Reducing and summarizing*

To illustrate the range of possible collector instances that can be created from the `Collectors` factory class, we'll reuse the domain we introduced in the previous chapter: a menu consisting of a list of delicious dishes!

As you just learned, collectors (the parameters to the `Stream` method `collect`) are typically used in cases where it's necessary to reorganize the stream's items into a collection. But more generally, they can be used every time you want to combine all the items in the stream into a single result. This result can be of any type, as complex as a multilevel map representing a tree or as simple as a single integer—perhaps representing the sum of all the calories in the menu. We'll look at both of these result types: single integers in section 6.2.2 and multilevel grouping in section 6.3.1.

As a first simple example, let's count the number of dishes in the menu, using the collector returned by the `counting` factory method:

```
long howManyDishes = menu.stream().collect(Collectors.counting());
```

You can write this far more directly as

```
long howManyDishes = menu.stream().count();
```

but the `counting` collector can be especially useful when used in combination with other collectors, as we demonstrate later.

In the rest of this chapter, we assume that you've imported all the static factory methods of the `Collectors` class with

```
import static java.util.stream.Collectors.*;
```

so you can write `counting()` instead of `Collectors.counting()` and so on.

Let's continue exploring simple predefined collectors by looking at how you can find the maximum and minimum values in a stream.

6.2.1 Finding maximum and minimum in a stream of values

Suppose you want to find the highest-calorie dish in the menu. You can use two collectors, `Collectors.maxBy` and `Collectors.minBy`, to calculate the maximum or minimum value in a stream. These two collectors take a `Comparator` as argument to compare the elements in the stream. Here you create a `Comparator` comparing dishes based on their calorie content and pass it to `Collectors.maxBy`:

```
Comparator<Dish> dishCaloriesComparator =
    Comparator.comparingInt(Dish::getCalories);

Optional<Dish> mostCalorieDish =
    menu.stream()
        .collect(maxBy(dishCaloriesComparator));
```

You may wonder what the `Optional<Dish>` is about. To answer this we need to ask the question "What if `menu` were empty?" There's no dish to return! Java 8 introduces `Optional`, which is a container that may or may not contain a value. Here it perfectly represents the idea that there may or may not be a dish returned. We briefly mentioned it in chapter 5 when you encountered the method `findAny`. Don't worry about it for now; we devote chapter 10 to the study of `Optional<T>` and its operations.

Another common reduction operation that returns a single value is to sum the values of a numeric field of the objects in a stream. Alternatively, you may want to average the values. Such operations are called *summarization* operations. Let's see how you can express them using collectors.

6.2.2 Summarization

The `Collectors` class provides a specific factory method for summing: `Collectors.summingInt`. It accepts a function that maps an object into the `int` that has to be summed and returns a collector that, when passed to the usual `collect` method, performs the requested summarization. So, for instance, you can find the total number of calories in your menu list with

```
int totalCalories = menu.stream().collect(summingInt(Dish::getCalories));
```

Here the collection process proceeds as illustrated in figure 6.2. While traversing the stream each dish is mapped into its number of calories, and this number is added to an accumulator starting from an initial value (in this case the value is `0`).

The `Collectors.summingLong` and `Collectors.summingDouble` methods behave exactly the same way and can be used where the field to be summed is respectively a `long` or a `double`.

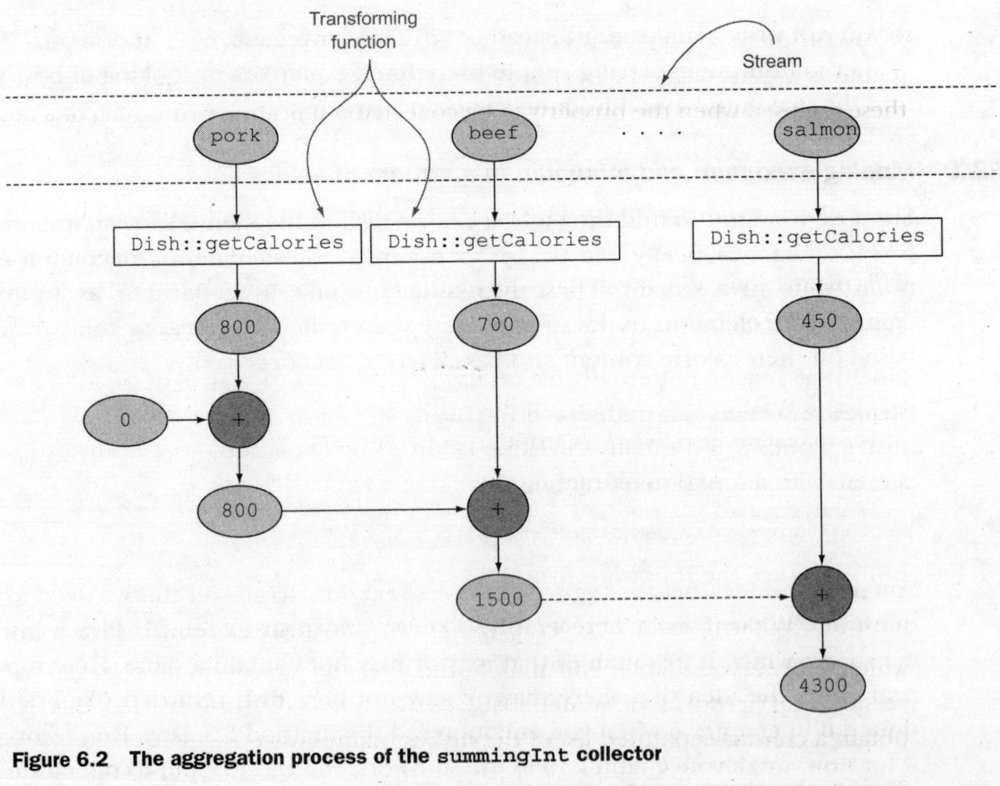

Figure 6.2 The aggregation process of the `summingInt` collector

But there's more to summarization than mere summing; also available is a `Collectors.averagingInt`, together with its `averagingLong` and `averagingDouble` counterparts, to calculate the average of the same set of numeric values:

```
double avgCalories =
    menu.stream().collect(averagingInt(Dish::getCalories));
```

So far, you've seen how to use collectors to count the elements in a stream, find the maximum and minimum values of a numeric property of those elements, and calculate their sum and average. Quite often, though, you may want to retrieve two or more of these results, and possibly you'd like to do it in a single operation. In this case, you can use the collector returned by the `summarizingInt` factory method. For example, you can count the elements in the menu and obtain the sum, average, maximum, and minimum of the calories contained in each dish with a single `summarizing` operation:

```
IntSummaryStatistics menuStatistics =
        menu.stream().collect(summarizingInt(Dish::getCalories));
```

This collector gathers all that information in a class called `IntSummaryStatistics` that provides convenient getter methods to access the results. Printing the `menuStatistic` object produces the following output:

```
IntSummaryStatistics{count=9, sum=4300, min=120,
                     average=477.777778, max=800}
```

As usual, there are corresponding `summarizingLong` and `summarizingDouble` factory methods with associated types `LongSummaryStatistics` and `DoubleSummaryStatistics`; these are used when the property to be collected is a primitive-type `long` or a `double`.

6.2.3 *Joining Strings*

The collector returned by the `joining` factory method concatenates into a single string all strings resulting from invoking the `toString` method on each object in the stream. This means you can concatenate the names of all the dishes in the menu as follows:

```
String shortMenu = menu.stream().map(Dish::getName).collect(joining());
```

Note that `joining` internally makes use of a `StringBuilder` to append the generated strings into one. Also note that if the `Dish` class had a `toString` method returning the dish's name, you'd obtain the same result without needing to map over the original stream with a function extracting the name from each dish:

```
String shortMenu = menu.stream().collect(joining());
```

Both produce the following string,

```
porkbeefchickenfrench friesriceseason fruitpizzaprawnssalmon
```

which isn't very readable. Fortunately, the `joining` factory method has an overloaded version that accepts a delimiter string between two consecutive elements, so you can obtain a comma-separated list of the dishes' names with

```
String shortMenu = menu.stream().map(Dish::getName).collect(joining(", "));
```

which, as expected, will generate

```
pork, beef, chicken, french fries, rice, season fruit, pizza, prawns, salmon
```

Until now, we've explored various collectors that reduce a stream to a single value. In the next section, we demonstrate how all the reduction processes of this form are special cases of the more general reduction collector provided by the `Collectors.reducing` factory method.

6.2.4 Generalized summarization with reduction

All the collectors we've discussed so far are, in reality, only convenient specializations of a reduction process that can be defined using the `reducing` factory method. The `Collectors.reducing` factory method is a generalization of all of them. The special cases discussed earlier are arguably provided only for programmer convenience. (But remember that programmer convenience and readability are of prime importance!) For instance, it's *possible* to calculate the total calories in your menu with a collector created from the `reducing` method as follows:

```
int totalCalories = menu.stream().collect(reducing(
                                   0, Dish::getCalories, (i, j) -> i + j));
```

It takes three arguments:

- The first argument is the starting value of the reduction operation and will also be the value returned in the case of a stream with no elements, so clearly `0` is the appropriate value in the case of a numeric sum.
- The second argument is the same function you used in section 6.2.2 to transform a dish into an `int` representing its calorie content.
- The third argument is a `BinaryOperator` that aggregates two items into a single value of the same type. Here, it just sums two `int`s.

Similarly, you could find the highest-calorie dish using the one-argument version of `reducing` as follows:

```
Optional<Dish> mostCalorieDish =
    menu.stream().collect(reducing(
        (d1, d2) -> d1.getCalories() > d2.getCalories() ? d1 : d2));
```

You can think of the collector created with the one-argument `reducing` factory method as a particular case of the three-argument method, which uses the first item in the stream as a starting point and an *identity function* (that is, a function doing nothing more than returning its input argument as is) as a transformation function. This also implies that the one-argument `reducing` collector won't have any starting point when passed to the `collect` method of an empty stream and, as we explained in section 6.2.1, for this reason it returns an `Optional<Dish>` object.

Collect vs. reduce

We've discussed reductions a lot in the previous chapter and this one. You may naturally wonder what the differences between the `collect` and `reduce` methods of the `Stream` interface are, because often you can obtain the same results using either method. For instance, you can achieve what is done by the `toList Collector` using the `reduce` method as follows:

```
Stream<Integer> stream = Arrays.asList(1, 2, 3, 4, 5, 6).stream();
List<Integer> numbers = stream.reduce(
                                     new ArrayList<Integer>(),
                                     (List<Integer> l, Integer e) -> {
                                              l.add(e);
                                              return l; },
                                     (List<Integer> l1, List<Integer> l2) -> {
                                              l1.addAll(l2);
                                              return l1; });
```

This solution has two problems: a semantic one and a practical one. The semantic problem lies in the fact that the `reduce` method is meant to combine two values and produce a new one; it's an immutable reduction. In contrast, the `collect` method is designed to mutate a container to accumulate the result it's supposed to produce. This means that the previous snippet of code is misusing the `reduce` method because it's mutating in place the `List` used as accumulator. As you'll see in more detail in the next chapter, using the `reduce` method with the wrong semantic is also the cause of a practical problem: this reduction process can't work in parallel because the concurrent modification of the same data structure operated by multiple threads can corrupt the `List` itself. In this case, if you want thread safety, you'll need to allocate a new `List` every time, which would impair performance by object allocation. This is the main reason why the `collect` method is useful for expressing reduction working on a mutable container but crucially in a parallel-friendly way, as you'll learn later in the chapter.

COLLECTION FRAMEWORK FLEXIBILITY: DOING THE SAME OPERATION IN DIFFERENT WAYS

You can further simplify the previous sum example using the `reducing` collector by using a reference to the `sum` method of the `Integer` class instead of the lambda expression you used to encode the same operation. This results in the following:

```
int totalCalories = menu.stream().collect(reducing(0,        <-- Initial value
                                 Dish::getCalories,          <-- Transformation function
                                 Integer::sum));             <-- Aggregating function
```

Logically, this reduction operation proceeds as shown in figure 6.3, where an accumulator, initialized with a starting value, is iteratively combined, using an aggregating function, with the result of the application of the transforming function on each element of the stream.

The `counting` collector we mentioned at the beginning of section 6.2 is, in reality, similarly implemented using the three-argument `reducing` factory method. It

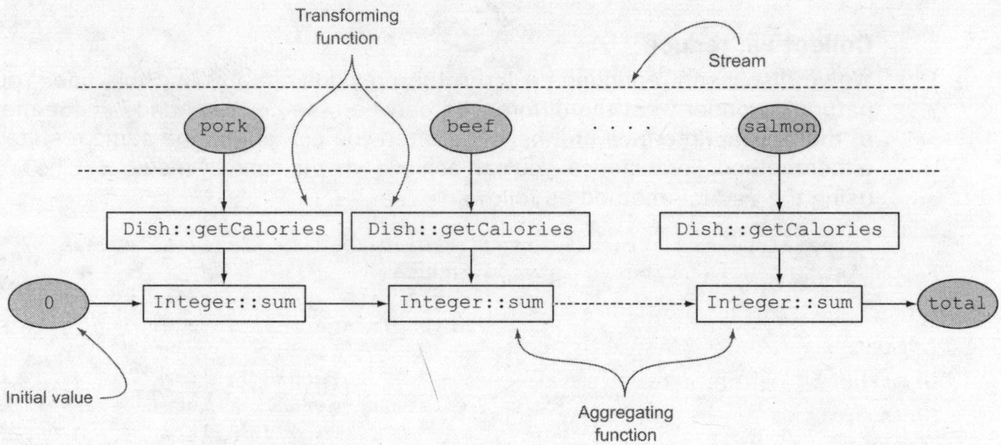

Figure 6.3 The reduction process calculating the total number of calories in the menu

transforms each element in the stream to an object of type `Long` with value `1` and then sums all these ones:

```
public static <T> Collector<T, ?, Long> counting() {
    return reducing(0L, e -> 1L, Long::sum);
}
```

> **Use of the generic ? wildcard**
>
> In the code snippet just shown, you probably noticed the `?` wildcard, used as the second generic type in the signature of the collector returned by the `counting` factory method. You should already be familiar with this notation, especially if you use the Java Collection Framework quite frequently. But here it means only that the type of the collector's accumulator is unknown, or in other words, the accumulator itself can be of any type. We used it here to exactly report the signature of the method as originally defined in the `Collectors` class, but in the rest of the chapter we avoid any wildcard notation to keep the discussion as simple as possible.

We already observed in chapter 5 that there's another way to perform the same operation without using a collector—by mapping the stream of dishes into the number of calories of each dish and then reducing this resulting stream with the same method reference used in the previous version:

```
int totalCalories =
    menu.stream().map(Dish::getCalories).reduce(Integer::sum).get();
```

Note that, like any one-argument `reduce` operation on a stream, the invocation `reduce(Integer::sum)` doesn't return an `int` but an `Optional<Integer>` to manage in a null-safe way the case of a reduction operation over an empty stream. Here you just extract the value inside the `Optional` object using its `get` method. Note that in this case using the get method is safe only because you're sure that the stream of dishes isn't empty. In general, as you'll learn in chapter 10, it's safer to unwrap the value eventually contained in an `Optional` using a method that also allows you to provide a default, such as `orElse` or `orElseGet`. Finally, and even more concisely, you can achieve the same result by mapping the stream to an `IntStream` and then invoking the `sum` method on it:

```
int totalCalories = menu.stream().mapToInt(Dish::getCalories).sum();
```

CHOOSING THE BEST SOLUTION FOR YOUR SITUATION

Once again, this demonstrates how functional programming in general (and the new API based on functional-style principles added to the `Collections` framework in Java 8 in particular) often provides multiple ways to perform the same operation. This example also shows that collectors are somewhat more complex to use than the methods directly available on the `Streams` interface, but in exchange they offer higher levels of abstraction and generalization and are more reusable and customizable.

Our suggestion is to explore the largest number of solutions possible for the problem at hand, but always choose the most specialized one that's general enough to solve it. This is often the best decision for both readability and performance reasons. For instance, to calculate the total calories in our menu, we'd prefer the last solution (using `IntStream`) because it's the most concise and likely also the most readable one. At the same time, it's also the one that performs best, because `IntStream` lets us avoid all the *auto-unboxing* operations, or implicit conversions from `Integer` to `int`, that are useless in this case.

Next, take the time to test your understanding of how `reducing` can be used as a generalization of other collectors by working through the exercise in Quiz 6.1.

Quiz 6.1: Joining strings with reducing

Which of the following statements using the `reducing` collector are valid replacements for this `joining` collector (as used in section 6.2.3)?

```
String shortMenu = menu.stream().map(Dish::getName).collect(joining());
```

```
1 String shortMenu = menu.stream().map(Dish::getName)
                    .collect( reducing( (s1, s2) -> s1 + s2 ) ).get();
2 String shortMenu = menu.stream()
  .collect( reducing( (d1, d2) -> d1.getName() + d2.getName() ) ).get();
3 String shortMenu = menu.stream()
        .collect( reducing( "", Dish::getName, (s1, s2) -> s1 + s2 ) );
```

Answer:

Statements 1 and 3 are valid, whereas 2 doesn't compile.

1 This converts each dish in its name, as done by the original statement using the `joining` collector, and then reduces the resulting stream of strings using a `String` as accumulator and appending to it the names of the dishes one by one.

(continued)

2 This doesn't compile because the one argument that `reducing` accepts is a `BinaryOperator<T>` that's a `BiFunction<T,T,T>`. This means that it wants a function taking two arguments and returns a value of the same type, but the lambda expression used there has two dishes as arguments but returns a string.

3 This starts the reduction process with an empty string as the accumulator, and when traversing the stream of dishes it converts each dish to its name and appends this name to the accumulator. Note that, as we mentioned, `reducing` doesn't need the three arguments to return an `Optional` because in the case of an empty stream it can return a more meaningful value, which is the empty string used as the initial accumulator value.

Note that even though statements 1 and 3 are valid replacements for the `joining` collector, they've been used here to demonstrate how the `reducing` one can be seen, at least conceptually, as a generalization of all other collectors discussed in this chapter. Nevertheless, for all practical purposes we always suggest using the `joining` collector for both readability and performance reasons.

6.3 Grouping

A common database operation is to group items in a set, based on one or more properties. As you saw in the earlier transactions-currency-grouping example, this operation can be cumbersome, verbose, and error prone when implemented with an imperative style. But it can be easily translated in a single, very readable statement by rewriting it in a more functional style as encouraged by Java 8. As a second example of how this feature works, suppose you want to classify the dishes in the menu according to their type, putting the ones containing meat in a group, the ones with fish in another group, and all others in a third group. You can easily perform this task using a collector returned by the `Collectors.groupingBy` factory method as follows:

```
Map<Dish.Type, List<Dish>> dishesByType =
                      menu.stream().collect(groupingBy(Dish::getType));
```

This will result in the following `Map`:

```
{FISH=[prawns, salmon], OTHER=[french fries, rice, season fruit, pizza],
 MEAT=[pork, beef, chicken]}
```

Here, you pass to the `groupingBy` method a `Function` (expressed in the form of a method reference) extracting the corresponding `Dish.Type` for each `Dish` in the stream. We call this `Function` a *classification* function because it's used to classify the elements of the stream into different groups. The result of this grouping operation, shown in figure 6.4, is a `Map` having as map key the value returned by the classification function and as corresponding map value a list of all the items in the stream having that classified value. In the menu-classification example a key is the type of dish, and its value is a list containing all the dishes of that type.

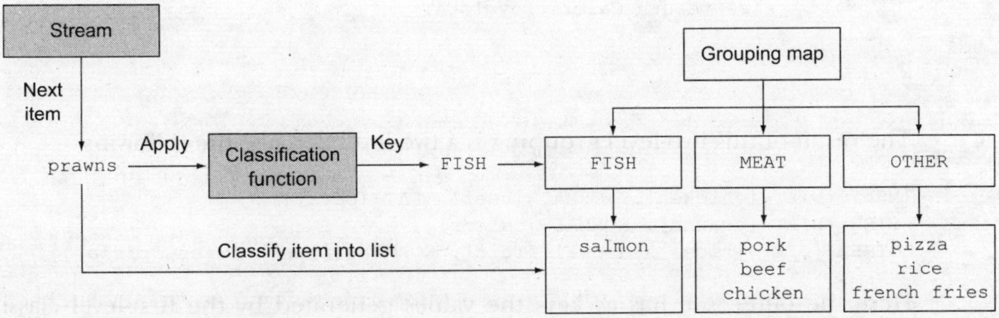

Figure 6.4 Classification of an item in the stream during the grouping process

But it isn't always possible to use a method reference as a classification function, because you may wish to classify using something more complex than a simple property accessor. For instance, you could decide to classify as "diet" all dishes with 400 calories or fewer, set to "normal" the dishes having between 400 and 700 calories, and set to "fat" the ones with more than 700 calories. Because the author of the `Dish` class unhelpfully didn't provide such an operation as a method, you can't use a method reference in this case, but you can express this logic in a lambda expression:

```
public enum CaloricLevel { DIET, NORMAL, FAT }
Map<CaloricLevel, List<Dish>> dishesByCaloricLevel = menu.stream().collect(
        groupingBy(dish -> {
               if (dish.getCalories() <= 400) return CaloricLevel.DIET;
               else if (dish.getCalories() <= 700) return
    CaloricLevel.NORMAL;
        else return CaloricLevel.FAT;
        } ));
```

Now you've seen how to group the dishes in the menu, both by their type and by calories, but what if you want to use both criteria at the same time? Grouping is powerful because it composes effectively. Let's see how to do this.

6.3.1 *Multilevel grouping*

You can achieve multilevel grouping by using a collector created with a two-argument version of the `Collectors.groupingBy` factory method, which accepts a second argument of type `collector` besides the usual classification function. So to perform a two-level grouping, you can pass an inner `groupingBy` to the outer `groupingBy`, defining a second-level criterion to classify the stream's items, as shown in the next listing.

Listing 6.2 Multilevel grouping

```
Map<Dish.Type, Map<CaloricLevel, List<Dish>>> dishesByTypeCaloricLevel =
menu.stream().collect(
      groupingBy(Dish::getType,
         groupingBy(dish -> {
            if (dish.getCalories() <= 400) return CaloricLevel.DIET;
                else if (dish.getCalories() <= 700) return CaloricLevel.NORMAL;
```

First-level classification function

Second-level classification function

```
            else return CaloricLevel.FAT;
        } )
    )
);
```

The result of this two-level grouping is a two-level `Map` like the following:

```
{MEAT={DIET=[chicken], NORMAL=[beef], FAT=[pork]},
 FISH={DIET=[prawns], NORMAL=[salmon]},
 OTHER={DIET=[rice, seasonal fruit], NORMAL=[french fries, pizza]}}
```

Here the outer `Map` has as keys the values generated by the first-level classification function: "fish, meat, other." The values of this `Map` are in turn other `Map`s, having as keys the values generated by the second-level classification function: "normal, diet, or fat." Finally, the second-level `Map`s have as values the `List` of the elements in the stream returning the corresponding first- and second-level key values when applied respectively to the first and second classification functions: "salmon, pizza, etc." This multilevel grouping operation can be extended to any number of levels, and an *n*-level grouping has as a result an *n*-level `Map` modeling an *n*-level tree structure.

Figure 6.5 shows how this structure is also equivalent to an *n*-dimensional table, highlighting the classification purpose of the grouping operation.

In general, it helps to think that `groupingBy` works in terms of "buckets." The first `groupingBy` creates a bucket for each key. You then collect the elements in each bucket with the downstream collector and so on to achieve *n*-level groupings!

Figure 6.5 Equivalence between *n*-level nested map and *n*-dimensional classification table

6.3.2 Collecting data in subgroups

In the previous section, you saw that it's possible to pass a second `groupingBy` collector to the outer one to achieve a multilevel grouping. But more generally, the second collector passed to the first `groupingBy` can be any type of collector, not just another `groupingBy`. For instance, it's possible to count the number of `Dishes` in the menu for each type, by passing the `counting` collector as a second argument to the `groupingBy` collector:

```
Map<Dish.Type, Long> typesCount = menu.stream().collect(
                groupingBy(Dish::getType, counting()));
```

The result is the following `Map`:

```
{MEAT=3, FISH=2, OTHER=4}
```

Also note that the regular one-argument `groupingBy(f)`, where `f` is the classification function, is in reality just shorthand for `groupingBy(f, toList())`.

To give another example, you could rework the collector you already used to find the highest-calorie dish in the menu to achieve a similar result, but now classified by the *type* of dish:

```
Map<Dish.Type, Optional<Dish>> mostCaloricByType =
    menu.stream()
        .collect(groupingBy(Dish::getType,
                    maxBy(comparingInt(Dish::getCalories))));
```

The result of this grouping is then clearly a `Map`, having as keys the available types of `Dishes` and as values the `Optional<Dish>`, wrapping the corresponding highest-calorie `Dish` for a given type:

```
{FISH=Optional[salmon], OTHER=Optional[pizza], MEAT=Optional[pork]}
```

> **NOTE** The values in this `Map` are `Optionals` because this is the resulting type of the collector generated by the `maxBy` factory method, but in reality if there's no `Dish` in the menu for a given type, that type won't have an `Optional.empty()` as value; it won't be present at all as a key in the `Map`. The `groupingBy` collector lazily adds a new key in the grouping `Map` only the first time it finds an element in the stream, producing that key when applying on it the grouping criteria being used. This means that in this case, the `Optional` wrapper isn't very useful, because it's not modeling a value that could be eventually absent but is there incidentally, only because this is the type returned by the reducing collector.

ADAPTING THE COLLECTOR RESULT TO A DIFFERENT TYPE

Because the `Optionals` wrapping all the values in the `Map` resulting from the last grouping operation aren't very useful in this case, you may want to get rid of them. To achieve this, or more generally, to adapt the result returned by a collector to a different type, you could use the collector returned by the `Collectors.collectingAndThen` factory method, as shown in the following listing.

Listing 6.3 Finding the highest-calorie Dish in each subgroup

```
Map<Dish.Type, Dish> mostCaloricByType =
    menu.stream()
        .collect(groupingBy(Dish::getType,          <-- Classification function
                 collectingAndThen(
                     maxBy(comparingInt(Dish::getCalories)),   <-- Wrapped collector
                 Optional::get)));                  <-- Transformation function
```

This factory method takes two arguments, the collector to be adapted and a transformation function, and returns another collector. This additional collector acts as a wrapper for the old one and maps the value it returns using the transformation function as the last step of the `collect` operation. In this case, the wrapped collector is the one created with `maxBy`, and the transformation function, `Optional::get`, extracts the value contained in the `Optional` returned. As we've said, here this is safe because the `reducing` collector will never return an `Optional.empty()`. The result is the following `Map`:

```
{FISH=salmon, OTHER=pizza, MEAT=pork}
```

It's quite common to use multiple nested collectors, and at first the way they interact may not always be obvious. Figure 6.6 helps you visualize how they work together. From the outermost layer and moving inward, note the following:

- The collectors are represented by the dashed lines, so `groupingBy` is the outermost one and groups the menu stream into three substreams according to the different dishes' types.
- The `groupingBy` collector wraps the `collectingAndThen` collector, so each substream resulting from the grouping operation is further reduced by this second collector.
- The `collectingAndThen` collector wraps in turn a third collector, the `maxBy` one.
- The reduction operation on the substreams is then performed by the reducing collector, but the `collectingAndThen` collector containing it applies the `Optional::get` transformation function to its result.
- The three transformed values, being the highest-calorie `Dishes` for a given type (resulting from the execution of this process on each of the three substreams), will be the values associated with the respective classification keys, the types of `Dishes`, in the `Map` returned by the `groupingBy` collector.

OTHER EXAMPLES OF COLLECTORS USED IN CONJUNCTION WITH GROUPINGBY

More generally, the collector passed as second argument to the `groupingBy` factory method will be used to perform a further reduction operation on all the elements in the stream classified into the same group. For example, you could also reuse the collector created to sum the calories of all the dishes in the menu to obtain a similar result, but this time for each group of `Dishes`:

```
Map<Dish.Type, Integer> totalCaloriesByType =
                menu.stream().collect(groupingBy(Dish::getType,
                          summingInt(Dish::getCalories)));
```

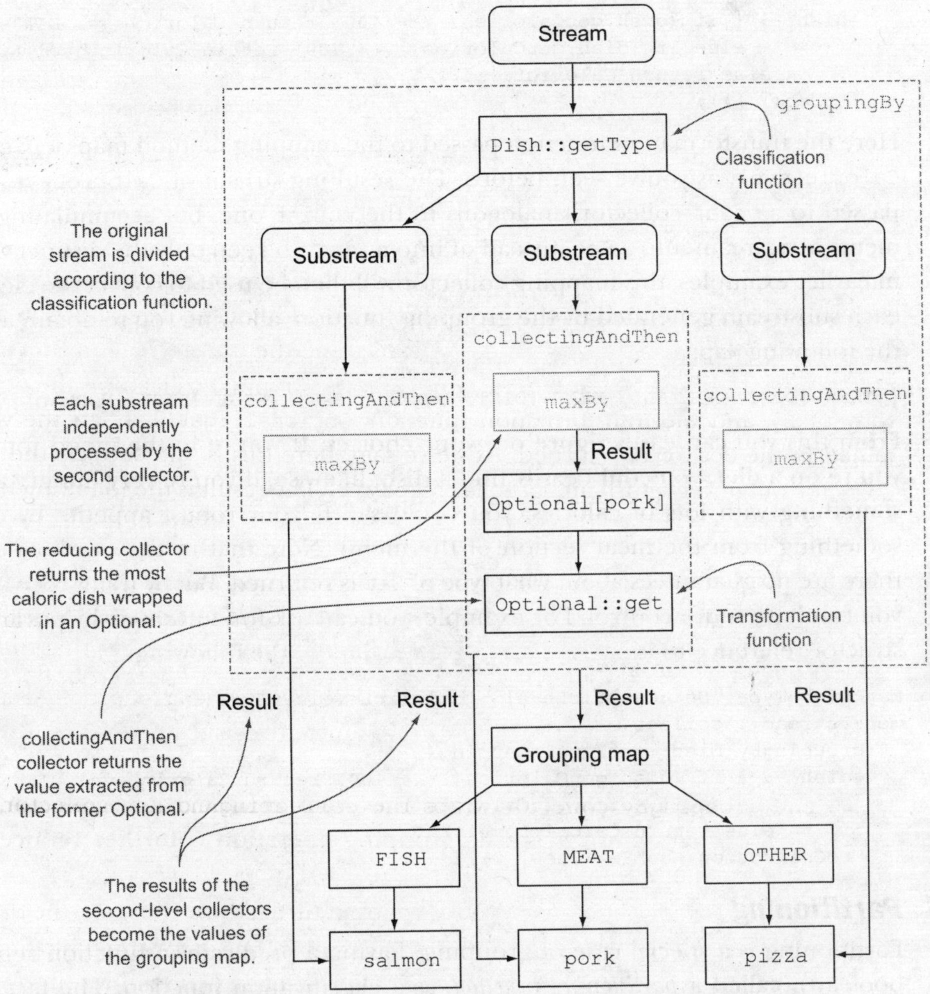

Figure 6.6 Combining the effect of multiple collectors by nesting one inside the other

Yet another collector, commonly used in conjunction with `groupingBy`, is one generated by the `mapping` method. This method takes two arguments: a function transforming the elements in a stream and a further collector accumulating the objects resulting from this transformation. Its purpose is to adapt a collector accepting elements of a given type to one working on objects of a different type, by applying a mapping function to each input element before accumulating them. To see a practical example of using this collector, suppose you want to know which `CaloricLevels` are available in the menu for each type of Dish. You could achieve this result combining a `groupingBy` and a `mapping` collector as follows:

```
Map<Dish.Type, Set<CaloricLevel>> caloricLevelsByType =
menu.stream().collect(
   groupingBy(Dish::getType, mapping(
```

```
dish -> { if (dish.getCalories() <= 400) return CaloricLevel.DIET;
        else if (dish.getCalories() <= 700) return CaloricLevel.NORMAL;
      else return CaloricLevel.FAT; },
toSet() )));
```

Here the transformation function passed to the mapping method maps a `Dish` into its `CaloricLevel`, as you've seen before. The resulting stream of `CaloricLevels` is then passed to a `toSet` collector, analogous to the `toList` one, but accumulating the elements of a stream into a `Set` instead of into a `List`, to keep only the distinct values. As in earlier examples, this mapping collector will then be used to collect the elements in each substream generated by the grouping function, allowing you to obtain as a result the following `Map`:

```
{OTHER=[DIET, NORMAL], MEAT=[DIET, NORMAL, FAT], FISH=[DIET, NORMAL]}
```

From this you can easily figure out your choices. If you're in the mood for fish and you're on a diet, you could easily find a dish; likewise, if you're very hungry and want something with lots of calories, you could satisfy your robust appetite by choosing something from the meat section of the menu. Note that in the previous example, there are no guarantees about what type of `Set` is returned. But by using `toCollection`, you can have more control. For example, you can ask for a `HashSet` by passing a constructor reference to it:

```
Map<Dish.Type, Set<CaloricLevel>> caloricLevelsByType =
menu.stream().collect(
   groupingBy(Dish::getType, mapping(
    dish -> { if (dish.getCalories() <= 400) return CaloricLevel.DIET;
           else if (dish.getCalories() <= 700) return CaloricLevel.NORMAL;
         else return CaloricLevel.FAT; },
    toCollection(HashSet::new) )));
```

6.4 Partitioning

Partitioning is a special case of grouping: having a predicate (a function returning a boolean), called a *partitioning function*, as a classification function. The fact that the partitioning function returns a boolean means the resulting grouping `Map` will have a `Boolean` as a key type and therefore there can be at most two different groups—one for `true` and one for `false`. For instance, if you're vegetarian or have invited a vegetarian friend to have dinner with you, you may be interested in partitioning the menu into vegetarian and nonvegetarian dishes:

```
Map<Boolean, List<Dish>> partitionedMenu =
             menu.stream().collect(partitioningBy(Dish::isVegetarian));
```

Partitioning function

This will return the following `Map`:

```
{false=[pork, beef, chicken, prawns, salmon],
 true=[french fries, rice, season fruit, pizza]}
```

So you could retrieve all the vegetarian dishes by getting from this `Map` the value indexed with the key `true`:

```
List<Dish> vegetarianDishes = partitionedMenu.get(true);
```

Note that you could achieve the same result by just filtering the stream created from the menu `List` with the same predicate used for partitioning and then collecting the result in an additional `List`:

```
List<Dish> vegetarianDishes =
            menu.stream().filter(Dish::isVegetarian).collect(toList());
```

6.4.1 Advantages of partitioning

Partitioning has the advantage of keeping both lists of the stream elements, for which the application of the partitioning function returns `true` or `false`. So in the previous example, you can obtain the `List` of the nonvegetarian `Dishes` by accessing the value of the key `false` in the `partitionedMenu` `Map`, using two separate filtering operations: one with the predicate and one with its negation. Also, as you already saw for grouping, the `partitioningBy` factory method has an overloaded version to which you can pass a second collector, as shown here:

```
Map<Boolean, Map<Dish.Type, List<Dish>>> vegetarianDishesByType =
menu.stream().collect(
        partitioningBy(Dish::isVegetarian,          <-- Partitioning function
                       groupingBy(Dish::getType)));  <-- Second collector
```

This will produce a two-level `Map`:

```
{false={FISH=[prawns, salmon], MEAT=[pork, beef, chicken]},
 true={OTHER=[french fries, rice, season fruit, pizza]}}
```

Here the grouping of the dishes by their type is applied individually to both of the substreams of vegetarian and nonvegetarian dishes resulting from the partitioning, producing a two-level `Map` that's similar to the one you obtained when you performed the two-level grouping in section 6.3.1. As another example, you can reuse your earlier code to find the most caloric dish among both vegetarian and nonvegetarian dishes:

```
Map<Boolean, Dish> mostCaloricPartitionedByVegetarian =
menu.stream().collect(
    partitioningBy(Dish::isVegetarian,
        collectingAndThen(
                        maxBy(comparingInt(Dish::getCalories)),
                        Optional::get)));
```

That will produce the following result:

```
{false=pork, true=pizza}
```

We started this section by saying that you can think of partitioning as a special case of grouping. The analogies between the `groupingBy` and `partitioningBy` collectors don't end here; as you'll see in the next quiz, you can also perform multilevel partitioning in a way similar to what you did for grouping in section 6.3.1.

Quiz 6.2: Using partitioningBy

As you've seen, like the `groupingBy` collector, the `partitioningBy` collector can be used in combination with other collectors. In particular it could be used with a second `partitioningBy` collector to achieve a multilevel partitioning. What will be the result of the following multilevel partitionings?

```
1 menu.stream().collect(partitioningBy(Dish::isVegetarian,
                          partitioningBy(d -> d.getCalories() > 500)));
2 menu.stream().collect(partitioningBy(Dish::isVegetarian,
                          partitioningBy(Dish::getType)));
3 menu.stream().collect(partitioningBy(Dish::isVegetarian,
                          counting()));
```

Answer:

1. This is a valid multilevel partitioning, producing the following two-level `Map`:

```
{ false={false=[chicken, prawns, salmon], true=[pork, beef]},
  true={false=[rice, season fruit], true=[french fries, pizza]}}
```

2. This won't compile because `partitioningBy` requires a predicate, a function returning a boolean. And the method reference `Dish::getType` can't be used as a predicate.
3. This counts the number of items in each partition, resulting in the following `Map`:

```
{false=5, true=4}
```

To give one last example of how you can use the `partitioningBy` collector, we'll put aside the menu data model and look at something a bit more complex but also more interesting: partitioning numbers into prime and nonprime.

6.4.2 *Partitioning numbers into prime and nonprime*

Suppose you want to write a method accepting as argument an `int` *n* and partitioning the first *n* natural numbers into prime and nonprime. But first, it will be useful to develop a predicate that tests to see if a given candidate number is prime or not:

```
public boolean isPrime(int candidate) {
    return IntStream.range(2, candidate)
                    .noneMatch(i -> candidate % i == 0);
}
```

Generate a range of natural numbers starting from and including 2 up to but excluding candidate.

Return `true` if the candidate isn't divisible for any of the numbers in the stream.

A simple optimization is to test only for factors less than or equal to the square root of the candidate:

```
public boolean isPrime(int candidate) {
    int candidateRoot = (int) Math.sqrt((double) candidate);
    return IntStream.rangeClosed(2, candidateRoot)
                    .noneMatch(i -> candidate % i == 0);
}
```

Now the biggest part of the job is done. To partition the first *n* numbers into prime and nonprime, it's enough to create a stream containing those *n* numbers and reduce it with a `partitioningBy` collector using as predicate the `isPrime` method you just developed:

```
public Map<Boolean, List<Integer>> partitionPrimes(int n) {
    return IntStream.rangeClosed(2, n).boxed()
                    .collect(
                       partitioningBy(candidate -> isPrime(candidate)));
}
```

We've now covered all the collectors that can be created using the static factory methods of the `Collectors` class, showing practical examples of how they work. Table 6.1 brings them all together, with the type they return when applied to a `Stream<T>` and a practical example of their use on a `Stream<Dish>` named `menuStream`.

Table 6.1 The static factory methods of the `Collectors` class

Factory method	Returned type	Used to
`toList`	`List<T>`	Gather all the stream's items in a `List`.
Example use: `List<Dish> dishes = menuStream.collect(toList());`		
`toSet`	`Set<T>`	Gather all the stream's items in a `Set`, eliminating duplicates.
Example use: `Set<Dish> dishes = menuStream.collect(toSet());`		
`toCollection`	`Collection<T>`	Gather all the stream's items in the collection created by the provided supplier.
Example use: `Collection<Dish> dishes = menuStream.collect(toCollection(), ArrayList::new);`		
`counting`	`Long`	Count the number of items in the stream.
Example use: `long howManyDishes = menuStream.collect(counting());`		
`summingInt`	`Integer`	Sum the values of an Integer property of the items in the stream.
Example use: `int totalCalories = menuStream.collect(summingInt(Dish::getCalories));`		
`averagingInt`	`Double`	Calculate the average value of an `Integer` property of the items in the stream.
Example use: `double avgCalories = menuStream.collect(averagingInt(Dish::getCalories));`		
`summarizingInt`	`IntSummaryStatistics`	Collect statistics regarding an `Integer` property of the items in the stream, such as the maximum, minimum, total, and average.
Example use: `IntSummaryStatistics menuStatistics = menuStream.collect(summarizingInt(Dish::getCalories));`		

Table 6.1 The static factory methods of the Collectors class *(continued)*

Factory method	Returned type	Used to
joining	String	Concatenate the strings resulting from the invocation of the toString method on each item of the stream.
Example use: String shortMenu = menuStream.map(Dish::getName).collect(joining(", "));		
maxBy	Optional<T>	An Optional wrapping the maximal element in this stream according to the given comparator or Optional.empty() if the stream is empty.
Example use: Optional<Dish> fattest = menuStream.collect(maxBy(comparingInt(Dish::getCalories)));		
minBy	Optional<T>	An Optional wrapping the minimal element in this stream according to the given comparator or Optional.empty() if the stream is empty.
Example use: Optional<Dish> lightest = menuStream.collect(minBy(comparingInt(Dish::getCalories)));		
reducing	The type produced by the reduction operation	Reduce the stream to a single value starting from an initial value used as accumulator and iteratively combining it with each item of the stream using a BinaryOperator.
Example use: int totalCalories = menuStream.collect(reducing(0, Dish::getCalories, Integer::sum));		
collectingAndThen	The type returned by the transforming function	Wrap another collector and apply a transformation function to its result.
Example use: int howManyDishes = menuStream.collect(collectingAndThen(toList(), List::size));		
groupingBy	Map<K, List<T>>	Group the items in the stream based on the value of one of their properties and use those values as keys in the resulting Map.
Example use: Map<Dish.Type, List<Dish>> dishesByType = menuStream.collect(groupingBy(Dish::getType));		
partitioningBy	Map<Boolean, List<T>>	Partition the items in the stream based on the result of the application of a predicate to each of them.
Example use: Map<Boolean, List<Dish>> vegetarianDishes = menuStream.collect(partitioningBy(Dish::isVegetarian));		

As we mentioned at the beginning of the chapter, all these collectors implement the Collector interface, so in the remaining part of the chapter we investigate this interface in more detail. We investigate the methods in that interface and then explore how you can implement your own collectors.

6.5 The Collector interface

The `Collector` interface consists of a set of methods that provide a blueprint for how to implement specific reduction operations (that is, collectors). You've seen many collectors that implement the `Collector` interface, such as `toList` or `groupingBy`. This also implies that you're free to create customized reduction operations by providing your own implementation of the `Collector` interface. In section 6.6 we show how you can implement the `Collector` interface to create a collector to partition a stream of numbers into prime and nonprime more efficiently than what you've seen so far.

To get started with the `Collector` interface, we focus on one of the first collectors you encountered at the beginning of this chapter: the `toList` factory method, which gathers all the elements of a stream in a `List`. We said that you'll frequently use this collector in your day-to-day job, but it's also one that, at least conceptually, is straightforward to develop. Investigating in more detail how this collector is implemented is a good way to understand how the `Collector` interface is defined and how the functions returned by its methods are internally used by the `collect` method.

Let's start by taking a look at the definition of the `Collector` interface in the next listing, which shows the interface signature together with the five methods it declares.

Listing 6.4 The `Collector` interface

```
public interface Collector<T, A, R> {
    Supplier<A> supplier();
    BiConsumer<A, T> accumulator();
    Function<A, R> finisher();
    BinaryOperator<A> combiner();
    Set<Characteristics> characteristics();
}
```

In this listing, the following definitions apply:

- `T` is the generic type of the items in the stream to be collected.
- `A` is the type of the accumulator, the object on which the partial result will be accumulated during the collection process.
- `R` is the type of the object (typically, but not always, the collection) resulting from the collect operation.

For instance, you could implement a `ToListCollector<T>` class that gathers all the elements of a `Stream<T>` into a `List<T>` having the following signature

```
public class ToListCollector<T> implements Collector<T, List<T>, List<T>>
```

where, as we'll clarify shortly, the object used for the accumulation process will also be the final result of the collection process.

6.5.1 Making sense of the methods declared by Collector interface

We can now analyze one by one the five methods declared by the `Collector` interface. When we do so, you'll notice that each of the first four methods returns a function that will be invoked by the `collect` method, whereas the fifth one, `characteristics`, provides a set of characteristics that's a list of hints used by the `collect` method itself to know which optimizations (for example, parallelization) it's allowed to employ while performing the reduction operation.

MAKING A NEW RESULT CONTAINER: THE SUPPLIER METHOD

The `supplier` method has to return a `Supplier` of an empty result—a parameterless function that when invoked creates an instance of an empty accumulator used during the collection process. Clearly, for a collector returning the accumulator itself as result, like our `ToListCollector`, this empty accumulator will also represent the result of the collection process when performed on an empty stream. In our `ToListCollector` the `supplier` will then return an empty `List` as follows:

```
public Supplier<List<T>> supplier() {
    return () -> new ArrayList<T>();
}
```

Note that you could also just pass a constructor reference:

```
public Supplier<List<T>> supplier() {
    return ArrayList::new;
}
```

ADDING AN ELEMENT TO A RESULT CONTAINER: THE ACCUMULATOR METHOD

The `accumulator` method returns the function that performs the reduction operation. When traversing the *n*th element in the stream, this function is applied with two arguments, the accumulator being the result of the reduction (after having collected the first *n*–1 items of the stream) and the *n*th element itself. The function returns `void` because the accumulator is modified in place, meaning that its internal state is changed by the function application to reflect the effect of the traversed element. For `ToListCollector`, this function merely has to add the current item to the list containing the already traversed ones:

```
public BiConsumer<List<T>, T> accumulator() {
    return (list, item) -> list.add(item);
```

You could instead use a method reference, which is more concise:

```
public BiConsumer<List<T>, T> accumulator() {
    return List::add;
}
```

APPLYING THE FINAL TRANSFORMATION TO THE RESULT CONTAINER: THE FINISHER METHOD

The `finisher` method has to return a function that's invoked at the end of the accumulation process, after having completely traversed the stream, in order to transform the accumulator object into the final result of the whole collection operation. Often,

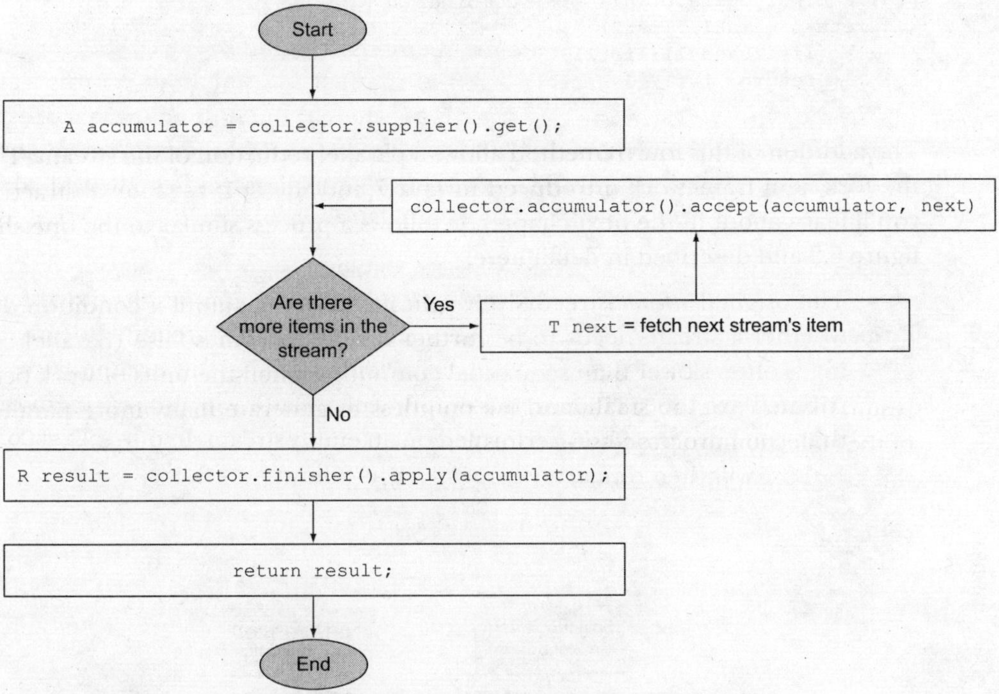

Figure 6.7 Logical steps of the sequential reduction process

as in the case of the `ToListCollector`, the accumulator object already coincides with the final expected result. As a consequence, there's no need to perform a transformation, so the `finisher` method just has to return the `identity` function:

```
public Function<List<T>, List<T>> finisher() {
    return Function.identity();
}
```

These first three methods are enough to execute a sequential reduction of the stream that, at least from a logical point of view, could proceed as in figure 6.7. The implementation details are a bit more difficult in practice due to both the lazy nature of the stream, which could require a pipeline of other intermediate operations to execute before the `collect` operation, and the possibility, in theory, of performing the reduction in parallel.

MERGING TWO RESULT CONTAINERS: THE COMBINER METHOD

The `combiner` method, the last of the four methods that return a function used by the reduction operation, defines how the accumulators resulting from the reduction of different subparts of the stream are combined when the subparts are processed in parallel. In the `toList` case, the implementation of this method is simple; just add the list containing the items gathered from the second subpart of the stream to the end of the list obtained when traversing the first subpart:

```
public BinaryOperator<List<T>> combiner() {
    return (list1, list2) -> {
        list1.addAll(list2);
        return list1; }
}
```

The addition of this fourth method allows a parallel reduction of the stream. This uses the fork/join framework introduced in Java 7 and the `Spliterator` abstraction that you'll learn about in the next chapter. It follows a process similar to the one shown in figure 6.8 and described in detail here:

- The original *stream* is recursively split in substreams until a condition defining whether a stream needs to be further divided becomes false (parallel computing is often slower than sequential computing when the units of work being distributed are too small, and it's pointless to generate many more parallel tasks than you have processing cores).

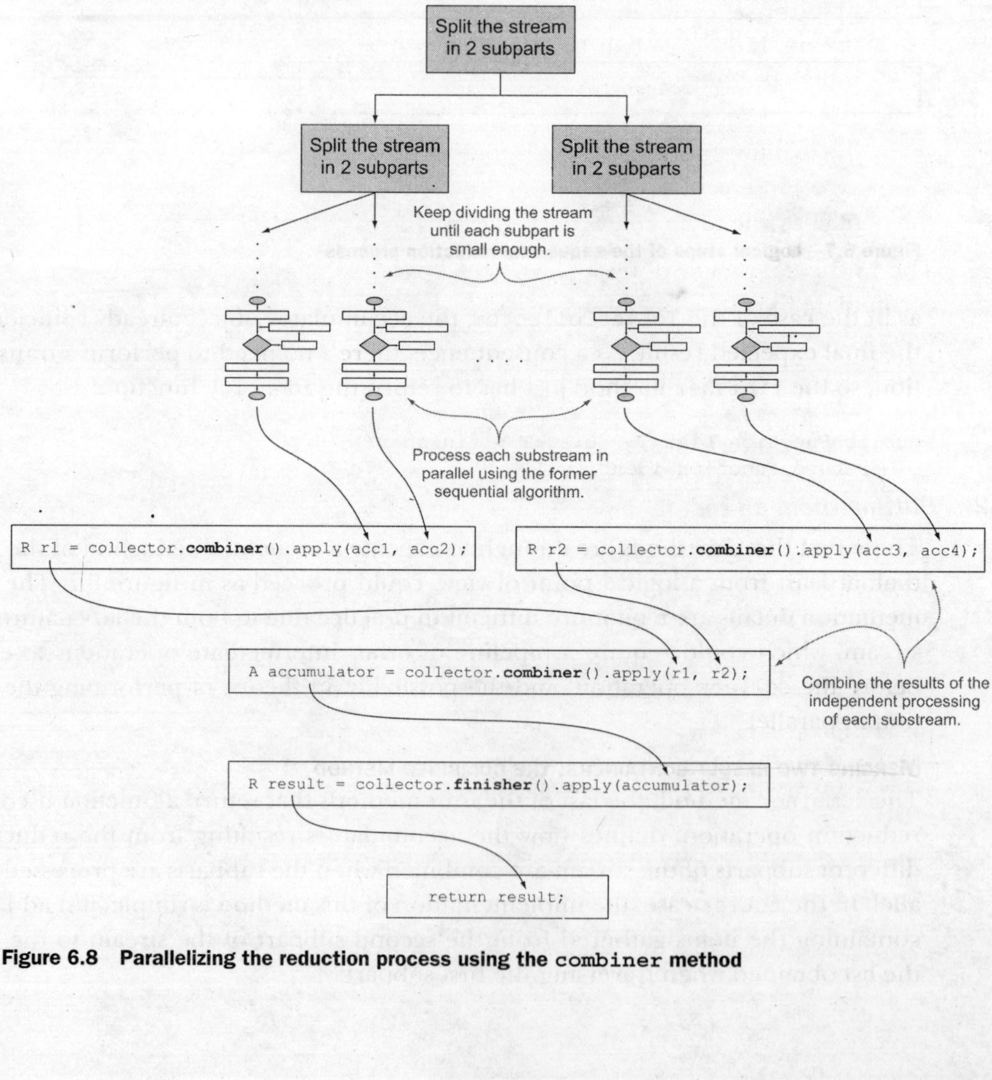

Figure 6.8 Parallelizing the reduction process using the `combiner` method

- At this point all *substreams* can be processed in parallel, each of them using the sequential reduction algorithm shown in figure 6.7.
- Finally, all the partial results are combined pairwise using the function returned by the `combiner` method of the collector. This is done by combining results corresponding to substreams associated with each split of the original stream.

CHARACTERISTICS METHOD

The last method, `characteristics`, returns an immutable set of `Characteristics`, defining the behavior of the collector—in particular providing hints about whether the stream can be reduced in parallel and which optimizations are valid when doing so. `Characteristics` is an enumeration containing three items:

- `UNORDERED`—The result of the reduction isn't affected by the order in which the items in the stream are traversed and accumulated.
- `CONCURRENT`—The `accumulator` function can be called concurrently from multiple threads, and then this collector can perform a parallel reduction of the stream. If the collector isn't also flagged as `UNORDERED`, it can perform a parallel reduction only when it's applied to an unordered data source.
- `IDENTITY_FINISH`—This indicates the function returned by the finisher method is the identity one, and its application can be omitted. In this case, the accumulator object is directly used as the final result of the reduction process. This also implies that it's safe to do an unchecked cast from the accumulator `A` to the result `R`.

The `ToListCollector` developed so far is `IDENTITY_FINISH`, because the `List` used to accumulate the elements in the stream is already the expected final result and doesn't need any further transformation, but it isn't `UNORDERED` because if you apply it to an ordered stream you want this ordering to be preserved in the resulting `List`. Finally, it's `CONCURRENT`, but following what we just said, the stream will be processed in parallel only if its underlying data source is unordered.

6.5.2 *Putting them all together*

The five methods analyzed in the preceding subsection are everything you need to develop your own `ToListCollector`, so you can impiement it by putting all of them together, as the next listing shows.

Listing 6.5 The `ToListCollector`

```
import java.util.*;
import java.util.function.*;
import java.util.stream.Collector;
import static java.util.stream.Collector.Characteristics.*;

public class ToListCollector<T> implements Collector<T, List<T>, List<T>> {

    @Override
    public Supplier<List<T>> supplier() {
        return ArrayList::new;            <-- Creates the collection operation starting point
    }
```

```
    @Override
    public BiConsumer<List<T>, T> accumulator() {
        return List::add;                              <-- Accumulates the traversed item, modifying the accumulator in place
    }
    @Override
    public Function<List<T>, List<T>> finisher() {
        return Function.indentity();                   <-- Identity function
    }

    @Override
    public BinaryOperator<List<T>> combiner() {
        return (list1, list2) -> {
            list1.addAll(list2);                       <-- Modifies the first accumulator, combining it with the content of the second one
            return list1;                              <-- Returns the modified first accumulator
        };
    }
    @Override
    public Set<Characteristics> characteristics() {
        return Collections.unmodifiableSet(EnumSet.of(
            IDENTITY_FINISH, CONCURRENT));             <-- Flags the collector as IDENTITY_FINISH and CONCURRENT
    }
}
```

Note that this implementation isn't identical to the one returned by the `Collectors.toList` method, but it differs only in some minor optimizations. These optimizations are mostly related to the fact that the collector provided by the Java API uses the `Collections.emptyList()` singleton when it has to return an empty list. This means that it could be safely used in place of the original Java as an example to gather a list of all the `Dish`es of a menu stream:

```
List<Dish> dishes = menuStream.collect(new ToListCollector<Dish>());
```

The remaining difference from this and the standard

```
List<Dish> dishes = menuStream.collect(toList());
```

formulation is that `toList` is a factory, whereas you have to use `new` to instantiate your `ToListCollector`.

PERFORMING A CUSTOM COLLECT WITHOUT CREATING A COLLECTOR IMPLEMENTATION

In the case of an `IDENTITY_FINISH` collection operation, there's a further possibility of obtaining the same result without developing a completely new implementation of the `Collector` interface. `Stream` has an overloaded `collect` method accepting the three other functions—`supplier`, `accumulator`, and `combiner`—having exactly the same semantics as the ones returned by the corresponding methods of the `Collector` interface. So, for instance, it's possible to collect in a `List` all the items in a stream of dishes as follows:

```
List<Dish> dishes = menuStream.collect(
                        ArrayList::new,        <-- Supplier
                        List::add,             <-- Accumulator
                        List::addAll);         <-- Combiner
```

We believe that this second form, even if more compact and concise than the former one, is rather less readable. Also, developing an implementation of your custom collector in a proper class promotes its reuse and helps avoid code duplication. It's also worth noting that you're not allowed to pass any `Characteristics` to this second `collect` method, so it always behaves as an `IDENTITY_FINISH` and `CONCURRENT` but not `UNORDERED` collector.

In the next section, you'll take your new knowledge of implementing collectors to the next level. You'll develop your own custom collector for a more complex but hopefully more specific and compelling use case.

6.6 Developing your own collector for better performance

In section 6.4, where we discussed partitioning, you created a collector, using one of the many convenient factory methods provided by the `Collectors` class, which divides the first *n* natural numbers into primes and nonprimes, as shown in the following listing.

Listing 6.6 Partitioning the first *n* natural numbers into primes and nonprimes

```
public Map<Boolean, List<Integer>> partitionPrimes(int n) {
return IntStream.rangeClosed(2, n).boxed()
                .collect(partitioningBy(candidate -> isPrime(candidate));
}
```

There you achieved an improvement over the original `isPrime` method by limiting the number of divisors to be tested against the candidate prime to those not bigger than the candidate's square root:

```
public boolean isPrime(int candidate) {
    int candidateRoot = (int) Math.sqrt((double) candidate);
    return IntStream.rangeClosed(2, candidateRoot)
                    .noneMatch(i -> candidate % i == 0);
}
```

Is there a way to obtain even better performances? The answer is yes, but for this you'll have to develop a custom collector.

6.6.1 Divide only by prime numbers

One possible optimization is to test only if the candidate number is divisible by prime numbers. It's pointless to test it against a divisor that's not itself prime! So you can limit the test to only the prime numbers found before the current candidate. The problem with the predefined collectors you've used so far, and the reason you have to develop a custom one, is that during the collecting process you don't have access to the partial result. This means that when testing whether a given candidate number is prime or not, you don't have access to the list of the other prime numbers found so far.

Suppose you had this list; you could pass it to the `isPrime` method and rewrite it as follows:

```
public static boolean isPrime(List<Integer> primes, int candidate) {
    return primes.stream().noneMatch(i -> candidate % i == 0);
}
```

Also, you should implement the same optimization you used before and test only with primes smaller than the square root of the candidate number. So you need a way to stop testing whether the candidate is divisible by a prime as soon as the next prime is greater than the candidate's root. Unfortunately, there isn't such a method available in the Streams API. You could use `filter(p -> p <= candidateRoot)` to filter the prime numbers smaller than the candidate root. But `filter` would process the whole stream before returning the adequate stream. If both the list of primes and the candidate number were very large, this would be problematic. You don't need to do this; all you want is to stop once you find a prime that's greater than the candidate root! Therefore, you'll create a method called `takeWhile`, which, given a sorted list and a predicate, returns the longest prefix of this list whose elements satisfy the predicate:

```
public static <A> List<A> takeWhile(List<A> list, Predicate<A> p) {
    int i = 0;
    for (A item : list) {
        if (!p.test(item)) {
            return list.subList(0, i);
        }
        i++;
    }
    return list;
}
```

Check if the current item in the list satisfies the Predicate.

If it doesn't, return the sublist prefix until the item before the tested one.

All the items in the list satisfy the Predicate, so return the list itself.

Using this method, you can optimize the `isPrime` method by testing only the candidate prime against only the primes that are not greater than its square root:

```
public static boolean isPrime(List<Integer> primes, int candidate){
    int candidateRoot = (int) Math.sqrt((double) candidate);
    return takeWhile(primes, i -> i <= candidateRoot)
                .stream()
                .noneMatch(p -> candidate % p == 0);
}
```

Note that this is an eager implementation of `takeWhile`. Ideally you'd like a lazy version of `takeWhile` so it can be merged with the `noneMatch` operation. Unfortunately, implementing it would be beyond the scope of this chapter because you'd need to get a grip on the Streams API implementation.

With this new `isPrime` method in hand, you're now ready to implement your own custom collector. First, you need to declare a new class that implements the `Collector` interface. Then, you need to develop the five methods required by the `Collector` interface.

STEP 1: DEFINING THE COLLECTOR CLASS SIGNATURE

Let's start with the class signature, remembering that the `Collector` interface is defined as

```
public interface Collector<T, A, R>
```

where `T`, `A`, and `R` are respectively the type of the elements in the stream, the type of the object used to accumulate partial results, and the type of the final result of the `collect` operation. In this case, you want to collect streams of `Integers` while both the accumulator and the result types are `Map<Boolean, List<Integer>>` (the same `Map` you obtained as a result of the former partitioning operation in listing 6.6), having as keys `true` and `false` and as values respectively the `Lists` of prime and nonprime numbers:

```
public class PrimeNumbersCollector
        implements Collector<Integer,
                        Map<Boolean, List<Integer>>,
                        Map<Boolean, List<Integer>>>
```

The type of the elements in the stream

The type of the accumulator

The type of the result of the `collect` operation

STEP 2: IMPLEMENTING THE REDUCTION PROCESS

Next, you need to implement the five methods declared in the `Collector` interface. The `supplier` method has to return a function that when invoked creates the accumulator:

```
public Supplier<Map<Boolean, List<Integer>>> supplier() {
    return () -> new HashMap<Boolean, List<Integer>>() {{
        put(true, new ArrayList<Integer>());
        put(false, new ArrayList<Integer>());
    }};
}
```

Here you're not only creating the `Map` that you'll use as the accumulator, but you're also initializing it with two empty lists under the `true` and `false` keys. This is where you'll add respectively the prime and nonprime numbers during the collection process. The most important method of your collector is the `accumulator` method, because it contains the logic defining how the elements of the stream have to be collected. In this case, it's also the key to implementing the optimization we described previously. At any given iteration you can now access the partial result of the collection process, which is the accumulator containing the prime numbers found so far:

```
public BiConsumer<Map<Boolean, List<Integer>>, Integer> accumulator() {
    return (Map<Boolean, List<Integer>> acc, Integer candidate) -> {
            acc.get( isPrime(acc.get(true), candidate) )
               .add(candidate);
    };
}
```

Get the list of prime or nonprime numbers depending on the result of `isPrime`.

Add the candidate to the appropriate list.

In this method, you invoke the `isPrime` method, passing to it (together with the number for which you want to test whether it's prime or not) the list of the prime numbers found so far (these are the values indexed by the `true` key in the accumulating `Map`). The result of this invocation is then used as key to get the list of either the prime or nonprime numbers so you can add the new candidate to the right list.

STEP 3: MAKING THE COLLECTOR WORK IN PARALLEL (IF POSSIBLE)

The next method has to combine two partial accumulators in the case of a parallel collection process, so in this case it just has to merge the two `Maps` by adding all the numbers in the prime and nonprime lists of the second `Map` to the corresponding lists in the first `Map`:

```
public BinaryOperator<Map<Boolean, List<Integer>>> combiner() {
    return (Map<Boolean, List<Integer>> map1,
            Map<Boolean, List<Integer>> map2) -> {
                map1.get(true).addAll(map2.get(true));
                map1.get(false).addAll(map2.get(false));
                return map1;
    };
}
```

Note that in reality this collector can't be used in parallel, because the algorithm is inherently sequential. This means the `combiner` method won't ever be invoked, and you could leave its implementation empty (or better, throw an `UnsupportedOperationException`). We decided to implement it anyway only for completeness.

STEP 4: THE FINISHER METHOD AND THE COLLECTOR'S CHARACTERISTIC METHOD

The implementation of the last two methods is quite straightforward: as we said, the `accumulator` coincides with the collector's result so it won't need any further transformation, and the `finisher` method returns the `identity` function:

```
public Function<Map<Boolean, List<Integer>>,
                Map<Boolean, List<Integer>>> finisher() {
        return Function.identity();
}
```

As for the characteristic method, we already said that it's neither `CONCURRENT` nor `UNORDERED` but is `IDENTITY_FINISH`:

```
public Set<Characteristics> characteristics() {
    return Collections.unmodifiableSet(EnumSet.of(IDENTITY_FINISH));
}
```

The following listing shows the final implementation of `PrimeNumbersCollector`.

Listing 6.7 The `PrimeNumbersCollector`

```
public class PrimeNumbersCollector
    implements Collector<Integer,
               Map<Boolean, List<Integer>>,
               Map<Boolean, List<Integer>>> {
    @Override
    public Supplier<Map<Boolean, List<Integer>>> supplier() {
        return () -> new HashMap<Boolean, List<Integer>>() {{      <- Start the collection process with a Map containing two empty Lists.
            put(true, new ArrayList<Integer>());
            put(false, new ArrayList<Integer>());
        }};
    }
    @Override
    public BiConsumer<Map<Boolean, List<Integer>>, Integer> accumulator() {
        return (Map<Boolean, List<Integer>> acc, Integer candidate) -> {
            acc.get( isPrime( acc.get(true),      <- Pass to the isPrime method the list of already found primes.
                candidate) )
               .add(candidate);      <- Get from the Map the list of prime or nonprime numbers, according to what the isPrime method returned, and add to it the current candidate.
        };
    }
```

```
@Override
public BinaryOperator<Map<Boolean, List<Integer>>> combiner() {
    return (Map<Boolean, List<Integer>> map1,
            Map<Boolean, List<Integer>> map2) -> {        <-- Merge the second Map into the first one.
                map1.get(true).addAll(map2.get(true));
                map1.get(false).addAll(map2.get(false));
                return map1;
    };
}

@Override
public Function<Map<Boolean, List<Integer>>,
               Map<Boolean, List<Integer>>> finisher() {
    return Function.identity();        <-- No transformation is necessary at the end of the collection process, so terminate it with the identity function.
}

@Override
public Set<Characteristics> characteristics() {
    return Collections.unmodifiableSet(EnumSet.of(IDENTITY_FINISH));   <--
}
}
```

This collector is `IDENTITY_FINISH` but neither `UNORDERED` nor `CONCURRENT` because it relies on the fact that prime numbers are discovered in sequence.

You can now use this new custom collector in place of the former one created with the `partitioningBy` factory method in section 6.4 and obtain exactly the same result:

```
public Map<Boolean, List<Integer>>
                    partitionPrimesWithCustomCollector(int n) {
    return IntStream.rangeClosed(2, n).boxed()
                    .collect(new PrimeNumbersCollector());
}
```

6.6.2 Comparing collectors' performances

The collector created with the `partitioningBy` factory method and the custom one you just developed are functionally identical, but did you achieve your goal of improving the performance of the `partitioningBy` collector with your custom one? Let's write a quick harness to check this:

```
public class CollectorHarness {
    public static void main(String[] args) {
        long fastest = Long.MAX_VALUE;
        for (int i = 0; i < 10; i++) {           <-- Run the test 10 times.
            long start = System.nanoTime();
            partitionPrimes(1_000_000);          <-- Partition into primes and nonprimes the first million natural numbers.
            long duration = (System.nanoTime() - start) / 1_000_000;   <-- Take the duration in milliseconds.
            if (duration < fastest) fastest = duration;   <-- Check if this execution has been the fastest one.
        }
        System.out.println(
            "Fastest execution done in " + fastest + " msecs");
    }
}
```

Note that a more scientific benchmarking approach would be to use a framework such as JMH, but we didn't want to add the complexity of using such a framework here and, for this use case, the results provided by this small benchmarking class are accurate enough. This class partitions the first million natural numbers into primes and nonprimes, invoking the method using the collector created with the `partitioningBy` factory method 10 times and registering the fastest execution. Running it on an Intel i5 2.4 GHz, it prints the following result:

```
Fastest execution done in 4716 msecs
```

Now replace `partitionPrimes` with `partitionPrimesWithCustomCollector` in the harness, in order to test the performances of the custom collector you developed. Now the program prints

```
Fastest execution done in 3201 msecs
```

Not bad! This means you didn't waste your time developing this custom collector for two reasons: first, you learned how to implement your own collector when you need it, and second, you achieved a performance improvement of around 32%.

Finally, it's important to note that, as you did for the `ToListCollector` in listing 6.5, it's possible to obtain the same result by passing the three functions implementing the core logic of `PrimeNumbersCollector` to the overloaded version of the `collect` method, taking them as arguments:

```
public Map<Boolean, List<Integer>> partitionPrimesWithCustomCollector
                  (int n) {
    IntStream.rangeClosed(2, n).boxed()
        .collect(
                  () -> new HashMap<Boolean, List<Integer>>() {{       <-- Supplier
                      put(true, new ArrayList<Integer>());
                      put(false, new ArrayList<Integer>());
                  }},
                (acc, candidate) -> {                                  <-- Accumulator
                    acc.get( isPrime(acc.get(true), candidate) )
                       .add(candidate);
               },
                (map1, map2) -> {                                      <-- Combiner
                    map1.get(true).addAll(map2.get(true));
                    map1.get(false).addAll(map2.get(false));
               });
}
```

As you can see, in this way you can avoid creating a completely new class that implements the `Collector` interface; the resulting code is more compact, even if it's also probably less readable and certainly less reusable.

6.7 Summary

Following are the key concepts you should take away from this chapter:

- `collect` is a terminal operation that takes as argument various recipes (called collectors) for accumulating the elements of a stream into a summary result.

- Predefined collectors include reducing and summarizing stream elements into a single value, such as calculating the minimum, maximum, or average. Those collectors are summarized in table 6.1.
- Predefined collectors let you group elements of a stream with `groupingBy` and partition elements of a stream with `partitioningBy`.
- Collectors compose effectively to create multilevel groupings, partitions, and reductions.
- You can develop your own collectors by implementing the methods defined in the `Collector` interface.

7 Parallel data processing and performance

This chapter covers

- Processing data in parallel with parallel streams
- Performance analysis of parallel streams
- The fork/join framework
- Splitting a stream of data using a `Spliterator`

In the last three chapters, you've seen how the new `Stream` interface lets you manipulate collections of data in a declarative way. We also explained that the shift from external to internal iteration enables the native Java library to gain control over processing the elements of a stream. This approach relieves Java developers from explicitly implementing optimizations necessary to speed up the processing of collections of data. By far the most important benefit is the possibility of executing a pipeline of operations on these collections that automatically makes use of the multiple cores on your computer.

For instance, before Java 7, processing a collection of data in parallel was extremely cumbersome. First, you needed to explicitly split the data structure containing your data into subparts. Second, you needed to assign each of these subparts to a different thread. Third, you needed to synchronize them opportunely to avoid unwanted race conditions, wait for the completion of all threads, and finally combine the partial results. Java 7 introduced a framework called *fork/join* to perform these operations more consistently and in a less error-prone way. We explore this framework in section 7.2.

In this chapter, you'll discover how the `Stream` interface gives you the opportunity to execute operations in parallel on a collection of data without much effort. It lets you declaratively turn a sequential stream into a parallel one. Moreover, you'll see how Java can make this magic happen or, more practically, how parallel streams work under the hood by employing the fork/join framework introduced in Java 7. You'll also discover that it's important to know how parallel streams work internally, because if you ignore this aspect, you could obtain unexpected (and very likely wrong) results by misusing them.

In particular we'll demonstrate that the way a parallel stream gets divided into chunks, before processing the different chunks in parallel, can in some cases be the origin of these incorrect and apparently unexplainable results. For this reason, you'll learn how to take control of this splitting process by implementing and using your own `Spliterator`.

7.1 Parallel streams

In chapter 4, we briefly mentioned that the `Stream` interface allows you to process its elements in parallel in a very convenient way: it's possible to turn a collection into a parallel stream by invoking the method `parallelStream` on the collection source. A *parallel* stream is a stream that splits its elements into multiple chunks, processing each chunk with a different thread. Thus, you can automatically partition the workload of a given operation on all the cores of your multicore processor and keep all of them equally busy. Let's experiment with this idea by using a simple example.

Let's suppose you need to write a method accepting a number *n* as argument and returning the sum of all the numbers from 1 to the given argument. A straightforward (perhaps naïve) approach is to generate an infinite stream of numbers, limiting it to the passed number, and then reduce the resulting stream with a `BinaryOperator` that just sums two numbers, as follows:

```
public static long sequentialSum(long n) {
    return Stream.iterate(1L, i -> i + 1)      // Generate the infinite stream of natural numbers.
                 .limit(n)                      // Limit it to the first n numbers.
                 .reduce(0L, Long::sum);        // Reduce the stream by summing all the numbers.
}
```

In more traditional Java terms, this code is equivalent to its iterative counterpart:

```
public static long iterativeSum(long n) {
    long result = 0;
    for (long i = 1L; i <= n; i++) {
        result += i;
    }
    return result;
}
```

This operation seems to be a good candidate to leverage parallelization, especially for large values of *n*. But where do you start? Do you synchronize on the result variable? How many threads do you use? Who does the generation of numbers? Who adds them up?

Don't worry about all of this. It's a much simpler problem to solve if you adopt parallel streams!

7.1.1 Turning a sequential stream into a parallel one

You can make the former functional reduction process (that is, summing) run in parallel by turning the stream into a parallel one; call the method `parallel` on the sequential stream:

```
public static long parallelSum(long n) {
    return Stream.iterate(1L, i -> i + 1)
                 .limit(n)
                 .parallel()
                 .reduce(0L, Long::sum);
}
```

Turn the stream into a parallel one.

In the previous code, the reduction process used to sum all the numbers in the stream works in a way that's similar to what's described in section 5.4.1. The difference is that the `Stream` is internally divided into multiple chunks. As a result, the reduction operation can work on the various chunks independently and in parallel, as shown in figure 7.1.

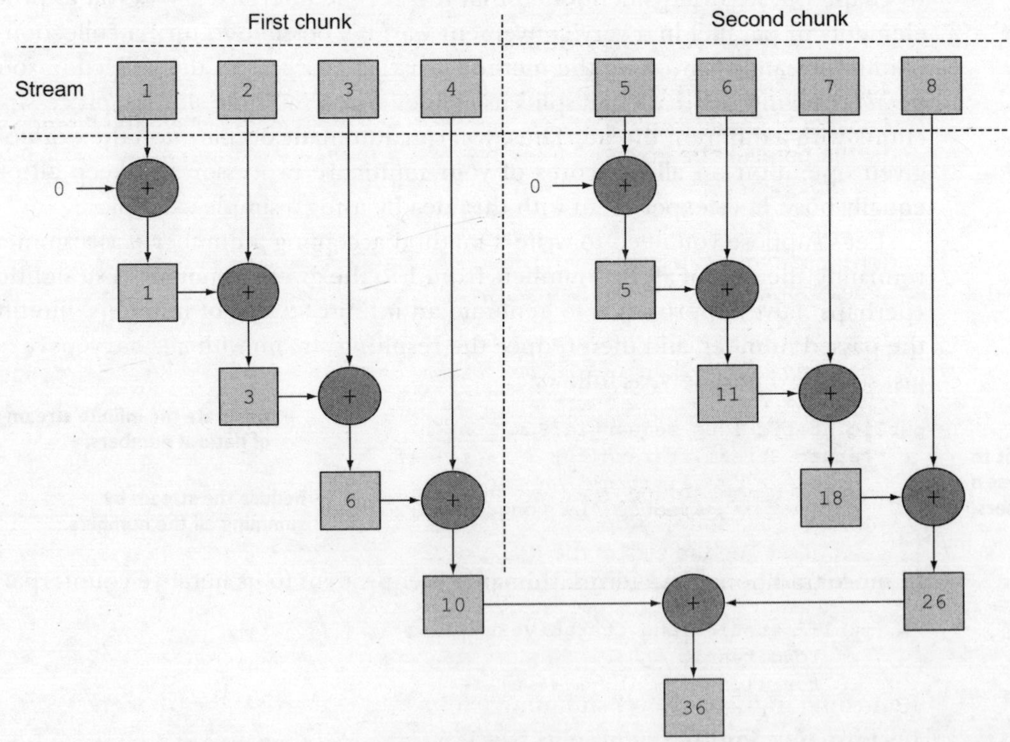

Figure 7.1 A parallel reduction operation

Finally, the same reduction operation combines the values resulting from the partial reductions of each substream, producing the result of the reduction process on the whole initial stream.

Note that, in reality, calling the method `parallel` on a sequential stream doesn't imply any concrete transformation on the stream itself. Internally, a `boolean` flag is set to signal that you want to run in parallel all the operations that follow the invocation to `parallel`. Similarly, you can turn a parallel stream into a sequential one by just invoking the method `sequential` on it. Note that you might think that you could achieve finer-grained control over which operations you want to perform in parallel and which one sequentially while traversing the stream by combining these two methods. For example, you could do something like the following:

```
stream.parallel()
      .filter(...)
      .sequential()
      .map(...)
      .parallel()
      .reduce();
```

But the last call to `parallel` or `sequential` wins and affects the pipeline globally. In this example, the pipeline will be executed in parallel because that's the last call in the pipeline.

Configuring the thread pool used by parallel streams

Looking at the stream's `parallel` method, you may wonder where the threads used by the parallel stream come from, how many there are, and how you can customize the process.

Parallel streams internally use the default `ForkJoinPool` (you'll learn more about the fork/join framework in section 7.2), which by default has as many threads as you have processors, as returned by `Runtime.getRuntime().availableProcessors()`.

But you can change the size of this pool using the system property `java.util.concurrent.ForkJoinPool.common.parallelism`, as in the following example:

```
System.setProperty("java.util.concurrent.ForkJoinPool.common.parallelism",
                   "12");
```

This is a global setting, so it will affect all the parallel streams in your code. Conversely, it currently isn't possible to specify this value for a single parallel stream. In general, having the size of the `ForkJoinPool` equal to the number of processors on your machine is a meaningful default, and we strongly suggest that you not modify it unless you have a very good reason for doing so.

Returning to the numbers-summing exercise, we said that you can expect a significant performance improvement in its parallel version when running it on a multicore processor. You now have three methods executing exactly the same operation in three different ways (iterative style, sequential reduction, and parallel reduction), so let's see which is the fastest one!

7.1.2 Measuring stream performance

We claimed that the parallelized summing method should perform better than the sequential and the iterative methods. Nevertheless, in software engineering guessing is never a good idea! Especially when optimizing performance you should always follow three golden rules: measure, measure, measure. To this purpose you can develop a method very similar to the basic harness you used in section 6.6.2 to compare the performances of the two collectors partitioning numbers into prime and nonprime, as shown in the following listing.

Listing 7.1 Measuring performance of a function summing the first *n* numbers

```
public long measureSumPerf(Function<Long, Long> adder, long n) {
    long fastest = Long.MAX_VALUE;
    for (int i = 0; i < 10; i++) {
        long start = System.nanoTime();
        long sum = adder.apply(n);
        long duration = (System.nanoTime() - start) / 1_000_000;
        System.out.println("Result: " + sum);
        if (duration < fastest) fastest = duration;
    }
    return fastest;
}
```

Here this method takes as arguments a function and a `long`. It applies the function 10 times on the `long` passed to the method, registers the time taken by each execution in milliseconds, and returns the duration of the fastest one. Supposing that you group all the methods you developed previously into a class named `ParallelStreams`, you can use this harness to check how long the sequential adder function takes to sum the first 10 million natural numbers:

```
System.out.println("Sequential sum done in: " +
    measureSumPerf(ParallelStreams::sequentialSum, 10_000_000) + " msecs");
```

Note that the results should be taken with a grain of salt. Many factors will influence the execution time, such as how many cores your machine supports! You can try this on your own machine by running the code available on the book's repository. Executing it on a MacBook pro Intel i7 2.3 GHz quad-core, it prints the following:

```
Sequential sum done in: 97 msecs
```

You should expect that the iterative version using a traditional `for` loop runs much faster because it works at a much lower level and, more important, doesn't need to perform any boxing or unboxing of the primitive values. If you try to measure its performance with

```
System.out.println("Iterative sum done in: " +
    measureSumPerf(ParallelStreams::iterativeSum, 10_000_000) + " msecs");
```

you'll obtain

```
Iterative sum done in: 2 msecs
```

Now let's do the same with the parallel version of that function

```
System.out.println("Parallel sum done in: " +
    measureSumPerf(ParallelStreams::parallelSum, 10_000_000) + " msecs" );
```

and see what happens:

```
Parallel sum done in: 164 msecs
```

This is quite disappointing: the parallel version of the summing method is much slower than the sequential one. How can you explain this unexpected result? There are actually two issues mixed together:

- `iterate` generates boxed objects, which have to be unboxed to numbers before they can be added.
- `iterate` is difficult to divide into independent chunks to execute in parallel.

The second issue is particularly interesting because you need to keep a mental model that some stream operations are more parallelizable than others. Specifically, the `iterate` operation is hard to split into chunks that can be executed independently because the input of one function application always depends on the result of the previous application, as illustrated in figure 7.2.

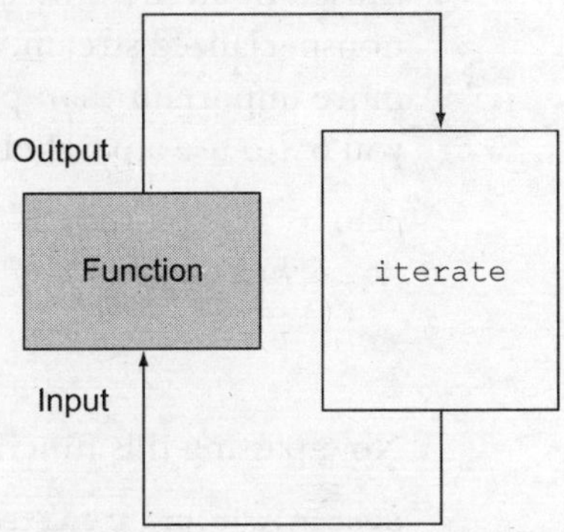

Figure 7.2 `iterate` **is inherently sequential.**

This means that in this specific case the reduction process isn't proceeding as depicted in figure 7.1: the whole list of numbers isn't available at the beginning of the reduction process, making it impossible to efficiently partition the stream in chunks to be processed in parallel. By flagging the stream as parallel, you're just adding to the sequential processing the overhead of allocating each sum operation on a different thread.

This demonstrates how parallel programming can be tricky and sometimes counterintuitive. When misused (for example, using an operation that's not parallel-friendly, like `iterate`) it can actually worsen the overall performance of your programs, so it's mandatory to understand what happens behind the scenes when you invoke that apparently magic `parallel` method.

USING MORE SPECIALIZED METHODS

So how can you leverage your multicore processors and use the stream to perform a parallel sum in an effective way? We discussed a method called `LongStream.rangeClosed` in chapter 5. This method has two benefits compared to `iterate`:

- `LongStream.rangeClosed` works on primitive `long` numbers directly so there's no boxing and unboxing overhead.
- `LongStream.rangeClosed` produces ranges of numbers, which can be easily split into independent chunks. For example, the range 1–20 can be split into 1–5, 6–10, 11–15, and 16–20.

Let's first see how it performs on a sequential stream to see if the overhead associated with unboxing is relevant:

```
public static long rangedSum(long n) {
    return LongStream.rangeClosed(1, n)
                     .reduce(0L, Long::sum);
}
```

This time the output is

```
Ranged sum done in: 17 msecs
```

The numeric stream is much faster than the earlier sequential version, generated with the `iterate` factory method, because the numeric stream avoids all the overhead caused by all the unnecessary autoboxing and unboxing operations performed by the nonspecialized stream. This is evidence that choosing the right data structures is often more important than parallelizing the algorithm that uses them. But what happens if you try to use a parallel stream in this new version that follows?

```
public static long parallelRangedSum(long n) {
    return LongStream.rangeClosed(1, n)
                     .parallel()
                     .reduce(0L, Long::sum);
}
```

Now, passing this function to your test method

```
System.out.println("Parallel range sum done in: " +
    measureSumPerf(ParallelStreams::parallelRangedSum, 10_000_000) +
    " msecs");
```

you obtain

```
Parallel range sum done in: 1 msecs
```

Finally, you obtain a parallel reduction that's faster than its sequential counterpart, because this time the reduction operation can actually be executed as shown in figure 7.1. This also demonstrates that using the right data structure *and* then making it work in parallel guarantees the best performance.

Nevertheless, keep in mind that parallelization doesn't come for free. The parallelization process itself requires you to recursively partition the stream, assign the reduction operation of each substream to a different thread, and then combine the results of these operations in a single value. But moving data between multiple cores is also more expensive than you might expect, so it's important that work to be done in parallel on another core takes longer than the time required to transfer the data from one core to another. In general, there are many cases where it isn't possible or convenient to use parallelization. But before you use a parallel `Stream` to make your code faster, you have to be sure that you're using it correctly; it's not helpful to produce a result in less time if the result will be wrong. Let's look at a common pitfall.

7.1.3 Using parallel streams correctly

The main cause of errors generated by misuse of parallel streams is the use of algorithms that mutate some shared state. Here's another way to implement the sum of the first *n* natural numbers but by mutating a shared accumulator:

```
public static long sideEffectSum(long n) {
    Accumulator accumulator = new Accumulator();
    LongStream.rangeClosed(1, n).forEach(accumulator::add);
    return accumulator.total;
}

public class Accumulator {
    public long total = 0;
    public void add(long value) { total += value; }
}
```

It's quite common to write this sort of code, especially for developers who are familiar with imperative programming paradigms. This code closely resembles what you're used to doing when iterating imperatively a list of numbers: you initialize an accumulator and traverse the elements in the list one by one, adding them on the accumulator.

What's wrong with this code? Unfortunately, it's irretrievably broken because it's fundamentally sequential. You have a data race on every access of `total`. And if you try to fix that with synchronization, you'll lose all your parallelism. To understand this, let's try to turn the `Stream` into a parallel one:

```
public static long sideEffectParallelSum(long n) {
    Accumulator accumulator = new Accumulator();
    LongStream.rangeClosed(1, n).parallel().forEach(accumulator::add);
    return accumulator.total;
}
```

Try to run this last method with the harness of listing 7.1, also printing the result of each execution:

```
System.out.println("SideEffect parallel sum done in: " +
    measurePerf(ParallelStreams::sideEffectParallelSum, 10_000_000L) + "
    msecs" );
```

You could obtain something like the following:

```
Result: 5959989000692
Result: 7425264100768
Result: 6827235020033
Result: 7192970417739
Result: 6714157975331
Result: 7497810541907
Result: 6435348440385
```

```
Result: 6999349840672
Result: 7435914379978
Result: 7715125932481
SideEffect parallel sum done in: 49 msecs
```

This time the performance of your method isn't important: the only relevant thing is that each execution returns a different result, all very distant from the correct value of `50000005000000`. This is caused by the fact that multiple threads are concurrently accessing the accumulator and in particular executing `total += value`, which, despite its appearance, isn't an atomic operation. The origin of the problem is that the method invoked inside the `forEach` block has the side effect of changing the mutable state of an object shared among multiple threads. It's mandatory to avoid these kinds of situations if you want to use parallel `Streams` without incurring similar bad surprises.

Now you know that shared mutable state doesn't play well with parallel streams and with parallel computations in general. We'll come back to this idea of avoiding mutation in chapters 13 and 14 when discussing functional programming in more detail. For now, keep in mind that avoiding shared mutable state ensures that your parallel `Stream` will produce the right result. Next, we'll look at some practical advice you can use to figure out when it's appropriate to use parallel streams to gain performance.

7.1.4 Using parallel streams effectively

In general it's impossible (and pointless) to try to give any quantitative hint on when to use a parallel stream because any suggestion like "use a parallel stream only if you have at least one thousand (or one million or whatever number you want) elements" could be correct for a specific operation running on a specific machine, but it could be completely wrong in an even marginally different context. Nonetheless, it's at least possible to provide some qualitative advice that could be useful when deciding whether it makes sense to use a parallel stream in a certain situation:

- If in doubt, measure. Turning a sequential stream into a parallel one is trivial but not always the right thing to do. As we already demonstrated in this section, a parallel stream isn't always faster than the corresponding sequential version. Moreover, parallel streams can sometimes work in a counterintuitive way, so the first and most important suggestion when choosing between sequential and parallel streams is to always check their performance with an appropriate benchmark.
- Watch out for boxing. Automatic boxing and unboxing operations can dramatically hurt performance. Java 8 includes primitive streams (`IntStream`, `LongStream`, and `DoubleStream`) to avoid such operations, so use them when possible.
- Some operations naturally perform worse on a parallel stream than on a sequential stream. In particular, operations such as `limit` and `findFirst` that rely on the order of the elements are expensive in a parallel stream. For example, `findAny` will perform better than `findFirst` because it isn't constrained to operate in the encounter order. You can always turn an ordered stream into an

unordered stream by invoking the method `unordered` on it. So, for instance, if you need *N* elements of your stream and you're not necessarily interested in the *first N* ones, calling `limit` on an unordered parallel stream may execute more efficiently than on a stream with an encounter order (for example, when the source is a `List`).

- Consider the total computational cost of the pipeline of operations performed by the stream. With *N* being the number of elements to be processed and *Q* the approximate cost of processing one of these elements through the stream pipeline, the product of *N*Q* gives a rough qualitative estimation of this cost. A higher value for *Q* implies a better chance of good performance when using a parallel stream.
- For a small amount of data, choosing a parallel stream is almost never a winning decision. The advantages of processing in parallel only a few elements aren't enough to compensate for the additional cost introduced by the parallelization process.
- Take into account how well the data structure underlying the stream decomposes. For instance, an `ArrayList` can be split much more efficiently than a `LinkedList`, because the first can be evenly divided without traversing it, as it's necessary to do with the second. Also, the primitive streams created with the `range` factory method can be decomposed quickly. Finally, as you'll learn in section 7.3, you can get full control of this decomposition process by implementing your own `Spliterator`.
- The characteristics of a stream, and how the intermediate operations through the pipeline modify them, can change the performance of the decomposition process. For example, a `SIZED` stream can be divided into two equal parts, and then each part can be processed in parallel more effectively, but a filter operation can throw away an unpredictable number of elements, making the size of the stream itself unknown.
- Consider whether a terminal operation has a cheap or expensive merge step (for example, the `combiner` method in a `Collector`). If this is expensive, then the cost caused by the combination of the partial results generated by each substream can outweigh the performance benefits of a parallel stream.

Table 7.1 gives a summary of the parallel-friendliness of certain stream sources in terms of their decomposability.

Table 7.1 Stream sources and decomposability

Source	Decomposability
`ArrayList`	Excellent
`LinkedList`	Poor
`IntStream.range`	Excellent

Table 7.1 Stream sources and decomposability *(continued)*

Source	Decomposability
`Stream.iterate`	Poor
`HashSet`	Good
`TreeSet`	Good

Finally, we need to emphasize that the infrastructure used behind the scenes by parallel streams to execute operations in parallel is the fork/join framework introduced in Java 7. The parallel summing example proved that it's vital to have a good understanding of the parallel stream internals in order to use them correctly, so we'll investigate in detail the fork/join framework in the next section.

7.2 The fork/join framework

The fork/join framework was designed to recursively split a parallelizable task into smaller tasks and then combine the results of each subtask to produce the overall result. It's an implementation of the `ExecutorService` interface, which distributes those subtasks to worker threads in a thread pool, called `ForkJoinPool`. Let's start by exploring how to define a task and subtasks.

7.2.1 Working with RecursiveTask

To submit tasks to this pool, you have to create a subclass of `RecursiveTask<R>`, where `R` is the type of the result produced by the parallelized task (and each of its subtasks) or of `RecursiveAction` if the task returns no result (it could be updating other nonlocal structures, though). To define `RecursiveTask`s you need only implement its single abstract method, `compute`:

```
protected abstract R compute();
```

This method defines both the logic of splitting the task at hand into subtasks and the algorithm to produce the result of a single subtask when it's no longer possible or convenient to further divide it. For this reason an implementation of this method often resembles the following pseudocode:

```
if (task is small enough or no longer divisible) {
    compute task sequentially
} else {
    split task in two subtasks
    call this method recursively possibly further splitting each subtask
    wait for the completion of all subtasks
    combine the results of each subtask
}
```

In general there are no precise criteria for deciding whether a given task should be further divided or not, but there are various heuristics that you can follow to help you

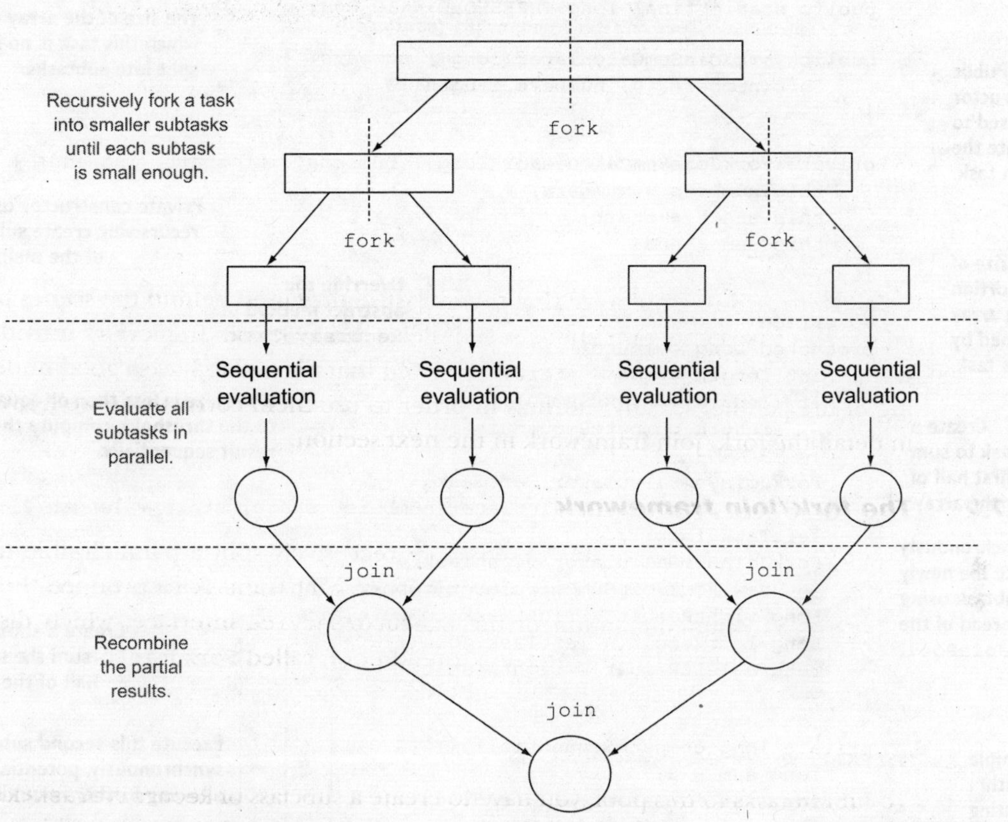

Figure 7.3 The fork/join process

with this decision. We clarify them in more detail in section 7.2.1. The recursive task-splitting process is visually synthesized by figure 7.3.

As you might have noticed, this is nothing more than the parallel version of the well-known divide-and-conquer algorithm. To demonstrate a practical example of how to use the fork/join framework and to build on our previous examples, let's try to calculate the sum of a range of numbers (here represented by an array of numbers `long[]`) using this framework. As explained, you need to first provide an implementation for the `RecursiveTask` class, as shown by the `ForkJoinSumCalculator` in the following listing.

Listing 7.2 Executing a parallel sum using the fork/join framework

```
public class ForkJoinSumCalculator
        extends java.util.concurrent.RecursiveTask<Long> {
    private final long[] numbers;
    private final int start;
    private final int end;
```

Extend `RecursiveTask` to create a task usable with the fork/join framework.

The array of numbers to be summed.

The initial and final positions of the portion of the array processed by this subtask.

```
    public static final long THRESHOLD = 10_000;

    public ForkJoinSumCalculator(long[] numbers) {
        this(numbers, 0, numbers.length);
    }

    private ForkJoinSumCalculator(long[] numbers, int start, int end) {
        this.numbers = numbers;
        this.start = start;
        this.end = end;
    }

    @Override
    protected Long compute() {
        int length = end - start;
        if (length <= THRESHOLD) {
            return computeSequentially();
        }
        ForkJoinSumCalculator leftTask =
            new ForkJoinSumCalculator(numbers, start, start + length/2);
        leftTask.fork();
        ForkJoinSumCalculator rightTask =
            new ForkJoinSumCalculator(numbers, start + length/2, end);
        Long rightResult = rightTask.compute();
        Long leftResult = leftTask.join();
        return leftResult + rightResult;
    }

    private long computeSequentially() {
        long sum = 0;
        for (int i = start; i < end; i++) {
            sum += numbers[i];
        }
        return sum;
    }
}
```

The size of the array under which this task is no longer split into subtasks.

Public constructor used to create the main task.

Private constructor used to recursively create subtasks of the main task.

The size of the portion of the array summed by this task.

Override the abstract method of `RecursiveTask`.

If the size is less than or equal to the threshold, compute the result sequentially.

Create a subtask to sum the first half of the array.

Asynchronously execute the newly created subtask using another thread of the `ForkJoinPool`.

Create a subtask to sum the second half of the array.

Execute this second subtask synchronously, potentially allowing further recursive splits.

Read the result of the first subtask or wait for it if it isn't ready.

The result of this task is the combination of the results of the two subtasks.

Simple algorithm calculating the result of a subtask when it's no longer divisible.

Writing a method performing a parallel sum of the first *n* natural numbers is now pretty straightforward. You just need to pass the desired array of numbers to the constructor of `ForkJoinSumCalculator`:

```
public static long forkJoinSum(long n) {
    long[] numbers = LongStream.rangeClosed(1, n).toArray();
    ForkJoinTask<Long> task = new ForkJoinSumCalculator(numbers);
    return new ForkJoinPool().invoke(task);
}
```

Here, you generate an array containing the first *n* natural numbers using a `LongStream`. Then you create a `ForkJoinTask` (the superclass of `RecursiveTask`), passing this array to the public constructor of the `ForkJoinSumCalculator` shown in listing 7.2. Finally, you create a new `ForkJoinPool` and pass that task to its `invoke` method. The value returned by this last method is the result of the task defined by the `ForkJoinSumCalculator` class when executed inside the `ForkJoinPool`.

Note that in a real-world application, it doesn't make sense to use more than one `ForkJoinPool`. For this reason, what you typically should do is instantiate it only once and keep this instance in a static field, making it a singleton, so it could be conveniently reused by any part of your software. Here, to create it you're using its default no-argument constructor, meaning that you want to allow the pool to use all the processors available to the JVM. More precisely, this constructor will use the value returned by `Runtime.availableProcessors` to determine the number of threads used by the pool. Note that the `availableProcessors` method, despite its name, in reality returns the number of available cores, including any virtual ones due to hyperthreading.

RUNNING THE FORKJOINSUMCALCULATOR

When you pass the `ForkJoinSumCalculator` task to the `ForkJoinPool`, this task is executed by a thread of the pool that in turn calls the `compute` method of the task. This method checks to see if the task is small enough to be performed sequentially; otherwise, it splits the array of numbers to be summed into two halves and assigns them to two new `ForkJoinSumCalculators` that are scheduled to be executed by the `ForkJoinPool`. As a result, this process can be recursively repeated, allowing the original task to be divided into smaller tasks, until the condition used to check if it's no longer convenient or no longer possible to further split it is met (in this case, if the number of items to be summed is less than or equal to 10,000). At this point, the result of each subtask is computed sequentially, and the (implicit) binary tree of tasks created by the forking process is traversed back toward its root. The result of the task is then computed, combining the partial results of each subtask. This process is shown in figure 7.4.

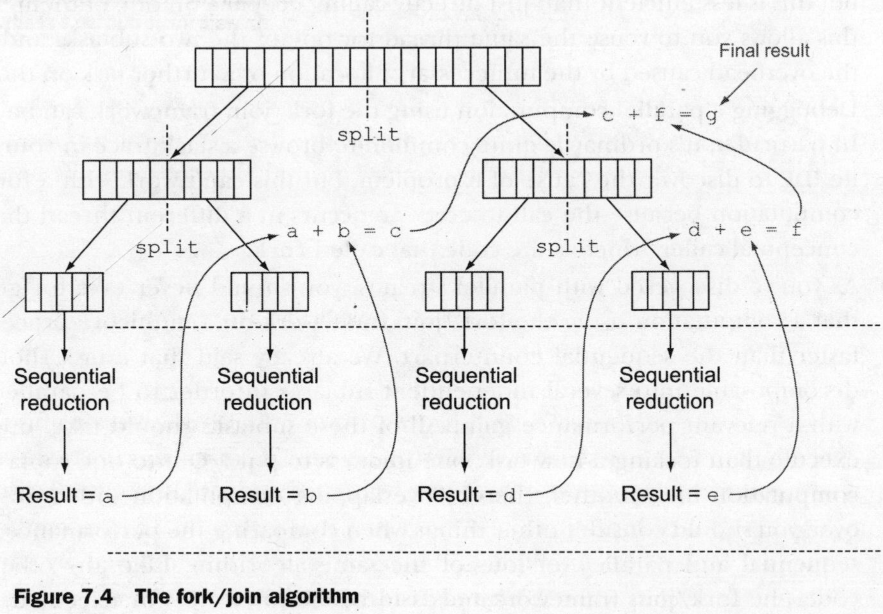

Figure 7.4 The fork/join algorithm

Once again you can check the performance of the summing method explicitly using the fork/join framework with the harness developed at the beginning of this chapter:

```
System.out.println("ForkJoin sum done in: " + measureSumPerf(
    ForkJoinSumCalculator::forkJoinSum, 10_000_000) + " msecs" );
```

In this case it produces the following output:

```
ForkJoin sum done in: 41 msecs
```

Here, the performance is worse than the version using the parallel stream, but only because you're obliged to put the whole stream of numbers into a `long[]` before being allowed to use it in the `ForkJoinSumCalculator` task.

7.2.2 Best practices for using the fork/join framework

Even though the fork/join framework is relatively easy to use, unfortunately it's also easy to misuse. Here are a few best practices to leverage it effectively:

- Invoking the `join` method on a task blocks the caller until the result produced by that task is ready. For this reason, it's necessary to call it after the computation of both subtasks has been started. Otherwise, you'll end up with a slower and more complex version of your original sequential algorithm because every subtask will have to wait for the other one to complete before starting.
- The `invoke` method of a `ForkJoinPool` shouldn't be used from within a `RecursiveTask`. Instead, you should always call the methods `compute` or `fork` directly; only sequential code should use `invoke` to begin parallel computation.
- Calling the `fork` method on a subtask is the way to schedule it on the `ForkJoinPool`. It might seem natural to invoke it on both the left and right subtasks, but this is less efficient than just directly calling `compute` on one of them. Doing this allows you to reuse the same thread for one of the two subtasks and avoid the overhead caused by the unnecessary allocation of a further task on the pool.
- Debugging a parallel computation using the fork/join framework can be tricky. In particular, it's ordinarily quite common to browse a stack trace in your favorite IDE to discover the cause of a problem, but this can't work with a fork-join computation because the call to `compute` occurs in a different thread than the conceptual caller, which is the code that called `fork`.
- As you've discovered with parallel streams, you should never take for granted that a computation using the fork/join framework on a multicore processor is faster than the sequential counterpart. We already said that a task should be decomposable into several independent subtasks in order to be parallelizable with a relevant performance gain. All of these subtasks should take longer to execute than forking a new task; one idiom is to put I/O into one subtask and computation into another, thereby overlapping computation with I/O. Moreover, you should consider other things when comparing the performance of the sequential and parallel versions of the same algorithm. Like any other Java code, the fork/join framework needs to be "warmed up," or executed, a few

times before being optimized by the JIT compiler. This is why it's always important to run the program multiple times before to measure its performance, as we did in our harness. Also be aware that optimizations built into the compiler could unfairly give an advantage to the sequential version (for example, by performing dead code analysis—removing a computation that's never used).

The fork/join splitting strategy deserves one last note: you must choose the criteria used to decide if a given subtask should be further split or is small enough to be evaluated sequentially. We give some hints about this in the next section.

7.2.3 Work stealing

In our `ForkJoinSumCalculator` example we decided to stop creating more subtasks when the array of numbers to be summed contained at most 10,000 items. This is an arbitrary choice, but in most cases it's difficult to find a good heuristic, other than trying to optimize it by making several attempts with different inputs. In our test case, we started with an array of 10 million items, meaning that the `ForkJoinSumCalculator` will fork at least 1,000 subtasks. This might seem like a waste of resources because we ran it on a machine that has only four cores. In this specific case, that's probably true because all tasks are CPU bound and are expected to take a similar amount of time.

But forking a quite large number of fine-grained tasks is in general a winning choice. This is because ideally you want to partition the workload of a parallelized task in such a way that each subtask takes exactly the same amount of time, keeping all the cores of your CPU equally busy. Unfortunately, especially in cases closer to real-world scenarios than the straightforward example we presented here, the time taken by each subtask can dramatically vary either due to the use of an inefficient partition strategy or because of unpredictable causes like slow access to the disk or the need to coordinate the execution with external services.

The fork/join framework works around this problem with a technique called *work stealing*. In practice, this means that the tasks are more or less evenly divided on all the threads in the `ForkJoinPool`. Each of these threads holds a doubly linked queue of the tasks assigned to it, and as soon as it completes a task it pulls another one from the head of the queue and starts executing it. For the reasons we listed previously, one thread might complete all the tasks assigned to it much faster than the others, which means its queue will become empty while the other threads are still pretty busy. In this case, instead of becoming idle, the thread randomly chooses a queue of a different thread and "steals" a task, taking it from the tail of the queue. This process continues until all the tasks are executed, and then all the queues become empty. That's why having many smaller tasks, instead of only a few bigger ones, can help in better balancing the workload among the worker threads.

More generally, this work-stealing algorithm is used to redistribute and balance the tasks among the worker threads in the pool. Figure 7.5 shows how this process occurs. When a task in the queue of a worker is divided into two subtasks, one of the two subtasks is stolen by another idle worker. As described previously, this process can

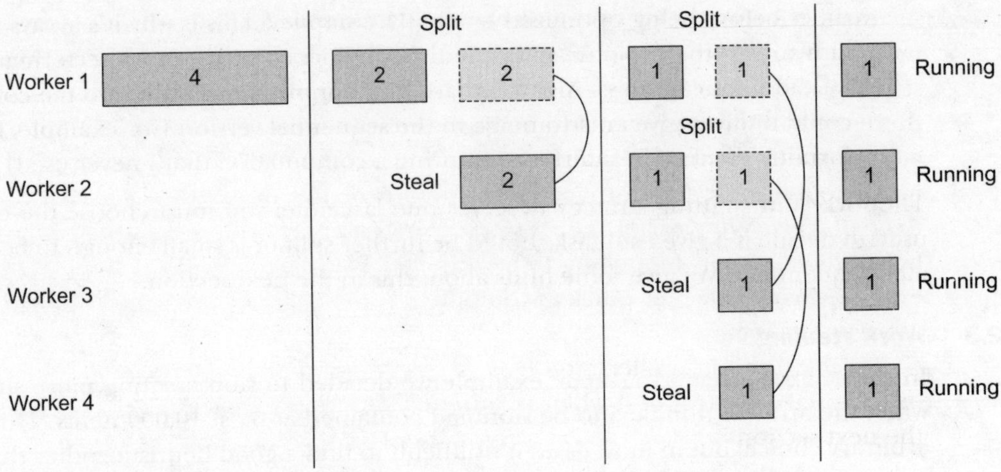

Figure 7.5 The work-stealing algorithm used by the fork/join framework

continue recursively until the condition used to define that a given subtask should be executed sequentially becomes true.

It should now be clear how a stream can use the fork/join framework to process its items in parallel, but there's still one missing ingredient. In this section, we analyzed an example where you explicitly developed the logic to split an array of numbers into multiple tasks. Nevertheless, you didn't have to do anything similar when you used the parallel streams at the beginning of this chapter, and this means that there must be an automatic mechanism splitting the stream for you. This new automatic mechanism is called the `Spliterator`, and we explore it in the next section.

7.3 Spliterator

The `Spliterator` is another new interface added to Java 8; its name stands for "splitable iterator." Like `Iterators`, `Spliterators` are used to traverse the elements of a source, but they're also designed to do this in parallel. Although you may not have to develop your own `Spliterator` in practice, understanding how to do so will give you a wider understanding about how parallel streams work. Java 8 already provides a default `Spliterator` implementation for all the data structures included in its Collections Framework. Collections now implements the interface `Spliterator`, which provides a method `spliterator`. This interface defines several methods, as shown in the following listing.

Listing 7.3 The `Spliterator` interface

```
public interface Spliterator<T> {
    boolean tryAdvance(Consumer<? super T> action);
    Spliterator<T> trySplit();
    long estimateSize();
    int characteristics();
}
```

As usual, `T` is the type of the elements traversed by the `Spliterator`. The `tryAdvance` method behaves in a way similar to a normal `Iterator` in the sense that it's used to sequentially consume the elements of the `Spliterator` one by one, returning `true` if there are still other elements to be traversed. But the `trySplit` method is more specific to the `Spliterator` interface because it's used to partition off some of its elements to a second `Spliterator` (the one returned by the method), allowing the two to be processed in parallel. A `Spliterator` may also provide an estimation of the number of the elements remaining to be traversed via its `estimateSize` method, because even an inaccurate but quick-to-compute value can be useful to split the structure more or less evenly.

It's important to understand how this splitting process is performed internally in order to take control of it when required. Therefore, we analyze it in more detail in the next section.

7.3.1 The splitting process

The algorithm that splits a `Stream` into multiple parts is a recursive process and proceeds as shown in figure 7.6. In the first step `trySplit` is invoked on the first `Spliterator` and generates a second one. Then in step 2 it's called again on these two `Spliterators`, which results in a total of four. The framework keeps invoking the method `trySplit` on a `Spliterator` until it returns `null` to signal that the data structure that it's processing is no longer divisible, as shown in step 3. Finally, this recursive

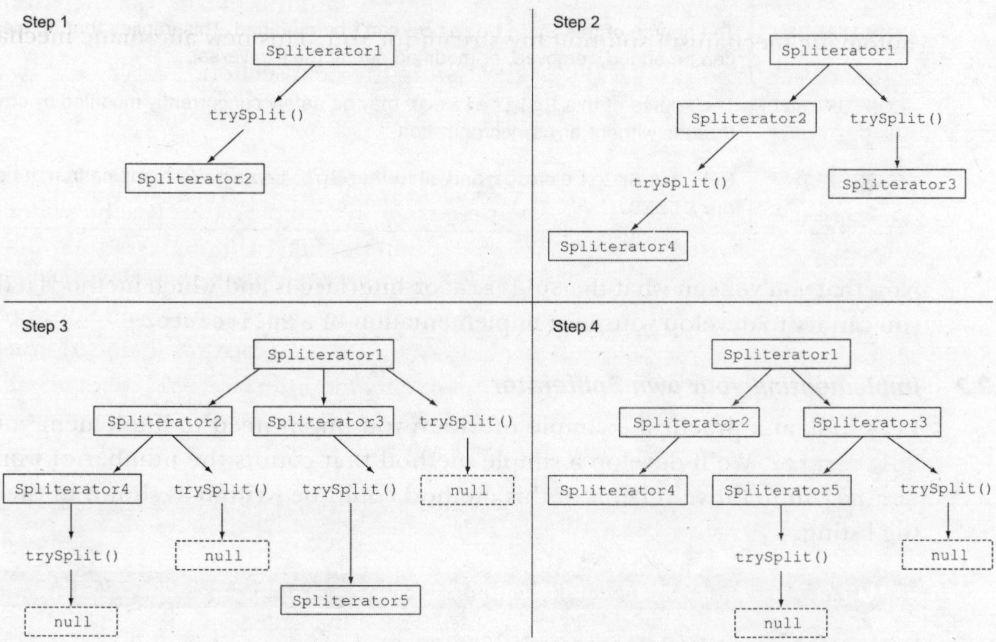

Figure 7.6 The recursive splitting process

splitting process terminates in step 4 when all `Spliterators` have returned `null` to a `trySplit` invocation.

This splitting process can also be influenced by the characteristics of the `Spliterator` itself, which are declared via the `characteristics` method.

THE SPLITERATOR CHARACTERISTICS

The last abstract method declared by the `Spliterator` interface is `characteristics`, which returns an `int` encoding the set of characteristics of the `Spliterator` itself. The `Spliterator` clients can use these characteristics to better control and optimize its usage. Table 7.2 summarizes them. (Unfortunately, although these conceptually overlap with characteristics of a collector, they're coded differently.)

Table 7.2 `Spliterator`'s characteristics

Characteristic	Meaning
`ORDERED`	Elements have a defined order (for example, a `List`), so the `Spliterator` enforces this order when traversing and partitioning them.
`DISTINCT`	For each pair of traversed elements `x` and `y`, `x.equals(y)` returns `false`.
`SORTED`	The traversed elements follow a predefined sort order.
`SIZED`	This `Spliterator` has been created from a source with a known size (for example, a `Set`), so the value returned by `estimatedSize()` is precise.
`NONNULL`	It's guaranteed that the traversed elements won't be `null`.
`IMMUTABLE`	The source of this `Spliterator` can't be modified. This implies that no elements can be added, removed, or modified during their traversal.
`CONCURRENT`	The source of this `Spliterator` may be safely concurrently modified by other threads without any synchronization.
`SUBSIZED`	Both this `Spliterator` and all further `Spliterators` resulting from its split are `SIZED`.

Now that you've seen what the `Spliterator` interface is and which methods it defines, you can try to develop your own implementation of a `Spliterator`.

7.3.2 *Implementing your own Spliterator*

Let's look at a practical example of where you might need to implement your own `Spliterator`. We'll develop a simple method that counts the number of words in a `String`. An iterative version of this method could be written as shown in the following listing.

Listing 7.4 An iterative word counter method

```
public int countWordsIteratively(String s) {
    int counter = 0;
    boolean lastSpace = true;
```

```
    for (char c : s.toCharArray()) {              <-- Traverse all the characters
        if (Character.isWhitespace(c)) {              in the String one by one.
            lastSpace = true;
        } else {
            if (lastSpace) counter++;             <-- Increase the word counter when
            lastSpace = false;                        the last character is a space and
        }                                             the currently traversed one isn't.
    }
    return counter;
}
```

Let's put this method to work on the first sentence of Dante's *Inferno*:[1]

```
final String SENTENCE =
            " Nel   mezzo del cammin  di nostra  vita " +
            "mi  ritrovai in una  selva oscura" +
            " ché la  dritta via era   smarrita ";

System.out.println("Found " + countWordsIteratively(SENTENCE) + " words");
```

Note that we added some additional random spaces in the sentence to demonstrate that the iterative implementation is working correctly even in the presence of multiple spaces between two words. As expected, this code prints out the following:

```
Found 19 words
```

Ideally you'd like to achieve the same result in a more functional style because this way you'll be able, as shown previously, to parallelize this process using a parallel `Stream` without having to explicitly deal with threads and their synchronization.

REWRITING THE WORDCOUNTER IN FUNCTIONAL STYLE

First, you need to convert the `String` into a stream. Unfortunately, there are primitive streams only for `int`, `long`, and `double`, so you'll have to use a `Stream<Character>`:

```
Stream<Character> stream = IntStream.range(0, SENTENCE.length())
                                    .mapToObj(SENTENCE::charAt);
```

You can calculate the number of words by performing a reduction on this stream. While reducing the stream, you'll have to carry a state consisting of two variables: an `int` counting the number of words found so far and a `boolean` to remember if the last-encountered `Character` was a space or not. Because Java doesn't have tuples (a construct to represent an ordered list of heterogeneous elements without the need of a wrapper object), you'll have to create a new class, `WordCounter`, which will encapsulate this state as shown in the following listing.

Listing 7.5 A class to count words while traversing a stream of `Characters`

```
class WordCounter {
    private final int counter;
    private final boolean lastSpace;
```

[1] See http://en.wikipedia.org/wiki/Inferno_(Dante).

```
    public WordCounter(int counter, boolean lastSpace) {
        this.counter = counter;
        this.lastSpace = lastSpace;
    }

    public WordCounter accumulate(Character c) {
        if (Character.isWhitespace(c)) {
            return lastSpace ?
                      this :
                      new WordCounter(counter, true);
        } else {
            return lastSpace ?
                      new WordCounter(counter+1, false) :
                      this;
        }
    }

    public WordCounter combine(WordCounter wordCounter) {
        return new WordCounter(counter + wordCounter.counter,
                                wordCounter.lastSpace);
    }

    public int getCounter() {
        return counter;
    }
}
```

The `accumulate` method traverses the `Characters` one by one as done by the iterative algorithm.

Increase the word counter when the last character is a space and the currently traversed one isn't.

Combine two `WordCounters` by summing their counters.

Use only the sum of the counters so you don't care about `lastSpace`.

In this listing, the accumulate method defines how to change the state of the WordCounter, or more precisely with which state to create a new WordCounter because it's an immutable class. The method accumulate is called whenever a new Character of the Stream is traversed. In particular, as you did in the countWordsIteratively method in listing 7.4, the counter is incremented when a new nonspace is met and the last character encountered is a space. Figure 7.7 shows the state transitions of the WordCounter when a new Character is traversed by the accumulate method.

The second method, combine, is invoked to aggregate the partial results of two WordCounters operating on two different subparts of the stream of Characters, so it combines two WordCounters by summing their internal counters.

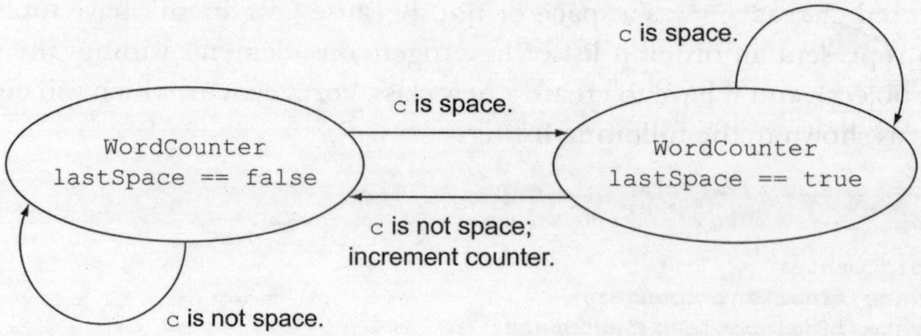

Figure 7.7 The state transitions of the `WordCounter` when a new `Character c` is traversed

Now that you've encoded the logic of how to accumulate characters on a `WordCounter` and how to combine them in the `WordCounter` itself, writing a method that will reduce the stream of `Characters` is straightforward:

```
private int countWords(Stream<Character> stream) {
    WordCounter wordCounter = stream.reduce(new WordCounter(0, true),
                                            WordCounter::accumulate,
                                            WordCounter::combine);
    return wordCounter.getCounter();
}
```

Now you can try this method with the stream created from the `String` containing the first sentence of Dante's *Inferno*:

```
Stream<Character> stream = IntStream.range(0, SENTENCE.length())
                                    .mapToObj(SENTENCE::charAt);
System.out.println("Found " + countWords(stream) + " words");
```

You can check that its output corresponds with the one generated by the iterative version:

```
Found 19 words
```

So far, so good, but we said that one of the main reasons for implementing the `WordCounter` in functional terms was to be able to easily parallelize this operation, so let's see how this works.

MAKING THE WORDCOUNTER WORK IN PARALLEL

You could try to speed up the word-counting operation using a parallel stream, as follows:

```
System.out.println("Found " + countWords(stream.parallel()) + " words");
```

Unfortunately, this time the output is

```
Found 25 words
```

Evidently something has gone wrong, but what? The problem isn't hard to discover. Because the original `String` is split at arbitrary positions, sometimes a word is divided in two and then counted twice. In general, this demonstrates that going from a sequential stream to a parallel one can lead to a wrong result if this result may be affected by the position where the stream is split.

How can you fix this issue? The solution consists of ensuring that the `String` isn't split at a random position but only at the end of a word. To do this, you'll have to implement a `Spliterator` of `Character` that splits a `String` only between two words, as shown in the following listing, and then creates the parallel stream from it.

Listing 7.6 The `WordCounterSpliterator`

```
class WordCounterSpliterator implements Spliterator<Character> {

    private final String string;
    private int currentChar = 0;

    public WordCounterSpliterator(String string) {
        this.string = string;
    }
```

```
    @Override
    public boolean tryAdvance(Consumer<? super Character> action) {
        action.accept(string.charAt(currentChar++));
        return currentChar < string.length();
    }
    @Override
    public Spliterator<Character> trySplit() {
        int currentSize = string.length() - currentChar;
        if (currentSize < 10) {
            return null;
        }
        for (int splitPos = currentSize / 2 + currentChar;
                 splitPos < string.length(); splitPos++) {
            if (Character.isWhitespace(string.charAt(splitPos))) {
                Spliterator<Character> spliterator =
                   new WordCounterSpliterator(string.substring(currentChar,
                                                               splitPos));
                currentChar = splitPos;
                return spliterator;
            }
        }
        return null;
    }

    @Override
    public long estimateSize() {
        return string.length() - currentChar;
    }

    @Override
    public int characteristics() {
        return ORDERED + SIZED + SUBSIZED + NONNULL + IMMUTABLE;
    }
}
```

Consume the current character.

Return `true` if there are further characters to be consumed.

Set the candidate's split position to be half of the `String` to be parsed.

Return `null` to signal that the `String` to be parsed is small enough to be processed sequentially.

Advance the split position until the next space.

Set the start position of this `WordCounter-Spliterator` to the split position.

Create a new `WordCounter-Spliterator` parsing the `String` from the start to the split position.

This `Spliterator` is created from the `String` to be parsed and iterates over its `Characters` by holding the index of the one currently being traversed. Let's quickly revisit the methods of the `WordCounterSpliterator` implementing the `Spliterator` interface:

- The `tryAdvance` method feeds the `Consumer` with the `Character` in the `String` at the current index position and increments this position. The `Consumer` passed as argument is an internal Java class forwarding the consumed `Character` to the set of functions that have to be applied to it while traversing the stream, which in this case is only a reducing function, namely, the `accumulate` method of the `WordCounter` class. The `tryAdvance` method returns `true` if the new cursor position is less than the total `String` length and there are further `Characters` to be iterated.
- The `trySplit` method is the most important one in a `Spliterator` because it's the one defining the logic used to split the data structure to be iterated. As you did in the `compute` method of the `RecursiveTask` implemented in listing 7.1

(on how to use the fork/join framework), the first thing you have to do here is set a limit under which you don't want to perform further splits. Here, you use a very low limit of 10 `Characters` only to make sure that your program will perform some splits with the relatively short `String` you're parsing, but in real-world applications you'll have to use a higher limit, as you did in the fork/join example, to avoid creating too many tasks. If the number of remaining `Characters` to be traversed is under this limit, you return `null` to signal that no further split is necessary. Conversely, if you need to perform a split, you set the candidate split position to the half of the `String` chunk remaining to be parsed. But you don't use this split position directly because you want to avoid splitting in the middle of a word, so you move forward until you find a blank `Character`. Once you find an opportune split position, you create a new `Spliterator` that will traverse the substring chunk going from the current position to the split one; you set the current position of `this` to the split one, because the part before it will be managed by the new `Spliterator`, and then you return it.

- The `estimatedSize` of elements still to be traversed is the difference between the total length of the `String` parsed by this `Spliterator` and the position currently iterated.
- Finally, the `characteristic` method signals to the framework that this `Spliterator` is `ORDERED` (the order is just the sequence of `Characters` in the `String`), `SIZED` (the value returned by the `estimatedSize` method is exact), `SUBSIZED` (the other `Spliterators` created by the `trySplit` method also have an exact size), `NONNULL` (there can be no `null` `Characters` in the `String`), and `IMMUTABLE` (no further `Characters` can be added while parsing the `String` because the `String` itself is an immutable class).

PUTTING THE WORDCOUNTERSPLITERATOR TO WORK

You can now use a parallel stream with this new `WordCounterSpliterator` as follows:

```
Spliterator<Character> spliterator = new WordCounterSpliterator(SENTENCE);
Stream<Character> stream = StreamSupport.stream(spliterator, true);
```

The second boolean argument passed to the `StreamSupport.stream` factory method means that you want to create a parallel stream. Passing this parallel stream to the `countWords` method

```
System.out.println("Found " + countWords(stream) + " words");
```

produces the correct output, as expected:

```
Found 19 words
```

You've seen how a `Spliterator` can let you to gain control over the policy used to split a data structure. One last notable feature of `Spliterators` is the possibility of binding the source of the elements to be traversed at the point of first traversal, first split, or first query for estimated size, rather than at the time of its creation. When this happens, it's called a *late-binding* `Spliterator`. We've dedicated appendix C to showing how you can develop a utility class capable of performing multiple operations on the same stream in parallel using this feature.

7.4 Summary

In this chapter, you've learned the following:

- Internal iteration allows you to process a stream in parallel without the need to explicitly use and coordinate different threads in your code.
- Even if processing a stream in parallel is so easy, there's no guarantee that doing so will make your programs run faster under all circumstances. Behavior and performance of parallel software can sometimes be counterintuitive, and for this reason it's always necessary to measure them and be sure that you're not actually slowing your programs down.
- Parallel execution of an operation on a set of data, as done by a parallel stream, can provide a performance boost, especially when the number of elements to be processed is huge or the processing of each single element is particularly time consuming.
- From a performance point of view, using the right data structure, for instance, employing primitive streams instead of nonspecialized ones whenever possible, is almost always more important than trying to parallelize some operations.
- The fork/join framework lets you recursively split a parallelizable task into smaller tasks, execute them on different threads, and then combine the results of each subtask in order to produce the overall result.
- `Spliterators` define how a parallel stream can split the data it traverses.

Part 3

Effective Java 8 programming

The third part of this book explores various Java 8 topics that will make you more effective at using Java 8 and enhance your codebase with modern idioms.

Chapter 8 explores how you can improve your existing code using new Java 8 features and a few recipes. In addition, it explores vital software development techniques such as design patterns, refactoring, testing, and debugging.

In chapter 9, you'll learn what default methods are, how you can use them to evolve APIs in a compatible way, some practical usage patterns, and rules for using default methods effectively.

Chapter 10 covers the new `java.util.Optional` class, which allows you to both design better APIs and reduce `null` pointer exceptions.

Chapter 11 explores `CompletableFuture`, which lets you express complex asynchronous computations in a declarative way—paralleling the design of the Streams API.

Chapter 12 investigates the new Date and Time API, which greatly improves the previous error-prone APIs for working with dates and time.

8 Refactoring, testing, and debugging

This chapter covers

- How to refactor code to use lambda expressions
- The impact of lambda expressions on object-oriented design patterns
- Testing lambda expressions
- Debugging code that uses lambda expressions and the Streams API

In the first seven chapters of this book, you saw the expressive power of lambdas and the Streams API. You were mainly creating new code that made use of these features. This is great if you have to start a new Java project—you can use lambdas and streams immediately.

Unfortunately, you don't always get to start a new project from scratch. Most of the time you'll have to deal with an existing codebase written in an older version of Java.

This is the purpose of this chapter. It presents several recipes showing how you can refactor existing code to make use of lambda expressions and gain more readability and flexibility. In addition, we discuss how several object-oriented design patterns including strategy, template method, observer, chain of responsibility, and factory can be made more concise thanks to lambda expressions. Finally, we explore how you can test and debug code that uses lambda expressions and the Streams API.

8.1 Refactoring for improved readability and flexibility

Right from the start of this book we've argued that lambda expressions can let you write more concise and flexible code. It's *more concise* because lambda expressions let you represent a piece of behavior in a more compact form in comparison to using anonymous classes. We also showed in chapter 3 that method references let you write even more concise code when all you want to do is pass an existing method as argument to another method.

Your code is *more flexible* because lambda expressions encourage the style of behavior parameterization that we introduced in chapter 2. Your code can use and execute multiple behaviors passed as arguments to cope with requirement changes.

In this section, we bring it all together and show you simple steps you can follow to refactor code to gain readability and flexibility, using the features you learned in the previous chapters: lambdas, method references, and streams.

8.1.1 Improving code readability

What does it mean to improve the readability of code? It's hard to define what *good readability* means, because it can be very subjective. The general view is that it means "how easily this code can be understood by another human." Improving code readability means ensuring your code is understandable and maintainable by people besides you. There are a few steps you can take to make sure your code is understandable by other people, such as making sure your code is well documented and follows coding standards.

Java 8 features can also help improve code readability compared to previous versions:

- You can reduce the verbosity of your code, making it easier to understand.
- You can improve the intent of your code by using method references and the Streams API.

We describe three simple refactorings that use lambdas, method references, and streams, which you can apply to your code to improve its readability:

- Refactoring anonymous classes to lambda expressions
- Refactoring lambda expressions to method references
- Refactoring imperative-style data processing to streams

8.1.2 From anonymous classes to lambda expressions

The first simple refactoring you should consider is converting uses of anonymous classes implementing one single abstract method to lambda expressions. Why? We hope we convinced you in earlier chapters that anonymous classes are extremely verbose and error-prone. By adopting lambda expressions, you produce code that is more succinct and readable. For example, as shown in chapter 3, here's an anonymous class for creating a `Runnable` object and its lambda expression counterpart:

```
Runnable r1 = new Runnable(){
    public void run(){
        System.out.println("Hello");
    }
};

Runnable r2 = () -> System.out.println("Hello");
```

Before, using an anonymous class

After, using a lambda expression

But converting anonymous classes to lambda expressions can be a difficult process in certain situations.[1] First, the meanings of `this` and `super` are different for anonymous classes and lambda expressions. Inside an anonymous class, `this` refers to the anonymous class itself, but inside a lambda it refers to the enclosing class. Second, anonymous classes are allowed to shadow variables from the enclosing class. Lambda expressions can't (they'll cause a compile error), as shown in the following code:

```
int a = 10;
Runnable r1 = () -> {
    int a = 2;
    System.out.println(a);
};

Runnable r2 = new Runnable(){
    public void run(){
        int a = 2;
        System.out.println(a);
    }
};
```

Compile error!

Everything is fine!

Finally, converting an anonymous class to a lambda expression can make the resulting code ambiguous in the context of overloading. Indeed, the type of anonymous class is explicit at instantiation, but the type of the lambda depends on its context. Here's an example of how this can be problematic. Let's say you've declared a functional interface with the same signature as `Runnable`, here called `Task` (this might occur when you need interface names that are more meaningful in your domain model):

```
interface Task{
    public void execute();
}
public static void doSomething(Runnable r){ r.run(); }
public static void doSomething(Task a){ r.execute(); }
```

You can now pass an anonymous class implementing `Task` without a problem:

```
doSomething(new Task() {
    public void execute() {
        System.out.println("Danger danger!!");
    }
});
```

[1] This excellent paper describes the process in more detail: http://dig.cs.illinois.edu/papers/lambda-Refactoring.pdf.

But converting this anonymous class to a lambda expression results in an ambiguous method call, because both `Runnable` and `Task` are valid target types:

```
doSomething(() -> System.out.println("Danger danger!!"));
```

Problem; both `doSomething(Runnable)` and `doSomething(Task)` match.

You can solve the ambiguity by providing an explicit cast `(Task)`:

```
doSomething((Task)() -> System.out.println("Danger danger!!"));
```

Don't be turned off by these issues though; there's good news! Most integrated development environments (IDEs) such as NetBeans and IntelliJ support this refactoring and will automatically ensure these gotchas don't arise.

8.1.3 From lambda expressions to method references

Lambda expressions are great for short code that needs to be passed around. But consider using method references when possible to improve code readability. A method name states more clearly the intent of your code. For example, in chapter 6 we showed you the following code to group dishes by caloric levels:

```
Map<CaloricLevel, List<Dish>> dishesByCaloricLevel =
  menu.stream()
      .collect(
          groupingBy(dish -> {
            if (dish.getCalories() <= 400) return CaloricLevel.DIET;
            else if (dish.getCalories() <= 700) return CaloricLevel.NORMAL;
            else return CaloricLevel.FAT;
          }));
```

You can extract the lambda expression into a separate method and pass it as argument to `groupingBy`. The code becomes more concise and its intent is now more explicit:

```
Map<CaloricLevel, List<Dish>> dishesByCaloricLevel =
    menu.stream().collect(groupingBy(Dish::getCaloricLevel));
```

The lambda expression is extracted into a method.

You need to add the method `getCaloricLevel` inside the `Dish` class itself for this to work:

```
public class Dish{
    …
    public CaloricLevel getCaloricLevel(){
        if (this.getCalories() <= 400) return CaloricLevel.DIET;
        else if (this.getCalories() <= 700) return CaloricLevel.NORMAL;
        else return CaloricLevel.FAT;
    }
}
```

In addition, consider making use of helper static methods such as `comparing` and `maxBy` when possible. These methods were designed for use with method references! Indeed, this code states much more clearly its intent than its counterpart using a lambda expression, as we showed in chapter 3:

```
inventory.sort(
    (Apple a1, Apple a2) -> a1.getWeight().compareTo(a2.getWeight()));

inventory.sort(comparing(Apple::getWeight));
```

Reads like problem statement.

You need to think about the implementation of comparison.

Moreover, for many common reduction operations such as *sum, maximum* there are built-in helper methods that can be combined with method references. For example, we showed that using the `Collectors` API you can find the maximum or sum in a clearer way than using a combination of a lambda expression and a lower-level `reduce` operation. Instead of writing

```
int totalCalories =
     menu.stream().map(Dish::getCalories)
                  .reduce(0, (c1, c2) -> c1 + c2);
```

try using alternative built-in collectors, which state more clearly what the problem statement is. Here we use the collector `summingInt` (names go a long way in documenting your code):

```
int totalCalories = menu.stream().collect(summingInt(Dish::getCalories));
```

8.1.4 From imperative data processing to Streams

Ideally, you should try to convert all code that processes a collection with typical data processing patterns with an iterator to use the Streams API instead. Why? The Streams API expresses more clearly the intent of a data processing pipeline. In addition, streams can be optimized behind the scenes making use of short-circuiting and laziness, as well as leveraging your multicore architecture, as we explained in chapter 7.

For example, the following imperative code expresses two patterns (filtering and extracting) that are mangled together, which forces the programmer to carefully understand the whole implementation before figuring out what the code does. In addition, an implementation that executes in parallel would be a lot more difficult to write (see section 7.2 in the previous chapter about the fork/join framework to get an idea):

```
List<String> dishNames = new ArrayList<>();
for(Dish dish: menu){
    if(dish.getCalories() > 300){
        dishNames.add(dish.getName());
    }
}
```

The alternative using the Streams API reads more like the problem statement, and it can be easily parallelized:

```
menu.parallelStream()
    .filter(d -> d.getCalories() > 300)
    .map(Dish::getName)
    .collect(toList());
```

Unfortunately, converting imperative code to the Streams API can be a difficult task, because you need to think about control-flow statements such as `break`, `continue`, and return and infer the right stream operations to use. The good news is that some tools can help you with this task as well.[2]

8.1.5 Improving code flexibility

We argued in chapters 2 and 3 that lambda expressions encourage the style of *behavior parameterization.* You can represent multiple different behaviors with different lambdas that you can then pass around to execute. This style lets you cope with requirement changes (for example, creating multiple different ways of filtering with a `Predicate` or comparing with a `Comparator`). We now look at a couple of patterns that you can apply to your codebase to immediately benefit from lambda expressions.

ADOPTING FUNCTIONAL INTERFACES

First, you can't use lambda expressions without functional interfaces. You should therefore start introducing them in your codebase. That sounds good, but in which situations? We discuss two common code patterns that can be refactored to leverage lambda expressions: *conditional deferred execution* and *execute around.* In addition, in the next section we show how many object-oriented design patterns such as strategy and template method can be rewritten more concisely using lambda expressions.

CONDITIONAL DEFERRED EXECUTION

It's common to see control-flow statements mangled inside business logic code. Typical scenarios include security checks and logging. For example, consider the following code that uses the built-in Java `Logger` class:

```
if (logger.isLoggable(Log.FINER)){
    logger.finer("Problem: " + generateDiagnostic());
}
```

What's wrong with it? A couple of things:

- The state of the logger (what level it supports) is exposed in the client code through the method `isLoggable`.
- Why should you have to query the state of the logger object every time before you can log a message? It just clutters your code.

A better alternative is to make use of the `log` method, which internally checks to see if the logger object is set to the right level before logging the message:

```
logger.log(Level.FINER, "Problem: " + generateDiagnostic());
```

This is a better approach because your code isn't cluttered with `if` checks, and the state of the logger is no longer exposed. Unfortunately, there's still an issue with this code. The logging message is always evaluated, even if the logger isn't enabled for the message level passed as argument.

This is where lambda expressions can help. What you need is a way to defer the construction of the message so it can be generated only under a given condition

[2] See http://refactoring.info/tools/LambdaFicator/.

(here, when the logger level is set to `FINER`). It turns out that the Java 8 API designers knew about this problem and introduced an overloaded alternative to `log` that takes a `Supplier` as argument. This alternative `log` method has the following signature:

```
public void log(Level level, Supplier<String> msgSupplier)
```

You can now call it as follows:

```
logger.log(Level.FINER, () -> "Problem: " + generateDiagnostic());
```

The `log` method will internally execute the lambda passed as argument only if the logger is of the right level. The internal implementation of the `log` method is along the lines of this:

```
public void log(Level level, Supplier<String> msgSupplier){
    if(logger.isLoggable(level)){
        log(level, msgSupplier.get());      <-- Executing the lambda
    }
}
```

What's the takeaway from the story? If you see yourself querying the state of an object many times in client code (for example, the state of the logger), only to call some method on this object with arguments (for example, log a message), then consider introducing a new method that calls that method (passed as a lambda or method reference) only after internally checking the state of the object. Your code will be more readable (less clutter) and better encapsulated (the state of the object isn't exposed in client code)!

EXECUTE AROUND

In chapter 3 we discussed another pattern that you can adopt: execute around. If you find yourself surrounding different code with the same preparation and cleanup phases, you can often pull that code into a lambda. The benefit is that you reuse the logic dealing with the preparation and cleanup phases, thus reducing code duplication.

To refresh, here's the code you saw in chapter 3. It reuses the same logic to open and close a file but can be parameterized with different lambdas to process the file:

```
String oneLine =
    processFile((BufferedReader b) -> b.readLine());      <-- Pass a lambda.
String twoLines =
    processFile((BufferedReader b) -> b.readLine() + b.readLine());      <-- Pass a different lambda.

public static String processFile(BufferedReaderProcessor p) throws
    IOException {
    try(BufferedReader br = new BufferedReader(new FileReader("java8inaction/
     chap8/data.txt"))){
        return p.process(br);      <-- Execute the BufferedReaderProcessor passed as argument.
    }
}

public interface BufferedReaderProcessor{      <-- A functional interface for a lambda, which can throw an IOException.
    String process(BufferedReader b) throws IOException;
}
```

This was made possible by introducing the functional interface `BufferedReader-Processor`, which lets you pass different lambdas to work with a `BufferedReader` object.

In this section, you've seen how to apply different recipes to improve the readability and flexibility of your code. You'll now see how lambda expressions can often remove boilerplate code associated with common object-oriented design patterns.

8.2 Refactoring object-oriented design patterns with lambdas

New language features often make existing code patterns or idioms less popular. For example, the introduction of the `for-each` loop in Java 5 has replaced many uses of explicit iterators because it's less error prone and more concise. The introduction of the diamond operator `<>` in Java 7 has reduced the use of explicit generics at instance creation (and slowly pushed Java programmers toward embracing type inference).

A specific class of patterns is called *design patterns*.[3] They're a reusable blueprint, if you will, for a common problem when designing software. It's a bit like how construction engineers have a set of reusable solutions to construct bridges for specific scenarios (such as suspension bridge, arch bridge, and so on). For example, the *visitor design pattern* is a common solution for separating an algorithm from a structure on which it needs to operate. The *singleton pattern* is a common solution to restrict the instantiation of a class to only one object.

Lambda expressions provide yet another new tool in the programmer's toolbox. They can provide alternative solutions to the problems the design patterns are tackling but often with less work and in a simpler way. Many existing object-oriented design patterns can be made redundant or written in a more concise way using lambda expressions. In this section, we explore five design patterns:

- Strategy
- Template method
- Observer
- Chain of responsibility
- Factory

We show how lambda expressions can provide an alternative way to solve the same problem each design pattern is intended for.

8.2.1 Strategy

The strategy pattern is a common solution for representing a family of algorithms and letting you choose among them at runtime. You briefly saw this pattern in chapter 2, when we showed you how to filter an inventory with different predicates (for example, heavy apples or green apples). You can apply this pattern to a multitude of scenarios, such as validating an input with different criteria, using different ways of parsing, or formatting an input.

---

3 See http://c2.com/cgi/wiki?GangOfFour.

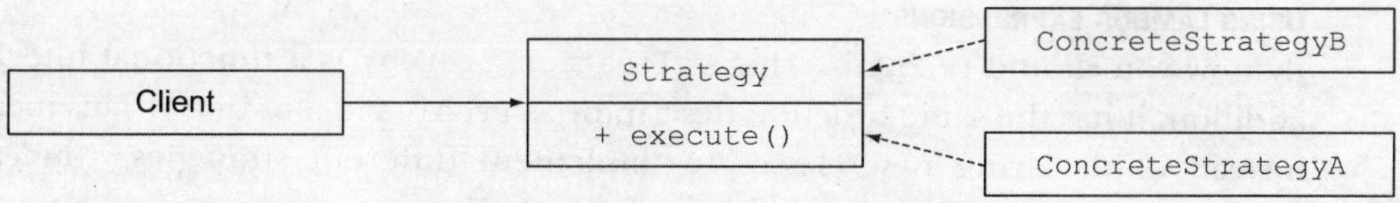

Figure 8.1 The strategy design pattern

The strategy pattern consists of three parts, as illustrated in figure 8.1:

- An interface to represent some algorithm (the interface `Strategy`)
- One or more concrete implementations of that interface to represent multiple algorithms (the concrete classes `ConcreteStrategyA`, `ConcreteStrategyB`)
- One or more clients that use the strategy objects

Let's say you'd like to validate whether a text input is properly formatted for different criteria (for example, it consists of only lowercase letters or is numeric). You start by defining an interface to validate the text (represented as a `String`):

```
public interface ValidationStrategy {
    boolean execute(String s);
}
```

Second, you define one or more implementation(s) of that interface:

```
public class IsAllLowerCase implements ValidationStrategy {
    public boolean execute(String s){
        return s.matches("[a-z]+");
    }
}

public class IsNumeric implements ValidationStrategy {
    public boolean execute(String s){
        return s.matches("\\d+");
    }
}
```

You can then use these different validation strategies in your program:

```
public class Validator{
    private final ValidationStrategy strategy;

    public Validator(ValidationStrategy v){
        this.strategy = v;
    }

    public boolean validate(String s){
        return strategy.execute(s);
    }
}

Validator numericValidator = new Validator(new IsNumeric());
boolean b1 = numericValidator.validate("aaaa");
Validator lowerCaseValidator = new Validator(new IsAllLowerCase ());
boolean b2 = lowerCaseValidator.validate("bbbb");
```

Returns `false` (b1)

Returns `true` (b2)

USING LAMBDA EXPRESSIONS

By now you should recognize that `ValidationStrategy` is a functional interface (in addition, it has the same function descriptor as `Predicate<String>`). This means that instead of declaring new classes to implement different strategies, you can pass lambda expressions directly, which are more concise:

```
Validator numericValidator =
    new Validator((String s) -> s.matches("[a-z]+"));
boolean b1 = numericValidator.validate("aaaa");
Validator lowerCaseValidator =
    new Validator((String s) -> s.matches("\\d+"));
boolean b2 = lowerCaseValidator.validate("bbbb");
```

Passing a lambda directly

As you can see, lambda expressions remove the boilerplate code inherent to the strategy design pattern. If you think about it, lambda expressions encapsulate a piece of code (or strategy), which is what the strategy design pattern was created for, so we recommend that you use lambda expressions instead for similar problems.

8.2.2 *Template method*

The template method design pattern is a common solution when you need to represent the outline of an algorithm and have the additional flexibility to change certain parts of it. Okay, it sounds a bit abstract. In other words, the template method pattern is useful when you find yourself in a situation such as "I'd love to use this algorithm but I need to change a few lines so it does what I want."

Let's look at an example of how this pattern works. Say you need to write a simple online banking application. Users typically enter a customer ID, and then the application fetches the customer's details from the bank database and finally does something to make the customer happy. Different online banking applications for different banking branches may have different ways of making a customer happy (for example, adding a bonus on their account or just sending them less paperwork). You can write the following abstract class to represent the online banking application:

```
abstract class OnlineBanking {

    public void processCustomer(int id){
        Customer c = Database.getCustomerWithId(id);
        makeCustomerHappy(c);
    }

    abstract void makeCustomerHappy(Customer c);
}
```

The `processCustomer` method provides a sketch for the online banking algorithm: fetch the customer given its ID and then make the customer happy. Different branches can now provide different implementations of the method `makeCustomerHappy` by subclassing the `OnlineBanking` class.

USING LAMBDA EXPRESSIONS

You can tackle the same problem (creating an outline of an algorithm and letting implementers plug in some parts) using your favorite lambdas! The different components of the algorithms you want to plug in can be represented by lambda expressions or method references.

Here we introduce a second argument to the method `processCustomer` of type `Consumer<Customer>` because it matches the signature of the method `makeCustomerHappy` defined earlier:

```
public void processCustomer(int id, Consumer<Customer> makeCustomerHappy){
    Customer c = Database.getCustomerWithId(id);
    makeCustomerHappy.accept(c);
}
```

You can now plug in different behaviors directly without subclassing the `OnlineBanking` class by passing lambda expressions:

```
new OnlineBankingLambda().processCustomer(1337, (Customer c) ->
     System.out.println("Hello " + c.getName());
```

This is another example of how lambda expressions can help you remove the boilerplate inherent to design patterns!

8.2.3 Observer

The observer design pattern is a common solution when an object (called the *subject*) needs to automatically notify a list of other objects (called *observers*) when some event happens (for example, a state change). You typically come across this pattern when working with GUI applications. You register a set of observers on a GUI component such as button. If the button is clicked, the observers are notified and can execute a specific action. But the observer pattern isn't limited to GUIs. For example, the observer design pattern is also suitable in a situation where several traders (observers) may wish to react to the change of price of a stock (subject). Figure 8.2 illustrates the UML diagram of the observer pattern.

Let's write some code to see how the observer pattern is useful in practice. You'll design and implement a customized notification system for an application like Twitter. The concept is simple: several newspaper agencies (*NY Times*, *The Guardian*, and *Le Monde*) are subscribed to a feed of news tweets and may want to receive a notification if a tweet contains a particular keyword.

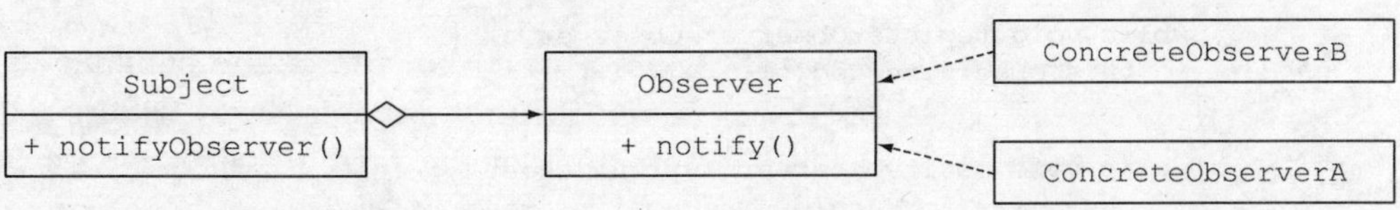

Figure 8.2 The observer design pattern

First, you need an Observer interface that groups the different observers. It has just one method called notify that will be called by the subject (Feed) when a new tweet is available:

```
interface Observer {
    void notify(String tweet);
}
```

You can now declare different observers (here, the three newspapers) that produce a different action for each different keyword contained in a tweet:

```
class NYTimes implements Observer{
    public void notify(String tweet) {
        if(tweet != null && tweet.contains("money")){
            System.out.println("Breaking news in NY! " + tweet);
        }
    }
}
class Guardian implements Observer{
    public void notify(String tweet) {
        if(tweet != null && tweet.contains("queen")){
            System.out.println("Yet another news in London... " + tweet);
        }
    }
}
class LeMonde implements Observer{
    public void notify(String tweet) {
        if(tweet != null && tweet.contains("wine")){
            System.out.println("Today cheese, wine and news! " + tweet);
        }
    }
}
```

You're still missing the crucial part: the subject! Let's define an interface for him:

```
interface Subject{
    void registerObserver(Observer o);
    void notifyObservers(String tweet);
}
```

The subject can register a new observer using the registerObserver method and notify his observers of a tweet with the notifyObservers method. Let's go ahead and implement the Feed class:

```
class Feed implements Subject{

    private final List<Observer> observers = new ArrayList<>();

    public void registerObserver(Observer o) {
        this.observers.add(o);
    }

    public void notifyObservers(String tweet) {
        observers.forEach(o -> o.notify(tweet));
    }
}
```

It's a pretty straightforward implementation: the feed keeps an internal list of observers that it can then notify when a tweet arrives. You can now create a demo application to wire up the subject and observers:

```
Feed f = new Feed();
f.registerObserver(new NYTimes());
f.registerObserver(new Guardian());
f.registerObserver(new LeMonde());
f.notifyObservers("The queen said her favourite book is Java 8 in Action!");
```

Unsurprisingly, *The Guardian* will pick up this tweet!

USING LAMBDA EXPRESSIONS

You may be wondering how lambda expressions are useful with the observer design pattern. Notice that the different classes implementing the `Observer` interface are all providing implementation for a single method: `notify`. They're all just wrapping a piece of behavior to execute when a tweet arrives! Lambda expressions are designed specifically to remove that boilerplate. Instead of instantiating three observer objects explicitly, you can pass a lambda expression directly to represent the behavior to execute:

```
f.registerObserver((String tweet) -> {
        if(tweet != null && tweet.contains("money")){
            System.out.println("Breaking news in NY! " + tweet);
        }
});

f.registerObserver((String tweet) -> {
        if(tweet != null && tweet.contains("queen")){
            System.out.println("Yet another news in London... " + tweet);
        }
});
```

Should you use lambda expressions all the time? The answer is no! In the example we described, lambda expressions work great because the behavior to execute is simple, so they're helpful to remove boilerplate code. But the observers may be more complex: they could have state, define several methods, and the like. In those situations, you should stick with classes.

8.2.4 Chain of responsibility

The chain of responsibility pattern is a common solution to create a chain of processing objects (such as a chain of operations). One processing object may do some work and pass the result to another object, which then also does some work and passes it on to yet another processing object, and so on.

Generally, this pattern is implemented by defining an abstract class representing a processing object that defines a field to keep track of a successor. Once it has finished its work, the processing object hands over its work to its successor. In code it looks like this:

```
public abstract class ProcessingObject<T> {

    protected ProcessingObject<T> successor;
```

```
    public void setSuccessor(ProcessingObject<T> successor){
        this.successor = successor;
    }

    public T handle(T input){
        T r = handleWork(input);
        if(successor != null){
            return successor.handle(r);
        }
        return r;
    }

    abstract protected T handleWork(T input);
}
```

Figure 8.3 illustrates the chain of responsibility pattern in UML.

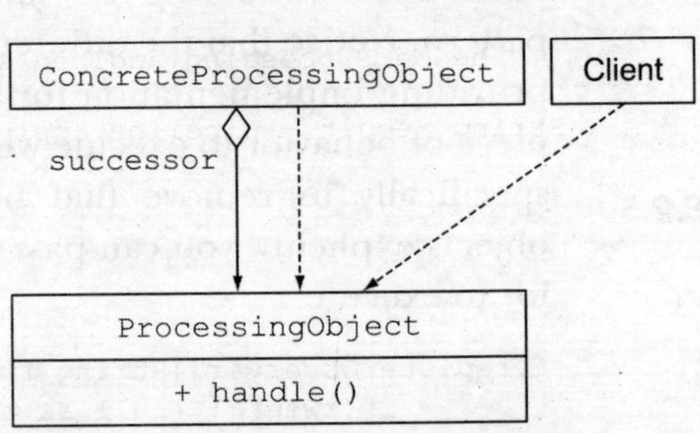

Figure 8.3 The chain of responsibility design pattern

Here you may recognize the template method design pattern, which we discussed in section 8.2.2. The method `handle` provides an outline of how to deal with a piece of work. Different kinds of processing objects can be created by subclassing the class `ProcessingObject` and by providing an implementation for the method `handleWork`.

Let's look at example of how to use this pattern. You can create two processing objects doing some text processing:

```
public class HeaderTextProcessing extends ProcessingObject<String> {
    public String handleWork(String text){
        return "From Raoul, Mario and Alan: " + text;
    }
}
public class SpellCheckerProcessing extends ProcessingObject<String> {
    public String handleWork(String text){
        return text.replaceAll("labda", "lambda");
    }
}
```

Oops, we forgot the 'm' in "lambda"!

You can now connect two processing objects to construct a chain of operations!

```
ProcessingObject<String> p1 = new HeaderTextProcessing();
ProcessingObject<String> p2 = new SpellCheckerProcessing();
p1.setSuccessor(p2);

String result = p1.handle("Aren't labdas really sexy?!!");
System.out.println(result);
```

Chaining two processing objects

Prints "From Raoul, Mario and Alan: Aren't lambdas really sexy?!!"

USING LAMBDA EXPRESSIONS

Wait a minute! This pattern looks like chaining (that is, composing) functions! We discussed how to compose lambda expressions in chapter 3. You can represent the processing objects as an instance of `Function<String, String>` or more precisely a `UnaryOperator<String>`. To chain them you just need to compose these functions by using the `andThen` method!

```
UnaryOperator<String> headerProcessing =
    (String text) -> "From Raoul, Mario and Alan: " + text;      <-- The first processing object.

UnaryOperator<String> spellCheckerProcessing =
    (String text) -> text.replaceAll("labda", "lambda");       <-- The second processing object.

Function<String, String> pipeline =
    headerProcessing.andThen(spellCheckerProcessing);          <-- Compose the two functions, resulting in a chain of operations.
String result = pipeline.apply("Aren't labdas really sexy?!!");
```

8.2.5 Factory

The factory design pattern lets you create objects without exposing the instantiation logic to the client. For example, let's say you're working for a bank and they need a way of creating different financial products: loans, bonds, stocks, and so on.

Typically you'd create a `Factory` class with a method that's responsible for the creation of different objects, as shown here:

```
public class ProductFactory {
    public static Product createProduct(String name){
        switch(name){
            case "loan": return new Loan();
            case "stock": return new Stock();
            case "bond": return new Bond();
            default: throw new RuntimeException("No such product " + name);
        }
    }
}
```

Here, `Loan`, `Stock`, and `Bond` are all subtypes of `Product`. The `createProduct` method could have additional logic to configure each created product. But the benefit is that you can now create these objects without exposing the constructor and the configuration to the client, which makes the creation of products simpler for the client:

```
Product p = ProductFactory.createProduct("loan");
```

USING LAMBDA EXPRESSIONS

You saw in chapter 3 that you can refer to constructors just like you refer to methods, by using method references. For example, here's how to refer to the `Loan` constructor:

```
Supplier<Product> loanSupplier = Loan::new;
Loan loan = loanSupplier.get();
```

Using this technique, you could rewrite the previous code by creating a `Map` that maps a product name to its constructor:

```
final static Map<String, Supplier<Product>> map = new HashMap<>();
static {
    map.put("loan", Loan::new);
    map.put("stock", Stock::new);
    map.put("bond", Bond::new);
}
```

You can now use this `Map` to instantiate different products, just as you did with the factory design pattern:

```
public static Product createProduct(String name){
    Supplier<Product> p = map.get(name);
    if(p != null) return p.get();
    throw new IllegalArgumentException("No such product " + name);
}
```

This is quite a neat way to make use of the Java 8 feature to achieve the same intent as the factory pattern. But this technique doesn't scale very well if the factory method `createProduct` needs to take multiple arguments to pass on to the product constructors! You'd have to provide a different functional interface than a simple `Supplier`.

For example, suppose you want to store constructors for products that take three arguments (two `Integer`s and a `String`); you'd need to create a special functional interface `TriFunction` to support this. As a result, the signature of the `Map` becomes more complex:

```
public interface TriFunction<T, U, V, R>{
    R apply(T t, U u, V v);
}
Map<String, TriFunction<Integer, Integer, String, Product>> map
    = new HashMap<>();
```

You've seen how to write and refactor code using lambda expressions. You'll now see how you can ensure your new code is correct.

8.3 Testing lambdas

You've now sprinkled your code with lambda expressions, and it looks nice and concise. But in most developer jobs you're not paid for writing nice code but for writing code that's correct.

Generally, good software engineering practice involves using *unit testing* to ensure that your program behaves as intended. You write test cases, which assert that small individual parts of your source code are producing the expected results. For example, consider a simple `Point` class for a graphical application:

```
public class Point{
    private final int x;
    private final int y;

    private Point(int x, int y) {
        this.x = x;
        this.y = y;
    }
```

```
    public int getX() { return x; }
    public int getY() { return y; }
    public Point moveRightBy(int x){
        return new Point(this.x + x, this.y);
    }
}
```

The following unit test checks whether the method `moveRightBy` behaves as expected:

```
@Test
public void testMoveRightBy() throws Exception {
    Point p1 = new Point(5, 5);
    Point p2 = p1.moveRightBy(10);
    assertEquals(15, p2.getX());
    assertEquals(5, p2.getY());
}
```

8.3.1 Testing the behavior of a visible lambda

This works nicely because the method `moveRightBy` is public. Therefore, it can be tested inside the test case. But lambdas don't have a name (they're anonymous functions, after all), so it's trickier to test them in your code because you can't refer to them by a name!

Sometime you may have access to a lambda via a field so you can reuse it, and you'd really like to test the logic encapsulated in that lambda. What can you do? You could test the lambda just like when calling methods. For example, let's say you add a static field `compareByXAndThenY` in the `Point` class that gives you access to a `Comparator` object that's generated from method references:

```
public class Point{
    public final static Comparator<Point> compareByXAndThenY =
        comparing(Point::getX).thenComparing(Point::getY);
    …
}
```

Remember that lambda expressions generate an instance of a functional interface. As a result, you can test the behavior of that instance. Here, you can now call the method `compare` on the `Comparator` object `compareByXAndThenY` with different arguments to test that its behavior is as intended:

```
@Test
public void testComparingTwoPoints() throws Exception {
    Point p1 = new Point(10, 15);
    Point p2 = new Point(10, 20);
    int result = Point.compareByXAndThenY.compare(p1 , p2);
    assertEquals(-1, result);
}
```

8.3.2 Focusing on the behavior of the method using a lambda

But the purpose of lambdas is to encapsulate a one-off piece of behavior to be used by another method. In that case you shouldn't make lambda expressions available publicly; they're only an implementation detail. Instead, we argue that you should test the behavior of the method that uses a lambda expression. For example, consider the method moveAllPointsRightBy shown here:

```
public static List<Point> moveAllPointsRightBy(List<Point> points, int x){
    return points.stream()
                 .map(p -> new Point(p.getX() + x, p.getY()))
                 .collect(toList());
}
```

There's no point (pun intended) in testing the lambda `p -> new Point(p.getX() + x, p.getY())`; it's only an implementation detail for the method moveAllPointsRightBy. Rather, you should focus on testing the behavior of the method moveAllPointsRightBy:

```
@Test
public void testMoveAllPointsRightBy() throws Exception{
    List<Point> points =
        Arrays.asList(new Point(5, 5), new Point(10, 5));
    List<Point> expectedPoints =
        Arrays.asList(new Point(15, 5), new Point(20, 5));
    List<Point> newPoints = Point.moveAllPointsRightBy(points, 10);
    assertEquals(expectedPoints, newPoints);
}
```

Note that in the unit test just shown, it's important that the Point class implement the equals method appropriately; otherwise it will rely on the default implementation from Object!

8.3.3 *Pulling complex lambdas into separate methods*

Perhaps you come across a really complicated lambda expression that contains a lot of logic (for example, a technical pricing algorithm with corner cases). What do you do, because you can't refer to the lambda expression inside your test? One strategy is to convert the lambda expression into a method reference (which involves declaring a new regular method), as we explained earlier in section 8.1.3. You can then test the behavior of the new method in your test as you would with any regular method.

8.3.4 *Testing high-order functions*

Methods that take a function as argument or return another function (so-called higher-order functions, explained more in chapter 14) are a little harder to deal with. One thing you can do if a method takes a lambda as argument is test its behavior with different lambdas. For example, you can test the filter method created in chapter 2 with different predicates:

```
@Test
public void testFilter() throws Exception{
    List<Integer> numbers = Arrays.asList(1, 2, 3, 4);
    List<Integer> even = filter(numbers, i -> i % 2 == 0);
    List<Integer> smallerThanThree = filter(numbers, i -> i < 3);
```

```
    assertEquals(Arrays.asList(2, 4), even);
    assertEquals(Arrays.asList(1, 2), smallerThanThree);
}
```

What if the method that needs to be tested returns another function? You can test the behavior of that function by treating it as an instance of a functional interface, as we showed earlier with a `Comparator`.

Unfortunately, not everything works the first time, and your tests may report some errors related to your use of lambda expressions. So we now turn to debugging!

8.4 Debugging

There are two main old-school weapons in a developer's arsenal to debug problematic code:

- Examining the stack trace
- Logging

Lambda expressions and streams can bring new challenges to your typical debugging routine. We explore these in this section.

8.4.1 Examining the stack trace

When your program has stopped (for example, because an exception was thrown), the first thing you need to know is where it stopped and how it got there. This is where stack frames are useful. Each time your program performs a method call, information about the call is generated, including the location of the call in your program, the arguments of the call, and the local variables of the method being called. This information is stored on a stack frame.

When your program fails, you get a *stack trace*, which is a summary of how your program got to that failure, stack frame by stack frame. In other words, you get a list of valuable method calls up to when the failure appeared. This helps you understand how the problem occurred.

LAMBDAS AND STACK TRACES

Unfortunately, due to the fact that lambda expressions don't have names, stack traces can be slightly puzzling. Consider the following simple code made to fail on purpose:

```
import java.util.*;

public class Debugging{
    public static void main(String[] args) {
        List<Point> points = Arrays.asList(new Point(12, 2), null);
        points.stream().map(p -> p.getX()).forEach(System.out::println);
    }
}
```

Running it will produce a stack trace along the lines of this:

```
Exception in thread "main" java.lang.NullPointerException
    at Debugging.lambda$main$0(Debugging.java:6)
    at Debugging$$Lambda$5/284720968.apply(Unknown Source)
```

What does $0 in this line mean?

```
    at java.util.stream.ReferencePipeline$3$1.accept(ReferencePipeline
        .java:193)
    at java.util.Spliterators$ArraySpliterator.forEachRemaining(Spliterators
        .java:948)
...
```

Yuck! What's going on? Of course the program will fail, because the second element of the list of points is `null`. You then try to process a `null` reference. Because the error occurs in a stream pipeline, the whole sequence of method calls that make a stream pipeline work is exposed to you. But notice that the stack trace produces the following cryptic lines:

```
at Debugging.lambda$main$0(Debugging.java:6)
    at Debugging$$Lambda$5/284720968.apply(Unknown Source)
```

They mean that the error occurred inside a lambda expression. Unfortunately, because lambda expressions don't have a name, the compiler has to make up a name to refer to them. In this case it's `lambda$main$0`, which isn't very intuitive. This can be problematic if you have large classes containing several lambda expressions.

Even if you use method references, it's still possible that the stack won't show you the name of the method you used. Changing the previous lambda `p -> p.getX()` to the method reference `Point::getX` will also result in a problematic stack trace:

```
points.stream().map(Point::getX).forEach(System.out::println);
Exception in thread "main" java.lang.NullPointerException
    at Debugging$$Lambda$5/284720968.apply(Unknown Source)       <-- What does this line mean?
    at java.util.stream.ReferencePipeline$3$1.accept(ReferencePipeline
        .java:193)
...
```

Note that if a method reference refers to a method declared in the same class as where it's used, then it will appear in the stack trace. For instance, in the following example

```
import java.util.*;

public class Debugging{
    public static void main(String[] args) {
        List<Integer> numbers = Arrays.asList(1, 2, 3);
        numbers.stream().map(Debugging::divideByZero).forEach(System
            .out::println);
    }

    public static int divideByZero(int n){
        return n / 0;
    }
}
```

the method `divideByZero` is reported correctly in the stack trace:

```
Exception in thread "main" java.lang.ArithmeticException: / by zero
    at Debugging.divideByZero(Debugging.java:10)       <-- divideByZero appears in the stack trace!
    at Debugging$$Lambda$1/999966131.apply(Unknown Source)
    at java.util.stream.ReferencePipeline$3$1.accept(ReferencePipeline
        .java:193)
...
```

In general, keep in mind that stack traces involving lambda expressions may be more difficult to understand. This is an area where the compiler can be improved in a future version of Java.

8.4.2 *Logging information*

Let's say you're trying to debug a pipeline of operations in a stream. What can you do? You could use `forEach` to print or log the result of a stream as follows:

```
List<Integer> numbers = Arrays.asList(2, 3, 4, 5);

numbers.stream()
        .map(x -> x + 17)
        .filter(x -> x % 2 == 0)
        .limit(3)
        .forEach(System.out::println);
```

It will produce the following output:

```
20
22
```

Unfortunately, once you call `forEach`, the whole stream is consumed. What would be really useful is to understand what each operation (`map`, `filter`, `limit`) produces in the pipeline of a stream.

This is where the stream operation `peek` can help. Its purpose is to execute an action on each element of a stream as it's consumed. But it doesn't consume the whole stream like `forEach` does; it forwards the element it performed an action on to the next operation in the pipeline. Figure 8.4 illustrates the `peek` operation.

In the following code, you use `peek` to print the intermediate value before and after each operation in the stream pipeline:

```
List<Integer> result =
  numbers.stream()
         .peek(x -> System.out.println("from stream: " + x))
         .map(x -> x + 17)
         .peek(x -> System.out.println("after map: " + x))
         .filter(x -> x % 2 == 0)
         .peek(x -> System.out.println("after filter: " + x))
         .limit(3)
         .peek(x -> System.out.println("after limit: " + x))
         .collect(toList());
```

Print the current element consumed from the source.

Print the result of the `map` operation.

Print the number selected after the `filter` operation.

Print the number selected after the `limit` operation.

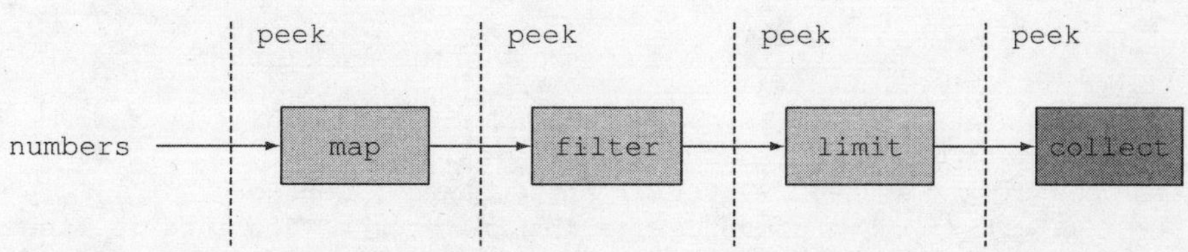

Figure 8.4 Examining values flowing in a stream pipeline with `peek`

This will produce a useful output at each step of the pipeline:

```
from stream: 2
after map: 19
from stream: 3
after map: 20
after filter: 20
after limit: 20
from stream: 4
after map: 21
from stream: 5
after map: 22
after filter: 22
after limit: 22
```

8.5 Summary

Following are the key concepts you should take away from this chapter:

- Lambda expressions can make your code more readable and flexible.
- Consider converting anonymous classes to lambda expressions, but be wary of subtle semantic differences such as the meaning of the keyword `this` and shadowing of variables.
- Method references can make your code more readable compared to lambda expressions.
- Consider converting iterative collection processing to use the Streams API.
- Lambda expressions can help remove boilerplate code associated with several object-oriented design patterns such as strategy, template method, observer, chain of responsibility, and factory.
- Lambda expressions can be unit tested, but in general you should focus on testing the behavior of the methods where the lambda expressions appear.
- Consider extracting complex lambda expressions into regular methods.
- Lambda expressions can make stack traces less readable.
- The `peek` method of a stream is useful to log intermediate values as they flow past at certain points in a stream pipeline.

9 Default methods

This chapter covers

- What default methods are
- Evolving APIs in a compatible way
- Usage patterns for default methods
- Resolution rules

Traditionally, a Java interface groups related methods together into a contract. Any class that implements an interface *must* provide an implementation for each method defined by the interface or inherit the implementation from a superclass. But this causes a problem when library designers need to update an interface to add a new method. Indeed, existing concrete classes (which may not be under their control) need to be modified to reflect the new interface contract. This is particularly problematic because the Java 8 API introduces many new methods on existing interfaces, such as the `sort` method on the `List` interface that you used in previous chapters. Imagine all the angry maintainers of alternative collection frameworks such as Guava and Apache Commons who now need to modify all the classes implementing the `List` interface to provide an implementation for the `sort` method too!

But don't worry. Java 8 introduces a new mechanism to tackle this problem. It might sound surprising, but interfaces in Java 8 can now declare methods with implementation code; this can happen in two ways. First, Java 8 allows *static methods* inside interfaces. Second, Java 8 introduces a new feature called *default methods* that allows you to provide a default implementation for methods in an interface. In other words, interfaces can provide concrete implementation for methods. As a result, existing classes implementing an interface will automatically inherit the default implementations if they don't provide one explicitly. This allows you to evolve interfaces non-intrusively. You've been using several default methods all along. Two examples you've seen are `sort` in the `List` interface and `stream` in the `Collection` interface.

The `sort` method in the `List` interface you saw in chapter 1 is new to Java 8 and is defined as follows:

```
default void sort(Comparator<? super E> c){
    Collections.sort(this, c);
}
```

Note the new `default` modifier before the return type. This is how you can tell that a method is a default method. Here the `sort` method calls the `Collections.sort` method to perform the sorting. Thanks to this new method, you can sort a list by calling the method directly:

```
List<Integer> numbers = Arrays.asList(3, 5, 1, 2, 6);
numbers.sort(Comparator.naturalOrder());
```

`sort` is a default method in the `List` interface.

There's something else that's new in this code. Notice that you call the `Comparator.naturalOrder` method. It's a new static method in the `Comparator` interface that returns a `Comparator` object to sort the elements in natural order (the standard alphanumerical sort).

The `stream` method in `Collection` you saw in chapter 4 looks like this:

```
default Stream<E> stream() {
    return StreamSupport.stream(spliterator(), false);
}
```

Here the `stream` method, which you used extensively in previous chapters to process collections, calls the `StreamSupport.stream` method to return a stream. Notice how the body of the `stream` method is calling the method `spliterator`, which is also a default method of the `Collection` interface.

Wow! Are interfaces like abstract classes now? Yes and no; there are fundamental differences, which we explain in this chapter. But more important, why should you care about default methods? The main users of default methods are library designers. As we explain later, default methods were introduced to evolve libraries such as the Java API in a compatible way, as illustrated in figure 9.1.

In a nutshell, adding a method to an interface is the source of many problems; existing classes implementing the interface need to be changed to provide an implementation for the method. If you're in control of the interface and all the implementations,

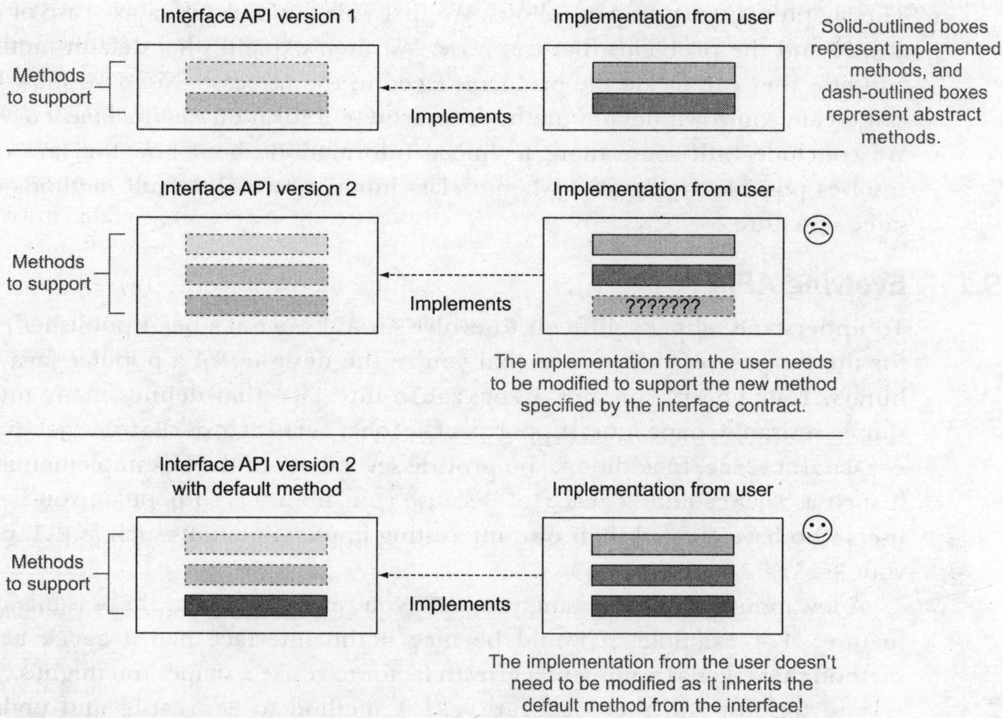

Figure 9.1 Adding a method to an interface

then it's not too bad. But this is often not the case. This is the motivation for default methods: they let classes automatically inherit a default implementation from an interface.

So if you're a library designer, this chapter is important because default methods provide a means to evolve interfaces without causing modifications to existing implementations. Also, as we explain later in the chapter, default methods can help structure your programs by providing a flexible mechanism for multiple inheritance of behavior: a class can inherit default methods from several interfaces. Therefore, you may still be interested in finding out about default methods even if you're not a library designer.

> **Static methods and interfaces**
>
> A common pattern in Java is to define both an interface and a utility companion class defining many static methods for working with instances of the interface. For example, `Collections` is a companion class to deal with `Collection` objects. Now that static methods can exist inside interfaces, such utility classes in your code can go away and their static methods can be moved inside an interface. These companion classes will remain in the Java API in order to preserve backward compatibility.

The chapter is structured as follows. We first walk you through a use case of evolving an API and the problems that can arise. We then explain what default methods are and how they can tackle the problems faced in the use case. Next, we show how you can create your own default methods to achieve a form of *multiple inheritance* in Java. We conclude with some more technical information about how the Java compiler resolves possible ambiguities when a class inherits several default methods with the same signature.

9.1 Evolving APIs

To understand why it's difficult to evolve an API once it's been published, let's say for the purpose of this section that you're the designer of a popular Java drawing library. Your library contains a `Resizable` interface that defines many methods a simple resizable shape must support: `setHeight`, `setWidth`, `getHeight`, `getWidth`, and `setAbsoluteSize`. In addition, you provide several out-of-the-box implementations for it such as `Square` and `Rectangle`. Because your library is so popular, you have some users who have created their own interesting implementations such as `Ellipse` using your `Resizable` interface.

A few months after releasing your API, you realize that `Resizable` is missing some features. For example, it would be nice if the interface had a `setRelativeSize` method that takes as argument a growth factor to resize a shape. You might say that it's easy to fix: just add the `setRelativeSize` method to `Resizable` and update your implementations of `Square` and `Rectangle`. Well, not so fast! What about all your users who created their own implementations of the `Resizable` interface? Unfortunately, you don't have access to and can't change their classes that implement `Resizable`. This is the same problem that the Java library designers face when they need to evolve the Java API. Let's look at an example in detail to see the consequences of modifying an interface that's already been published.

9.1.1 API version 1

The first version of your `Resizable` interface has the following methods:

```
public interface Resizable extends Drawable{
    int getWidth();
    int getHeight();
    void setWidth(int width);
    void setHeight(int height);
    void setAbsoluteSize(int width, int height);
}
```

USER IMPLEMENTATION

One of your most loyal users decides to create his own implementation of `Resizable` called `Ellipse`:

```
public class Ellipse implements Resizable {
    …
}
```

He's created a game that processes different types of Resizable shapes (including his own Ellipse):

```
public class Game{
    public static void main(String…args){
        List<Resizable> resizableShapes =
            Arrays.asList(new Square(), new Rectangle(), new Ellipse());
        Utils.paint(resizableShapes);
    }
}
public class Utils{
    public static void paint(List<Resizable> l){
        l.forEach(r -> {
                        r.setAbsoluteSize(42, 42);
                        r.draw();
                      });
    }
}
```

A list of shapes that are resizable

Calling the `setAbsoluteSize` method on each shape

9.1.2 API version 2

After your library has been in use for a few months, you receive many requests to update your implementations of Resizable: Square, Rectangle, and so on to support the setRelativeSize method. So you come up with version 2 of your API, as shown here and illustrated in figure 9.2:

```
public interface Resizable {
    int getWidth();
    int getHeight();
    void setWidth(int width);
    void setHeight(int height);
    void setAbsoluteSize(int width, int height);
    void setRelativeSize(int wFactor, int hFactor);
}
```

Adding a new method for API version 2

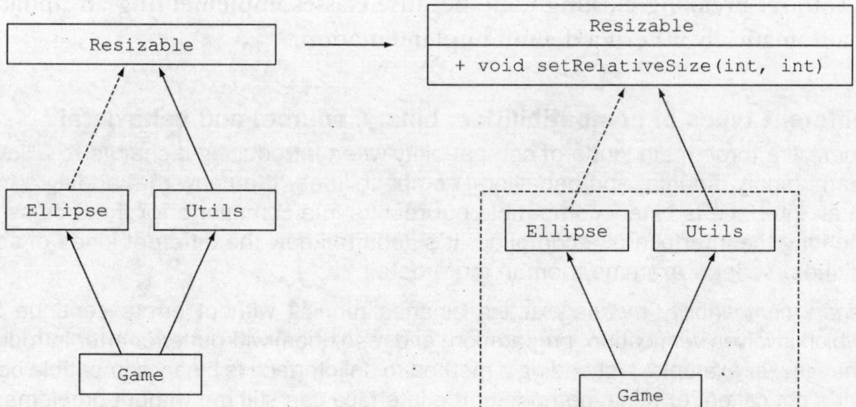

Figure 9.2 Evolving an API by adding a method to `Resizable`. Recompiling the application produces errors because it depends on the `Resizable` interface.

PROBLEMS FOR YOUR USERS

This update of `Resizable` creates a few problems. First, the interface now requires an implementation of `setRelativeSize`. But the `Ellipse` implementation your user created doesn't implement the method `setRelativeSize`. Adding a new method to an interface is *binary compatible*; this means existing class file implementations will still run without the implementation of the new method, if there's no attempt to recompile them. In this case the game will still run (unless it's recompiled) despite adding the method `setRelativeSize` to the `Resizable` interface. Nonetheless, the user could modify the method `Utils.paint` in his game to use the method `setRelativeSize` because the `paint` method expects a list of `Resizable` objects as argument. If an `Ellipse` object is passed, an error will be thrown at run-time because the `setRelativeSize` method isn't implemented:

```
Exception in thread "main" java.lang.AbstractMethodError:
    lambdasinaction.chap9.Ellipse.setRelativeSize(II)V
```

Second, if the user tries to rebuild his entire application (including `Ellipse`), he'll get the following compile error:

```
lambdasinaction/chap9/Ellipse.java:6: error: Ellipse is not abstract and does
    not override abstract method setRelativeSize(int,int) in Resizable
```

Consequently, updating a published API creates backward incompatibilities. This is why evolving existing APIs, such as the official Java Collections API, causes problems for users of the APIs. There are alternatives to evolving an API, but they're poor choices. For example, you could create a separate version of your API and maintain both the old and the new versions, but this is inconvenient for several reasons. First, it's more complex for you to maintain as a library designer. Second, your users may have to use both versions of your API in the same codebase, which impacts memory space and loading time because more class files are required for their projects.

This is where default methods come to the rescue. They let library designers evolve APIs without breaking existing code because classes implementing an updated interface automatically inherit a default implementation.

> **Different types of compatibilities: binary, source, and behavioral**
>
> There are three main kinds of compatibility when introducing a change to a Java program: binary, source, and behavioral compatibilities.[1] You saw that adding a method to an interface is binary compatible but results in a compiler error if the class implementing the interface is recompiled. It's good to know the different kinds of compatibilities, so let's examine them in more detail.
>
> *Binary compatibility* means existing binaries running without errors continue to link (which involves verification, preparation, and resolution) without error after introducing a change. For example, just adding a method to an interface is binary compatible because if it's not called, existing methods of the interface can still run without problems.

[1] See https://blogs.oracle.com/darcy/entry/kinds_of_compatibility.

> ***(continued)***
>
> In its simplest form, *source compatibility* means an existing program will still compile after introducing a change. For example, adding a method to an interface isn't source compatible; existing implementations won't recompile because they need to implement the new method.
>
> Finally, *behavioral compatibility* means running a program after a change with the same inputs results in the same behavior. For example, adding a method to an interface is behavioral compatible because the method is never called in the program (or it gets overridden by an implementation).

9.2 Default methods in a nutshell

You've seen how adding methods to a published API disrupts existing implementations. *Default methods* are a new feature added in Java 8 to help evolve APIs in a compatible way. An interface can now contain method signatures for which an implementing class doesn't provide an implementation. So who implements them? The missing method bodies are given as part of the interface (hence default implementations) rather than in the implementing class.

So how do you recognize a default method? It's very simple. It starts with a `default` modifier and contains a body just like a method declared in a class. For example, in the context of a collection library, you could define an interface `Sized` with one abstract method `size` and a default method `isEmpty` as follows:

```
public interface Sized {
    int size();
    default boolean isEmpty() {          <-- A default method
        return size() == 0;
    }
}
```

Now any class that implements the `Sized` interface will automatically inherit the implementation of `isEmpty`. Consequently, adding a method to an interface with a default implementation isn't a source incompatibility.

Let's go back to our initial example of the Java drawing library and your game. Concretely, to evolve your library in a compatible way (which means the users of your library don't have to modify all their classes that implement `Resizable`), use a default method and provide a default implementation for `setRelativeSize`:

```
default void setRelativeSize(int wFactor, int hFactor){
    setAbsoluteSize(getWidth() / wFactor, getHeight() / hFactor);
}
```

Because interfaces can now have methods with implementation, does that mean multiple inheritance has arrived in Java? What happens if an implementing class also defines the same method signature or if default methods can be overridden? Don't worry about these issues for now; there are a few rules to follow and mechanisms available for you to deal with these issues. We explore them in detail in section 9.5.

You may have guessed that default methods are used extensively in the Java 8 API. You saw in the introduction of this chapter that the `stream` method in the `Collection` interface we used extensively in previous chapters is a default method. The `sort` method in the `List` interface is also a default method. Many of the functional interfaces we presented in chapter 3 such as `Predicate`, `Function`, and `Comparator` also introduced new default methods such as `Predicate.and` or `Function.andThen` (remember, a functional interface contains only one abstract method; default methods are non-abstract methods).

Abstract classes vs. interfaces in Java 8

So what's the difference between an abstract class and an interface? They both can contain abstract methods and methods with a body.

First, a class can extend only *from one* abstract class, but a class can implement *multiple* interfaces.

Second, an abstract class can enforce a common state through instance variables (fields). An interface can't have instance variables.

To put your knowledge of default methods to use, have a go at Quiz 9.1.

Quiz 9.1: removeIf

For this quiz, pretend you're one of the masters of the Java language and API. You've received many requests for a `removeIf` method to use on `ArrayList`, `TreeSet`, `LinkedList`, and all other collections. The `removeIf` method should remove all elements from a collection that match a given predicate. Your task in this quiz is to figure out the best way to enhance the Collections API with this new method.

Answer:

What's the most disruptive way to enhance the `Collections` API? You could copy and paste the implementation of `removeIf` in each concrete class of the Collections API, but that would be a crime to the Java community. What else can you do? Well, all of the `Collection` classes implement an interface called `java.util.Collection`. Great; can you add a method there? Yes; you just learned that default methods are a way to add implementations inside an interface in a source-compatible way. And all classes implementing `Collection` (including classes from your users that aren't part of the Collections API) will be able to use the implementation of `removeIf`. The code solution for `removeIf` is as follows (which is roughly the implementation in the official Java 8 Collections API). It's a default method inside the `Collection` interface:

```
default boolean removeIf(Predicate<? super E> filter) {
    boolean removed = false;
    Iterator<E> each = iterator();
```

(continued)

```
    while(each.hasNext()) {
        if(filter.test(each.next())) {
            each.remove();
            removed = true;
        }
    }
    return removed;
}
```

9.3 Usage patterns for default methods

You've seen how default methods can be useful to evolve a library in a compatible way. Is there anything else you can do with them? You can *create your own interfaces that have default methods* too. You may want to do this for two use cases that we explore in this section: *optional methods* and *multiple inheritance of behavior.*

9.3.1 Optional methods

It's likely you've come across classes that implement an interface but leave empty some method implementations. Take, for example, the `Iterator` interface. It defines `hasNext` and `next` but also the `remove` method. Prior to Java 8, `remove` was often ignored because the user decided not to use that capability. As a result, many classes implementing `Iterator` have an empty implementation for `remove`, which results in unnecessary boilerplate code.

With default methods, you can provide a default implementation for such methods, so concrete classes don't need to explicitly provide an empty implementation. For example, the `Iterator` interface in Java 8 provides a default implementation for `remove` as follows:

```
interface Iterator<T> {
    boolean hasNext();
    T next();
    default void remove() {
        throw new UnsupportedOperationException();
    }
}
```

Consequently, you can reduce boilerplate code. Any class implementing the `Iterator` interface doesn't need to declare an empty `remove` method anymore to ignore it, because it now has a default implementation.

9.3.2 Multiple inheritance of behavior

Default methods enable something that wasn't possible in an elegant way before: *multiple inheritance of behavior.* This is the ability of a class to reuse code from multiple places, as illustrated in figure 9.3.

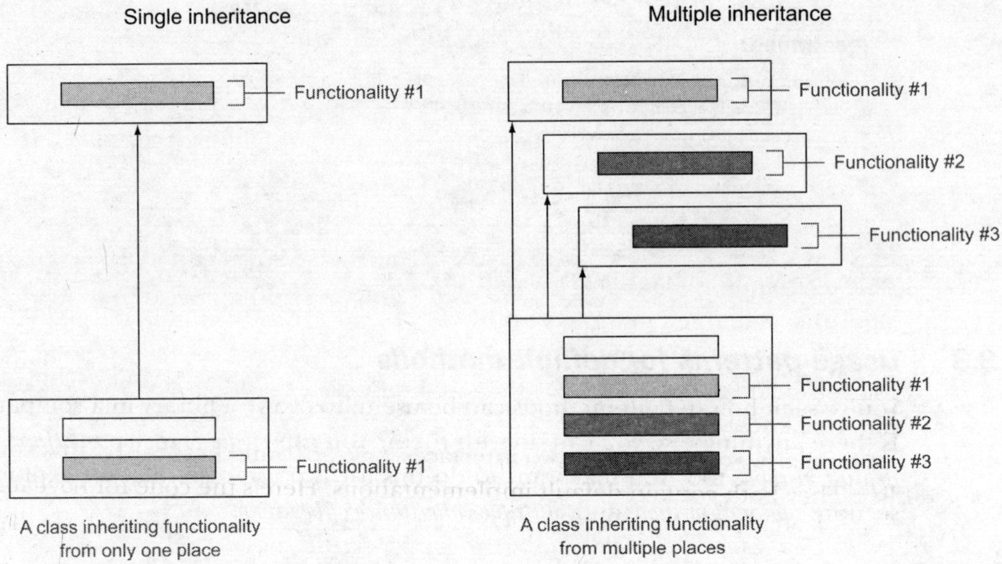

Figure 9.3 Single inheritance vs. multiple inheritance

Remember that classes in Java can inherit from only one other class, but classes have always been allowed to implement multiple interfaces. To confirm, here's how the class ArrayList is defined in the Java API:

```
public class ArrayList<E> extends AbstractList<E>          <- Inherits from one class
    implements List<E>, RandomAccess, Cloneable,
               Serializable, Iterable<E>, Collection<E> {  <- Implements six interfaces
}
```

MULTIPLE INHERITANCE OF TYPES

Here, ArrayList is extending one class and implementing six interfaces. As a result, an ArrayList is a direct *subtype* of seven types: AbstractList, List, RandomAccess, Cloneable, Serializable, Iterable, and Collection. So in a sense we already have multiple inheritance of types.

Because interface methods can have implementations in Java 8, classes can inherit behavior (implementation code) from multiple interfaces. Let's explore an example to see how you can use this capability to your benefit. Keeping interfaces minimal and orthogonal lets you achieve great reuse and composition of behavior inside your codebase.

MINIMAL INTERFACES WITH ORTHOGONAL FUNCTIONALITIES

Let's say you need to define several shapes with different characteristics for the game you're creating. Some shapes should be resizable but not rotatable; some should be rotatable and moveable but not resizable. How can you achieve great code reuse?

You can start by defining a standalone Rotatable interface with two abstract methods, setRotationAngle and getRotationAngle. The interface also declares a default rotateBy method that can be implemented using the setRotationAngle and getRotationAngle methods as follows:

```
public interface Rotatable {
    void setRotationAngle(int angleInDegrees);
    int getRotationAngle();
    default void rotateBy(int angleInDegrees){      <-- A default implementation for the method rotateBy
        setRotationAngle((getRotationAngle () + angle) % 360);
    }
}
```

This technique is somewhat related to the template design pattern where a skeleton algorithm is defined in terms of other methods that need to be implemented.

Now, any class that implements Rotatable will need to provide an implementation for setRotationAngle and getRotationAngle but will inherit the default implementation of rotateBy for free.

Similarly, you can define two interfaces, Moveable and Resizable, that you saw earlier. They both contain default implementations. Here's the code for Moveable:

```
public interface Moveable {
    int getX();
    int getY();
    void setX(int x);
    void setY(int y);

    default void moveHorizontally(int distance){
        setX(getX() + distance);
    }

    default void moveVertically(int distance){
        setY(getY() + distance);
    }
}
```

And here's the code for Resizable:

```
public interface Resizable {
    int getWidth();
    int getHeight();
    void setWidth(int width);
    void setHeight(int height);
    void setAbsoluteSize(int width, int height);

    default void setRelativeSize(int wFactor, int hFactor){
        setAbsoluteSize(getWidth() / wFactor, getHeight() / hFactor);
    }
}
```

COMPOSING INTERFACES

You can now create different concrete classes for your game by composing these interfaces. For example, monsters can be moveable, rotatable, and resizable:

```
public class Monster implements Rotatable, Moveable, Resizable {
...                     <-- Needs to provide implementations for all abstract methods but not the default methods
}
```

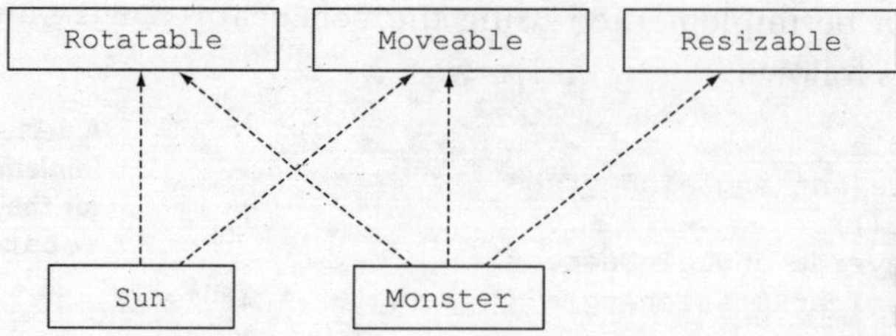

Figure 9.4 Multiple behavior composition

The Monster class will automatically inherit the default methods from the Rotatable, Moveable, and Resizable interfaces. In this case, Monster inherits the implementations of rotateBy, moveHorizontally, moveVertically, and setRelativeSize.

You can now call the different methods directly:

```
Monster m = new Monster();      <-- Constructor internally sets the coordinates, height, width, and default angle
m.rotateBy(180);                <-- Calling rotateBy from Rotatable
m.moveVertically(10);           <-- Calling moveVertically from Moveable
```

Say you now need to declare another class that's moveable and rotatable but not resizable, such as the sun. There's no need to copy and paste code; you can reuse the default implementations from the Moveable and Rotatable interfaces as shown here. Figure 9.4 illustrates the UML diagram of this scenario:

```
public class Sun implements Moveable, Rotatable {
...                                                   <-- Needs to provide implementations for all abstract methods but not the default methods
}
```

Here's another advantage of defining simple interfaces with default implementations like the ones for your game. Let's say you need to modify the implementation of moveVertically to make it more efficient. You can now change its implementation directly in the Moveable interface, and all classes implementing it will automatically inherit the code (provided they didn't implement the method themselves)!

> **Inheritance considered harmful**
>
> Inheritance shouldn't be your answer to everything when it comes down to reusing code. For example, inheriting from a class that has 100 methods and fields just to reuse one method is a bad idea, because it adds unnecessary complexity. You'd be better off using *delegation*: create a method that calls directly the method of the class you need via a member variable. This is why you'll sometime find classes that are declared "final" intentionally: they can't be inherited from to prevent this kind of anti-pattern or have their core behavior messed with. Note that sometimes final classes have a place; for example, String is final because we don't want anybody to be able to interfere with such core functionality.
>
> The same idea is applicable to interfaces with default methods. By keeping your interface minimal, you can achieve greater composition because you can select only the implementations you need.

You've seen that default methods are useful for many usage patterns. But here's some food for thought: what if a class implements two interfaces that have the same default method signature? Which method is the class allowed to use? We explore this problem in the next section.

9.4 Resolution rules

As you know, in Java a class can extend only one parent class but implement multiple interfaces. With the introduction of default methods in Java 8, there's the possibility of a class inheriting more than one method with the same signature. Which version of the method should be used? Such conflicts will probably be quite rare in practice, but when they do occur there must be rules that specify how to deal with the conflict. This section explains how the Java compiler resolves such potential conflicts. We aim to answer questions such as "In the code that follows, which `hello` method is `C` calling?" Note that the examples that follow are intended to explore problematic scenarios; it doesn't mean such scenarios will happen frequently in practice:

```
public interface A {
    default void hello() {
        System.out.println("Hello from A");
    }
}
public interface B extends A {
    default void hello() {
        System.out.println("Hello from B");
    }
}

public class C implements B, A {
    public static void main(String... args) {
        new C().hello();                          <-- What gets printed?
    }
}
```

In addition, you may have heard of the diamond problem in C++ where a class can inherit two methods with the same signature. Which one gets chosen? Java 8 provides resolution rules to solve this issue too. Read on!

9.4.1 Three resolution rules to know

There are three rules to follow when a class inherits a method with the same signature from multiple places (such as another class or interface):

1. Classes always win. A method declaration in the class or a superclass takes priority over any default method declaration.
2. Otherwise, sub-interfaces win: the method with the same signature in the most specific default-providing interface is selected. (If `B` extends `A`, `B` is more specific than `A`).
3. Finally, if the choice is still ambiguous, the class inheriting from multiple interfaces has to explicitly select which default method implementation to use by overriding it and calling the desired method explicitly.

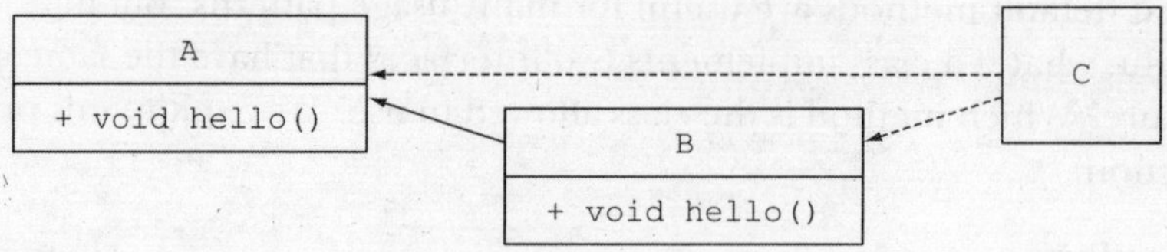

Figure 9.5 The most specific default-providing interface wins.

We promise, these are the only rules you need to know! Let's now look at some examples.

9.4.2 *Most specific default-providing interface wins*

Let's revisit our example from the beginning of this section where `C` implements both `B` and `A`, which define a default method called `hello`. In addition, `B` extends `A`. Figure 9.5 provides a UML diagram for the scenario.

Which declaration of the `hello` method will the compiler use? Rule 2 says that the method with the most specific default-providing interface is selected. Because `B` is more specific than `A`, the `hello` from `B` is selected. Consequently the program will print "Hello from B."

Now, consider what would happen if `C` were inheriting from `D` as follows (illustrated in figure 9.6):

```
public class D implements A{ }

public class C extends D implements B, A {
    public static void main(String... args) {
        new C().hello();
    }
}
```

What gets printed?

Rule 1 says that a method declaration in the class takes priority. But `D` doesn't override `hello`; it implements interface `A`. Consequently, it has a default method from interface `A`. Rule 2 says that if there are no methods in the class or superclass, then the method with the most specific default-providing interface is selected. The compiler therefore has the choice between the `hello` method from interface `A` and the `hello` method from interface `B`. Because `B` is more specific, the program will print "Hello from B" again. To check your understanding of the resolution rules, try Quiz 9.2.

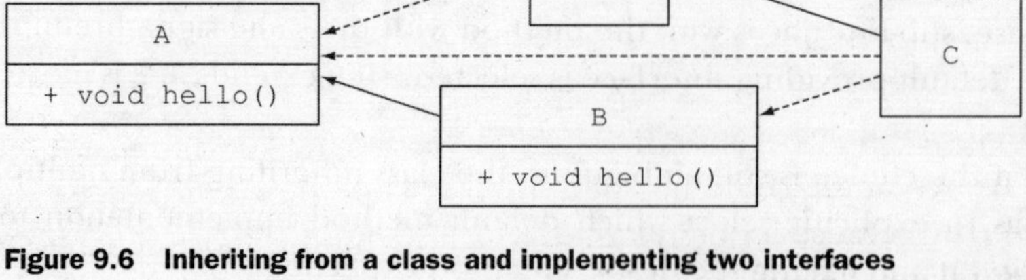

Figure 9.6 Inheriting from a class and implementing two interfaces

Quiz 9.2: Remember the resolution rules

For this quiz, let's reuse the previous example except that D explicitly overrides the hello method from A. What do you think will get printed?

```
public class D implements A{
    void hello(){
        System.out.println("Hello from D");
    }
}

public class C extends D implements B, A {
    public static void main(String... args) {
        new C().hello();
    }
}
```

Answer:

The program will print "Hello from D" because a method declaration from a superclass has priority, as stated by rule 1.

Note that if D was declared as follows,

```
public abstract class D implements A {
    public abstract void hello();
}
```

then C would be forced to implement the method hello itself, even though default implementations exist elsewhere in the hierarchy.

9.4.3 Conflicts and explicit disambiguation

The examples you've seen so far could be resolved using the first two resolution rules. Let's say now that B doesn't extend A anymore (illustrated in figure 9.7):

```
public interface A {
    void hello() {
        System.out.println("Hello from A");
    }
}

public interface B {
    void hello() {
        System.out.println("Hello from B");
    }
}

public class C implements B, A { }
```

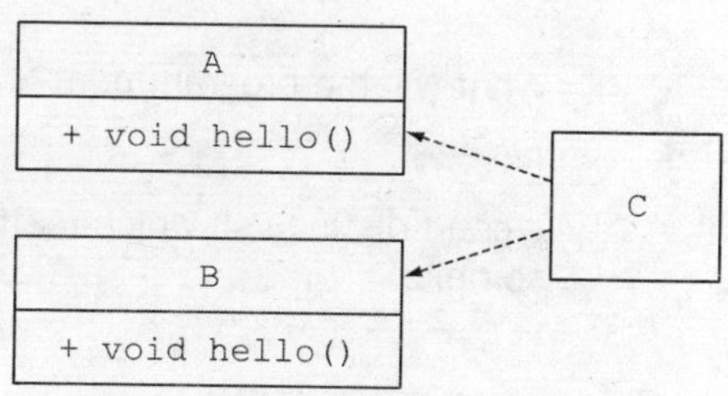

Figure 9.7 Implementing two interfaces

Rule 2 doesn't help you now because there's no more-specific interface to select. Both hello methods from A and B could be valid options. Thus, the Java compiler will produce a compile error because it doesn't know which method is more suitable: "Error: class C inherits unrelated defaults for hello() from types B and A."

RESOLVING THE CONFLICT

There aren't many solutions to resolve the conflict between the two possible valid methods; you have to explicitly decide which method declaration you want `C` to use. To do this, you can override the `hello` method in class `C` and then in its body explicitly call the method you wish to use. Java 8 introduces the new syntax `X.super.m(...)` where `X` is the superinterface whose method `m` you want to call. For example, if you want `C` to use the default method from `B`, it looks like this:

```
public class C implements B, A {
    void hello(){
        B.super.hello();        <-- Explicitly choosing to call the
    }                               method from interface B
}
```

Have a go at Quiz 9.3 to investigate another related tricky case.

> **Quiz 9.3: Almost the same signature**
>
> For this quiz, assume interfaces `A` and `B` are declared as follows:
>
> ```
> public interface A{
>     default Number getNumber(){
>         return 10;
>     }
> }
> public interface B{
>     default Integer getNumber(){
>         return 42;
>     }
> }
> ```
>
> And class `C` is declared as follows:
>
> ```
> public class C implements B, A {
>     public static void main(String... args) {
>         System.out.println(new C().getNumber());
>     }
> }
> ```
>
> What will the program print?
>
> Answer:
>
> `C` can't distinguish which method of `A` or `B` is more specific. This is why class `C` won't compile.

9.4.4 *Diamond problem*

Let's consider a final scenario that sends shivers through the C++ community:

```
public interface A{
    default void hello(){
        System.out.println("Hello from A");
    }
}
```

```
public interface B extends A { }

public interface C extends A { }

public class D implements B, C {
    public static void main(String... args) {
        new D().hello();
    }
}
```

What gets printed?

Figure 9.8 illustrates the UML diagram for this scenario. It's called a *diamond problem* because the shape of the diagram resembles a diamond. So what default method declaration does D inherit—the one from B or the one from C? There's actually only one method declaration to choose from. Only A declares a default method. Because the interface is a superinterface of D, the code will print "Hello from A."

Now what happens if B also has a default hello method with the same signature? Rule 2 says that you select the most specific default-providing interface. Because B is more specific than A, the default method declaration from B will be selected. If both B and C declare a hello method with the same signature, you have a conflict and need to solve it explicitly, as we showed earlier.

Just as a side note, you may be wondering what happens if you add an abstract hello method (one that's not default) in interface C as follows (still no methods in A and B):

```
public interface C extends A {
    void hello();
}
```

The new abstract hello method in C takes priority over the default hello method from interface A because C is more specific. Therefore, class D now needs to provide an explicit implementation for hello; otherwise the program won't compile.

C++ diamond problem

The diamond problem is more complicated in C++. First, C++ allows multiple inheritance of classes. By default, if a class D inherits from classes B and C, and classes B and C both inherit from A, then class D will actually have access to a copy of a B object and a copy of a C object. As a result, uses of methods from A have to be explicitly qualified: are they coming from B or are they coming from C? In addition, classes have state, so modifying member variables from B isn't reflected on the copy of the C object.

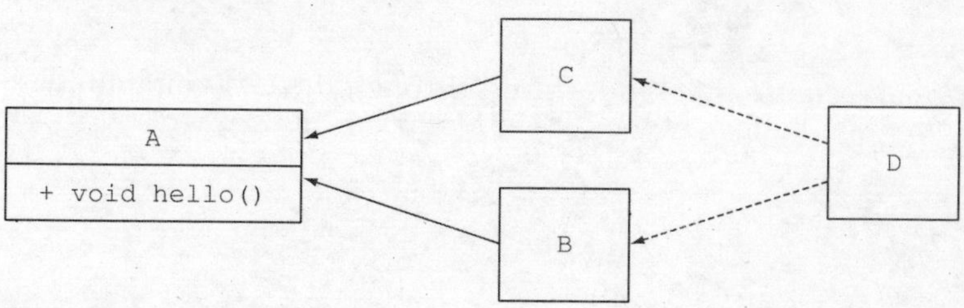

Figure 9.8 The diamond problem

You've seen that the default method's resolution mechanism is pretty simple if a class inherits from several methods with the same signature. You just need to follow three rules systematically to solve all possible conflicts:

- First, an explicit method declaration in the class or a superclass takes priority over any default method declaration.
- Otherwise, the method with the same signature in the most specific default-providing interface is selected.
- Finally, if there's still a conflict, you have to explicitly override the default methods and choose which one your class should use.

9.5 Summary

Following are the key concepts you should take away from this chapter:

- Interfaces in Java 8 can have implementation code through default methods and static methods.
- Default methods start with a `default` keyword and contain a body like class methods do.
- Adding an abstract method to a published interface is a source incompatibility.
- Default methods help library designers evolve APIs in a backward-compatible way.
- Default methods can be used for creating optional methods and multiple inheritance of behavior.
- There are resolution rules to resolve conflicts when a class inherits from several default methods with the same signature.
- A method declaration in the class or a superclass takes priority over any default method declaration. Otherwise, the method with the same signature in the most specific default-providing interface is selected.
- When two methods are equally specific, a class can explicitly override a method and select which one to call.

10 Using Optional as a better alternative to null

This chapter covers

- What's wrong with `null` references and why you should avoid them
- From `null` to `Optional`: rewriting your domain model in a null-safe way
- Putting optionals to work: removing null checks from your code
- Different ways to read the value possibly contained in an optional
- Rethinking programming given potentially missing values

Raise your hand if you ever got a `NullPointerException` during your life as a Java developer. Keep it up if this is the `Exception` you encounter most frequently. Unfortunately, we can't see you at this moment, but we believe there's a very high probability that your hand is raised now. We also guess you may possibly be thinking something like "Yes, I agree, `NullPointerException`s are a pain for any Java developer, novice, or expert, but there's not much we can do about them, because this is the price we pay to use such a convenient, and maybe unavoidable, construct as `null` references." This is a common feeling in the (imperative) programming world; nevertheless, it may not be the whole truth but more likely a bias with solid historical roots.

A British computer scientist named Tony Hoare introduced `null` references back in 1965 while designing ALGOL W, one of the first typed programming languages with heap-allocated records, "simply because it was so easy to implement." Despite his goal "to ensure that all use of references could be absolutely safe, with checking performed automatically by the compiler," he decided to make an exception for `null` references, because he thought this was the most convenient way to model *the absence of a value.* After many years he regretted this decision, calling it "my billion-dollar mistake." We've all seen the effect—we examine a field of an object, perhaps to determine whether its value is one of two expected forms, only to instead find we're examining not an object but a `null` pointer that promptly raises that annoying `NullPointerException`.

In reality, Hoare's statement could underestimate the costs incurred by millions of developers fixing bugs caused by `null` references in the last 50 years. Indeed, the vast majority of the languages[1] created in recent decades, including Java, have been built with the same design decision, maybe for reasons of compatibility with older languages, or more probably, as Hoare states, "simply because it was so easy to implement." Let's start by looking at a simple example to understand the problems with `null`.

10.1 How do you model the absence of a value?

Imagine you have the following nested object structure for a person owning a car and having car insurance.

Listing 10.1 The `Person/Car/Insurance` data model

```
public class Person {
    private Car car;
    public Car getCar() { return car; }
}

public class Car {
    private Insurance insurance;
    public Insurance getInsurance() { return insurance; }
}

public class Insurance {
    private String name;
    public String getName() { return name; }
}
```

Then, what's possibly problematic with the following code?

```
public String getCarInsuranceName(Person person) {
    return person.getCar().getInsurance().getName();
}
```

1 Notable exceptions include most typed functional languages, such as Haskell and ML; these include *algebraic data types* that allow data types to be succinctly expressed, including explicit specification of whether special values such as `null` are to be included on a type-by-type basis.

This code looks pretty reasonable, but many people don't own a car. So what's the result of calling the method `getCar`? A common unfortunate practice is to return the `null` reference to indicate the absence of a value, here to indicate the absence of a car. As a consequence, the call to `getInsurance` will return the insurance of a `null` reference, which will result in a `NullPointerException` at run-time and stop your program from running further. But that's not all. What if `person` was `null`? What if the method `getInsurance` returned `null` too?

10.1.1 Reducing NullPointerExceptions with defensive checking

What can you do to avoid running into an unexpected `NullPointerException`? Typically, you can add `null` checks where necessary (and sometimes, in an excess of defensive programming, even where not necessary) and often with different styles. A first attempt to write a method preventing a `NullPointerException` is shown in the following listing.

Listing 10.2 Null-safe attempt 1: deep doubts

```
public String getCarInsuranceName(Person person) {
    if (person != null) {
        Car car = person.getCar();
        if (car != null) {
            Insurance insurance = car.getInsurance();
            if (insurance != null) {
                return insurance.getName();
            }
        }
    }
    return "Unknown";
}
```

Each `null` check increases the nesting level of the remaining part of the invocation chain.

This method performs a `null` check every time it dereferences a variable, returning the string "Unknown" if any of the variables traversed in this dereferencing chain is a `null` value. The only exception to this is that you're not checking to see if the name of the insurance company is `null` because, like any other company, you *know* it must have a name. Note that you can avoid this last check only because of your knowledge of the business domain, but that isn't reflected in the Java classes modeling your data.

We labeled the method in listing 10.2 "deep doubts" because it shows a recurring pattern: every time you have a doubt that a variable could be `null`, you're obliged to add a further nested `if` block, increasing the indentation level of the code. This clearly scales poorly and compromises the readability, so maybe you'd like to attempt another solution. Let's try to avoid this problem by doing something different in the next listing.

Listing 10.3 Null-safe attempt 2: too many exits

```
public String getCarInsuranceName(Person person) {
    if (person == null) {
        return "Unknown";
    }
```

Each `null` check adds a further exit point.

```
    Car car = person.getCar();
    if (car == null) {
        return "Unknown";
    }
    Insurance insurance = car.getInsurance();
    if (insurance == null) {
        return "Unknown";
    }
    return insurance.getName();
}
```

Each `null` check adds a further exit point.

In this second attempt, you try to avoid the deeply nested `if` blocks, adopting a different strategy: every time you meet a null variable, you return the string "Unknown." Nevertheless, this solution is also far from ideal; now the method has four distinct exit points, making it hardly maintainable. Even worse, the default value to be returned in case of a `null`, the string "Unknown," is repeated in three places—and hopefully not misspelled! Of course, you may wish to extract it into a constant to avoid this problem.

Furthermore, it's an error-prone process; what if you forget to check that one property could be `null`? We argue in this chapter that using `null` to represent the absence of a value is the wrong approach. What you need is a better way to model the absence and presence of a value.

10.1.2 Problems with null

To recap our discussion so far, the use of `null` references in Java causes both theoretical and practical problems:

- It's a source of error.
  `NullPointerException` is by far the most common exception in Java.
- It bloats your code.
  It worsens readability by making it necessary to fill your code with often deeply nested `null` checks.
- It's meaningless.
  It doesn't have any semantic meaning, and in particular it represents the wrong way to model the absence of a value in a statically typed language.
- It breaks Java philosophy.
  Java always hides pointers from developers except in one case: the `null` pointer.
- It creates a hole in the type system.
  `null` carries no type or other information, meaning it can be assigned to any reference type. This is a problem because, when it's propagated to another part of the system, you have no idea what that `null` was initially supposed to be.

To provide some context for what other solutions are out there for this problem, let's briefly look at what other programming languages have to offer.

10.1.3 What are the alternatives to null in other languages?

In recent years other languages like Groovy worked around this problem by introducing a *safe navigation operator*, represented by `?.`, to safely navigate through potentially `null` values. To understand how this works, consider the following Groovy code to retrieve the name of the insurance company used by a given person to insure their car:

```
def carInsuranceName = person?.car?.insurance?.name
```

What this statement does should be pretty clear. A person might not have a car and you tend to model this possibility by assigning a `null` to the car reference of the `Person` object. Similarly, a `car` might not have insurance. The Groovy safe navigation operator allows you to safely navigate through these potentially `null` references without throwing a `NullPointerException`, by just propagating the `null` reference through the invocations chain, returning a `null` in the event that any value in the chain is a `null`.

A similar feature was proposed and then discarded for Java 7. Somehow, though, we don't seem to miss a safe navigation operator in Java; the first temptation of all Java developers when confronted with a `NullPointerException` is to quickly fix it by adding an `if` statement, checking that a value is not `null` before invoking a method on it. If you solve this problem in this way, without wondering if it's correct that your algorithm or your data model could present a `null` value in that specific situation, you're not fixing a bug but hiding it, making its discovery and fix far more difficult for whoever will be called to work on it next time; it very likely will be you in the next week or month. You're just sweeping the dirt under the carpet. Groovy's null-safe dereferencing operator is only a bigger and more powerful broom for making this mistake, without worrying too much about its consequences.

Other functional languages, such as Haskell and Scala, take a different view. Haskell includes a `Maybe` type, which essentially encapsulates an optional value. A value of type `Maybe` can contain either a value of a given type or nothing. There's no concept of a `null` reference. `Scala` has a similar construct called `Option[T]` to encapsulate the presence or absence of a value of type `T`, which we discuss in chapter 15. You then have to explicitly check whether a value is present or not using operations available on the `Option` type, which enforces the idea of "`null` checking." You can no longer forget to do it because it's enforced by the type system.

Okay, we diverged a bit, and all this sounds fairly abstract. You might now wonder "So, what about Java 8?" Well actually, Java 8 takes inspiration from this idea of an "optional value" by introducing a new class called `java.util.Optional<T>`! In this chapter, we show the advantages of using it to model potentially absent values instead of assigning a `null` reference to them. We also clarify how this migration from `null`s to `Optional`s requires you to rethink the way you deal with optional values in your domain model. Finally, we explore the features of this new `Optional` class and provide a few practical examples showing how to use it effectively. Ultimately, you'll learn how to design better APIs in which—just by reading the signature of a method—users can tell whether to expect an optional value.

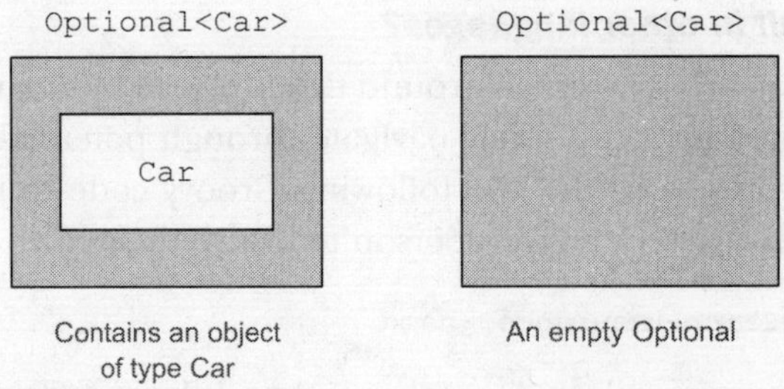

Figure 10.1 An optional `Car`

10.2 Introducing the Optional class

Java 8 introduces a new class called `java.util.Optional<T>` that's inspired by the ideas of Haskell and Scala. It's a class that encapsulates an optional value. This means, for example, that if you know a person might or might not have a car, the `car` variable inside the `Person` class shouldn't be declared type `Car` and assigned to a `null` reference when the person doesn't own a car, but instead should be type `Optional<Car>`, as illustrated in figure 10.1.

When a value is present, the `Optional` class just wraps it. Conversely, the absence of a value is modeled with an "empty" optional returned by the method `Optional.empty`. It's a static factory method that returns a special singleton instance of the `Optional` class. You might wonder what the difference is between a `null` reference and `Optional.empty()`. Semantically, they could be seen as the same thing, but in practice the difference is huge: trying to dereference a `null` will invariably cause a `NullPointerException`, whereas `Optional.empty()` is a valid, workable object of type `Optional` that can be invoked in useful ways. You'll soon see how.

An important, practical semantic difference in using optionals instead of nulls is that in the first case, declaring a variable of type `Optional<Car>` instead of `Car` clearly signals that a missing value is permitted there. Conversely, always using the type `Car` and possibly assigning a `null` reference to a variable of that type implies you don't have any help, other than your knowledge of the business model, to understand whether the `null` belongs to the valid domain of that given variable or not.

With this in mind, you can rework the original model from listing 10.1, using the `Optional` class as follows.

Listing 10.4 Redefining the `Person`/`Car`/`Insurance` data model using `Optional`

```
public class Person {
    private Optional<Car> car;
    public Optional<Car> getCar() { return car; }
}

public class Car {
    private Optional<Insurance> insurance;
    public Optional<Insurance> getInsurance() { return insurance; }
}
```

A person might or might not own a car, so you declare this field `Optional`.

A car might or might not be insured, so you declare this field `Optional`.

```
public class Insurance {
    private String name;
    public String getName() { return name; }
}
```

An insurance company must have a name.

Note how the use of the `Optional` class enriches the semantics of your model. The fact that a person references an `Optional<Car>`, and a car an `Optional<Insurance>`, makes it explicit in the domain that a person *might* or *might not* own a car, and that car *might* or *might not* be insured.

At the same time, the fact that the name of the insurance company is declared of type `String` instead of `Optional<String>` makes it evident that it's mandatory for an insurance company to have a name. This way you know for certain whether you'll get a `NullPointerException` when dereferencing the name of an insurance company; you don't have to add a `null` check because doing so will just hide the problem instead of fixing it. An insurance company must have a name, so if you find one without, you'll have to work out what's wrong in your data instead of adding a piece of code covering up this circumstance. Using optionals consistently disambiguates beyond any doubt the case of a value that can be structurally missing from the case of a value that's absent only because of a bug in your algorithm or a problem in your data. It's important to note that the intention of the `Optional` class is not to replace every single `null` reference. Instead, its purpose is to help you design more-comprehensible APIs so that by just reading the signature of a method, you can tell whether to expect an optional value. This forces you to actively unwrap an optional to deal with the absence of a value.

10.3 Patterns for adopting Optional

So far, so good; you've learned how to employ optionals in types to clarify your domain model and the advantages this offers over representing missing values with `null` references. But how can you use them now? What can you do with them, or more specifically how can you actually use a value wrapped in an optional?

10.3.1 Creating Optional objects

The first step before working with `Optional` is to learn how to create optional objects! There are several ways.

EMPTY OPTIONAL

As mentioned earlier, you can get hold of an empty optional object using the static factory method `Optional.empty`:

```
Optional<Car> optCar = Optional.empty();
```

OPTIONAL FROM A NON-NULL VALUE

You can also create an optional from a non-null value with the static factory method `Optional.of`:

```
Optional<Car> optCar = Optional.of(car);
```

If car were null, a NullPointerException would be immediately thrown (rather than getting a latent error once you try to access properties of the car).

OPTIONAL FROM NULL

Finally, by using the static factory method Optional.ofNullable, you can create an Optional object that may hold a null value:

```
Optional<Car> optCar = Optional.ofNullable(car);
```

If car were null, the resulting Optional object would be empty.

You might imagine we'll continue by investigating "how to get a value out of an optional." In particular, there's a get method that does precisely this, and we'll talk more about it later. But get raises an exception when the optional is empty, and so using it in an ill-disciplined manner effectively re-creates all the maintenance problems caused by using null. So instead we start by looking at ways of using optional values that avoid explicit tests; these are inspired by similar operations on streams.

10.3.2 Extracting and transforming values from optionals with map

A common pattern is to extract information from an object. For example, you may want to extract the name from an insurance company. You'd need to check whether insurance is null before extracting the name as follows:

```
String name = null;
if(insurance != null){
    name = insurance.getName();
}
```

Optional supports a map method for this pattern. It works as follows (from here on we use the model presented in listing 10.4):

```
Optional<Insurance> optInsurance = Optional.ofNullable(insurance);
Optional<String> name = optInsurance.map(Insurance::getName);
```

It's conceptually similar to the stream's map method you saw in chapters 4 and 5. The map operation applies the provided function to each element of a stream. You could also think of an Optional object as a particular collection of data, containing at most a single element. If the Optional contains a value, then the function passed as argument to map transforms that value. If the Optional is empty, then nothing happens. Figure 10.2 illustrates this similarity, showing what happens when passing a function that transforms a square into a triangle to the map methods of both a stream of square and an optional of square.

This looks useful, but how could you use this to write the previous code, which was chaining several method calls in a safe way?

```
public String getCarInsuranceName(Person person) {
    return person.getCar().getInsurance().getName();
}
```

We have to look at another method supported by Optional called flatMap!

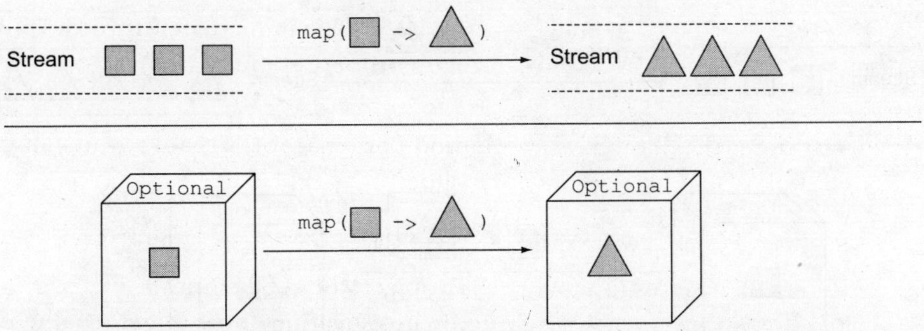

Figure 10.2 Comparing the map methods of Streams and Optionals

10.3.3 *Chaining Optional objects with flatMap*

Because you've just learned how to use map, your first reaction may be that you can rewrite the previous code using map as follows:

```
Optional<Person> optPerson = Optional.of(person);
Optional<String> name =
        optPerson.map(Person::getCar)
                 .map(Car::getInsurance)
                 .map(Insurance::getName);
```

Unfortunately, this code doesn't compile. Why? The variable optPeople is of type Optional<People>, so it's perfectly fine to call the map method. But getCar returns an object of type Optional<Car> (as presented in listing 10.4). This means the result of the map operation is an object of type Optional<Optional<Car>>. As a result, the call to getInsurance is invalid because the outermost optional contains as its value another optional, which of course doesn't support the getInsurance method. Figure 10.3 illustrates the nested optional structure you'd get.

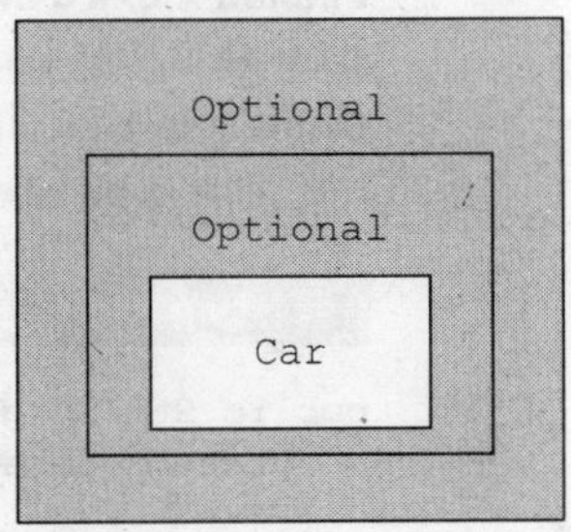

Figure 10.3 A two-level optional

So how can we solve this problem? Again, we can look at a pattern you've used previously with streams: the flatMap method. With streams, the flatMap method takes a function as an argument, which returns another stream. This function is applied to each element of a stream, which would result in a stream of streams. But flatMap has the effect of replacing each generated stream by the contents of that stream. In other words, all the separate streams that are generated by the function get amalgamated or flattened into a single stream. What you want here is something similar, but you want to flatten a two-level optional into one.

Like figure 10.2 for the map method, figure 10.4 illustrates the similarities between the flatMap methods of the Stream and Optional classes.

Here the function passed to the stream's flatMap method transforms each square into another stream containing two triangles. The result of a simple map would then

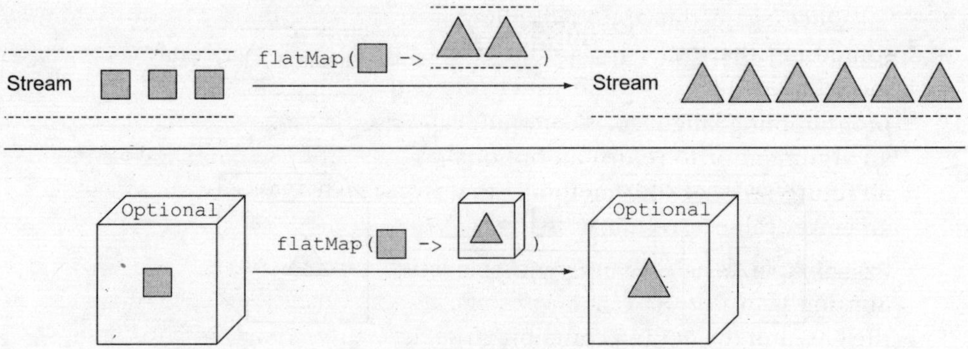

Figure 10.4 Comparing the `flatMap` methods of `Stream` and `Optional`

be a stream containing three other streams, each of them having two triangles, but the `flatMap` method flattens this two-level stream into a single stream containing six triangles in total. In the same way, the function passed to the optional's `flatMap` method transforms the square contained in the original optional into an optional containing a triangle. If this function was passed to the `map` method, the result would be an optional containing another optional that, in turn, contains a triangle, but the `flatMap` method flattens this two-level optional into a single optional containing a triangle.

FINDING A CAR'S INSURANCE COMPANY NAME WITH OPTIONALS

Now that you know the theory of the `map` and `flatMap` methods of `Optional`, let's put them into practice. The ugly attempts we made in listings 10.2 and 10.3 can be rewritten using the optional-based data model of listing 10.4 as follows.

Listing 10.5 Finding a car's insurance company name with `Optionals`

```
public String getCarInsuranceName(Optional<Person> person) {
    return person.flatMap(Person::getCar)
                 .flatMap(Car::getInsurance)
                 .map(Insurance::getName)
                 .orElse("Unknown");
}
```

A default value if the resulting `Optional` is empty

Comparing listing 10.5 with the two former attempts shows the advantages of using optionals when dealing with potentially missing values. This time, you can obtain what you want with an easily comprehensible statement—instead of increasing the code complexity with conditional branches.

In implementation terms, first note that you modify the signature of the `getCarInsuranceName` method from listings 10.2 and 10.3, because we explicitly said there could also be a case where a nonexistent `Person` is passed to this method, such as when that `Person` is retrieved from a database using an identifier, and you want to model the possibility that no `Person` exists in your data for the given identifier. You model this additional requirement, changing the type of the method's argument from `Person` to `Optional<Person>`.

Once again this approach allows you to make explicit through the type system something that otherwise would remain implicit in your knowledge of the domain model, namely, you should never forget that the first purpose of a language, even a programming language, is communication. Declaring a method to take an optional as an argument or to return an optional as a result documents to your colleagues—and all future users of your method—that it can take an empty value or that it might give an empty value as result.

PERSON/CAR/INSURANCE DEREFERENCING CHAIN USING OPTIONALS

Starting with this `Optional<Person>`, the `Car` from the `Person`, the `Insurance` from the `Car`, and the `String` containing the insurance company name from the `Insurance` are dereferenced with a combination of the `map` and `flatMap` methods introduced earlier. Figure 10.5 illustrates this pipeline of operations.

Here you begin with the optional wrapping the `Person` and invoking `flatMap(Person::getCar)` on it. As we said, you can logically think of this invocation as something that happens in two steps. In step 1, a `Function` is applied to the `Person` inside the optional to transform it. In this case, the `Function` is expressed with a method reference invoking the method `getCar` on that `Person`. Because that method returns an `Optional<Car>`, the `Person` inside the optional is transformed into an instance of that type, resulting in a two-level optional that's flattened as part of the `flatMap` operation. From a theoretical point of view, you can think of this flattening operation as the operation that combines two optionals, resulting in an empty optional, if at least one of them is empty. What happens in reality is that if you invoke `flatMap` on an empty optional, nothing is changed, and it's returned as is. Conversely, if the optional wraps a `Person`, the `Function` passed to the `flatMap` method is applied to that `Person`. Because the value produced by that `Function` application is already an optional, the `flatMap` method can return it as is.

The second step is similar to the first one, transforming the `Optional<Car>` into an `Optional<Insurance>`. Step 3 turns the `Optional<Insurance>` into an `Optional<String>`:

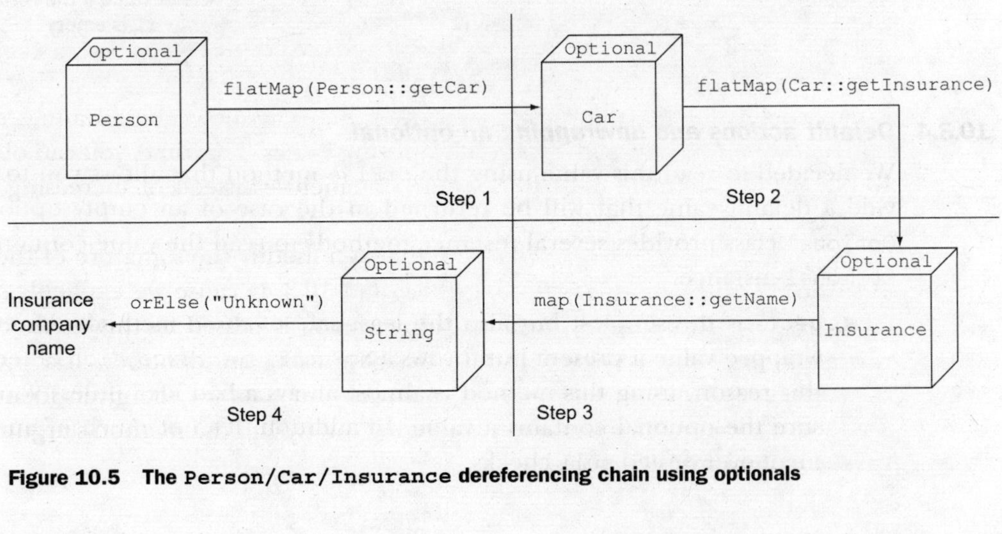

Figure 10.5 The `Person/Car/Insurance` dereferencing chain using optionals

because the `Insurance.getName()` method returns a `String`, in this case a `flatMap` isn't necessary.

At this point the resulting optional will be empty if any of the methods in this invocation chain returns an empty optional or will contain the desired insurance company name otherwise. So how do you read that value? After all, you'll end up getting an `Optional<String>` that may or may not contain the name of the insurance company. In listing 10.5, we used another method called `orElse`, which provides a default value in case the optional is empty. There are many methods to provide default actions or unwrap an optional. Let's look at them in more detail.

Using optionals in a domain model and why they're not Serializable

In listing 10.4, we showed how to use `Optionals` in your domain model in order to mark with a specific type the values that are allowed to be missing or remain undefined. However, the designers of the `Optional` class developed it from different assumptions and with a different use case in mind. In particular, Java Language Architect Brian Goetz clearly stated the purpose of `Optional` is to support the optional-return idiom only.

Because the `Optional` class wasn't intended for use as a field type, it also doesn't implement the `Serializable` interface. For this reason, using `Optionals` in your domain model could break applications using tools or frameworks that require a serializable model to work. Nevertheless, we believe that we showed why using `Optionals` as a proper type in your domain is a good idea, especially when you have to traverse a graph of objects that could be, all or in part, potentially not present. Alternatively, if you need to have a serializable domain model, we suggest you at least provide a method allowing access also to any possibly missing value as an optional, as in the following example:

```
public class Person {
    private Car car;
    public Optional<Car> getCarAsOptional() {
        return Optional.ofNullable(car);
    }
}
```

10.3.4 Default actions and unwrapping an optional

We decided to read this value using the `orElse` method that allows you to also provide a default value that will be returned in the case of an empty optional. The `Optional` class provides several instance methods to read the value contained by an `Optional` instance.

- `get()` is the simplest but also the least safe of these methods. It returns the wrapped value if present but throws a `NoSuchElementException` otherwise. For this reason, using this method is almost always a bad idea unless you're really sure the optional contains a value. In addition, it's not much of an improvement over nested `null` checks.

- `orElse(T other)` is the method used in listing 10.5, and as we noted there, it allows you to provide a default value for when the optional doesn't contain a value.
- `orElseGet(Supplier<? extends T> other)` is the lazy counterpart of the `orElse` method, because the supplier is invoked only if the optional contains no value. You should use this method either when the default value is time-consuming to create (to gain a little efficiency) or you want to be sure this is done only if the optional is empty (in which case it's strictly necessary).
- `orElseThrow(Supplier<? extends X> exceptionSupplier)` is similar to the `get` method in that it throws an exception when the optional is empty, but in this case it allows you to choose the type of exception that you want to throw.
- `ifPresent(Consumer<? super T> consumer)` lets you execute the action given as argument if a value is present; otherwise no action is taken.

The analogies between the `Optional` class and the `Stream` interface aren't limited to the `map` and `flatMap` methods. There's a third method, `filter`, that behaves in a similar fashion, and we explore it in section 10.3.6.

10.3.5 Combining two optionals

Let's now suppose that you have a method that given a `Person` and a `Car` queries some external services and implements some quite complex business logic to find the insurance company offering the cheapest policy for that combination:

```
public Insurance findCheapestInsurance(Person person, Car car) {
    // queries services provided by the different insurance companies
    // compare all those data
    return cheapestCompany;
}
```

Let's also suppose that you want to develop a null-safe version of this method taking two optionals as arguments and then returning an `Optional<Insurance>` that will be empty if at least one of the values passed in to it is also empty. The `Optional` class also provides an `isPresent` method returning `true` if the optional contains a value, so your first attempt could be to implement this method as follows:

```
public Optional<Insurance> nullSafeFindCheapestInsurance(
                              Optional<Person> person, Optional<Car> car) {
    if (person.isPresent() && car.isPresent()) {
        return Optional.of(findCheapestInsurance(person.get(), car.get()));
    } else {
        return Optional.empty();
    }
}
```

This method has the advantage of making clear in its signature that both the person and the car values passed to it could be missing and that for this reason it couldn't return any value. Unfortunately, its implementation resembles too closely the `null` checks that you'd write if the method took as arguments a `Person` and a `Car` and both those arguments could be potentially `null`. Is there a better and more idiomatic way to implement this method using the features of the `Optional` class? Take a few minutes to go through Quiz 10.1 and try to find an elegant solution.

Quiz 10.1: Combining two optionals without unwrapping them

Using a combination of the `map` and `flatMap` methods you learned in this section, rewrite the implementation of the former `nullSafeFindCheapestInsurance()` method in a single statement.

Answer:

You can implement that method in a single statement and without using any conditional constructs like the ternary operator as follows:

```
public Optional<Insurance> nullSafeFindCheapestInsurance(
                              Optional<Person> person, Optional<Car> car) {
    return person.flatMap(p -> car.map(c -> findCheapestInsurance(p, c)));
}
```

Here you invoke a `flatMap` on the first optional, so if this is empty, the lambda expression passed to it won't be executed at all and this invocation will just return an empty optional. Conversely, if the person is present, it uses it as the input of a `Function` returning an `Optional<Insurance>` as required by the `flatMap` method. The body of this function invokes a `map` on the second optional, so if it doesn't contain any car, the `Function` will return an empty optional and so will the whole `nullSafeFindCheapestInsurance` method. Finally, if both the person and the car are present, the lambda expression passed as argument to the `map` method can safely invoke the original `findCheapestInsurance` method with them.

The analogies between the `Optional` class and the `Stream` interface aren't limited to the `map` and `flatMap` methods. There's a third method, `filter`, that behaves in a similar fashion on both classes, and we explore it next.

10.3.6 Rejecting certain values with filter

Often you need to call a method on an object and check some property. For example, you might need to check whether the insurance's name is equal to "CambridgeInsurance." To do this in a safe way, you first need to check whether the reference pointing to an `Insurance` object is `null` and then call the `getName` method, as follows:

```
Insurance insurance = ...;
if(insurance != null && "CambridgeInsurance".equals(insurance.getName())){
  System.out.println("ok");
}
```

This pattern can be rewritten using the `filter` method on an `Optional` object, as follows:

```
Optional<Insurance> optInsurance = ...;
optInsurance.filter(insurance ->
                        "CambridgeInsurance".equals(insurance.getName()))
            .ifPresent(x -> System.out.println("ok"));
```

The `filter` method takes a predicate as an argument. If a value is present in the `Optional` object and it matches the predicate, the `filter` method returns that value; otherwise, it returns an empty `Optional` object. If you remember that you can think of an optional as a stream containing at most a single element, the behavior of this method should be pretty clear. If the optional is already empty, it doesn't have any effect; otherwise, it applies the predicate to the value contained in the optional. If this application returns `true`, the optional returns unchanged; otherwise, the value is filtered away, leaving the optional empty. You can test your understanding of how the `filter` method works by working through Quiz 10.2.

Quiz 10.2: Filtering an optional

Supposing the `Person` class of our `Person/Car/Insurance` model also has a method `getAge` to access the age of the person, modify the `getCarInsuranceName` method in listing 10.5 using the following signature

```
public String getCarInsuranceName(Optional<Person> person, int minAge)
```

so that the insurance company name is returned *only* if the person has an age greater than or equal to the `minAge` argument.

Answer:

You can filter from the `Optional` the person it eventually contains if the age of the person is greater than the `minAge` argument by encoding this condition in a predicate and passing this predicate to the `filter` method as follows:

```
public String getCarInsuranceName(Optional<Person> person, int minAge) {
    return person.filter(p -> p.getAge() >= minAge)
                 .flatMap(Person::getCar)
                 .flatMap(Car::getInsurance)
                 .map(Insurance::getName)
                 .orElse("Unknown");
}
```

In the next section, we investigate the remaining features of the `Optional` class and give more practical examples showing various techniques you could use to reimplement the code you write to manage missing values.

Table 10.1 summarizes the methods of the `Optional` class.

Table 10.1 The methods of the `Optional` class

Method	Description
`empty`	Returns an empty `Optional` instance
`filter`	If the value is present and matches the given predicate, returns this `Optional`; otherwise returns the empty one
`flatMap`	If a value is present, returns the `Optional` resulting from the application of the provided mapping function to it; otherwise returns the empty `Optional`

Table 10.1 The methods of the `Optional` class *(continued)*

Method	Description
`get`	Returns the value wrapped by this `Optional` if present; otherwise throws a `NoSuchElementException`
`ifPresent`	If a value is present, invokes the specified consumer with the value; otherwise does nothing
`isPresent`	Returns `true` if there is a value present; otherwise `false`
`map`	If a value is present, applies the provided mapping function to it
`of`	Returns an `Optional` wrapping the given value or throws a `NullPointerException` if this value is `null`
`ofNullable`	Returns an `Optional` wrapping the given value or the empty `Optional` if this value is `null`
`orElse`	Returns the value if present or the given default value otherwise
`orElseGet`	Returns the value if present or the one provided by the given `Supplier` otherwise
`orElseThrow`	Returns the value if present or throws the exception created by the given `Supplier` otherwise

10.4 Practical examples of using Optional

As you've learned, effective use of the new `Optional` class implies a complete rethink of how you deal with potentially missing values. This rethink involves not only the code you write but, possibly even more important, how you interact with native Java APIs.

Indeed, we believe that many of those APIs would have been written differently if the `Optional` class had been available at the time they were developed. For backward-compatibility reasons, old Java APIs can't be changed to make proper use of optionals, but all is not lost. You can fix, or at least work around, this issue by adding into your code small utility methods that allow you to benefit from the power of optionals. You'll see how to do this with a couple of practical examples.

10.4.1 Wrapping a potentially null value in an optional

An existing Java API almost always returns a `null` to signal the absence of the required value or that the computation to obtain it failed for some reason. For instance, the `get` method of a `Map` returns `null` as its value if it contains no mapping for the requested key. But for the reasons we listed earlier, in most cases like this, you'd prefer that these methods could return an optional. You can't modify the signature of these methods, but you can easily wrap the value they return with an optional. Continuing with the `Map` example, and supposing you have a `Map<String, Object>`, then accessing the value indexed by `key` with

```
Object value = map.get("key");
```

will return `null` if there's no value in the `map` associated with the `String` "key." You can improve this by wrapping in an optional the value returned by the `map`. You can do this in two ways: either with an ugly `if-then-else` adding to code complexity or by using the method `Optional.ofNullable` that we discussed earlier:

```
Optional<Object> value = Optional.ofNullable(map.get("key"));
```

You can use this method every time you want to safely transform a value that could be potentially `null` into an optional.

10.4.2 Exceptions vs. Optional

Throwing an exception is another common alternative in the Java API to returning a `null` when, for any reason, a value can't be provided. A typical example of this is the conversion of `String` into an `int`, provided by the `Integer.parseInt(String)` static method. In this case, if the `String` doesn't contain a parseable integer, this method throws a `NumberFormatException`. The net effect is once again that the code signals an invalid argument in the case of a `String` not representing an integer, the only difference being that this time you have to check it with a `try/catch` block instead of using an `if` condition controlling whether a value is not `null`.

You could also model the invalid value caused by nonconvertible `String`s with an empty optional, so you'd prefer that `parseInt` could return an optional. You can't change the original Java method, but nothing prevents you from implementing a tiny utility method, wrapping it, and returning an optional as desired, as shown in this next listing.

Listing 10.6 Converting a `String` into an `Integer` returning an optional

```
public static Optional<Integer> stringToInt(String s) {
    try {
        return Optional.of(Integer.parseInt(s));      <-- If the String can be converted into an Integer, return an optional containing it.
    } catch (NumberFormatException e) {
        return Optional.empty();      <-- Otherwise return an empty optional.
    }
}
```

Our suggestion is to collect several methods similar to this in a utility class; let's call it `OptionalUtility`. In this way, from now on you'll always be allowed to convert a `String` into an `Optional<Integer>`, using this `OptionalUtility.stringToInt` method. You can forget that you encapsulated the ugly `try/catch` logic in it.

PRIMITIVE OPTIONALS AND WHY YOU SHOULDN'T USE THEM

Note that, like streams, optionals also have primitive counterparts—`OptionalInt`, `OptionalLong`, and `OptionalDouble`—so the method in listing 10.6 could have returned an `OptionalInt` instead of `Optional<Integer>`. In chapter 5, we encouraged the use of primitive streams, especially when they could contain a huge number of elements, for performance reasons, but because an `Optional` can have at most a single value, that justification doesn't apply here.

We discourage using primitive optionals because they lack the `map`, `flatMap`, and `filter` methods, which, as you saw in section 10.2, are the most useful methods of the `Optional` class. Moreover, as happens for streams, an optional can't be composed with its primitive counterpart, so, for example, if the method of listing 10.6 returned `OptionalInt`, you couldn't pass it as a method reference to the `flatMap` method of another optional.

10.4.3 Putting it all together

To demonstrate how the methods of the `Optional` class presented so far can be used together in a more compelling use case, suppose you have some `Properties` that are passed as configuration arguments to your program. For the purpose of this example and to test the code you'll develop, create some sample `Properties` as follows:

```
Properties props = new Properties();
props.setProperty("a", "5");
props.setProperty("b", "true");
props.setProperty("c", "-3");
```

Now let's also suppose your program needs to read a value from these `Properties` that it will interpret as a duration in seconds. Because a duration has to be a positive number, you'll want a method with the following signature

```
public int readDuration(Properties props, String name)
```

that, when the value of a given property is a `String` representing a positive integer, returns that integer, but returns zero in all other cases. To clarify this requirement you can formalize it with a few JUnit assertions:

```
assertEquals(5, readDuration(param, "a"));
assertEquals(0, readDuration(param, "b"));
assertEquals(0, readDuration(param, "c"));
assertEquals(0, readDuration(param, "d"));
```

These assertions reflect the original requirement: the `readDuration` method returns `5` for the property `"a"` because the value of this property is a `String` that's convertible in a positive number; it returns `0` for `"b"` because it isn't a number, returns `0` for `"c"` because it's a number but it's negative, and returns `0` for `"d"` because a property with that name doesn't exist. Let's try to implement the method satisfying this requirement in imperative style, as shown in the following listing.

Listing 10.7 Reading duration from a property imperatively

```
public int readDuration(Properties props, String name) {
    String value = props.getProperty(name);
    if (value != null) {
        try {
            int i = Integer.parseInt(value);
            if (i > 0) {
                return i;
            }
```

Make sure a property exists with the required name.

Try to convert the `String` property into a number.

Check if the resulting number is positive.

```
    } catch (NumberFormatException nfe) { }
    }
    return 0;                          <-- Return 0 if any of
}                                          the conditions fail.
```

As you might expect, the resulting implementation is quite convoluted and not very readable, presenting multiple nested conditions coded both as `if` statements and as a `try/catch` block. Take a few minutes to figure out in Quiz 10.3 how you can achieve the same result using what you've learned in this chapter.

Quiz 10.3: Reading duration from a property using an optional

Using the features of the `Optional` class and the utility method of listing 10.6, try to reimplement the imperative method of listing 10.7 with a single fluent statement.

Answer:

Because the value returned by the `Properties.getProperty(String)` method is a `null` when the required property doesn't exist, it's convenient to turn this value into an optional with the `ofNullable` factory method. You can then convert the `Optional<String>` into an `Optional<Integer>`, passing to its `flatMap` method a reference to the `OptionalUtility.stringToInt` method developed in listing 10.6. Finally, you can easily filter away the negative number. In this way, if any of these operations will return an empty optional, the method will return the `0` that's passed as the default value to the `orElse` method; otherwise, it will return the positive integer contained in the optional. This is then simply implemented as follows:

```
public int readDuration(Properties props, String name) {
    return Optional.ofNullable(props.getProperty(name))
                   .flatMap(OptionalUtility::stringToInt)
                   .filter(i -> i > 0)
                   .orElse(0);
}
```

Note the common style in using optionals and streams; both are reminiscent of a database query where several operations are chained together.

10.5 Summary

In this chapter, you've learned the following:

- `null` references have been historically introduced in programming languages to generally signal the absence of a value.
- Java 8 introduces the class `java.util.Optional<T>` to model the presence or absence of a value.
- You can create `Optional` objects with the static factory methods `Optional.empty`, `Optional.of`, and `Optional.ofNullable`.
- The `Optional` class supports many methods such as `map`, `flatMap`, and `filter`, which are conceptually similar to the methods of a stream.

- Using `Optional` forces you to actively unwrap an optional to deal with the absence of a value; as a result, you protect your code against unintended `null` pointer exceptions.
- Using `Optional` can help you design better APIs in which, just by reading the signature of a method, users can tell whether to expect an optional value.

11

CompletableFuture: composable asynchronous programming

This chapter covers

- Creating an asynchronous computation and retrieving its result
- Increasing throughput using non-blocking operations
- Designing and implementing an asynchronous API
- Consuming asynchronously a synchronous API
- Pipelining and merging two or more asynchronous operations
- Reacting to the completion of an asynchronous operation

In recent years, two trends are obliging us to rethink the way we write software. The first trend is related to the hardware on which we run our applications, and the second trend concerns how applications are structured and particularly how they interact with each other. We discussed the impact of the hardware trend in chapter 7. We noted that since the advent of multicore processors, the most effective way to speed up your applications is to write software that's able to fully exploit the multicore processors. You saw that this is possible by splitting large tasks and making each subtask run in parallel with the others; you also learned how the fork/join framework (available since Java 7) and parallel streams (new in Java 8) allow you to accomplish this in a simpler and more effective way than by directly working with threads.

The second trend reflects the increasing availability and use by applications of internet services accessible through public APIs, made available by known providers such as Google (for example, localization information), Facebook (for example, social information), and Twitter (for example, news). Nowadays it's relatively rare to develop a website or a network application that works in total isolation. It's far more likely that your next web application will be a mash-up: it will use content from multiple sources and aggregate it to ease the life of your end users.

For instance, you might like to provide the collective sentiment about a given topic to your French users; to do this you could ask the Facebook or Twitter API for the most trending comments about that topic in any language and maybe rank the most relevant ones with your internal algorithms. Then you might use Google Translate to translate them into French, or even Google Maps to geolocate where their authors live, and finally aggregate all this information and display it on your website.

Oh, and of course, if any of these external network services are slow to respond, then you'll wish to provide partial results to your users, for example, showing your text results alongside a generic map with a question mark in it, instead of showing a totally blank screen until the map server responds or times out. Figure 11.1 illustrates how this typical mash-up application interacts with the remote services it needs to work with.

To implement a similar application, you'll have to contact multiple web services across the internet. But what you don't want to do is block your computations and waste billions of precious clock cycles of your CPU waiting for an answer from these services. For example, you shouldn't have to wait for data from Facebook to start processing the data coming from Twitter.

This situation represents the other side of the multitask-programming coin. The fork/join framework and parallel streams discussed in chapter 7 are valuable tools for parallelism; they split an operation into multiple suboperations and perform those suboperations in parallel on different cores, CPUs, or even machines.

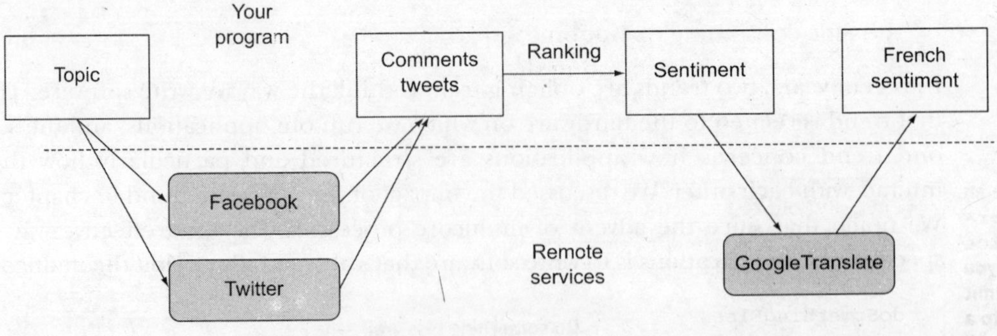

Figure 11.1 A typical mash-up application

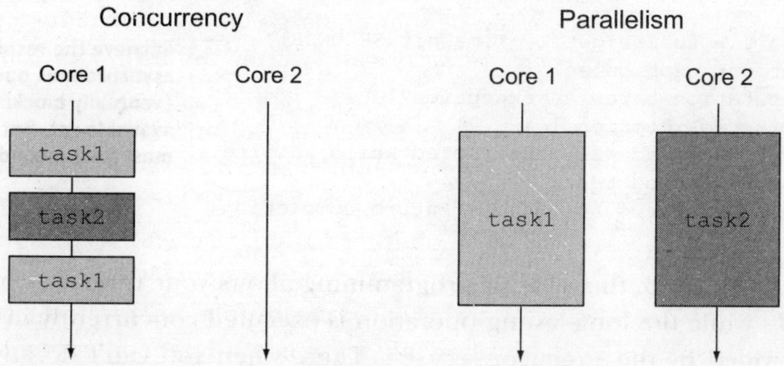

Figure 11.2 Concurrency vs. parallelism

Conversely, when dealing with concurrency instead of parallelism, or when your main goal is to perform several loosely related tasks on the same CPUs, keeping their cores as busy as possible to maximize the throughput of your application, what you really want to achieve is to avoid blocking a thread and wasting its computational resources while waiting, potentially for quite a while, for a result from a remote service or from interrogating a database. As you'll see in this chapter, the `Future` interface and particularly its new `CompletableFuture` implementation are your best tools in such circumstances. Figure 11.2 illustrates the difference between parallelism and concurrency.

11.1 Futures

The `Future` interface was introduced in Java 5 to model a result made available at some point in the future. It models an asynchronous computation and provides a reference to its result that will be available when the computation itself is completed. Triggering a potentially time-consuming action inside a `Future` allows the caller `Thread` to continue doing useful work instead of just waiting for the operation's result. You can think of it as taking a bag of clothes to your favorite dry cleaner. They will give you a receipt to tell you when your clothes are cleaned (a `Future`). In the meantime, you can do some other activities. Another advantage of `Future` is that it's friendlier to work with than lower-level `Thread`s. To work with a `Future`, you typically have to wrap the time-consuming operation inside a `Callable` object and submit it to an `ExecutorService`. The following listing shows an example written before Java 8.

Listing 11.1 Executing a long-lasting operation asynchronously in a `Future`

```
ExecutorService executor = Executors.newCachedThreadPool();
Future<Double> future = executor.submit(new Callable<Double>() {
        public Double call() {
            return doSomeLongComputation();
        }});
doSomethingElse();
```

- Create an ...ecutorService ...wing you ...o submit ...asks to a ...d pool. (left margin, partly cut off)
- **Submit a `Callable` to the `ExecutorService`.**
- **Execute a long operation asynchronously in a separate thread.**
- **Do something else while the asynchronous operation is progressing.**

```
try {
    Double result = future.get(1, TimeUnit.SECONDS);
} catch (ExecutionException ee) {
    // the computation threw an exception
} catch (InterruptedException ie) {
    // the current thread was interrupted while waiting
} catch (TimeoutException te) {
    // the timeout expired before the Future completion
}
```

Retrieve the result of the asynchronous operation, eventually blocking if it isn't available yet, but waiting at most for 1 second.

As depicted in figure 11.3, this style of programming allows your thread to perform some other tasks while the long-lasting operation is executed concurrently in a separate thread provided by the `ExecutorService`. Then, when you can't do any other meaningful work without having the result of that asynchronous operation, you can retrieve it from the `Future` by invoking its `get` method. This method immediately returns the result of the operation if it's already completed or blocks your thread, waiting for its result to be available.

Can you think of a problem with this scenario? What if the long operation never returns? To handle this possibility, even though there also exists a `get` method that doesn't take a parameter, it's almost always a good idea to use its overloaded version, accepting a timeout defining the maximum time your thread has to wait for the `Future`'s result, as you did in listing 11.1, instead of waiting indefinitely.

11.1.1 Futures limitations

This first small example shows that the `Future` interface provides methods to check if the asynchronous computation is complete (using the `isDone` method), to wait for its completion, and to retrieve its result. But these features aren't enough to let you write concise concurrent code. For example, it's difficult to express dependencies between results of a `Future`; declaratively it's easy to say, "When the result of the long computation is available, please send its result to another long computation, and when that's done, combine its result with the result from another query." But implementing this with the operations available in a `Future` is a different story. This is why more declarative features would be useful, such as these:

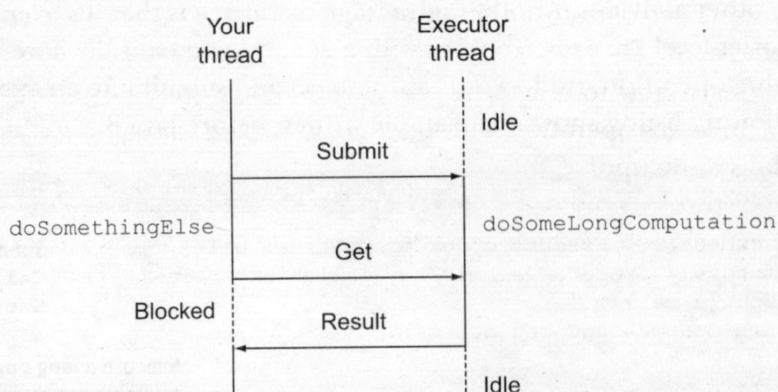

Figure 11.3 Using a `Future` to execute a long operation asynchronously

- Combining two asynchronous computations in one—both when they're independent and when the second depends on the result of the first
- Waiting for the completion of all tasks performed by a set of `Futures`
- Waiting for the completion of only the quickest task in a set of `Futures` (possibly because they're trying to calculate the same value in different ways) and retrieving its result
- Programmatically completing a `Future` (that is, by manually providing the result of the asynchronous operation)
- Reacting to a `Future` completion (that is, being notified when the completion happens and then having the ability to perform a further action using the result of the `Future`, instead of being blocked waiting for its result)

In this chapter, you'll learn how the new `CompletableFuture` class (which implements the `Future` interface) makes all of this possible in a declarative way using Java 8's new features. The designs of `Stream` and `CompletableFuture` follow similar patterns: both use lambda expressions and the idea of pipelining. For this reason you could say that `CompletableFuture` is to a plain `Future` what `Stream` is to a `Collection`.

11.1.2 Using CompletableFutures to build an asynchronous application

To demonstrate the `CompletableFuture` features, we incrementally develop a best-price-finder application that contacts multiple online shops to find the lowest price for a given product or service. Along the way, you'll learn several important skills:

- First, you'll learn how to provide an asynchronous API for your customers (useful if you're the owner of one of the online shops).
- Second, you'll learn how to make your code non-blocking when you're a consumer of a synchronous API. You'll discover how to pipeline two subsequent asynchronous operations, merging them into a single asynchronous computation. This situation would arise, for example, when the online shop returns a discount code along with the original price of the item you wanted to buy—so you have to contact a second remote discount service to find out the percentage discount associated with this discount code before finally calculating the actual price of that item.
- You'll also learn how to reactively process events representing the completion of an asynchronous operation and how that allows the best-price-finder application to constantly update the best-buy quote for the item you want to buy as each shop returns its price, instead of having to wait for all the shops to return their respective quotes (which also risks giving the user a blank screen forever if one of the shops' servers is down).

> **Synchronous vs. asynchronous API**
>
> The phrase *synchronous API* is just another way of talking about a traditional call to a method: you call it, the caller then waits while the method computes, the method then returns, and the caller continues with the returned value. Even if the caller and callee were executed on different threads, the caller would still wait for the callee to complete; this gives rise to the phrase *blocking call*.
>
> In contrast, in an *asynchronous API* the method returns immediately, or at least before its computation is complete, delegating its remaining computation to a thread, which runs asynchronously to the caller—hence the phrase *non-blocking call*. The remaining computation gives its value to the caller, either by calling a callback method or by the caller invoking a further "wait until the computation is complete" method. This style of computation is common for I/O systems programming: you initiate a disc access, which happens asynchronously while you do more computation, and when you have nothing more useful to do, you simply wait until the disc blocks are loaded into memory.

11.2 Implementing an asynchronous API

To start implementing the best-price-finder application, let's begin by defining the API that each single shop should provide. First, a shop declares a method that returns the price of a product given its name:

```
public class Shop {
    public double getPrice(String product) {
        // to be implemented
    }
}
```

The internal implementation of this method would query the shop's database but probably also perform other time-consuming tasks, such as contacting various other external services (for example, the shop's suppliers or manufacturer-related promotional discounts). To fake such a long-running method execution, in the rest of this chapter we simply use a `delay` method, which introduces an artificial delay of 1 second, defined in the following listing.

Listing 11.2 A method to simulate a 1-second delay

```
public static void delay() {
    try {
        Thread.sleep(1000L);
    } catch (InterruptedException e) {
        throw new RuntimeException(e);
    }
}
```

For the purpose of this chapter, the `getPrice` method can be modeled by calling `delay` and then returning a randomly calculated value for the price, as shown in the next listing. The code for returning a randomly calculated price may look like a bit of a hack. It randomizes the price based on the product name by using the result of charAt as a number.

Listing 11.3 Introducing a simulated delay in the getPrice method

```
public double getPrice(String product) {
    return calculatePrice(product);
}
private double calculatePrice(String product) {
    delay();
    return random.nextDouble() * product.charAt(0) + product.charAt(1);
}
```

This implies that when the consumer of this API (in this case, the best-price-finder application) invokes this method, it will remain blocked and then idle for 1 second while waiting for its synchronous completion. This is unacceptable, especially considering that the best-price-finder application will have to repeat this operation for all the shops in its network. In the subsequent sections of this chapter, you'll discover how you can resolve this problem by consuming this synchronous API in an asynchronous way. But for the purpose of learning how to design an asynchronous API, we continue this section by pretending to be on the other side of the barricade: you're a wise shop owner who realizes how painful this synchronous API is for its users and you want to rewrite it as an asynchronous API to make your customers' lives easier.

11.2.1 Converting a synchronous method into an asynchronous one

To achieve this you first have to turn the getPrice method into a getPriceAsync method and change its return value:

```
public Future<Double> getPriceAsync(String product) { ... }
```

As we mentioned in the introduction of this chapter, the java.util.concurrent.Future interface was introduced in Java 5 to represent the result of an asynchronous computation (that is, the caller thread is allowed to proceed without blocking). This means a Future is just a handle for a value that isn't yet available but can be retrieved by invoking its get method after its computation has finally terminated. As a result, the getPriceAsync method can return immediately, giving the caller thread a chance to perform other useful computations in the meantime. The new CompletableFuture class gives you various possibilities to implement this method in an easy way, for example, as shown in the next listing.

Listing 11.4 Implementing the getPriceAsync method

Create the CompletableFuture that will contain the result of the computation.

Execute the computation asynchronously in a different Thread.

```
public Future<Double> getPriceAsync(String product) {
    CompletableFuture<Double> futurePrice = new CompletableFuture<>();
    new Thread( () -> {
                double price = calculatePrice(product);
```

```
                futurePrice.complete(price);          <-- Set the value returned by the long
    }).start();                                           computation on the Future
    return futurePrice;                 <--               when it becomes available.
}
        Return the Future without waiting
        for the computation of the result it
        contains to be completed.
```

Here you create an instance of CompletableFuture, representing an asynchronous computation and containing a result when it becomes available. Then you fork a different Thread that will perform the actual price calculation and return the Future instance without waiting for that long-lasting calculation to terminate. When the price of the requested product is finally available, you can complete the CompletableFuture using its complete method to set the value. Obviously this feature also explains the name of this new Future implementation. A client of this API can invoke it, as shown in the next listing.

Listing 11.5 Using an asynchronous API

```
Shop shop = new Shop("BestShop");
long start = System.nanoTime();
Future<Double> futurePrice = shop.getPriceAsync("my favorite product");    <--
long invocationTime = ((System.nanoTime() - start) / 1_000_000);
System.out.println("Invocation returned after " + invocationTime
                                                + " msecs");
// Do some more tasks, like querying other shops                Query the shop to
doSomethingElse();                                              retrieve the price
// while the price of the product is being calculated              of a product.
try {
    double price = futurePrice.get();                   <--  Read the price from the
    System.out.printf("Price is %.2f%n", price);             Future or block until it
} catch (Exception e) {                                      won't be available.
    throw new RuntimeException(e);
}
long retrievalTime = ((System.nanoTime() - start) / 1_000_000);
System.out.println("Price returned after " + retrievalTime + " msecs");
```

As you can see, the client asks the shop to get the price of a certain product. Because the shop provides an asynchronous API, this invocation almost immediately returns the Future, through which the client can retrieve the product's price at a later time. This allows the client to do other tasks, like querying other shops, instead of remaining blocked waiting for the first shop to produce the requested result. Later, when there are no other meaningful jobs that the client could do without having the product price, it can invoke get on the Future. By doing so the client either unwraps the value contained in the Future (if the asynchronous task is already finished) or remains blocked until that value is available. The output produced by the code in listing 11.5 could be something like this:

```
Invocation returned after 43 msecs
Price is 123.26
Price returned after 1045 msecs
```

You can see that the invocation of the getPriceAsync method returns far sooner than when the price calculation eventually finishes. In section 11.4 you'll learn that it's also possible for the client to avoid any risk of being blocked. Instead it can just be notified when the Future is completed, and execute a callback code, defined through a lambda expression or a method reference, only when the result of the computation is available. For now we'll address another problem: how to correctly manage the possibility of an error occurring during the execution of the asynchronous task.

11.2.2 Dealing with errors

The code we developed so far works correctly if everything goes smoothly. But what happens if the price calculation generates an error? Unfortunately, in this case you'll get a particularly negative outcome: the exception raised to signal the error will remain confined in the thread, which is trying to calculate the product price, and will ultimately kill it. As a consequence, the client will remain blocked forever, waiting for the result of the get method to arrive.

The client can prevent this problem by using an overloaded version of the get method that also accepts a timeout. It's a good practice to always use a timeout to avoid similar situations elsewhere in your code. This way the client will at least avoid waiting indefinitely, but when the timeout expires, it will just be notified with a TimeoutException. As a consequence, it won't have a chance to discover what really caused that failure inside the thread that was trying to calculate the product price. To make the client aware of the reason the shop wasn't able to provide the price of the requested product, you have to propagate the Exception that caused the problem inside the CompletableFuture through its completeExceptionally method. This refines listing 11.4 to give the code shown in the listing that follows.

Listing 11.6 Propagating an error inside the CompletableFuture

```
public Future<Double> getPriceAsync(String product) {
    CompletableFuture<Double> futurePrice = new CompletableFuture<>();
    new Thread( () -> {
                try {
                    double price = calculatePrice(product);
                    futurePrice.complete(price);
                } catch (Exception ex) {
                    futurePrice.completeExceptionally(ex);
                }
    }).start();
    return futurePrice;
}
```

If the price calculation completed normally, complete the Future with the price.

Otherwise, complete it exceptionally with the Exception that caused the failure.

The client will now be notified with an ExecutionException (which takes an Exception parameter containing the cause—the original Exception thrown by the price calculation method). So, for example, if that method throws a RuntimeException saying "product not available," the client will get an ExecutionException like the following:

```
java.util.concurrent.ExecutionException: java.lang.RuntimeException: product
    not available
   at java.util.concurrent.CompletableFuture.get(CompletableFuture.java:2237)
   at lambdasinaction.chap11.AsyncShopClient.main(AsyncShopClient.java:14)
   ... 5 more
Caused by: java.lang.RuntimeException: product not available
   at lambdasinaction.chap11.AsyncShop.calculatePrice(AsyncShop.java:36)
   at lambdasinaction.chap11.AsyncShop.lambda$getPrice$0(AsyncShop.java:23)
   at lambdasinaction.chap11.AsyncShop$$Lambda$1/24071475.run(Unknown Source)
   at java.lang.Thread.run(Thread.java:744)
```

CREATING A COMPLETABLEFUTURE WITH THE SUPPLYASYNC FACTORY METHOD

Until now you've created `CompletableFuture`s and completed them programmatically, when it seemed convenient to do so, but the `CompletableFuture` class itself comes with lots of handy factory methods that can make this process far easier and less verbose. For example, the `supplyAsync` method can let you rewrite the `getPriceAsync` method in listing 11.4 with a single statement, as shown in the following listing.

Listing 11.7 Creating a `CompletableFuture` with the `supplyAsync` factory method

```
public Future<Double> getPriceAsync(String product) {
    return CompletableFuture.supplyAsync(() -> calculatePrice(product));
}
```

The `supplyAsync` method accepts a `Supplier` as argument and returns a `CompletableFuture` that will be asynchronously completed with the value obtained by invoking that `Supplier`. This `Supplier` will be run by one of the `Executors` in the `ForkJoinPool`, but you can specify a different `Executor` by passing it as a second argument to the overloaded version of this method. More generally, it's possible to optionally pass an `Executor` to all other `CompletableFuture` factory methods, and you'll use this capability in section 11.3.4, where we demonstrate that using an `Executor` that fits the characteristics of your application can have a positive effect on its performance.

Also note that the `CompletableFuture` returned by the `getPriceAsync` method in listing 11.7 is totally equivalent to the one you created and completed manually in listing 11.6, meaning it provides the same error management you carefully added.

For the rest of this chapter, we'll suppose you sadly have no control over the API implemented by the `Shop` class and that it provides only synchronous blocking methods. This is also what typically happens when you want to consume an HTTP API provided by some service. You'll learn how it's still possible to query multiple shops asynchronously, thus avoiding becoming blocked on a single request and thereby increasing the performance and the throughput of your best-price-finder application.

11.3 Make your code non-blocking

So you've been asked to develop a best-price-finder application, and all the shops you have to query provide only the same synchronous API implemented as shown at the beginning of section 11.2. In other words, you have a list of shops, like this one:

```
List<Shop> shops = Arrays.asList(new Shop("BestPrice"),
                                 new Shop("LetsSaveBig"),
                                 new Shop("MyFavoriteShop"),
                                 new Shop("BuyItAll"));
```

You have to implement a method with the following signature, that given the name of a product returns a `List` of strings, where each string contains the name of a shop and the price of the requested product in that shop:

```
public List<String> findPrices(String product);
```

Your first idea will probably be to use the `Stream` features you learned in chapters 4, 5, and 6. You may be tempted to write something like what's shown in the next listing (yes, it's good if you're already thinking this first solution is bad!).

Listing 11.8 A `findPrices` implementation sequentially querying all the shops

```
public List<String> findPrices(String product) {
    return shops.stream()
        .map(shop -> String.format("%s price is %.2f",
                                   shop.getName(), shop.getPrice(product)))
        .collect(toList());
}
```

Okay, this was straightforward. Now try to put the method `findPrices` to work with the only product you want madly these days (yes, you guessed it; it's the myPhone27S). In addition, record how long the method takes to run, as shown in the following listing; this will let you compare its performance with the improved method we develop later.

Listing 11.9 Checking `findPrices` correctness and performance

```
long start = System.nanoTime();
System.out.println(findPrices("myPhone27S"));
long duration = (System.nanoTime() - start) / 1_000_000;
System.out.println("Done in " + duration + " msecs");
```

The code in listing 11.9 produces output like this:

```
[BestPrice price is 123.26, LetsSaveBig price is 169.47, MyFavoriteShop price
    is 214.13, BuyItAll price is 184.74]
Done in 4032 msecs
```

As you may have expected, the time taken by the `findPrices` method to run is just a few milliseconds longer than 4 seconds, because the four shops are queried sequentially and blocking one after the other, and each of them takes 1 second to calculate the price of the requested product. How can you improve on this result?

11.3.1 Parallelizing requests using a parallel Stream

After reading chapter 7, the first and quickest improvement that should occur to you would be to avoid this sequential computation using a parallel `Stream` instead of a sequential, as shown in the next listing.

Listing 11.10 Parallelizing the `findPrices` method

```
public List<String> findPrices(String product) {
    return shops.parallelStream()
        .map(shop -> String.format("%s price is %.2f",
                                   shop.getName(), shop.getPrice(product)))
        .collect(toList());
}
```

Use a parallel `Stream` to retrieve the prices from the different shops in parallel.

Find out if this new version of `findPrices` is any better by again running the code in listing 11.9:

```
[BestPrice price is 123.26, LetsSaveBig price is 169.47, MyFavoriteShop price
    is 214.13, BuyItAll price is 184.74]
Done in 1180 msecs
```

Well done! It looks like this was a simple but very effective idea: now the four different shops are queried in parallel, so it takes in total just a bit more than a second to complete. Can you do even better? Let's try to turn all the synchronous invocations to the different shops in the `findPrices` method into asynchronous invocations, using what you learned so far about `CompletableFuture`s.

11.3.2 Making asynchronous requests with CompletableFutures

You saw that you can use the factory method `supplyAsync` to create `CompletableFuture` objects. Let's use it:

```
List<CompletableFuture<String>> priceFutures =
        shops.stream()
        .map(shop -> CompletableFuture.supplyAsync(
             () -> String.format("%s price is %.2f",
             shop.getName(), shop.getPrice(product))))
        .collect(toList());
```

Using this approach, you obtain a `List<CompletableFuture<String>>`, where each `CompletableFuture` in the `List` will contain the `String` name of a shop when its computation is completed. But because the `findPrices` method you're trying to reimplement using `CompletableFuture`s has to return just a `List<String>`, you'll have to wait for the completion of all these futures and extract the value they contain before returning the `List`.

To achieve this result, you can apply a second `map` operation to the original `List<CompletableFuture<String>>`, invoking a `join` on all the futures in the `List` and then waiting for their completion one by one. Note that the `join` method of the `CompletableFuture` class has the same meaning as the `get` method also declared in the `Future` interface, with the only difference being that `join` doesn't throw any checked exception. By using it you don't have to bloat the lambda expression passed to this second `map` with a `try/catch` block. Putting everything together, you can rewrite the `findPrices` method as follows.

Listing 11.11 Implementing the findPrices method with CompletableFutures

```
public List<String> findPrices(String product) {
    List<CompletableFuture<String>> priceFutures =
            shops.stream()
            .map(shop -> CompletableFuture.supplyAsync(
                         () -> shop.getName() + " price is " +
                               shop.getPrice(product)))
            .collect(Collectors.toList());

    return priceFutures.stream()
            .map(CompletableFuture::join)
            .collect(toList());
}
```

Calculate each price asynchronously with a `CompletableFuture`.

Wait for the completion of all asynchronous operations.

Note that you use two separate stream pipelines, instead of putting the two map operations one after the other in the same stream-processing pipeline—and for a very good reason. Given the lazy nature of intermediate stream operations, if you had processed the stream in a single pipeline, you would have succeeded only in executing all the requests to different shops synchronously and sequentially. This is because the creation of each CompletableFuture to interrogate a given shop would start only when the computation of the previous one had completed, letting the join method return the result of that computation. Figure 11.4 clarifies this important detail.

The top half of figure 11.4 shows that processing the stream with a single pipeline implies the evaluation order (identified by the dotted line) is sequential. In fact, a new CompletableFuture is created only after the former one has been completely

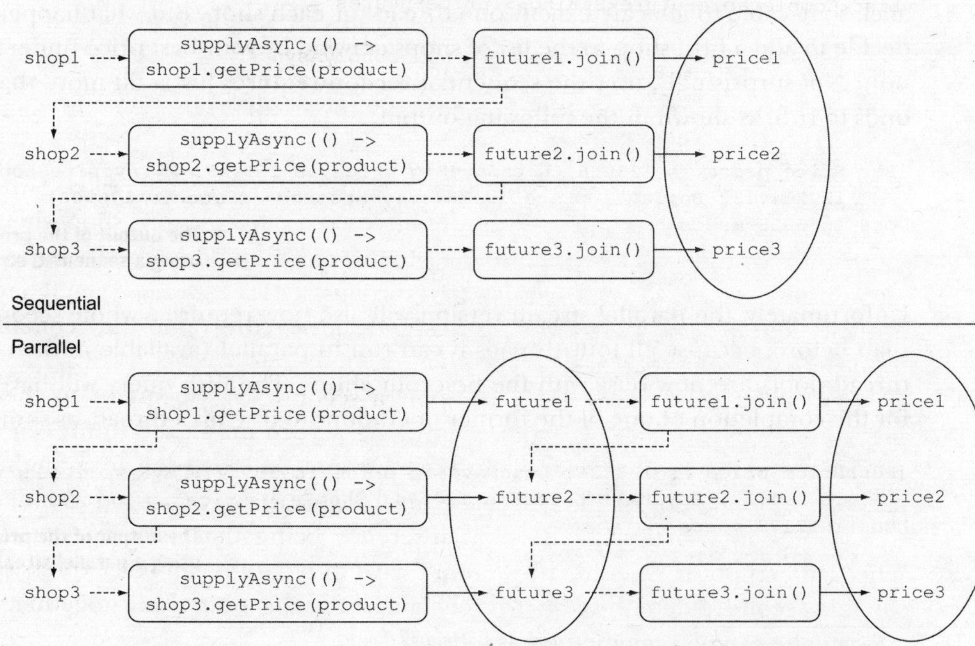

Figure 11.4 Why Stream's laziness causes a sequential computation and how to avoid it

evaluated. Conversely, the bottom half of the figure demonstrates how gathering the `CompletableFutures` in a list first, represented by the oval, allows all of them to start before waiting for their completion.

Running the code in listing 11.11 to check the performance of this third version of the `findPrices` method, you could obtain output along the lines of this:

```
[BestPrice price is 123.26, LetsSaveBig price is 169.47, MyFavoriteShop price
    is 214.13, BuyItAll price is 184.74]
Done in 2005 msecs
```

This is quite disappointing, isn't it? More than 2 seconds means this implementation using `CompletableFutures` is faster than the original naïve sequential and blocking implementation from listing 11.8. But it's also almost twice as slow as the previous implementation using a parallel stream. Moreover, it's even more disappointing considering you obtained the parallel stream version with a trivial change to the sequential version.

In comparison, our newer version using `CompletableFutures` required quite a bit of work! But is this the whole truth? Is using `CompletableFutures` in this scenario really a waste of time? Or are we perhaps overlooking something important? Take a few minutes before going forward, particularly recalling that you're testing the code samples on a machine capable of running four threads in parallel.[1]

11.3.3 Looking for the solution that scales better

The parallel stream version performs so well only because it can run four tasks in parallel, so it's able to allocate exactly one thread for each shop. But what happens if you decide to add a fifth shop to the list of shops crawled by your best-price-finder application? Not surprisingly, now the sequential version requires just a bit more than 5 seconds to run, as shown in the following output:

```
[BestPrice price is 123.26, LetsSaveBig price is 169.47, MyFavoriteShop price
    is 214.13, BuyItAll price is 184.74, ShopEasy price is 176.08]
Done in 5025 msecs
```

The output of the program using a sequential stream

Unfortunately, the parallel stream version will also now require a whole second more than before, because all four threads it can run in parallel (available in the common thread pool) are now busy with the first four shops. The fifth query will have to wait for the completion of one of the former operations to free up a thread, as shown here:

```
[BestPrice price is 123.26, LetsSaveBig price is 169.47, MyFavoriteShop price
    is 214.13, BuyItAll price is 184.74, ShopEasy price is 176.08]
Done in 2177 msecs
```

The output of the program using a parallel stream

[1] If you're using a machine capable of running more threads in parallel (for example, eight), then it will require more shops and processes in parallel to reproduce the behavior shown in these pages.

What about the `CompletableFuture` version? Let's also give it a try with the additional fifth shop:

```
[BestPrice price is 123.26, LetsSaveBig price is 169.47, MyFavoriteShop price
    is 214.13, BuyItAll price is 184.74, ShopEasy price is 176.08]
Done in 2006 msecs
```

The output of the program using `CompletableFutures`

The `CompletableFuture` version seems just a bit faster than the one using parallel stream. But this last version isn't satisfying either. For instance, if you try to run your code with nine shops, the parallel stream version takes 3143 milliseconds, whereas the `CompletableFuture` one requires 3009 milliseconds. They look equivalent and for a very good reason: they both internally use the same common pool that by default has a fixed number of threads equal to the one returned by `Runtime.getRuntime().availableProcessors()`. Nevertheless, CompletableFutures have an advantage because, in contrast to what's offered by the parallel Streams API, they allow you to specify a different `Executor` to submit their tasks to. This allows you to configure this `Executor`, and in particular to size its thread pool, in a way that better fits the requirements of your application. Let's see if you can translate this better level of configurability into practical performance gain for your application.

11.3.4 Using a custom Executor

In this case, a sensible choice seems to be to create an `Executor` with a number of threads in its pool that takes into account the actual workload you could expect in your application, but how do you correctly size it?

> **Sizing thread pools**
>
> In the great book *Java Concurrency in Practice* (http://mng.bz/979c), Brian Goetz and coauthors give some advice to find the optimal size for a thread pool. This is important because if the number of threads in the pool is too big, they'll end up competing for scarce CPU and memory resources, wasting their time performing context switching. Conversely, if this number is too small (as it very likely is in your application), some of the cores of the CPU will remain underutilized. In particular, Goetz suggests that the right pool size to approximate a desired CPU utilization rate can be calculated with the following formula:
>
> $N_{threads} = N_{CPU} * U_{CPU} * (1 + W/C)$
>
> where
>
> - N_{CPU} is the number of cores, available through `Runtime.getRuntime().availableProcessors()`
> - U_{CPU} is the target CPU utilization (between 0 and 1), and
> - W/C is the ratio of wait time to compute time

The application is spending about the 99% of the time waiting for the shops' responses, so you could estimate a W/C ratio of 100. This means that if your target is 100% CPU utilization, you should have a pool with 400 threads. In practice it will be wasteful to have more threads than shops, because in doing so you'll have threads in your pool that are never used. For this reason, you need to set up an `Executor` with a fixed number of threads equal to the number of shops you have to query, so there will be exactly one thread for each shop. But you must also set an upper limit of 100 threads in order to avoid a server crash for a larger number of shops, as shown in the following listing.

Listing 11.12 A custom `Executor` fitting our best-price-finder application

```
private final Executor executor =
        Executors.newFixedThreadPool(Math.min(shops.size(), 100),
                                     new ThreadFactory() {
            public Thread newThread(Runnable r) {
                Thread t = new Thread(r);
                t.setDaemon(true);
                return t;
            }
});
```

Create a thread pool with a number of threads equal to the minimum between 100 and the number of shops.

Use daemon threads—they don't prevent the termination of the program.

Note that you're creating a pool made of *daemon threads*. A Java program can't terminate or exit while a normal thread is executing, so a leftover thread waiting for a never-satisfiable event causes problems. By contrast, marking a thread as a daemon means it can be killed on program termination. There's no performance difference. You can now pass the new `Executor` as the second argument of the `supplyAsync` factory method. For example, you should now create the `CompletableFuture` retrieving the price of the requested product from a given shop as follows:

```
CompletableFuture.supplyAsync(() -> shop.getName() + " price is " +
                                    shop.getPrice(product), executor);
```

After this improvement, the solution using the `CompletableFutures` takes only 1021 ms to process five shops and 1022 ms to process nine. In general this trend carries on until the number of shops reaches that threshold of 400 we calculated earlier. This demonstrates that it was a good idea to create an `Executor` that better fits the characteristics of your application and to make use of `CompletableFutures` to submit their tasks to it. This is almost always an effective strategy and something to consider when making intensive use of asynchronous operations.

Parallelism—via Streams or CompletableFutures?

You've now seen two different ways to do parallel computing on a collection: either convert it to a parallel stream and use operations like `map` on it, or iterate over the collection and spawn operations within a `CompletableFuture`. The latter provides more control using resizing of thread pools, which helps ensure that your overall computation doesn't block just because all of your fixed number of threads are waiting for I/O.

> **(continued)**
>
> Our advice for using these APIs is as follows:
>
> - If you're doing computation-heavy operations with no I/O, then the `Stream` interface gives the simplest implementation and one likely to be the most efficient (if all threads are compute-bound, then there's no point in having more threads than processor cores).
> - On the other hand, if your parallel units of work involve waiting for I/O (including network connections), then `CompletableFutures` give more flexibility and the ability to match the number of threads to the wait/computer, or W/C, ratio as discussed previously. Another reason to avoid using parallel streams when I/O waits are involved in the stream-processing pipeline is that the laziness of streams can make it harder to reason about when the waits actually happen.

You've learned how to take advantage of `CompletableFutures` both to provide an asynchronous API to your clients and as the client of a synchronous but slow server. But we performed only a single time-consuming operation in each `Future`. In the next section, you'll see how you can use `CompletableFutures` to pipeline multiple asynchronous operations, in a declarative style similar to what you've already learned using the Streams API.

11.4 Pipelining asynchronous tasks

Let's now suppose that all the shops have agreed to use a centralized discount service. This service uses five different discount codes, and each code has a different discount percentage. You represent this idea by defining a `Discount.Code` enumeration, as shown in the following listing.

Listing 11.13 An enumeration defining the discount codes

```
public class Discount {
    public enum Code {
        NONE(0), SILVER(5), GOLD(10), PLATINUM(15), DIAMOND(20);

        private final int percentage;

        Code(int percentage) {
            this.percentage = percentage;
        }
    }
    // Discount class implementation omitted, see Listing 11.14
}
```

Also suppose the shops have agreed to change the format of the result of the `getPrice` method. It now returns a `String` in the format *`ShopName:price:DiscountCode`*. Our sample implementation will return a random `Discount.Code` together with the random price already calculated:

```
public String getPrice(String product) {
    double price = calculatePrice(product);
    Discount.Code code = Discount.Code.values()[
                            random.nextInt(Discount.Code.values().length)];
    return String.format("%s:%.2f:%s", name, price, code);
}
private double calculatePrice(String product) {
    delay();
    return random.nextDouble() * product.charAt(0) + product.charAt(1);
}
```

Invoking `getPrice` might then return a `String` such as

```
BestPrice:123.26:GOLD
```

11.4.1 Implementing a discount service

Your best-price-finder application should now obtain the prices from the different shops, parse the resulting `Strings`, and for each `String`, query the discount server's needs. This process determines the final discounted price of the requested product (the actual discount percentage associated with each discount code could change, so this is why you query the server each time). We've encapsulated the parsing of the `Strings` produced by the shop in the following `Quote` class:

```
public class Quote {

    private final String shopName;
    private final double price;
    private final Discount.Code discountCode;

    public Quote(String shopName, double price, Discount.Code code) {
        this.shopName = shopName;
        this.price = price;
        this.discountCode = code;
    }

    public static Quote parse(String s) {
        String[] split = s.split(":");
        String shopName = split[0];
        double price = Double.parseDouble(split[1]);
        Discount.Code discountCode = Discount.Code.valueOf(split[2]);
        return new Quote(shopName, price, discountCode);
    }

    public String getShopName() { return shopName; }
    public double getPrice() { return price; }
    public Discount.Code getDiscountCode() { return discountCode; }
}
```

You can obtain an instance of the `Quote` class, which contains the name of the shop, the nondiscounted price, and the discount code, by simply passing the `String` produced by a shop to the static `parse` factory method.

The `Discount` service will also have an `applyDiscount` method accepting a `Quote` object and returning a `String` stating the discounted price for the shop that produced that quote, as shown in the next listing.

Listing 11.14 The Discount service

```
public class Discount {
    public enum Code {
        // source omitted ...
    }

    public static String applyDiscount(Quote quote) {
        return quote.getShopName() + " price is " +
                Discount.apply(quote.getPrice(),
                               quote.getDiscountCode());
    }
    private static double apply(double price, Code code) {
        delay();
        return format(price * (100 - code.percentage) / 100);
    }
}
```

Apply the discount code to the original price.

Simulate a delay in the Discount service response.

11.4.2 Using the Discount service

Because the Discount service is a remote service, you again add a simulated delay of 1 second to it, as shown in the following listing. As you did in section 11.3, first try to reimplement the findPrices method to fit these new requirements in the most obvious (but sadly sequential and synchronous) way.

Listing 11.15 Simplest findPrices implementation that uses the Discount service

```
public List<String> findPrices(String product) {
    return shops.stream()
            .map(shop -> shop.getPrice(product))
            .map(Quote::parse)
            .map(Discount::applyDiscount)
            .collect(toList());
}
```

Retrieve the nondiscounted price from each shop.

Transform the Strings returned by the shops in Quote objects.

Contact the Discount service to apply the discount on each Quote.

The desired result is obtained by pipelining three map operations on the stream of shops:

- The first operation transforms each shop into a String that encodes the price and discount code of the requested product for that shop.
- The second operation parses those Strings, converting each of them in a Quote object.
- Finally, the third one contacts the remote Discount service that will calculate the final discounted price and return another String containing the name of the shop with that price.

As you may imagine, the performance of this implementation will be far from optimal, but try to measure it, as usual, by running your benchmark:

```
[BestPrice price is 110.93, LetsSaveBig price is 135.58, MyFavoriteShop price
    is 192.72, BuyItAll price is 184.74, ShopEasy price is 167.28]
Done in 10028 msecs
```

As expected, it takes 10 seconds, because the 5 seconds used in sequentially querying the five shops is now added to the 5 seconds consumed by the discount service to apply the discount code to the prices returned by the five shops. You already know you can easily improve this result by converting the stream into a parallel one. However, you also learned in section 11.3 that this solution doesn't scale very well when you increase the number of shops to be queried, due to the fixed common thread pool that streams rely on. Conversely, you learned that you could better utilize your CPU by defining a custom `Executor` that will schedule the tasks performed by the `CompletableFuture`s.

11.4.3 Composing synchronous and asynchronous operations

Let's try to reimplement the `findPrices` method asynchronously, again using the features provided by `CompletableFuture`. Here's the code for it. Don't worry if there's something that looks unfamiliar; we explain it shortly.

Listing 11.16 Implementing the `findPrices` method with `CompletableFutures`

```
public List<String> findPrices(String product) {
    List<CompletableFuture<String>> priceFutures =
        shops.stream()
            .map(shop -> CompletableFuture.supplyAsync(
                        () -> shop.getPrice(product), executor))
            .map(future -> future.thenApply(Quote::parse))
            .map(future -> future.thenCompose(quote ->
                     CompletableFuture.supplyAsync(
                        () -> Discount.applyDiscount(quote), executor)))
            .collect(toList());

    return priceFutures.stream()
            .map(CompletableFuture::join)
            .collect(toList());
}
```

Asynchronously retrieve the nondiscounted price from each shop.

Transform the `String` returned by a shop into a `Quote` object when it becomes available.

Compose the resulting `Future` with another asynchronous task, applying the discount code.

Wait for all the `Futures` in the stream to be completed and extract their respective results.

Things look a bit more complex this time, so try to understand what's going on here, step by step. The sequence of these three transformations is depicted in figure 11.5.

You're performing the same three `map` operations as you did in the synchronous solution of listing 11.15, but you make those operations asynchronous when necessary, using the feature provided by the `CompletableFuture` class.

GETTING THE PRICES

You've already seen the first of these three operations in various examples in this chapter; you just query the shop asynchronously by passing a lambda expression to the `supplyAsync` factory method. The result of this first transformation is a `Stream<CompletableFuture<String>>`, where each `CompletableFuture` will contain, once completed, the `String` returned by the corresponding shop. Note that you configure the `CompletableFutures` with the custom `Executor` developed in listing 11.12.

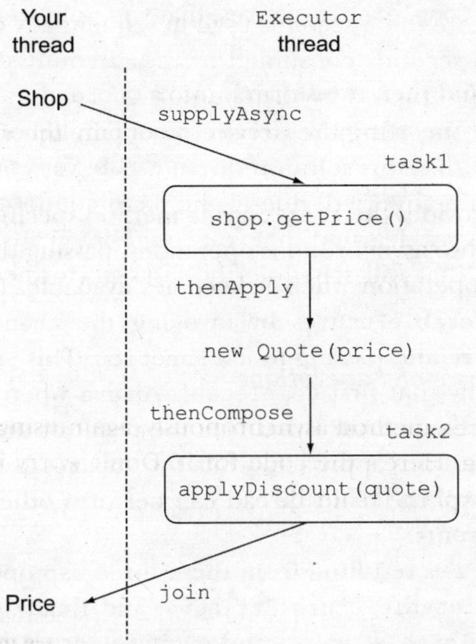

Figure 11.5 Composing synchronous operations and asynchronous tasks

PARSING THE QUOTES

Now you have to convert those Strings into Quotes with a second transformation. But because this parsing operation isn't invoking any remote service or doing any I/O in general, it can be performed almost instantaneously and can be done synchronously without introducing any delay. For this reason, you implement this second transformation by invoking the thenApply method on the CompletableFutures produced by the first step and passing to it a Function converting a String into an instance of Quote.

Note that using the thenApply method doesn't block your code until the CompletableFuture on which you're invoking it is completed. This means that when the CompletableFuture finally completes, you want to transform the value it contains using the lambda expression passed to the thenApply method, thus transforming each CompletableFuture<String> in the stream into a corresponding CompletableFuture<Quote>. You can see this as building a recipe of what to do with the result of the CompletableFuture, just like when you were working with a stream pipeline.

COMPOSING THE FUTURES FOR CALCULATING THE DISCOUNTED PRICE

The third map operation involves contacting the remote Discount service to apply the appropriate discount percentage to the nondiscounted prices received from the shops. This transformation is different from the previous one because it will have to be executed remotely (or, in this case, it will have to simulate the remote invocation with a delay), and for this reason you also want to perform it asynchronously.

To achieve this, as you did with the first invocation of supplyAsync with getPrice, you pass this operation as a lambda expression to the supplyAsync factory method, which will return another CompletableFuture. At this point you have two asynchronous operations, modeled with two distinct CompletableFutures, that you want to perform in a cascade:

- Retrieve the price from a shop and then transform it into a Quote
- Take this Quote and pass it to the Discount service to obtain the final discounted price

The Java 8 CompletableFutures API provides the thenCompose method specifically for this purpose, allowing you to pipeline two asynchronous operations, passing the result of the first operation to the second operation when it becomes available. In other words, you can compose two CompletableFutures by invoking the thenCompose method on the first CompletableFuture and passing to it a Function. This Function has as argument the value returned by that first CompletableFuture when it completes, and it returns a second CompletableFuture that uses the result of the first as input for its computation. Note that with this approach, while the Futures are retrieving the quotes from the different shops, the main thread can perform other useful operations such as responding to UI events.

Collecting the elements of the Stream resulting from these three map operations into a List, you obtain a List<CompletableFuture<String>>, and finally you can wait for the completion of those CompletableFutures and extract their values using join, exactly as you did in listing 11.11. This new version of the findPrices method implemented in listing 11.8 might produce output like this:

```
[BestPrice price is 110.93, LetsSaveBig price is 135.58, MyFavoriteShop price
     is 192.72, BuyItAll price is 184.74, ShopEasy price is 167.28]
Done in 2035 msecs
```

The thenCompose method you used in listing 11.16, like other methods of the CompletableFuture class, also has a variant with an Async suffix, thenComposeAsync. In general, a method without the Async suffix in its name executes its task in the same thread as the previous task, whereas a method terminating with Async always submits the succeeding task to the thread pool, so each of the tasks can be handled by a different thread. In this case, the result of the second CompletableFuture depends on the first, so it makes no difference to the final result or to its broad-brush timing whether you compose the two CompletableFutures with one or the other variant of this method. We chose to use the one with thenCompose only because it's slightly more efficient due to less thread-switching overhead.

11.4.4 Combining two CompletableFutures—dependent and independent

In listing 11.16, you invoked the thenCompose method on one CompletableFuture and passed to it a second CompletableFuture, which needed as input the value resulting from the execution of the first. But another frequently occurring case is where you need to combine the results of the operations performed by two completely independent CompletableFutures, and you don't want to wait for the first to complete before starting on the second.

In situations like this, use the thenCombine method; this takes as second argument a BiFunction, which defines how the results of the two CompletableFutures are to be combined when they both become available. Just like thenCompose, the thenCombine method also comes with an Async variant. In this case, using the thenCombineAsync method will cause the combination operation defined by the BiFunction to be submitted to the thread pool and then executed asynchronously in a separate task.

Turning to our running example, you may know that one of the shops provides prices in € (EUR), but you always want to communicate them in $ (USD) to your customers. You can asynchronously ask the shop the price of a given product *and* retrieve, from a remote exchange-rate service, the current exchange rate between € and $. After both have completed, you can combine the results by multiplying the price by the exchange rate. With this approach, you'll obtain a third CompletableFuture that will complete when the results of the two CompletableFutures are both available and have been combined using the BiFunction, as done in the following listing.

Listing 11.17 Combining two independent CompletableFutures

```
Future<Double> futurePriceInUSD =
        CompletableFuture.supplyAsync(() -> shop.getPrice(product))
        .thenCombine(
            CompletableFuture.supplyAsync(
                () ->  exchangeService.getRate(Money.EUR, Money.USD)),
            (price, rate) -> price * rate
        ));
```

Create a first task querying the shop to obtain the price of a product.

Create a second independent task to retrieve the conversion rate between USD and EUR.

Combine the price and exchange rate by multiplying them.

Here, because the combination operation is a simple multiplication, performing it in a separate task would have been a waste of resources, so you need to use the thenCombine method instead of its asynchronous thenCombineAsync counterpart. Figure 11.6 shows how the different tasks created in listing 11.17 are executed on the different threads of the pool and how their results are combined.

11.4.5 Reflecting on Future vs. CompletableFuture

The last two examples in listings 11.16 and 11.17 clearly show one of the biggest advantages of CompletableFutures over the other pre-Java 8 Future implementations. CompletableFutures use lambda expressions to provide a declarative API that offers the possibility of easily defining a recipe that combines and composes different synchronous and asynchronous tasks to perform a complex operation in the most effective way. To get a more tangible idea of the code readability benefits of CompletableFuture, try to obtain the same result of listing 11.17 purely in Java 7. Listing 11.18 shows you how to do it.

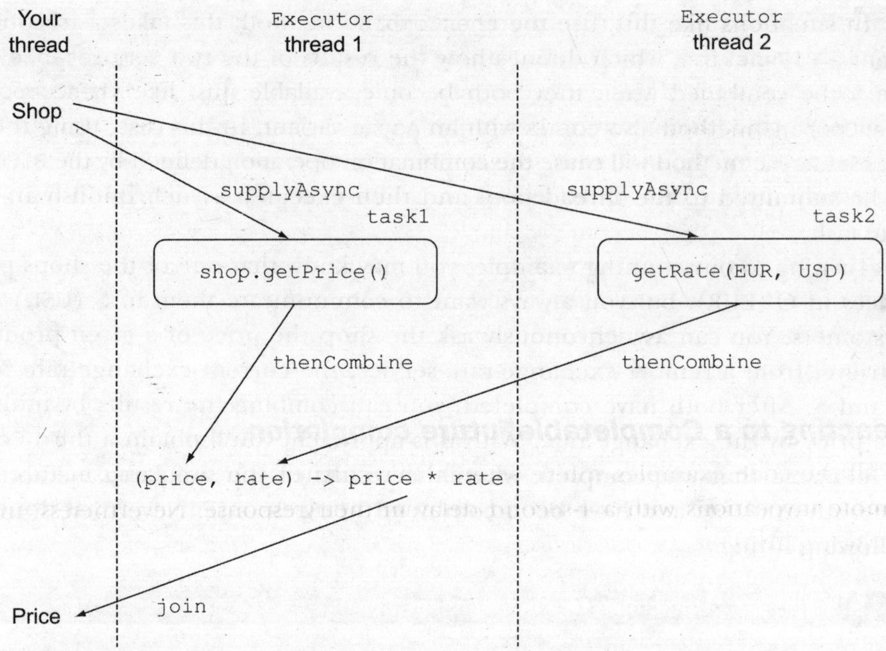

Figure 11.6 Combining two independent asynchronous tasks

Listing 11.18 Combining two Futures in Java 7

```
ExecutorService executor = Executors.newCachedThreadPool();
final Future<Double> futureRate = executor.submit(new Callable<Double>() {
        public Double call() {
            return exchangeService.getRate(Money.EUR, Money.USD);
    }});
Future<Double> futurePriceInUSD = executor.submit(new Callable<Double>() {
        public Double call() {
            double priceInEUR = shop.getPrice(product);
            return priceInEUR * futureRate.get();
    }});
```

Create an ExecutorService allowing you to submit tasks to a thread pool.

Create a Future retrieving the exchange rate between EUR and USD.

Find the price of the requested product for a given shop in a second Future.

Multiply the price and exchange rate in the same Future used to find the price.

In listing 11.18, you create a first Future, submitting a Callable to an Executor querying an external service to find the exchange rate between EUR and USD. Then you create a second Future, retrieving the price in EUR of the requested product for a given shop. Finally, as you did in listing 11.17, you multiply the exchange rate by the price in the same future that also queried the shop to retrieve the price in EUR. Note that using thenCombineAsync instead of thenCombine in listing 11.17 would have been equivalent to performing the price by rate multiplication in a third Future in listing 11.18. The difference between these two implementations might seem small, but this is because you're just combining two Futures. Listings 11.19 and 11.20 show how easy it is to create a pipeline that mixes synchronous and asynchronous operations, and the advantages of this declarative style are more evident when the number of tasks to be performed and results to be combined increases.

You're almost finished with your best-price-finder application, but there's still one ingredient missing. You'd like to show your users the prices provided by the different shops as soon as they become available (car insurance or flight-comparison websites typically do this), instead of waiting for all the price requests to complete, as you did until now. In the next section, you'll discover how to achieve this by *reacting* to the completion of a CompletableFuture instead of invoking get or join on it and thereby remaining blocked until the CompletableFuture itself completes.

11.5 Reacting to a CompletableFuture completion

In all the code examples you've seen in this chapter, you simulated methods doing remote invocations with a 1-second delay in their response. Nevertheless, in a real-world scenario, the various remote services you need to contact from your application are likely to have unpredictable delays, caused by everything from server load to network delays, and perhaps even how valuable the server regards your application's business compared to other applications that perhaps pay more per query.

For these reasons it's likely the prices of the products you want to buy will be available for some shops far earlier than for others. For the purpose of this section, we simulate this scenario in the following listing by introducing a random delay between 0.5 and 2.5 seconds, using the randomDelay method instead of the previous delay method that always waited 1 second.

Listing 11.19 A method to simulate a random delay between 0.5 and 2.5 seconds

```
private static final Random random = new Random();
public static void randomDelay() {
    int delay = 500 + random.nextInt(2000);
    try {
        Thread.sleep(delay);
    } catch (InterruptedException e) {
        throw new RuntimeException(e);
    }
}
```

Until now, you've implemented the findPrices method so it shows the prices provided by the different shops only when all of them are available. What you want to do now is have the best-price-finder application display the price for a given shop as soon as it becomes available, without waiting for the slowest one (which perhaps even times out). How can you achieve this further improvement?

11.5.1 Refactoring the best-price-finder application

The first thing to avoid is waiting for the creation of a List already containing all the prices. You'll need to work directly with the stream of CompletableFutures, where each CompletableFuture is executing the sequence of operations necessary for a given shop. To do this, in the next listing you'll refactor the first part of the implementation from listing 11.12 into a findPricesStream method to produce this stream of CompletableFutures.

Listing 11.20 Refactoring the findPrices method to return a stream of Futures

```
public Stream<CompletableFuture<String>> findPricesStream(String product) {
    return shops.stream()
            .map(shop -> CompletableFuture.supplyAsync(
                                   () -> shop.getPrice(product), executor))
            .map(future -> future.thenApply(Quote::parse))
            .map(future -> future.thenCompose(quote ->
                        CompletableFuture.supplyAsync(
                            () -> Discount.applyDiscount(quote), executor)));
}
```

At this point, you add a fourth map operation on the Stream returned by the findPricesStream method to the three already performed inside that method. This new operation simply *registers* an action on each CompletableFuture; this action consumes the value of the CompletableFuture as soon as it completes. The Java 8 CompletableFuture API provides this feature via the thenAccept method, which take as argument a Consumer of the value with which it completes. In this case, this value is the String returned by the discount services and containing the name of a shop together with the discounted price of the requested product for that shop, and the only action you want to perform to consume this value is to print it:

```
findPricesStream("myPhone").map(f -> f.thenAccept(System.out::println));
```

Note that, as you've already seen for the thenCompose and thenCombine methods, the thenAccept method also has an Async variant named thenAcceptAsync. The Async variant schedules the execution of the Consumer passed to it on a new thread from the thread pool instead of directly performing it using the same thread that completed the CompletableFuture. Because you want to avoid an unnecessary context switch, and more importantly you want to react to the completion of the CompletableFuture as soon as possible (instead of risking having to wait for a new thread to be available), you don't use this variant here.

Because the thenAccept method already specifies how to consume the result produced by the CompletableFuture when it becomes available, it returns a CompletableFuture<Void>. As a result, the map operation will return a Stream<CompletableFuture<Void>>. There's not much you can do on a CompletableFuture<Void> except wait for its completion, but this is exactly what you need. You also want to give the slowest shop a chance to provide its response and print its returned price. To do this, you can put all the CompletableFuture<Void>s of the stream into an array and then wait for the completion of all of them, as in the following listing.

Listing 11.21 Reacting to `CompletableFuture` completion

```
CompletableFuture[] futures = findPricesStream("myPhone")
        .map(f -> f.thenAccept(System.out::println))
        .toArray(size -> new CompletableFuture[size]);
CompletableFuture.allOf(futures).join();
```

The `allOf` factory method takes as input an array of `CompletableFuture`s and returns a `CompletableFuture<Void>` that's completed only when all the `CompletableFuture`s passed have completed. This means that invoking `join` on the `CompletableFuture` returned by the `allOf` method provides an easy way to wait for the completion of all the `CompletableFuture`s in the original stream. This is useful for the best-price-finder application because it can then display a message saying "All shops returned results or timed out," so a user doesn't keep wondering whether more prices might become available.

Conversely, in other applications you may wish to wait for the completion of only one of the `CompletableFuture`s in an array, perhaps if you're consulting two currency-exchange servers and are happy to take the result of the first to respond. In this case, you can similarly use the `anyOf` factory method. As a matter of detail, this method takes as input an array of `CompletableFuture`s and returns a `CompletableFuture<Object>` that completes with the same value as the first-to-complete `CompletableFuture`.

11.5.2 Putting it to work

As we discussed at beginning of this section, you'll now suppose that all the methods simulating a remote invocation will use the `randomDelay` method of listing 11.19, introducing a random delay distributed between 0.5 and 2.5 seconds instead of a delay of 1 second. Running the code in listing 11.21 with this change, you'll see that the prices provided by the different shops don't appear all at the same time as happened before but are printed incrementally as soon as the discounted price for a given shop is available. To make the result of this change more obvious, we slightly modified the code to report a timestamp showing the time taken for each price to be calculated:

```
long start = System.nanoTime();
CompletableFuture[] futures = findPricesStream("myPhone27S")
        .map(f -> f.thenAccept(
             s -> System.out.println(s + " (done in " +
                  ((System.nanoTime() - start) / 1_000_000) + " msecs)")))
        .toArray(size -> new CompletableFuture[size]);
CompletableFuture.allOf(futures).join();
System.out.println("All shops have now responded in "
                   + ((System.nanoTime() - start) / 1_000_000) + " msecs");
```

Running this code produces output similar to the following:

```
BuyItAll price is 184.74 (done in 2005 msecs)
MyFavoriteShop price is 192.72 (done in 2157 msecs)
LetsSaveBig price is 135.58 (done in 3301 msecs)
ShopEasy price is 167.28 (done in 3869 msecs)
BestPrice price is 110.93 (done in 4188 msecs)
All shops have now responded in 4188 msecs
```

You can see that, due to the effect of the random delays, the first price is now printed more than twice as fast as the last!

11.6 Summary

In this chapter, you learned the following:

- Executing relatively long-lasting operations using asynchronous tasks can increase the performance and responsiveness of your application, especially if it relies on one or more remote external services.
- You should consider providing an asynchronous API to your clients. You can easily implement it using `CompletableFuture`s features.
- A `CompletableFuture` also allows you to propagate and manage errors generated within an asynchronous task.
- You can asynchronously consume from a synchronous API by simply wrapping its invocation in a `CompletableFuture`.
- You can compose or combine multiple asynchronous tasks both when they're independent and when the result of one of them is used as the input to another.
- You can register a callback on a `CompletableFuture` to reactively execute some code when the `Future` completes and its result becomes available.
- You can determine when all values in a list of `CompletableFuture`s have completed, or alternatively you can wait for just the first to complete.

12 New Date and Time API

This chapter covers

- Why we needed a new date and time library in Java 8
- Representing date and time for both humans and machines
- Defining an amount of time
- Manipulating, formatting, and parsing dates
- Dealing with different time zones and calendars

The Java API includes many useful components to help you build complex applications. Unfortunately, the Java API isn't always perfect. We believe the majority of experienced Java developers will agree that date and time support before Java 8 was far from ideal. Don't worry, though; Java 8 introduces a brand new Date and Time API to tackle this issue.

In Java 1.0 the only support for date and time was the `java.util.Date` class. Despite its name, this class doesn't represent a date but a point in time with milliseconds precision. Even worse, the usability of this class is harmed by some nebulous design decisions like the choice of its offsets: the years start from 1900, whereas the months start at index 0. This means that if you want to represent the release date of Java 8, which is March 18, 2014, you have to create an instance of `Date` as follows:

```
Date date = new Date(114, 2, 18);
```

Printing this date produces

```
Tue Mar 18 00:00:00 CET 2014
```

Not very intuitive, is it? Moreover even the `String` returned by the `toString` method of the `Date` class could be quite misleading. It also includes the JVM's default time zone, CET, which is Central Europe Time in our case. But this doesn't mean the `Date` class itself is in any way aware of the time zone!

The problems and limitations of the `Date` class were immediately clear when Java 1.0 came out, but it was also clear that it wasn't fixable without breaking its backward compatibility. As a consequence, in Java 1.1 many of the `Date` class's methods were deprecated, and it was replaced with the alternative `java.util.Calendar` class. Unfortunately, `Calendar` has similar problems and design flaws that lead to error-prone code. For instance, months also start at index 0 (at least `Calendar` got rid of the 1900 offset for the year). Even worse, the presence of *both* the `Date` and `Calendar` classes increases confusion among developers. Which one should you use? In addition, some other features such as the `DateFormat`, used to format and parse dates or time in a language-independent manner, work only with the `Date` class.

The `DateFormat` also comes with its own set of problems. For example, it isn't thread-safe. This means that if two threads try to parse a date using the same formatter at the same time, you may receive unpredictable results.

Finally, both `Date` and `Calendar` are mutable classes. What does it mean to mutate the 18th of March 2014 to the 18th of April? This design choice can lead you into a maintenance nightmare, as you'll learn in more detail in the next chapter, which is about functional programming.

The consequence is that all these flaws and inconsistencies have encouraged the use of third-party date and time libraries, such as Joda-Time. For these reasons Oracle decided to provide high-quality date and time support in the native Java API. As a result, Java 8 integrates many of the Joda-Time features in the `java.time` package.

In this chapter, we explore the features introduced by the new Date and Time API. We start with basic use cases such as creating dates and times that are suitable to be used by both humans and machines, and gradually explore more advanced applications of the new Date and Time API, like manipulating, parsing, and printing date-time objects and working with different time zones and alternative calendars.

12.1 LocalDate, LocalTime, Instant, Duration, and Period

Let's start by exploring how to create simple dates and intervals. The `java.time` package includes many new classes to help you: `LocalDate`, `LocalTime`, `LocalDateTime`, `Instant`, `Duration`, and `Period`.

12.1.1 Working with LocalDate and LocalTime

The class `LocalDate` is probably the first one you'll come across when you start using the new Date and Time API. An instance of this class is an immutable object representing just a plain date without the time of day. In particular, it doesn't carry any information about the time zone.

You can create a `LocalDate` instance using the `of` static factory method. A `LocalDate` instance provides many methods to read its most commonly used values such as year, month, day of the week, and so on, as shown in the listing that follows.

Listing 12.1 Creating a `LocalDate` and reading its values

```
LocalDate date = LocalDate.of(2014, 3, 18);      <- 2014-03-18
int year = date.getYear();                       <- 2014
Month month = date.getMonth();                   <- MARCH
int day = date.getDayOfMonth();                  <- 18
DayOfWeek dow = date.getDayOfWeek();             <- TUESDAY
int len = date.lengthOfMonth();                  <- 31 (days in March)
boolean leap = date.isLeapYear();                <- false (not a leap year)
```

It's also possible to obtains the current date from the system clock using the `now` factory method:

```
LocalDate today = LocalDate.now();
```

All the other date-time classes we'll investigate in the remaining part of this chapter provide a similar factory method. You can also access the same information by passing a `TemporalField` to the `get` method. The `TemporalField` is an interface defining how to access the value of a specific field of a temporal object. The `ChronoField` enumeration implements this interface, so you can conveniently use an element of that enumeration with the `get` method, as shown in the next listing.

Listing 12.2 Reading `LocalDate` values using a `TemporalField`

```
int year = date.get(ChronoField.YEAR);
int month = date.get(ChronoField.MONTH_OF_YEAR);
int day = date.get(ChronoField.DAY_OF_MONTH);
```

Similarly, the time of day, such as 13:45:20, is represented by the `LocalTime` class. You can create instances of `LocalTime` using two overloaded static factory methods named `of`. The first one accepts an hour and a minute and the second one also accepts a second. Just like the `LocalDate` class, the `LocalTime` class provides some getter methods to access its values, as shown in the following listing.

Listing 12.3 Creating a `LocalTime` and reading its values

```
LocalTime time = LocalTime.of(13, 45, 20);       <- 13:45:20
int hour = time.getHour();                       <- 13
int minute = time.getMinute();                   <- 45
int second = time.getSecond();                   <- 20
```

Both `LocalDate` and `LocalTime` can be created by parsing a `String` representing them. You can achieve this using their `parse` static methods:

```
LocalDate date = LocalDate.parse("2014-03-18");
LocalTime time = LocalTime.parse("13:45:20");
```

It's possible to pass a `DateTimeFormatter` to the `parse` method. An instance of this class specifies how to format a date and/or a time object. It's intended as a replacement for the old `java.util.DateFormat` that we mentioned earlier. We show in more detail how you can use a `DateTimeFormatter` in section 12.2. Also note that these `parse` methods both throw a `DateTimeParseException`, which extends `RuntimeException` in case the `String` argument can't be parsed as a valid `LocalDate` or `LocalTime`.

12.1.2 Combining a date and a time

The composite class called `LocalDateTime` pairs a `LocalDate` and a `LocalTime`. It represents both a date and a time, without a time zone, and can be created either directly or by combining a date and time, as shown in the next listing.

Listing 12.4 Creating a `LocalDateTime` directly or by combining a date and a time

```
// 2014-03-18T13:45:20
LocalDateTime dt1 = LocalDateTime.of(2014, Month.MARCH, 18, 13, 45, 20);
LocalDateTime dt2 = LocalDateTime.of(date, time);
LocalDateTime dt3 = date.atTime(13, 45, 20);
LocalDateTime dt4 = date.atTime(time);
LocalDateTime dt5 = time.atDate(date);
```

Note that it's possible to create a `LocalDateTime` by passing a time to a `LocalDate`, or conversely a date to a `LocalTime`, using respectively their `atTime` or `atDate` methods. You can also extract the `LocalDate` or `LocalTime` component from a `LocalDateTime` using the `toLocalDate` and `toLocalTime` methods:

```
LocalDate date1 = dt1.toLocalDate();    <-- 2014-03-18
LocalTime time1 = dt1.toLocalTime();    <-- 13:45:20
```

12.1.3 Instant: a date and time for machines

As humans we're used to thinking of dates and time in terms of weeks, days, hours, and minutes. Nonetheless, this representation isn't easy for a computer to deal with. From a machine point of view, the most natural format to model time is with a single large number representing a point on a continuous timeline. This is the approach used by the new `java.time.Instant` class, which basically represents the number of seconds passed since the Unix epoch time, set by convention to midnight of January 1, 1970 UTC.

You can create an instance of this class by passing the number of seconds to its `ofEpochSecond` static factory method. In addition, the `Instant` class supports nanosecond precision. There's a supplementary overloaded version of the `ofEpochSecond` static factory method that accepts a second argument that's a nanosecond adjustment to the passed number of seconds. This overloaded version adjusts the nanosecond argument, ensuring that the stored nanosecond fraction is between 0 and 999,999,999. This means all the following invocations of the `ofEpochSecond` factory method will return exactly the same `Instant`:

```
Instant.ofEpochSecond(3);
Instant.ofEpochSecond(3, 0);
Instant.ofEpochSecond(2, 1_000_000_000);   <-- One billion nanoseconds (1 second) after 2 seconds
Instant.ofEpochSecond(4, -1_000_000_000);  <-- One billion nanoseconds (1 second) before 4 seconds
```

As you've already seen for the `LocalDate` and the other human-readable date-time classes, the `Instant` class also supports another static factory method named `now`, which allows you to capture a timestamp of the current moment. It's important to reinforce that an `Instant` is intended for use only by a machine. It consists of a number of seconds and nanoseconds. As a consequence, it doesn't provide any ability to handle units of time that are meaningful to humans. For example, this statement

```
int day = Instant.now().get(ChronoField.DAY_OF_MONTH);
```

will just throw an exception like

```
java.time.temporal.UnsupportedTemporalTypeException: Unsupported field:
    DayOfMonth
```

But you can work with `Instants` by using the `Duration` and `Period` classes, which we look at next.

12.1.4 Defining a Duration or a Period

All the classes you've seen so far implement the `Temporal` interface, which defines how to read and manipulate the values of an object modeling a generic point in time. We've shown you a few ways to create different `Temporal` instances. The next natural step is to create a duration between two temporal objects. The `between` static factory method of the `Duration` class serves exactly this purpose. You can create a duration between two `LocalTimes`, two `LocalDateTimes`, or two `Instants` as follows:

```
Duration d1 = Duration.between(time1, time2);
Duration d1 = Duration.between(dateTime1, dateTime2);
Duration d2 = Duration.between(instant1, instant2);
```

Because `LocalDateTime` and `Instant` are made for different purposes, one to be used by humans and the other by machines, you're not allowed to mix them. If you try to create a duration between them, you'll only obtain a `DateTimeException`. Moreover, because the `Duration` class is used to represent an amount of time measured in seconds and eventually nanoseconds, you can't pass a `LocalDate` to the `between` method.

When you need to model an amount of time in terms of years, months, and days, you can use the `Period` class. You can find out the difference between two `LocalDates` with the `between` factory method of that class:

```
Period tenDays = Period.between(LocalDate.of(2014, 3, 8),
                                LocalDate.of(2014, 3, 18));
```

Finally, both the Duration and Period classes have other convenient factory methods to create instances of them directly, in other words, without defining them as the difference between two temporal objects, as shown in the next listing.

Listing 12.5 Creating Durations and Periods

```
Duration threeMinutes = Duration.ofMinutes(3);
Duration threeMinutes = Duration.of(3, ChronoUnit.MINUTES);

Period tenDays = Period.ofDays(10);
Period threeWeeks = Period.ofWeeks(3);
Period twoYearsSixMonthsOneDay = Period.of(2, 6, 1);
```

Both the Duration and Period classes share many similar methods, and table 12.1 lists these.

Table 12.1 The common methods of date-time classes representing an interval

Method	Static	Description
between	Yes	Creates an interval between two points in time
from	Yes	Creates an interval from a temporal unit
of	Yes	Creates an instance of this interval from its constituent parts
parse	Yes	Creates an instance of this interval from a String
addTo	No	Creates a copy of this interval adding to it the specified temporal object
get	No	Reads part of the state of this interval
isNegative	No	Checks if this interval is negative, excluding zero
isZero	No	Checks if this interval is zero length
minus	No	Creates a copy of this interval with an amount of time subtracted
multipliedBy	No	Creates a copy of this interval multiplied by the given scalar
negated	No	Creates a copy of this interval with the length negated
plus	No	Creates a copy of this interval with an amount of time added
subtractFrom	No	Subtracts this interval from the specified temporal object

All the classes we've investigated so far are immutable, and this is a great design choice to allow a more functional programming style, ensure thread-safety, and preserve the consistency of the domain model. Nevertheless, the new Date and Time API offers some handy methods to create a modified version of those objects. For example, you may wish to add three days to an existing LocalDate instance. We explore how to do this in the next section. In addition, we explore how to create a date-time formatter from a given pattern, such as dd/MM/yyyy, or even programmatically, and how to use this formatter for both parsing and printing a date.

12.2 Manipulating, parsing, and formatting dates

The most immediate and easiest way to create a modified version of an existing LocalDate is changing one of its attributes, using one of its withAttribute methods. Note that all the methods return a new object with the modified attribute, as shown in the following listing. They don't mutate the existing object!

Listing 12.6 Manipulating the attributes of a LocalDate in an absolute way

```
LocalDate date1 = LocalDate.of(2014, 3, 18);           <-- 2014-03-18
LocalDate date2 = date1.withYear(2011);                <-- 2011-03-18
LocalDate date3 = date2.withDayOfMonth(25);            <-- 2011-03-25
LocalDate date4 = date3.with(ChronoField.MONTH_OF_YEAR, 9);  <-- 2011-09-25
```

You can also do this with the more generic with method, taking a TemporalField as first argument, as in the last statement of listing 12.6. This last with method is the dual of the get method used in listing 12.2. Both of these methods are declared in the Temporal interface implemented by all the classes of the Date and Time API, which define a single point in time such as LocalDate, LocalTime, LocalDateTime, and Instant. More precisely, the get and with methods let you respectively read and modify the value of a field of a Temporal object. They throw an Unsupported-TemporalTypeException if the requested field isn't supported by the specific Temporal, for example, a ChronoField.MONTH_OF_YEAR on an Instant or a ChronoField.NANO_OF_SECOND on a LocalDate.

It's even possible to manipulate a LocalDate in a declarative manner. For example, you can add or subtract a given amount of time, as shown in the next listing.

Listing 12.7 Manipulating the attributes of a LocalDate in a relative way

```
LocalDate date1 = LocalDate.of(2014, 3, 18);           <-- 2014-03-18
LocalDate date2 = date1.plusWeeks(1);                  <-- 2014-03-18
LocalDate date3 = date2.minusYears(3);                 <-- 2011-03-25
LocalDate date4 = date3.plus(6, ChronoUnit.MONTHS);    <-- 2011-09-25
```

Similarly to what we've explained about the with and get methods, the generic plus method used in the last statement of listing 12.7, together with the analogous minus method, is declared in the Temporal interface. These methods allow you to move a Temporal back or forward a given amount of time, defined by a number plus a TemporalUnit, where the ChronoUnit enumeration offers a convenient implementation of the TemporalUnit interface.

As you may have anticipated, all the date-time classes representing a point in time like LocalDate, LocalTime, LocalDateTime, and Instant have many methods in common; table 12.2 summarizes these.

Table 12.2 The common methods of date-time classes representing a point in time

Method	Static	Description
`from`	Yes	Creates an instance of this class from the passed temporal object
`now`	Yes	Creates a temporal object from the system clock
`of`	Yes	Creates an instance of this temporal object from its constituent parts
`parse`	Yes	Creates an instance of this temporal object from a `String`
`atOffset`	No	Combines this temporal object with a zone offset
`atZone`	No	Combines this temporal object with a time zone
`format`	No	Converts this temporal object into a `String` using the specified formatter (not available for `Instant`)
`get`	No	Reads part of the state of this temporal object
`minus`	No	Creates a copy of this temporal object with an amount of time subtracted
`plus`	No	Creates a copy of this temporal object with an amount of time added
`with`	No	Creates a copy of this temporal object with part of the state changed

Check what you've learned up to now about manipulating dates with Quiz 12.1.

Quiz 12.1: Manipulating a LocalDate

What will the value of the `date` variable be after the following manipulations?

```
LocalDate date = LocalDate.of(2014, 3, 18);
date = date.with(ChronoField.MONTH_OF_YEAR, 9);
date = date.plusYears(2).minusDays(10);
date.withYear(2011);
```

Answer:

```
2016-09-08
```

As you've seen, you can manipulate the date both in an absolute way and in a relative way. You can also concatenate more manipulations in a single statement, because every change will create a new `LocalDate` object, and the subsequent invocation will manipulate the object created by the former one. Finally, the last statement in this code snippet has no observable effect because, as usual, it creates a new `LocalDate` instance, but we're not assigning this new value to any variable.

12.2.1 Working with TemporalAdjusters

All the date manipulations you've seen so far are relatively straightforward. Sometimes, you may need to perform more advanced operations, such as adjusting a date to the next Sunday, the next working day, or the last day of the month. In such cases you can pass to an overloaded version of the `with` method a `TemporalAdjuster` that provides a more customizable way to define the manipulation needed to operate on a specific date. The Date and Time API already provides many predefined `TemporalAdjusters` for the most common use cases. You can access them using the static factory methods contained in the `TemporalAdjusters` class, as shown next.

Listing 12.8 Using the predefined `TemporalAdjusters`

```
import static java.time.temporal.TemporalAdjusters.*;
LocalDate date1 = LocalDate.of(2014, 3, 18);                       <- 2014-03-18
LocalDate date2 = date1.with(nextOrSame(DayOfWeek.SUNDAY));         <- 2014-03-23
LocalDate date3 = date2.with(lastDayOfMonth());                     <- 2014-03-31
```

Table 12.3 provides a list of the `TemporalAdjusters` that can be created with these factory methods.

Table 12.3 The factory methods of the `TemporalAdjusters` class

Method	Description
`dayOfWeekInMonth`	Creates a new date in the same month with the ordinal day of week
`firstDayOfMonth`	Creates a new date set to the first day of the current month
`firstDayOfNextMonth`	Creates a new date set to the first day of the next month
`firstDayOfNextYear`	Creates a new date set to the first day of the next year
`firstDayOfYear`	Creates a new date set to the first day of the current year
`firstInMonth`	Creates a new date in the same month with the first matching day of week
`lastDayOfMonth`	Creates a new date set to the last day of the current month
`lastDayOfNextMonth`	Creates a new date set to the last day of the next month
`lastDayOfNextYear`	Creates a new date set to the last day of the next year
`lastDayOfYear`	Creates a new date set to the last day of the current year
`lastInMonth`	Creates a new date in the same month with the last matching day of week
`next` `previous`	Creates a new date set to the first occurrence of the specified day of week after/before the date being adjusted
`nextOrSame` `previousOrSame`	Creates a new date set to the first occurrence of the specified day of week after/before the date being adjusted unless it's already on that day, in which case the same object is returned

As you can see, `TemporalAdjusters` allow you to perform more complex date manipulations that still read like the problem statement. Moreover, it's relatively simple to create your own custom `TemporalAdjuster` implementation if you can't find a predefined `TemporalAdjuster` that fits your need. In fact, the `TemporalAdjuster` interface declares only a single method (this makes it a functional interface), defined as follows.

Listing 12.9 The TemporalAdjuster interface

```
@FunctionalInterface
public interface TemporalAdjuster {
    Temporal adjustInto(Temporal temporal);
}
```

This means an implementation of the `TemporalAdjuster` interface defines how to convert a `Temporal` object into another `Temporal`. You can think of it as being like a `UnaryOperator<Temporal>`. Take a few minutes to practice what you've learned so far and implement your own `TemporalAdjuster` in Quiz 12.2.

Quiz 12.2: Implementing a custom TemporalAdjuster

Develop a class named `NextWorkingDay`, implementing the `TemporalAdjuster` interface that moves a date forward by one day but skips Saturdays and Sundays. Doing the following

```
date = date.with(new NextWorkingDay());
```

should move the date to the next day, if this day is between Monday and Friday, but to the next Monday if it's a Saturday or a Sunday.

Answer:

You can implement the `NextWorkingDay` adjuster as follows:

```
public class NextWorkingDay implements TemporalAdjuster {
    @Override
    public Temporal adjustInto(Temporal temporal) {
        DayOfWeek dow =
                DayOfWeek.of(temporal.get(ChronoField.DAY_OF_WEEK));   <- Read the current day.
        int dayToAdd = 1;                                               <- Normally add one day.
        if (dow == DayOfWeek.FRIDAY) dayToAdd = 3;                      <- But add three days if today is a Friday.
        else if (dow == DayOfWeek.SATURDAY) dayToAdd = 2;               <- Or two if it's a Saturday.
        return temporal.plus(dayToAdd, ChronoUnit.DAYS);                <- Return the modified date adding the right number of days.
    }
}
```

This `TemporalAdjuster` normally moves a date forward one day, except if today is a Friday or Saturday, in which case it advances the dates three or two days, respectively. Note that since a `TemporalAdjuster` is a functional interface, you could just pass the behavior of this adjuster in a lambda expression:

```
date = date.with(temporal -> {
        DayOfWeek dow =
                DayOfWeek.of(temporal.get(ChronoField.DAY_OF_WEEK));
    int dayToAdd = 1;
    if (dow == DayOfWeek.FRIDAY) dayToAdd = 3;
    else if (dow == DayOfWeek.SATURDAY) dayToAdd = 2;
    return temporal.plus(dayToAdd, ChronoUnit.DAYS);
});
```

(continued)

It's likely that you may want to apply this manipulation to a date in several points of your code, and for this reason we suggest encapsulating its logic in a proper class as we did here. Do the same for all the manipulations you use frequently. You'll end up with a small library of adjusters you and your team could easily reuse in your codebase.

If you want to define the `TemporalAdjuster` with a lambda expression, it's preferable to do it using the `ofDateAdjuster` static factory of the `TemporalAdjusters` class that accepts a `UnaryOperator<LocalDate>` as follows:

```
TemporalAdjuster nextWorkingDay = TemporalAdjusters.ofDateAdjuster(
    temporal -> {
        DayOfWeek dow =
                DayOfWeek.of(temporal.get(ChronoField.DAY_OF_WEEK));
        int dayToAdd = 1;
        if (dow == DayOfWeek.FRIDAY) dayToAdd = 3;
        if (dow == DayOfWeek.SATURDAY) dayToAdd = 2;
        return temporal.plus(dayToAdd, ChronoUnit.DAYS);
    });
date = date.with(nextWorkingDay);
```

Another common operation you may want to perform on your date and time objects is printing them in different formats specific to your business domain. Similarly, you may want to convert `String`s representing dates in those formats into actual date objects. In the next section, we demonstrate the mechanisms provided by the new `Date` and `Time` API to accomplish these tasks.

12.2.2 Printing and parsing date-time objects

Formatting and parsing is another relevant feature when working with dates and times. The new `java.time.format` package is entirely devoted to this purpose. The most important class of this package is `DateTimeFormatter`. The easiest way to create a formatter is through its static factory methods and constants. The constants such as `BASIC_ISO_DATE` and `ISO_LOCAL_DATE` are just predefined instances of the `DateTimeFormatter` class. All `DateTimeFormatter`s can be used to create a `String` representing a given date or time in a specific format. For example, here we produce a `String` using two different formatters:

```
LocalDate date = LocalDate.of(2014, 3, 18);
String s1 = date.format(DateTimeFormatter.BASIC_ISO_DATE);     <-- 20140318
String s2 = date.format(DateTimeFormatter.ISO_LOCAL_DATE);     <-- 2014-03-18
```

You can also parse a `String` representing a date or a time in that format to re-create the date object itself. You can achieve this by using the `parse` factory method provided by all the classes of the Date and Time API representing a point in time or an interval:

```
LocalDate date1 = LocalDate.parse("20140318",
                                 DateTimeFormatter.BASIC_ISO_DATE);
LocalDate date2 = LocalDate.parse("2014-03-18",
                                 DateTimeFormatter.ISO_LOCAL_DATE);
```

In comparison to the old java.util.DateFormat class, all the DateTimeFormatter instances are thread-safe. Therefore, you can create singleton formatters, like the ones defined by the DateTimeFormatter constants, and share them among multiple threads. The DateTimeFormatter class also supports a static factory method that lets you create a formatter from a specific pattern, as shown in the next listing.

Listing 12.10 Creating a DateTimeFormatter from a pattern

```
DateTimeFormatter formatter = DateTimeFormatter.ofPattern("dd/MM/yyyy");
LocalDate date1 = LocalDate.of(2014, 3, 18);
String formattedDate = date1.format(formatter);
LocalDate date2 = LocalDate.parse(formattedDate, formatter);
```

Here the LocalDate's format method produces a String representing the date with the requested pattern. Next, the static parse method re-creates the same date by parsing the generated String using the same formatter. The ofPattern method also has an overloaded version allowing you to create a formatter for a given Locale, as shown in the following listing.

Listing 12.11 Creating a localized DateTimeFormatter

```
DateTimeFormatter italianFormatter =
                   DateTimeFormatter.ofPattern("d. MMMM yyyy", Locale.ITALIAN);
LocalDate date1 = LocalDate.of(2014, 3, 18);
String formattedDate = date.format(italianFormatter); // 18. marzo 2014
LocalDate date2 = LocalDate.parse(formattedDate, italianFormatter);
```

Finally, in case you need even more control, the DateTimeFormatterBuilder class lets you define complex formatters step by step using meaningful methods. In addition, it provides you with the ability to have case-insensitive parsing, lenient parsing (allowing the parser to use heuristics to interpret inputs that don't precisely match the specified format), padding, and optional sections of the formatter. For example, you can programmatically build the same italianFormatter we used in listing 12.11 through the DateTimeFormatterBuilder as follows.

Listing 12.12 Building a DateTimeFormatter

```
DateTimeFormatter italianFormatter = new DateTimeFormatterBuilder()
        .appendText(ChronoField.DAY_OF_MONTH)
        .appendLiteral(". ")
        .appendText(ChronoField.MONTH_OF_YEAR)
        .appendLiteral(" ")
        .appendText(ChronoField.YEAR)
        .parseCaseInsensitive()
        .toFormatter(Locale.ITALIAN);
```

So far you've learned how to create, manipulate, format, and parse both points in time and intervals. But you haven't seen how to deal with subtleties involving dates and time. For example, you may need to deal with different time zones or work with alternative calendar systems. In the next sections, we explore these topics using the new Date and Time API.

12.3 Working with different time zones and calendars

None of the classes you've seen so far contained any information about time zones. Dealing with time zones is another important issue that's been vastly simplified by the new Date and Time API. The new `java.time.ZoneId` class is the replacement for the old `java.util.TimeZone` class. It aims to better shield you from the complexities related to time zones, such as dealing with Daylight Saving Time (DST). Like the other classes of the Date and Time API, it's immutable.

A time zone is a set of rules corresponding to a region in which the standard time is the same. There are about 40 of them held in instances of the `ZoneRules` class. You can simply call `getRules()` on a `ZoneId` to obtain the rules for that given time zone. A specific `ZoneId` is identified by a region ID, for example:

```
ZoneId romeZone = ZoneId.of("Europe/Rome");
```

The region IDs are all in the format "{area}/{city}" and the set of available locations is the one supplied by the IANA Time Zone Database. You can also convert an old `TimeZone` object to a `ZoneId` by using the new method `toZoneId`:

```
ZoneId zoneId = TimeZone.getDefault().toZoneId();
```

Once you have a `ZoneId` object, you can combine it with a `LocalDate`, a `LocalDateTime`, or an `Instant`, to transform it into `ZoneDateTime` instances, which represent points in time relative to the specified time zone, as shown in the next listing.

Listing 12.13 Applying a time zone to a point in time

```
LocalDate date = LocalDate.of(2014, Month.MARCH, 18);
ZonedDateTime zdt1 = date.atStartOfDay(romeZone);

LocalDateTime dateTime = LocalDateTime.of(2014, Month.MARCH, 18, 13, 45);
ZonedDateTime zdt2 = dateTime.atZone(romeZone);

Instant instant = Instant.now();
ZonedDateTime zdt3 = instant.atZone(romeZone);
```

Figure 12.1 illustrates the components of a `ZonedDateTime` to help you understand the differences between `LocaleDate`, `LocalTime`, `LocalDateTime`, and `ZoneId`.

You can also convert a `LocalDateTime` to an `Instant` by using a `ZoneId`:

```
LocalDateTime dateTime = LocalDateTime.of(2014, Month.MARCH, 18, 13, 45);
Instant instantFromDateTime = dateTime.toInstant(romeZone);
```

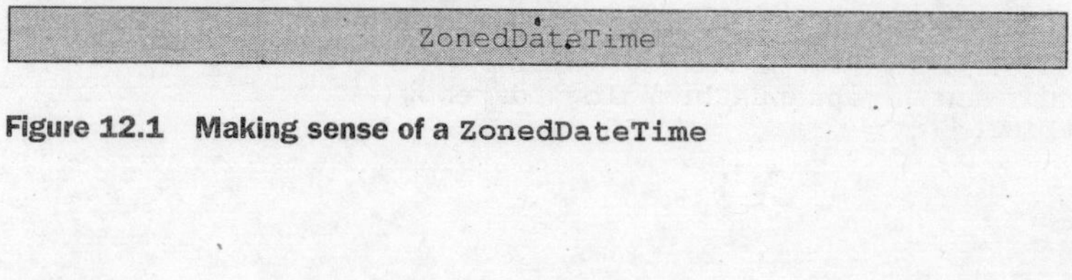

Figure 12.1 Making sense of a `ZonedDateTime`

Or you can do it the other way around:

```
Instant instant = Instant.now();
LocalDateTime timeFromInstant = LocalDateTime.ofInstant(instant, romeZone);
```

12.3.1 Fixed offset from UTC/Greenwich

Another common way to express a time zone is with a fixed offset from UTC/Greenwich. For instance, you can use this notation to say that "New York is five hours behind London." In cases like this you can use the `ZoneOffset` class, a subclass of `ZoneId` that represents the difference between a time and the zero meridian of Greenwich, London:

```
ZoneOffset newYorkOffset = ZoneOffset.of("-05:00");
```

The -05:00 offset indeed corresponds to the US Eastern Standard Time. Be aware that a `ZoneOffset` defined in this way doesn't have any Daylight Saving Time management, and for this reason it isn't suggested in the majority of cases. Because a `ZoneOffset` is also a `ZoneId`, you can use it as shown in listing 12.13. You can also create an `OffsetDateTime`, which represents a date-time with an offset from UTC/Greenwich in the ISO-8601 calendar system:

```
LocalDateTime dateTime = LocalDateTime.of(2014, Month.MARCH, 18, 13, 45);
OffsetDateTime dateTimeInNewYork = OffsetDateTime.of(date, newYorkOffset);
```

Another advanced feature supported by the new Date and Time API is support for non-ISO calendaring systems.

12.3.2 Using alternative calendar systems

The ISO-8601 calendar system is the de facto world civil calendar system. But four additional calendar systems are provided in Java 8. Each of these calendar systems has a dedicated date class: `ThaiBuddhistDate`, `MinguoDate`, `JapaneseDate`, and `HijrahDate`. All these classes together with `LocalDate` implement the `ChronoLocalDate` interface intended to model a date in an arbitrary chronology. You can create an instance of one of these classes out of a `LocalDate`. More generally, you can create any other `Temporal` instance using their `from` static factory methods as follows:

```
LocalDate date = LocalDate.of(2014, Month.MARCH, 18);
JapaneseDate japaneseDate = JapaneseDate.from(date);
```

Alternatively, you can explicitly create a calendar system for a specific `Locale` and create an instance of a date for that `Locale`. In the new Date and Time API, the `Chronology` interface models a calendar system, and you can obtain an instance of it using its `ofLocale` static factory method:

```
Chronology japaneseChronology = Chronology.ofLocale(Locale.JAPAN);
ChronoLocalDate now = japaneseChronology.dateNow();
```

The designers of the Date and Time API advise using `LocalDate` instead of `Chrono-LocalDate` for most cases; this is because a developer could make assumptions in their code that unfortunately aren't true in a multicalendar system. Such assumptions might include that the value of a day or month will never be higher than 31, that a year contains 12 months, or even that a year has a fixed number of months. For these reasons, it's recommended to use `LocalDate` throughout your application, including all storage, manipulation, and interpretation of business rules, whereas you should employ `ChronoLocalDate` only when you need to localize the input or output of your program.

ISLAMIC CALENDAR

Out of the new calendars added to Java 8, the `HijrahDate` (Islamic calendar) seems to be the most complex because it can have variants. The Hijrah calendar system is based on lunar months. There are a variety of methods to determine a new month, such as a new moon that could be visible anywhere in the world or that must be visible first in Saudi Arabia. The `withVariant` method is used to choose the desired variant. Java 8 has included the Umm Al-Qura variant for `HijrahDate` as standard.

The following code illustrates an example of displaying the start and end dates of Ramadan for the current Islamic year in ISO date:

```
HijrahDate ramadanDate =
    HijrahDate.now().with(ChronoField.DAY_OF_MONTH, 1)
                    .with(ChronoField.MONTH_OF_YEAR, 9);
System.out.println("Ramadan starts on " +
                   IsoChronology.INSTANCE.date(ramadanDate) +
                   " and ends on " +
                   IsoChronology.INSTANCE.date(
                       ramadanDate.with(
                           TemporalAdjusters.lastDayOfMonth())));
```

Get current Hijrah date; then change it to have the first day of Ramadan, which is the 9th month.

`IsoChronology.INSTANCE` is a static instance of the `IsoChronology` class.

Ramadan starts on 2014-06-28 and ends on 2014-07-27.

12.4 Summary

In this chapter, you've learned the following:

- The old `java.util.Date` class and all other classes used to model date and time in Java before Java 8 have many inconsistencies and design flaws, including their mutability and some poorly chosen offsets, defaults, and naming.
- The date-time objects of the new Date and Time API are all immutable.
- This new API provides two different time representations to manage the different needs of humans and machines when operating on it.
- You can manipulate date and time objects in both an absolute and relative manner, and the result of these manipulations is always a new instance, leaving the original one unchanged.
- `TemporalAdjusters` allow you to manipulate a date in a more complex way than just changing one of its values, and you can define and use your own custom date transformations.

- You can define a formatter to both print and parse date-time objects in a specific format. These formatters can be created from a pattern or programmatically and they're all thread-safe.
- You can represent a time zone, both relative to a specific region/location and as a fixed offset from UTC/Greenwich, and apply it to a date-time object in order to localize it.
- You can use calendar systems different from the ISO-8601 standard system.

Part 4

Beyond Java 8

In the final part of this book, we draw back a little with a tutorial introduction to writing effective functional-style programs in Java, along with a comparison of Java 8 features with those of Scala.

Chapter 13 gives a full tutorial on functional programming, introduces some of its terminology, and explains how to write functional-style programs in Java 8.

Chapter 14 covers more advanced functional programming techniques including higher-order functions, currying, persistent data structures, lazy lists, and pattern matching. You can view this chapter as a mix of practical techniques to apply in your codebase as well as academic information that will make you a more knowledgeable programmer.

Chapter 15 follows by discussing how Java 8 features compare to features in the Scala language—a language that, like Java, is implemented on top of the JVM and that has evolved quickly to threaten some aspects of Java's niche in the programming language ecosystem.

Finally, chapter 16 reviews the journey of learning about Java 8 and the gentle push toward functional-style programming. In addition, we speculate on what future enhancements and great new features may be in Java's pipeline beyond Java 8.

13 Thinking functionally

This chapter covers

- Why functional programming?
- What defines functional programming?
- Declarative programming and referential transparency
- Guidelines for writing functional-style Java
- Iteration vs. recursion

You've seen the term *functional* quite frequently throughout this book. By now, you may have some ideas of what being functional entails. Is it about lambdas and first-class functions? Or is it about restricting your right to mutate objects? In which case, what do you achieve from adopting a functional style? In this chapter, we shed light on these questions. We explain what functional programming is and introduce some of its terminology. We first examine the concepts behind functional programming such as side effects, immutability, declarative programming, and referential transparency and relate these to Java 8. In the next chapter, we look more closely at functional programming techniques such as higher-order functions, currying, persistent data structures, lazy lists, pattern matching, and combinators.

13.1 Implementing and maintaining systems

Let's start by imagining you've been asked to manage an upgrade to a large preexisting software system, which you haven't yet seen. Should you accept this job maintaining such a software system? A seasoned Java contractor's only slightly tongue-in-cheek maxim for deciding is "Start by searching for the keyword `synchronized`; if you find it, then just say no (reflecting the difficulty of fixing concurrency bugs); otherwise consider the structure of the system in more detail." We provide more detail in the next paragraphs, but first observe that, as you've seen in previous chapters, Java 8's addition of streams allows you to exploit parallelism without worrying about locking, provided you embrace stateless behaviors (that is, functions in your stream-processing pipeline don't interact by one reading from or writing to a variable that's written by another).

What else might you wish the program to look like so it's easy to work with? You'd want it to be well structured, with an understandable class hierarchy reflecting the structure of the system; there are even ways to estimate such structure by using software engineering metrics of coupling (how interdependent parts of the system are) and cohesion (how related the various parts of the system are).

But for many programmers, the key day-to-day concern is debugging during maintenance: this code crashed because it observed some unexpected value. Why is it this way and how did it get this way? Just think of how many of your maintenance concerns fall into this category![1] It turns out that the ideas of *no side effects* and *immutability*, which functional programming promotes, can help. Let's examine this in more detail.

13.1.1 Shared mutable data

Ultimately, the reason for the unexpected variable value problems just discussed is that shared mutable data structures are read and updated by more than one of the methods your maintenance centers on. Suppose several classes keep a reference to a list. Who owns this list? What if one class modifies it? Do other classes expect this change? How do other classes learn of this change? Do they need to be notified of this change to satisfy all assumptions on this list, or should they make a defensive copy for themselves? In other words, shared mutable data structures make it harder to track changes in different parts of your program. Figure 13.1 illustrates this idea.

Consider a system that doesn't mutate any data structures. It would be a dream to maintain because you wouldn't have any bad surprises about some object somewhere that unexpectedly modifies a data structure! A method, which modifies neither the state of its enclosing class nor the state of any other objects and returns its entire results using `return`, is called *pure* or *side-effect free.*

What constitutes a side effect more concretely? In a nutshell, a side effect is an action that's not totally enclosed within the function itself. Here are some examples:

---

[1] We recommend reading *Working Effectively with Legacy Code* (Prentice Hall, 2004) by Michael Feathers for further discussion on this topic.

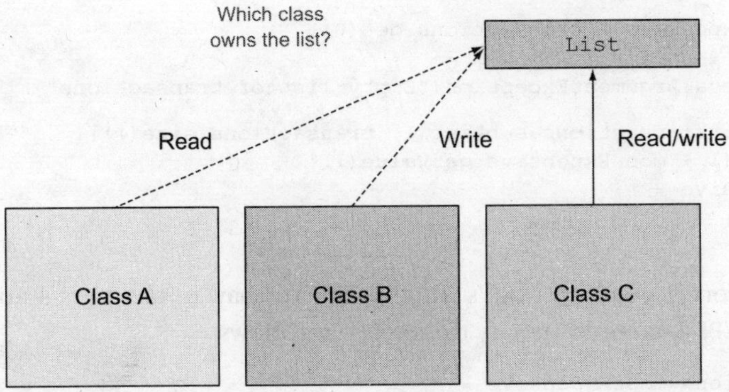

Figure 13.1 A mutable shared across multiple classes. It's difficult to understand who the owner is.

- Modifying a data structure in place, including assigning to any field, apart from initialization inside a constructor (for example, setter methods)
- Throwing an exception
- Doing I/O operations such as writing to a file

Another way to look at this idea of no side effects is to consider immutable objects. An immutable object is an object that can't change its state after it's instantiated so it can't be affected by the actions of a function. This means that once immutable objects are instantiated, they can never go into an unexpected state. You can share them without having to copy them, and they're thread-safe because they can't be modified.

The idea of no side effects might appear as a pretty severe restriction, and you may doubt whether real systems *can* be built in this way. We hope to convince you of this by the end of the chapter. The good news is that components of systems that embrace this idea can use multicore parallelism without using locking, because the methods can no longer interfere with each other. In addition, this is great for immediately understanding which parts of the program are independent.

These ideas come from functional programming, which we turn to in the next section. But first, let's explore the idea of *declarative programming*, upon which functional programming is based.

13.1.2 Declarative programming

There are two ways of thinking about implementing a system by writing a program. One way centers on how things are done: "first do this, then update that, then …." For example, if you want to calculate the most expensive transaction in a list, you'll typically execute a sequence of commands: take a transaction from the list and compare it with the provisional most expensive transaction; if it's more expensive, then it becomes the provisional most expensive; repeat with the next transaction in the list and so on.

This "how" style of programming is an excellent match for classic object-oriented programming, sometimes called imperative programming, because it has instructions that mimic the low-level vocabulary of a computer (for example, assignment, conditional branching, and loops), as shown in this code:

```
Transaction mostExpensive = transactions.get(0);
if(mostExpensive == null)
    throw new IllegalArgumentException("Empty list of transactions")

for(Transaction t: transactions.subList(1, transactions.size())){
    if(t.getValue() > mostExpensive.getValue()){
        mostExpensive = t;
    }
}
```

The other way centers instead on what's to be done. You saw in chapters 4 and 5 that using the Streams API you could specify this query as follows:

```
Optional<Transaction> mostExpensive =
    transactions.stream()
                .max(comparing(Transaction::getValue));
```

The fine detail of how this query is implemented is left to the library. We refer to this idea as *internal iteration*. The great advantage is that your query reads like the problem statement, and because of that it's clear to understand immediately in comparison to trying to understand what a sequence of commands does.

This "what" style is often called declarative programming. You give rules saying what you want, and you expect the system to decide how to achieve it. It's great because it reads closer to the problem statement.

13.1.3 Why functional programming?

Functional programming exemplifies this idea of declarative programming ("just say what you want, using expressions that don't interact, and for which the system can choose the implementation") and side-effect-free computation explained previously. As we discussed, these two ideas can help you implement and maintain systems more easily.

Note that certain language features such as composing operations and passing behaviors, which we presented in chapter 3 using lambda expressions, are required to help read and write code in a natural way using a declarative style. Using streams, you were able to chain several operations together to express a complicated query. These features are what characterize functional programming languages; we look at them more carefully under the guise of combinators in the next chapter, in section 14.5.

To make things tangible and connect them with the new features in Java 8, we now concretely define the idea of functional programming and its representation in Java. What we'd like to impart is that by using functional-programming style, you can write serious programs without relying on side effects.

13.2 What's functional programming?

The oversimplistic answer to "What is functional programming?" is "programming using functions." So what's a function?

It's easy to imagine a method taking an `int` and a `double` as arguments and producing a double—and also having the side effect of counting the number of times it has been called by updating a mutable variable, as illustrated in figure 13.2.

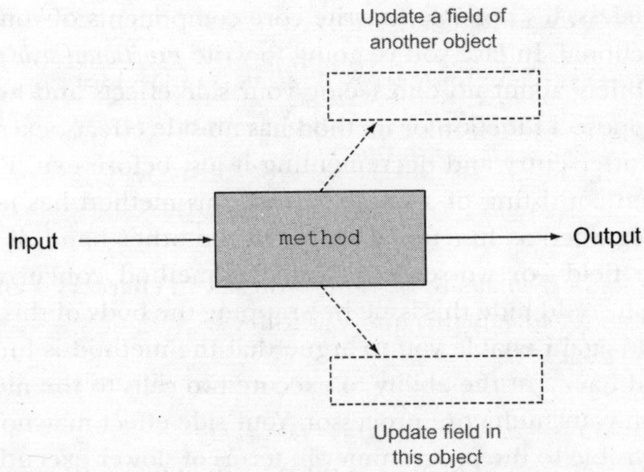

Figure 13.2 A function with side effects

But in the context of functional programming a *function* corresponds to a mathematical function: it takes zero or more arguments, gives one or more results, *and has no side effects.* You can see it as a black box, which takes some inputs and produces some outputs, as illustrated in figure 13.3.

The distinction between this sort of function and the methods you see in programming languages like Java is central. (The idea of the mathematical functions like `log` or `sin` having such side effects in unthinkable.) In particular, mathematical functions when repeatedly called with the same arguments always return the same results. This rules out methods such as `Random.nextInt`, and we further discuss this idea later under the concept of referential transparency.

When we say *functional* we mean "like mathematics—no side effects." Now a programming subtlety appears. Do we mean that every function is built *only* using functions and of course mathematical ideas such as `if-then-else`? Or might we allow a function to do nonfunctional things internally, as long as it doesn't *expose* any of these side effects to the rest of the system? In other words, if we as programmers perform a side effect that can't be observed by callers, does that side effect actually exist? The caller doesn't need to know or care, because it can't affect them.

When we wish to emphasize the difference, we refer to the first as pure functional programming (we return to this later in the chapter) and the latter as functional-style programming.

13.2.1 Functional-style Java

In practice, you can't completely program in pure functional style in Java. For example, Java's I/O model consists of side-effecting methods (calling `Scanner.nextLine` has the side effect of consuming a line from a file, so calling it twice typically gives

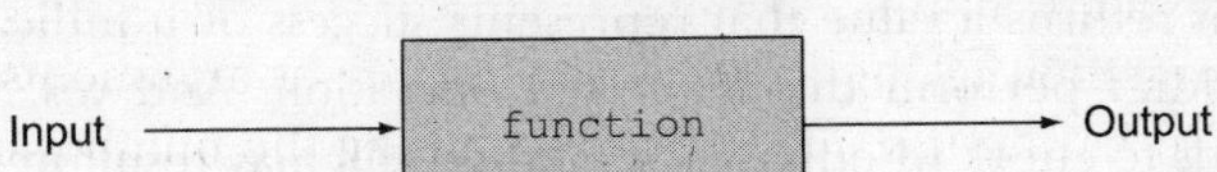

Figure 13.3 A function with no side effects

different results). Nonetheless, it's possible to write core components of your system as if they were purely functional. In Java you're going to write *functional-style programs.* First, there's a further subtlety about no one seeing your side effects and hence the meaning of *functional.* Suppose a function or method has no side effects, except for it incrementing a field just after entry and decrementing it just before exit. From the point of view of a program consisting of a single thread, this method has no visible side effects and can be regarded as functional style. On the other hand, if another thread could inspect the field—or worse could call the method concurrently—it wouldn't be functional. You could hide this issue by wrapping the body of this method with a lock, and this would again enable you to argue that the method is functional. But in doing so you would have lost the ability to execute two calls to the method in parallel using two cores on your multicore processor. Your side effect may not be visible to a program, but it's visible to the programmer in terms of slower execution!

Our guideline is that to be regarded as *functional style,* a function or method can mutate only local variables. In addition, objects it references should be immutable. By this we mean all fields are `final`, and all fields of reference type refer transitively to other immutable objects. Later you may also permit updates to fields of objects that are freshly created in the method, and so aren't visible from elsewhere, and that aren't saved to affect the result of a subsequent call.

Our previous guideline is incomplete, and there's an additional requirement on being functional, which feels less important at first. To be regarded as functional style, *a function or method shouldn't throw any exceptions.* There's a simple overlegalistic explanation: you can't throw an exception because this means a result is being signaled other than being passed as a proper result via `return` as in the black-box model discussed previously. But then this seems countered by practical mathematical use: although legally a *mathematical function* gives exactly one result for each possible argument value, many common mathematical operations are what we should properly call *partial functions.* That is, for some or most input values they give exactly one result, but for other input values they're *undefined* and don't give a result at all. An example is division when the second operand is zero or `sqrt` when its argument is negative. It might seem natural to model these situations by throwing an exception as Java does. There's some scope for debate here, with some authors arguing that uncaught exceptions representing fatal errors are okay, but it's the act of catching an exception that represents nonfunctional control flow, in that it breaks the simple "pass arguments, return result" metaphor pictured in the black-box model, leading to a third arrow representing an exception, as illustrated in figure 13.4.

So how might you express functions like division without using exceptions? The answer is to use types like `Optional<T>`: instead of `sqrt` having signature "`double sqrt(double)` but may raise an exception," it would have signature "`Optional<Double> sqrt(double)`"—either it returns a value that represents success or it indicates in its return value that it couldn't perform the requested operation. And yes, this does mean that the caller needs to check whether each method call may result in an empty

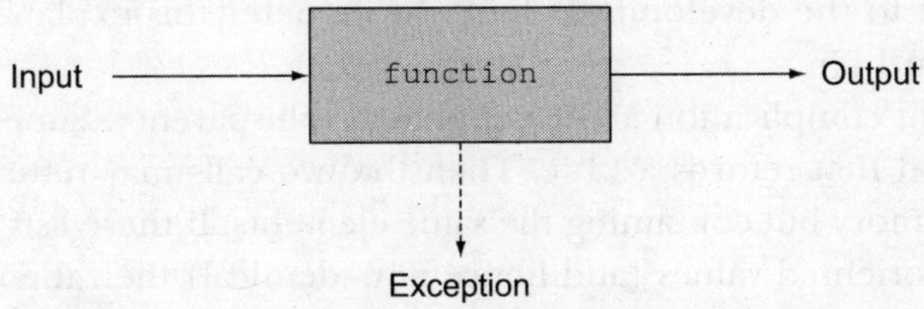

Figure 13.4 A function throwing an exception

`Optional`. This may sound like a huge deal, but pragmatically, given our guidance on functional-style programming versus pure functional programming, you may choose to use exceptions locally but not expose them via large-scale interfaces, thereby gaining the advantages of functional style without the risk of code bloat.

Finally, to be regarded as functional, your function or method should call only those side-effecting library functions for which you can hide their nonfunctional behavior (that is, ensuring that any mutation they make on data structures is hidden from your caller, perhaps by copying first and by catching any exceptions they might raise). In section 13.2.4, "Functional style in practice," you'll see an example where we hide the use of side-effecting library function `List.add` inside our method `insertAll` by copying the list.

These prescriptions can often be marked using comments or by declaring a method with a marker annotation—and match the restrictions we placed on functions we passed to parallel stream-processing operations such as `Stream.map` in chapters 4–7.

Finally, for pragmatic reasons, you may find it convenient for functional-style code still to be able to output debugging information to some form of log file. Yes, this means the code can't be strictly described as functional, but in practice you retain most of the benefits of functional-style programming.

13.2.2 Referential transparency

The restrictions on "no visible side-effects" (no mutating structure visible to callers, no I/O, no exceptions) encode the concept of *referential transparency*. A function is referentially transparent if it always returns the same result value when called with the same argument value. The method `String.replace` is referentially transparent because `"raoul".replace('r', 'R')` will always produce the same result (the method `replace` returns a *new* `String` with all lowercase `'r'` replaced with uppercase `'R'`) rather than updating its `this` object so it can be considered a function.

Put another way, a function consistently produces the same result given the same input, no matter where and when it's invoked. It also explains why we don't regard `Random.nextInt` as functional. In Java using a `Scanner` object to get the input from a user's keyboard violates referential transparency because calling the method `nextLine` may produce a different result at each call. But adding together two `final int` variables always produces the same result, because the content of the variables can never change.

Referential transparency is a great property for program understanding. It also encompasses a save-instead-of-recompute optimization for expensive or long-lived operations, which goes under the name *memoization* or *caching*. Although important, this is slightly at a tangent to the development here, so we defer this explanation to the next chapter, in section 14.5.

In Java there's one slight complication about referential transparency. Suppose you make two calls to a method that returns a `List`. Then the two calls may return references to distinct lists in memory but containing the same elements. If these lists were to be seen as mutable object-oriented values (and hence non-identical) then the method wouldn't be referentially transparent. If you plan to use these lists as pure (immutable) values, then it makes sense to see the values as equal and hence the function as referentially transparent. In general, *in functional-style code you choose to regard such functions as referentially transparent.* We discuss this issue again in the next chapter, in section 14.5. We now explore the issue of whether to mutate from a wider perspective.

13.2.3 Object-oriented vs. functional-style programming

We start by contrasting functional-style programming with (extreme) classical object-oriented programming before observing that Java 8 sees these styles as mere extremes of the object-oriented spectrum. As a Java programmer, without consciously thinking about it, you almost certainly use some aspects of functional-style programming and some aspects of what we'll call extreme object-oriented programming. As we remarked in chapter 1, changes in both hardware (for example, multicore) and programmer expectation (for example, database-like queries to manipulate data) are pushing Java software-engineering styles somewhat more to the functional end of this spectrum, and one of the aims of this book is to help you adapt to the changing climate.

At one end of the spectrum is the extreme object-oriented view: everything is an object and programs operate by updating fields and calling methods that update their associated object. At the other end of the spectrum lies the referentially transparent functional-programming style of no (visible) mutation. In practice, Java programmers have always mixed these styles. You might traverse a data structure using an `Iterator` containing mutable internal state but use this to calculate, say, the sum of values in the data structure in a functional-style manner (in Java, as discussed, this can include mutating local variables). One of the aims of the next sections in this chapter and more generally in the next chapter is to discuss programming techniques and introduce features from functional programming to enable you to write programs that are more modular and more suitable for multicore processors. Think of these ideas as additional weapons in your programming armory.

13.2.4 Functional style in practice

Let's start by solving a programming exercise given to beginning students exemplifying functional style: Given a `List<Integer>` value, for example, {1, 4, 9}, construct a `List<List<Integer>>` value whose members are all the subsets of {1, 4, 9}—in any order. The subsets of {1, 4, 9} are {1, 4 ,9}, {1, 4}, {1, 9}, {4, 9}, {1}, {4}, {9}, and {}.

There are eight subsets including the empty subset, written {}. Each subset is represented as type `List<Integer>`, which means the answer is of type `List<List<Integer>>`.

Students often have problems thinking how to start and need prompting[2] with the remark that "the subsets of {1, 4, 9} either contain 1 or do not." The ones that don't are simply subsets of {4, 9}, and the ones that do can be obtained by taking the subsets of {4, 9} and inserting 1 into each of them. This gives an easy, natural, top-down, functional-programming-style encoding in Java. (A common programmer error is to say that an empty list has no subsets.)

```
static List<List<Integer>> subsets(List<Integer> list) {
    if (list.isEmpty()) {
        List<List<Integer>> ans = new ArrayList<>();
        ans.add(Collections.emptyList());
        return ans;
    }
    Integer first = list.get(0);
    List<Integer> rest = list.subList(1,list.size());
    List<List<Integer>> subans = subsets(rest);
    List<List<Integer>> subans2 = insertAll(first, subans);
    return concat(subans, subans2);
}
```

If the input list is empty, it has exactly one subset, the empty list itself!

Otherwise take one element out, `first`, and find all subsets of the rest to give `subans`; `subans` forms half of the answer.

Then concatenate the two subanswers. Easy?

The other half of the answer, `subans2`, consists of all the lists in `subans` but adjusted by prefixing each of these element lists with `first`.

The solution program produces {{}, {9}, {4}, {4, 9}, {1}, {1, 9}, {1, 4}, {1, 4, 9}} when given {1, 4, 9} as input. Do try it when you've defined the two missing methods.

Let's review what you've just done. You've assumed that the missing methods `insertAll` and `concat` are themselves functional and deduced that your function `subsets` is also, because no operation in it mutates any existing structure. (If you're familiar with mathematics, then you'll recognize this argument as being *by induction.*)

Now let's look at defining `insertAll`. Here's the first danger point. Suppose you defined `insertAll` so that it mutated its arguments, perhaps by updating all the elements of `subans` to contain `first`. Then the program would incorrectly cause `subans` to be modified in the same way as `subans2`, resulting in an answer mysteriously containing eight copies of {1,4,9}. You instead define `insertAll` functionally as follows:

```
static List<List<Integer>> insertAll(Integer first,
                                     List<List<Integer>> lists) {
    List<List<Integer>> result = new ArrayList<>();
    for (List<Integer> list : lists) {
        List<Integer> copyList = new ArrayList<>();
        copyList.add(first);
        copyList.addAll(list);
        result.add(copyList);
    }
    return result;
}
```

Copy the list to allow you to add to it. You wouldn't copy the lower-level structure even if it were mutable (`Integer`s are not).

[2] Troublesome (bright!) students occasionally point out a neat coding trick involving binary representation of numbers (the Java solution code corresponds to 000,001,010,011,100,101,110,111). We tell such students to calculate instead the list of all *permutations* of a list; for the example {1,4,9} there are six of these.

Note that you're creating a new List that contains all the elements of subans. You take advantage of the fact that an Integer object is immutable (otherwise you'd have to clone each element too). The focus caused by thinking of methods like insertAll as functional gives you a natural place to put all this careful copying code—inside insertAll rather in its callers.

Finally, you need to define the method concat. In this case, there's a simple solution, *which we beg you not to use* (we show it only so you can compare the different styles):

```
static List<List<Integer>> concat(List<List<Integer>> a,
                                  List<List<Integer>> b) {
    a.addAll(b);
    return a;
}
```

Instead, we suggest you write this:

```
static List<List<Integer>> concat(List<List<Integer>> a,
                                  List<List<Integer>> b) {
    List<List<Integer>> r = new ArrayList<>(a);
    r.addAll(b);
    return r;
}
```

Why? The second version of concat is a pure function. It may be using mutation (adding elements to the list r) internally, but it returns a result based on its arguments and modifies neither of them. By contrast, the first version relies on the fact that after the call concat(subans, subans2), no one refers to the value of subans ever again. It turns out that, for our definition of subsets, this is indeed the case, so surely using the cheaper version of concat is better. Well, it depends on how you value your time spent later searching for obscure bugs compared with the additional cost of making a copy.

No matter how well you comment that the impure concat is "only to be used when the first argument can be arbitrarily overwritten, and only intended to be used in the subsets method, and any change to subsets must be reviewed in the light of this comment," somebody sometime will find it useful in some piece of code where it apparently seems to work, and your future nightmare debugging problem has just been born. We revisit this issue in the next chapter in section 14.2, "Persistent data structures."

Takeaway point: thinking of programming problems in terms of function-style methods that are characterized only by their input arguments, and their output result (that is, what to do) is often more productive than thinking how to do it and what to mutate too early in the design cycle. We now turn to recursion in more detail, a technique promoted in functional programming to let you think more in terms of this what to do style.

13.3 Recursion vs. iteration

Pure functional programming languages typically don't include iterative constructs like while and for loops. Why? Because such constructs are often a hidden invitation to use mutation. For example, the condition in a while loop needs to be updated;

otherwise the loop would execute zero or an infinite number of times. But for a lot of use cases loops are perfectly fine. We've argued that to be functional style you're allowed mutation if no one can see you doing it, meaning it's acceptable to mutate local variables. Using the `for-each` loop in Java, `for(Apple a : apples { }` decodes into the `Iterator` shown here:

```
Iterator<Apple> it = apples.iterator();
while (it.hasNext()) {
   Apple apple = it.next();
   // ...
}
```

This isn't a problem because the mutations (both changing the state of the `Iterator` with the method `next` and assigning to the variable `apple` inside the `while` body) aren't visible to the caller of the method where the mutations happen. But using a `for-each` loop, such as a search algorithm, as follows is problematic because the loop body is updating a data structure that's shared with the caller:

```
public void searchForGold(List<String> l, Stats stats){
    for(String s: l){
        if("gold".equals(s)){
            stats.incrementFor("gold");
        }
    }
}
```

Indeed, the body of the loop has a side effect that can't be dismissed as functional style: it mutates the state of the `stats` object, which is shared with other parts of the program.

For this reason, pure functional programming languages such as Haskell omit such side-effecting operations entirely! How then are you to write programs? The theoretical answer is that every program can be rewritten to avoid iteration by using recursion instead, which doesn't require mutability. Using recursion lets you get rid of iteration variables that are updated step by step. A classic school problem is calculating the factorial function (for positive arguments) in an iterative way and in a recursive way (we assume the input is > 1), as shown in the following two listings.

Listing 13.1 Iterative factorial

```
static int factorialIterative(int n) {
    int r = 1;
    for (int i = 1; i <= n; i++) {
        r *= i;
    }
    return r;
}
```

Listing 13.2 Recursive factorial

```
static long factorialRecursive(long n) {
    return n == 1 ? 1 : n * factorialRecursive(n-1);
}
```

The first listing demonstrates a standard loop-based form: the variables `r` and `i` are updated at each iteration. The second listing shows a recursive definition (the function calls itself) in a more mathematically familiar form. In Java, recursive forms are typically less efficient, and we discuss this shortly.

But if you've read the earlier chapters of this book, then you know that Java 8 streams provide an even simpler declarative way of defining factorial, as the next listing shows.

Listing 13.3 Stream factorial

```
static long factorialStreams(long n){
    return LongStream.rangeClosed(1, n)
                     .reduce(1, (long a, long b) -> a * b);
}
```

Now let's turn to efficiency. As Java users, you should beware of functional-programming zealots who tell you that you should always use recursion instead of iteration. In general, making a recursive function call is much more expensive than the single machine-level branch instruction needed to iterate. Why? Every time the `factorialRecursive` function is called, a new stack frame is created on the call stack to hold the state of each function call (the multiplication it needs to do) until the recursion is done. This means your recursive definition of factorial will take memory proportional to its input. This is why if you run `factorialRecursive` with a large input, you're likely to receive a `StackOverflowError`:

```
Exception in thread "main" java.lang.StackOverflowError
```

Does this mean recursion is useless? Of course not! Functional languages provide an answer to this problem: *tail-call optimization.* The basic idea is that you can write a recursive definition of factorial where the recursive call is the last thing that happens in the function (we say the call is in a tail position). This different form of recursion style can be optimized to run fast. To exemplify, here's a tail-recursive definition of factorial

Listing 13.4 Tail-recursive factorial

```
static long factorialTailRecursive(long n) {
    return factorialHelper(1, n);
}
static long factorialHelper(long acc, long n) {
    return n == 1 ? acc : factorialHelper(acc * n, n-1);
}
```

The function `factorialHelper` is tail recursive because the recursive call is the last thing that happens in the function. By contrast in our previous definition of `factorialRecursive`, the last thing was a multiplication of `n` and the result of a recursive call.

This form of recursion is useful because instead of storing each intermediate result of the recursion onto different stack frames, the compiler can decide to reuse a single

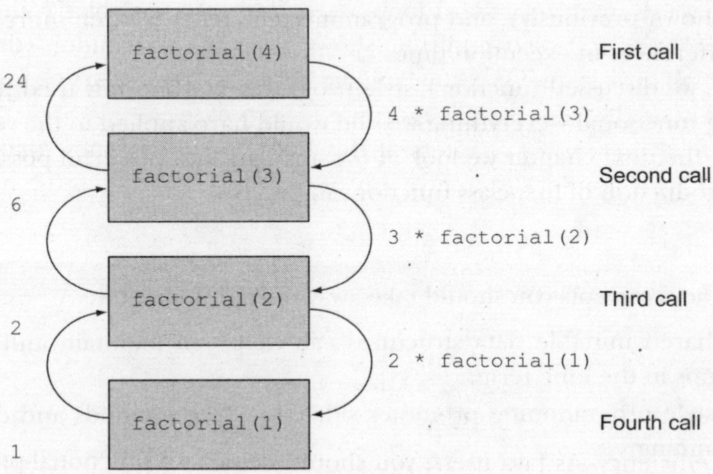

Figure 13.5 Recursive definition of factorial, which requires several stack frames

stack frame. Indeed, in the definition of `factorialHelper`, the intermediate results (the partial results of the factorial) are passed directly as arguments to the function. There's no need to keep track of the intermediate result of each recursive call on a separate stack frame—it's accessible directly through the argument of the function.

Figures 13.5 and 13.6 illustrate the difference between the recursive and tail-recursive definitions of factorial.

The bad news is that Java doesn't support this kind of optimization. But adopting tail recursion may be a better practice than classic recursion because it opens the way to eventual compiler optimization. Many modern JVM languages such as Scala and Groovy can optimize those uses of recursion, which are equivalent to iteration (they'll execute at the same speed). This means that pure-functional adherents can have their purity cake and eat it efficiently too.

The guidance when writing Java 8 is that you can often replace iteration with streams to avoid mutation. In addition, iteration can be replaced with recursion when it lets you write an algorithm in a more concise and side-effect-free way. Indeed, recursion can make examples easier to read, write, and understand (for example, in the

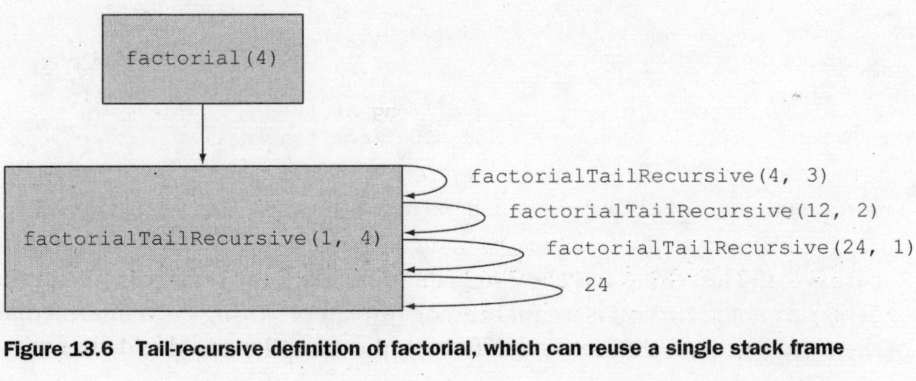

Figure 13.6 Tail-recursive definition of factorial, which can reuse a single stack frame

subsets example shown previously), and programmer efficiency is often more important than small differences in execution time.

In this section, we discussed functional-style programming but only used the idea of a method being functional—everything we said would have applied to the very first version of Java. In the next chapter we look at the amazing and powerful possibilities offered by the introduction of first-class functions in Java 8.

13.4 Summary

Following are the key concepts you should take away from this chapter:

- Reducing shared mutable data structures can help you maintain and debug your programs in the long term.
- Functional-style programming promotes side-effect-free methods and declarative programming.
- Function-style methods are characterized only by their input arguments and their output result.
- A function is referentially transparent if it always returns the same result value when called with the same argument value. Iterative constructs such as `while` loops can be replaced by recursion.
- Tail recursion may be a better practice than classic recursion in Java because it opens the way to eventual compiler optimization.

14 Functional programming techniques

This chapter covers

- First-class citizens, higher-order functions, currying, and partial application
- Persistent data structures
- Lazy evaluation and lazy lists as generalizing Java streams
- Pattern matching and how to simulate it in Java
- Referential transparency and caching

In chapter 13 you saw how to think functionally; thinking in terms of side-effect-free methods can help you write more maintainable code. In this chapter, we introduce more advanced functional programming techniques. You can view this chapter as a mix of practical techniques to apply in your codebase as well as academic information that will make you a more knowledgeable programmer. We discuss higher-order functions, currying, persistent data structures, lazy lists, pattern matching, caching with referential transparency, and combinators.

14.1 Functions everywhere

In chapter 13 we used the phrase *functional-style programming* to mean that the behavior of functions and methods should be like that of mathematical-style functions—no side effects. Functional-language programmers often use the phrase with more generality to mean that functions may be used like other values: passed as arguments, returned as results, and stored in data structures. Such functions that may be used like other values are referred to as *first-class functions*. This is exactly what Java 8 adds over previous versions of Java: you may use any method as a function value, using the `::` operator to create *a method reference*, and lambda expressions (for example, `(int x) -> x + 1`) to directly express function values. In Java 8 it's perfectly valid to store the method `Integer.parseInt` in a variable by using a method reference as follows:

```
Function<String, Integer> strToInt = Integer::parseInt;
```

14.1.1 Higher-order functions

So far we've mainly used the fact that function values are first class only in order to pass them to Java 8 stream-processing operations (as in chapters 4–7) and to achieve the very similar effect of behavior parameterization when we passed `Apple::isGreenApple` as a function value to `filterApples` in chapters 1 and 2. But this was just a start. Another interesting example was the use of the static method `Comparator.comparing`, which takes a function as parameter and returns another function (a `Comparator`), as illustrated in the following code and figure 14.1:

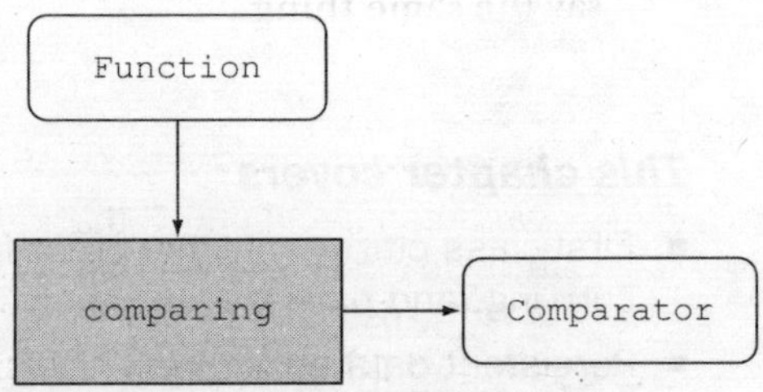

Figure 14.1 `comparing` **takes a function as parameter and returns another function.**

```
Comparator<Apple> c = comparing(Apple::getWeight);
```

We did something similar when we were composing functions in chapter 3 to create a pipeline of operations:

```
Function<String, String> transformationPipeline
  = addHeader.andThen(Letter::checkSpelling)
             .andThen(Letter::addFooter);
```

Functions (like `Comparator.comparing`) that can do at least one of the following are called *higher-order functions* within the functional programming community:

- Take one or more functions as parameter
- Return a function as result

This directly relates to Java 8 functions because they can not only be passed as arguments but also returned as results, assigned to local variables, or even inserted into structures. For example, a pocket calculator program might have a `Map<String,`

Function<Double, Double>>, which maps the String "sin" to Function<Double, Double> to hold the method reference Math::sin. We did something similar when we introduced the factory design pattern in chapter 8.

For readers who liked the calculus example at the end of chapter 3, you can regard the type of differentiation as

```
Function<Function<Double,Double>, Function<Double,Double>>
```

because it takes a function as argument (for example, (Double x) -> x * x) and returns a function as result (in this example (Double x) -> 2 * x). We've written this as a function type (the leftmost Function) to explicitly affirm the fact that you could pass this differentiating function to yet another function. But it's good to recall that the *type* for differentiating and the *signature*

```
Function<Double,Double> differentiate(Function<Double,Double> func)
```

say the same thing.

> **Side effects and higher-order functions**
>
> We noted in chapter 7 that functions passed to stream operations should generally be side-effect free, and we noted the problems that arise otherwise (such as incorrect results, perhaps even unpredictable results due to race conditions we hadn't thought of). This principle also applies in general when you use higher-order functions. When writing a higher-order function or method, you don't know in advance what arguments it will be passed—and if the arguments have side effects, then what these might do! It becomes far too complicated to reason about what your code does if it uses functions passed as arguments that make unpredictable changes to the state of your program; they might even interfere with your code in some hard-to-debug way. So it's a good design principle to document what side effects you're willing to accept from functions passed as parameters, and "none" is the best of all!

We now turn to *currying*: a technique that can help you modularize functions and reuse code.

14.1.2 Currying

Before we give the theoretical definition of currying, let's look at an example. Applications almost always need to be internationalized, and so converting from one set of units to another set is a problem that comes up repeatedly.

Unit conversion always involves a conversion factor and from time to time a baseline adjustment factor. For example, the formula to convert Celsius to Fahrenheit is CtoF(x) = x*9/5 + 32.

The basic pattern of all unit conversion is as follows:

1. Multiply by the conversion factor.
2. Adjust the baseline if relevant.

You can express this pattern with the following general method:

```
static double converter(double x, double f, double b) {
    return x * f + b;
}
```

Here `x` is the quantity you want to convert, `f` is the conversion factor, and `b` is the baseline. But this method is a bit too general. You'll typically find you require a lot of conversions between the same pair of units, kilometers to miles, for example. You could obviously call the `converter` method with three arguments on each occasion, but supplying the factor and baseline each time would be tedious and you might accidentally mistype them.

You could write a completely new method for each application, but that would miss the reuse of the underlying logic.

Here's an easy way to benefit from the existing logic while tailoring the converter for particular applications. You can define a "factory" that manufactures one-argument conversion functions to exemplify the idea of currying. Here it is:

```
static DoubleUnaryOperator curriedConverter(double f, double b){
    return (double x) -> x * f + b;
}
```

Now all you have to do is pass it the conversion factor and baseline (`f` and `b`), and it will obligingly return a function (of `x`) to do exactly what you asked for. For example, you can now use the factory to produce any converter you require:

```
DoubleUnaryOperator convertCtoF = curriedConverter(9.0/5, 32);

DoubleUnaryOperator convertUSDtoGBP = curriedConverter(0.6, 0);

DoubleUnaryOperator convertKmtoMi = curriedConverter(0.6214, 0);
```

Because `DoubleUnaryOperator` defines a method `applyAsDouble`, you can use your converters as follows:

```
double gbp = convertUSDtoGBP.applyAsDouble(1000);
```

As a result, your code is more flexible and it reuses the existing conversion logic! Let's reflect on what you're doing here. Instead of passing all the arguments `x`, `f`, and `b` all at once to the `converter` method, you only ask for the arguments `f` and `b` and return another function, which when given an argument `x` returns `x * f + b`. This enables you to reuse the conversion logic and create different functions with different conversion factors.

> **Theoretical definition of currying**
>
> Currying is a technique where a function `f` of two arguments (`x` and `y`, say) is seen instead as a function `g` of one argument that returns a function also of one argument. The value returned by the latter function is the same as the value of the original function, that is, `f(x,y) = (g(x))(y)`.

> Of course, this generalizes: you can curry a six-argument function to first take arguments numbered 2, 4, and 6 returning a function taking argument 5, which returns a function taking the remaining arguments, 1 and 3.
>
> When some but fewer than the full complement of arguments have been passed, we often say the function is *partially applied*.

Now we turn to another aspect of functional-style programming. Can you really program using data structures if you're forbidden from modifying them?

14.2 Persistent data structures

In this section, we explore the use of data structures used in functional-style programs. These come under various names, such as functional data structures and immutable data structures, but perhaps most common is persistent data structures (unfortunately this terminology clashes with the notion of *persistent* in databases, meaning "outliving one run of the program").

The first thing to note is that a functional-style method isn't allowed to update any global data structure or any structure passed as a parameter. Why? Because calling it twice is likely to produce different answers—violating referential transparency and the ability to understand the method as a simple mapping from arguments to results.

14.2.1 Destructive updates vs. functional

Let's consider the problems that can otherwise arise. Suppose you represent train journeys from A to B as a *mutable* `TrainJourney` class (a simple implementation of a singly linked list), with an `int` field modeling some detail of the journey such as the price of the current leg of the journey. Journeys requiring you to change trains will have several linked `TrainJourney` objects using the `onward` field; a direct train or final leg of a journey will have `onward` being `null`:

```
class TrainJourney {
    public int price;
    public TrainJourney onward;
    public TrainJourney(int p, TrainJourney t) {
        price = p;
        onward = t;
    }
}
```

Now suppose you have separate `TrainJourney` objects representing a journey from X to Y and from Y to Z. You may wish to create one journey that links the two `TrainJourney` objects (that is, X to Y to Z).

A simple traditional imperative method to `link` these train journeys is as follows:

```
static TrainJourney link(TrainJourney a, TrainJourney b){
    if (a==null) return b;
    TrainJourney t = a;
```

```
    while(t.onward != null){
        t = t.onward;
    }
    t.onward = b;
    return a;
}
```

This works by finding the last leg in the `TrainJourney` for `a` and replacing the `null` marking the end of a's list with list `b` (you need a special case if `a` has no elements).

Here's the problem: suppose a variable `firstJourney` contains the route from X to Y and a variable `secondJourney` contains the route from Y to Z. If you call `link(firstJourney, secondJourney)`, this code destructively updates `firstJourney` to also contain `secondJourney`, so in addition to the single user who requests a trip from X to Z seeing the combined journey as intended, the journey from X to Y has been destructively updated. Indeed, the `firstJourney` variable is no longer a route from X to Y but one from X to Z! This will break code that depends on `firstJourney` not being modified! Suppose `firstJourney` represented the early morning London–Brussels train, which all subsequent users trying to get to Brussels will be surprised to see as requiring an onward leg, perhaps to Cologne. We've all fought battles with such bugs concerning how visible a change to a data structure should be.

The functional-style approach to this problem is to ban such side-effecting methods. If you need a data structure to represent the result of a computation, you should make a new one and not mutate an existing data structure as done previously. This is often best practice in standard object-oriented programming too. A common objection to the functional approach is that it causes excess copying and that the programmer says, "I'll just remember" or "I'll just document" that it has side effects. But this leaves traps for maintenance programmers who later will have to deal with your code. Thus the functional-style solution is as follows:

```
static TrainJourney append(TrainJourney a, TrainJourney b){
    return a==null ? b : new TrainJourney(a.price, append(a.onward, b));
}
```

This code is clearly functional style (it uses no mutation at all, even locally) and doesn't modify any existing data structures. Note, however, that the code does *not* create an entirely new `TrainJourney`—if `a` is a sequence of n elements and `b` a sequence of m elements, then it returns a sequence of $n+m$ elements of which the first n elements are new nodes and the final m elements share with the `TrainJourney` `b`. Note that users are also required not to mutate the result of `append` because in doing so they may corrupt the trains passed as sequence `b`. Figures 14.2 and 14.3 illustrate the difference between the destructive `append` and the functional-style `append`.

14.2.2 Another example with Trees

Before leaving this topic, let's consider another data structure—that of a binary search tree that might be used to implement a similar interface to a `HashMap`. The idea is that

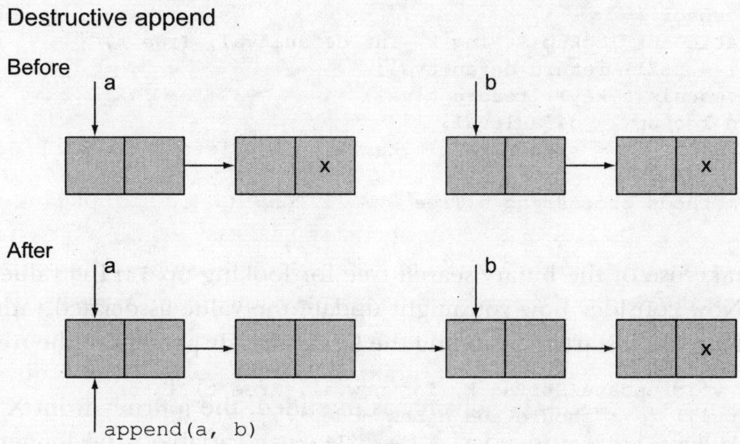

Figure 14.2 The data structure is destructively updated.

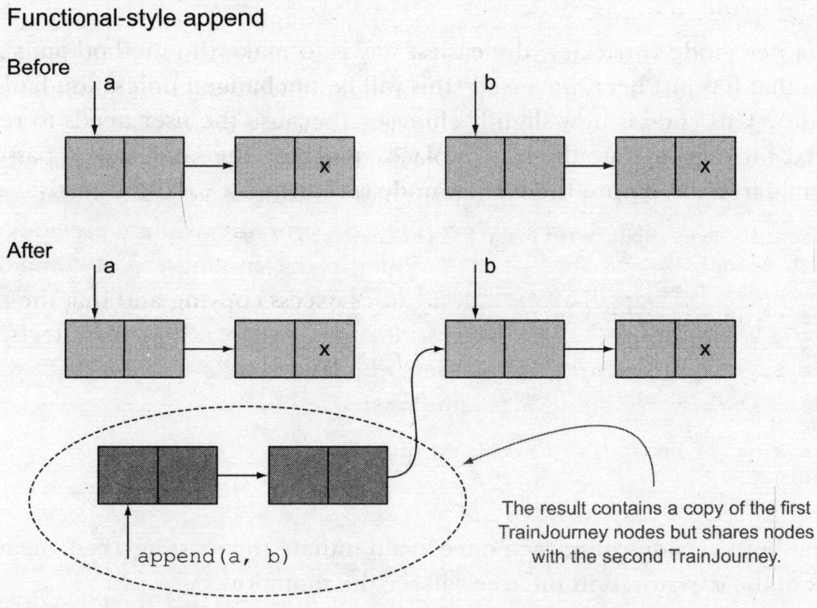

Figure 14.3 Functional style, no modifications to the data structure

a `Tree` contains a `String` representing a key and an `int` representing its value, perhaps names and ages:

```
class Tree {
   private String key;
   private int val;
   private Tree left, right;
   public Tree(String k, int v, Tree l, Tree r) {
     key = k; val = v; left = l; right = r;
   }
}
```

```
class TreeProcessor {
    public static int lookup(String k, int defaultval, Tree t) {
        if (t == null) return defaultval;
        if (k.equals(t.key)) return t.val;
        return lookup(k, defaultval,
                      k.compareTo(t.key) < 0 ? t.left : t.right);
    }
    // other methods processing a Tree
}
```

You want to make use of the binary search tree for looking up String values to produce an int. Now consider how you might update the value associated with a given key (for simplicity you'll start by assuming the key is already present in the tree):

```
public static void update(String k, int newval, Tree t) {
    if (t == null) { /* should add a new node */ }
    else if (k.equals(t.key)) t.val = newval;
    else update(k, newval, k.compareTo(t.key) < 0 ? t.left : t.right);
}
```

Adding a new node is trickier; the easiest way is to make the method update return the Tree that has just been traversed (this will be unchanged unless you had to add a new node). This code is now slightly clumsier (because the user needs to remember that update tries to update the tree in place, returning the same tree as passed, but if the original tree was empty, then a new node is returned as result instead):

```
public static Tree update(String k, int newval, Tree t) {
    if (t == null)
       t = new Tree(k, newval, null, null);
    else if (k.equals(t.key))
       t.val = newval;
    else if (k.compareTo(t.key) < 0)
       t.left = update(k, newval, t.left);
    else
       t.right = update(k, newval, t.right);
    return t;
}
```

Note that both versions of update once again mutate the existing Tree, meaning that all users of the map stored in the tree will see the mutation.

14.2.3 Using a functional approach

So how might you do this functionally? You need to create a new node for the new key-value pair, but you also need to create new nodes on the path from the root of the tree to the new node (in general this isn't very expensive, if the tree is of depth d and reasonably well balanced, then it can have 2^d entries, so you re-create only a small fraction of it):

```
public static Tree fupdate(String k, int newval, Tree t) {
    return (t == null) ?
        new Tree(k, newval, null, null) :
          k.equals(t.key) ?
            new Tree(k, newval, t.left, t.right) :
```

```
    k.compareTo(t.key) < 0 ?
      new Tree(t.key, t.val, fupdate(k,newval, t.left), t.right) :
      new Tree(t.key, t.val, t.left, fupdate(k,newval, t.right));
}
```

We've written this as a single conditional expression instead of using `if-then-else` to emphasize the idea that the body is only a single expression with no side effects, but you may prefer to write an equivalent `if-then-else` chain, each containing a `return`.

So what's the difference between `update` and `fupdate`? We noted previously that the method `update` assumes every user wants to share the identical data structure and see updates caused by any part of the program. Hence it's vital (but often overlooked) in nonfunctional code that whenever you add some form of structured value to a tree, you copy it, because, who knows, someone may later assume they can update it. By contrast, `fupdate` is purely functional. It creates a new `Tree` as a result but *sharing as much as it can with its argument.* Figure 14.4 illustrates this idea. You have a tree consisting of nodes storing a name and an age of a person. Calling `fupdate` doesn't modify the existing tree but creates new nodes "living at the side of" the tree without harming the existing data structure.

Such functional data structures are often called *persistent*—their values persist and are isolated from changes happening elsewhere—so as a programmer you're sure `fupdate` won't mutate the data structures passed as its arguments. There's just one proviso: the other side of the treaty is you require all users of persistent data structures to follow the *do-not-mutate requirement.* If not, a programmer who disregards this might mutate the result of `fupdate` (for example, changing Emily's 20). This would then be visible as an (almost certainly unwanted) unexpected and delayed change to the data structure passed as argument to `fupdate`!

Seen in these terms, `fupdate` can often be more efficient: the "no mutation of existing structure" rule allows structures that differ only slightly from each other (for example, the `Tree` seen by user A and the modified version seen by user B) to share storage for common parts of their structure. You can get the compiler to help enforce

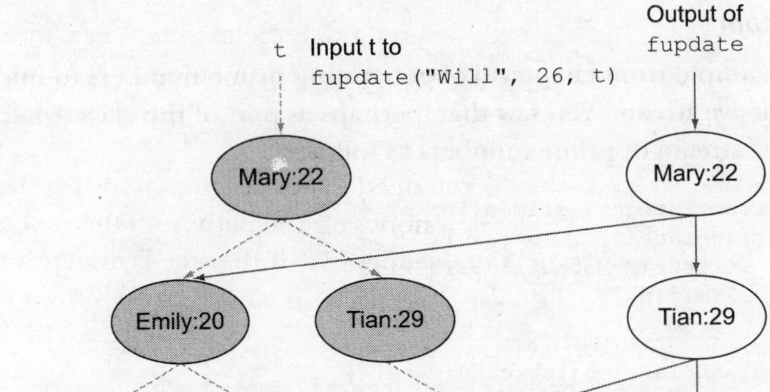

Figure 14.4 No existing data structure was harmed during the making of this update to the `Tree`.

this "no mutation of existing structure" rule by declaring fields `key`, `val`, `left`, and `right` of class `Tree` to be `final`; but remember that `final` protects only a field and not the object pointed to, which may need its own fields to be `final` to protect it, and so on.

Ah, but you might say, "I *want* updates to the tree to be seen by some users (but admittedly not by some others)." Well, there are two choices: one is the classical Java solution (be very careful when updating something to check whether you need to copy it first). The other is the functional-style solution: you logically make a new data structure whenever you do an update (so nothing is ever mutated) and just arrange to pass the correct version of the data structure to users as appropriate. This idea could be enforced through an API. If certain clients of the data structure need to have updates visible, they should go through an API that returns the latest version. Clients who don't want updates visible (such as for long-running statistical analysis) simply use whatever copy they retrieved, knowing that it can't be mutated from under them.

One might remark that this technique is like "updating" a file on a CD-R, which allows a file to be written only once by burning with a laser; multiple versions of the file are *all* stored on the CD (smart CD authoring software might even share common parts of multiple versions), and you pass the appropriate block address of the start of file (or a filename encoding the version within its name) to select which version you want to use. In Java things are rather better than on a CD, in that old versions of the data structure that can no longer be used will be garbage collected.

14.3 Lazy evaluation with streams

You saw in previous chapters that streams are a great way to process a collection of data. But for various reasons, including efficient implementation, the Java 8 designers added streams to Java in a rather specific way. In particular, one limitation is that you can't define a stream recursively because a stream can be consumed only once. We show in the coming section how this can sometimes be problematic.

14.3.1 Self-defining stream

Let's revisit our example from chapter 6 of generating prime numbers to understand this idea of a recursive stream. You saw that, perhaps as part of the class `MyMathUtils`, you can compute a stream of prime numbers as follows:

```
public static Stream<Integer> primes(int n) {
    return Stream.iterate(2, i -> i + 1)
                 .filter(MyMathUtils::isPrime)
                 .limit(n);
}

public static boolean isPrime(int candidate) {
    int candidateRoot = (int) Math.sqrt((double) candidate);
    return IntStream.rangeClosed(2, candidateRoot)
                    .noneMatch(i -> candidate % i == 0);
}
```

But this solution is somewhat awkward: you have to iterate through every number every time to see if it can be exactly divided by a candidate number. (Actually you need only test with numbers that have been already classified as prime.)

Ideally the stream should filter out numbers divisible by the prime it's producing on the go! This sounds crazy, so we'll try to sketch out how this might work:

1. You need a stream of numbers from which you'll select prime numbers.
2. From that stream you take the first number (the head of the stream), which will be a prime number (at the initial step this will be 2).
3. You then filter all the numbers divisible by that number from the tail of the stream.
4. The resulting tail is the new stream of numbers that you can use to find prime numbers. Essentially you go back to step 1, so this algorithm is recursive.

Note that this algorithm is "poor" for a few reasons.[1] But it's simple to reason about algorithms for the purpose of working with streams. Let's try to write this algorithm using the Streams API.

STEP 1: GET A STREAM OF NUMBERS

You can get an infinite stream of numbers starting from 2 using the method `IntStream.iterate`, which we described in chapter 5 as follows:

```
static Intstream numbers(){
    return IntStream.iterate(2, n -> n + 1);
}
```

STEP 2: TAKE THE HEAD

An `IntStream` comes with the method `findFirst`, which can be used to return the first element:

```
static int head(IntStream numbers){
    return numbers.findFirst().getAsInt();
}
```

STEP 3: FILTER THE TAIL

Define a method to get the tail of a stream:

```
static IntStream tail(IntStream numbers){
    return numbers.skip(1);
}
```

Given the head of the stream, you can filter the numbers as follows:

```
IntStream numbers = numbers();
int head = head(numbers);
IntStream filtered = tail(numbers).filter(n -> n % head != 0);
```

[1] More information about why the algorithm is poor can be found at www.cs.hmc.edu/~oneill/papers/Sieve-JFP.pdf.

STEP 4: RECURSIVELY CREATE A STREAM OF PRIMES

Here comes the tricky part. You might be tempted to try passing back the resulting filtered stream so you can take its head and filter more numbers, like this:

```
static IntStream primes(IntStream numbers) {
    int head = head(numbers);
    return IntStream.concat(
             IntStream.of(head),
             primes(tail(numbers).filter(n -> n % head != 0))
           );
}
```

BAD NEWS

Unfortunately, if you run the code in step 4, you'll get the following error: "java.lang.IllegalStateException: stream has already been operated upon or closed." Indeed, you're using two terminal operations to split the stream into its head and tail: `findFirst` and `skip`. Remember from chapter 4 that once you call a terminal operation on a stream, it's consumed forever!

LAZY EVALUATION

There's an additional, more important problem: the static method `IntStream.concat` expects two instances of a stream. But its second argument is a direct recursive call to `primes`, resulting in an infinite recursion! For many Java purposes, restrictions on Java 8 streams such as "no recursive definitions" are unproblematic and give your database-like queries expressivity and the ability to parallelize. Thus, the Java 8 designers chose a sweet spot. Nonetheless, the more-general features and models of streams from functional languages such as Scala and Haskell can be a useful addition to your programming tool box. What you need is a way to lazily evaluate the call to the method `primes` in the second argument of `concat`. (In a more technical programming language vocabulary we refer to this as *lazy evaluation*, *nonstrict evaluation*, or even *call by name.*) Only when you need to process the prime numbers (for example, with the method `limit`) should the stream be evaluated. Scala (which we explore in the next chapter) provides support for this idea. In Scala you can write the previous algorithm as follows, where the operator `#::` does lazy concatenation (the arguments are evaluated only when you need to actually consume the stream):

```
def numbers(n: Int): Stream[Int] = n #:: numbers(n+1)

def primes(numbers: Stream[Int]): Stream[Int] = {
  numbers.head #:: primes(numbers.tail filter (n -> n % numbers.head != 0))
}
```

Don't worry about this code. Its only purpose is to show you an area of difference between Java and other functional programming languages. It's good to reflect just a moment about how the arguments are evaluated. In Java when you call a method, all its arguments are fully evaluated immediately. But in Scala using `#::`, the concatenation returns immediately and the elements are evaluated only when needed. Now we turn to implementing this idea of lazy lists directly in Java.

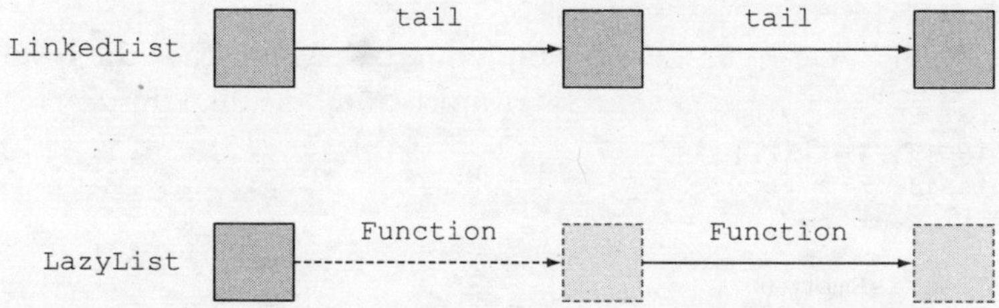

Figure 14.5 Elements of a `LinkedList` exist (are spread out) in memory. But elements of a `LazyList` are created on demand by a `Function`—you can see them as spread out in time.

14.3.2 Your own lazy list

Java 8 streams are often described as lazy. They're lazy in one particular aspect: a stream behaves like a black box that can generate values on request. When you apply a sequence of operations to a stream, these are merely saved up. Only when you apply *a terminal operation* to a stream is anything actually computed. This has the great advantage when you apply several operations (perhaps a `filter` and a `map` followed by a terminal operation `reduce`) to a stream; then the stream has to be traversed only once instead of for each operation.

In this section we consider the notion of lazy lists, which are a form of a more general stream (lazy lists form a similar concept to stream). Lazy lists also provide an excellent way of thinking about higher-order functions; you place a function value into a data structure so most of the time it can sit there unused, but when it's called (that is, on demand) it can create more of the data structure. Figure 14.5 illustrates this idea.

Enough talking—let's see how this works. What you want to achieve is to generate an infinite list of prime numbers using the algorithm we described earlier.

A BASIC LINKED LIST

Recall that you can define a simple linked-list-style class called `MyLinkedList` in Java by writing it as follows (here we only consider a minimal `MyList` interface):

```
interface MyList<T> {
    T head();

    MyList<T> tail();

    default boolean isEmpty() {
        return true;
    }
}

class MyLinkedList<T> implements MyList<T> {
    private final T head;
    private final MyList<T> tail;
    public MyLinkedList(T head, MyList<T> tail) {
        this.head = head;
        this.tail = tail;
    }
```

```
    public T head() {
        return head;
    }

    public MyList<T> tail() {
        return tail;
    }

    public boolean isEmpty() {
        return false;
    }
}

class Empty<T> implements MyList<T> {

    public T head() {
        throw new UnsupportedOperationException();
    }
    public MyList<T> tail() {
        throw new UnsupportedOperationException();
    }
}
```

You can now construct a sample MyLinkedList value as follows:

```
MyList<Integer> l =
    new MyLinkedList<>(5, new MyLinkedList<>(10, new Empty<>()));
```

A BASIC LAZY LIST

An easy way to adapt this class to the concept of a lazy list is to cause the tail not to be present in memory all at once but to have a Supplier<T> that you saw in chapter 3 (you can also see it as a factory with a function descriptor void -> T), which produces the next node of the list. This leads to the following:

```
import java.util.function.Supplier;
class LazyList<T> implements MyList<T>{
    final T head;
    final Supplier<MyList<T>> tail;
    public LazyList(T head, Supplier<MyList<T>> tail) {
        this.head = head;
        this.tail = tail;
    }

    public T head() {
        return head;
    }

    public MyList<T> tail() {
        return tail.get();        <-- Note how tail using a Supplier encodes laziness, compared to head above.
    }

    public boolean isEmpty() {
        return false;
    }
}
```

Calling the method get from the Supplier causes the creation of a node of the LazyList (as a factory would create a new object).

You can now create the infinite lazy list of numbers starting at *n* as follows by passing a Supplier as the tail argument of the LazyList constructor, which creates the next element in the series of numbers:

```
public static LazyList<Integer> from(int n) {
    return new LazyList<Integer>(n, () -> from(n+1));
}
```

If you try the following code for yourself, you'll see that the following calls will print "2 3 4." Indeed, the numbers are generated on demand. You can check this by inserting System.out.println appropriately or just by noting that from(2) would run forever if it tried to eagerly calculate all the numbers starting from 2!

```
LazyList<Integer> numbers = from(2);
int two = numbers.head();
int three = numbers.tail().head();
int four = numbers.tail().tail().head();

System.out.println(two + " " + three + " " + four);
```

BACK TO GENERATING PRIMES

See if you can use what you've done so far to generate a self-defining lazy list of prime numbers (something you were unable to do with the Streams API). If you were to translate the code that was using the Streams API earlier using our new LazyList, it would look like something like this:

```
public static MyList<Integer> primes(MyList<Integer> numbers) {
    return new LazyList<>(
                numbers.head(),
                () -> primes(
                        numbers.tail()
                               .filter(n -> n % numbers.head() != 0)
                            )
    );
}
```

IMPLEMENTING A LAZY FILTER

Unfortunately, a LazyList (more accurately the List interface) doesn't define a filter method, so the previous code won't compile! Let's fix this and declare one:

```
public MyList<T> filter(Predicate<T> p) {
    return isEmpty() ?
           this :
           p.test(head()) ?
               new LazyList<>(head(), () -> tail().filter(p)) :
               tail().filter(p);
}
```

You could return new Empty<>() but this is just as good and empty.

Your code now compiles and is ready for use! You can calculate the first three prime numbers by chaining calls to tail and head:

```
LazyList<Integer> numbers = from(2);
int two = primes(numbers).head();
int three = primes(numbers).tail().head();
int five = primes(numbers).tail().tail().head();
System.out.println(two + " " + three + " " + five);
```

This will print "2 3 5," which are the first three prime numbers. You can now have some fun; for example, you could print all the prime numbers (the program will run infinitely by writing a `printAll` method, which iteratively prints the head and tail of a list:

```
static <T> void printAll(MyList<T> list){
    while (!list.isEmpty()){
        System.out.println(list.head());
        list = list.tail();
    }
}
printAll(primes(from(2)));
```

This being a functional programming chapter, we should explain that you could do this neatly recursively:

```
static <T> void printAll(MyList<T> list){
    if (list.isEmpty())
        return;
    System.out.println(list.head());
    printAll(list.tail());
}
```

But this program wouldn't run infinitely; sadly it would eventually fail due to stack overflow because Java doesn't support tail call elimination, as discussed in chapter 13.

WHEW!

So you've built a whole lot of technology: lazy lists and functions using them just to define a data structure containing all the primes. Why? What's the practical use? Well, you've seen how to place functions inside data structures (because Java 8 allows you to), and these functions can be used to create parts of the data structure on demand instead of when the structure is created. This might be useful if you're writing a game-playing program, perhaps for chess; you can have a data structure that notionally represents the whole tree of possible moves (far too big to calculate eagerly) but that can be created on demand. This would be a lazy tree as opposed to a lazy list. We concentrated on lazy lists because they provide a link back to another Java 8 feature, streams, and we could then discuss the pros and cons of streams compared to lazy lists.

There remains the question of performance. It's easy to assume that doing things lazily will be better than doing things eagerly—surely it's better to calculate only the values and data structures needed by a program on demand than to create all those values (and perhaps some more) as done under traditional execution. Unfortunately, the real world isn't so simple. The overhead of doing things lazily (for example, the additional `Suppliers` between each item in your `LazyList`) outweighs the notional benefit unless you explore, say, less than 10% of the data structure. Finally, there's a subtle way in which your `LazyList` values aren't truly lazy. If you traverse a `LazyList` value such as `from(2)`, perhaps up to the 10th item, then it also creates all the nodes twice, thus creating 20 nodes rather than 10. This is hardly lazy. The issue is that the `Supplier` in `tail` is repeatedly called on each on-demand exploration of the `LazyList`; you can fix this by arranging that the `Supplier` in `tail` is called only on the first on-demand exploration—and its resulting value is cached—in effect solidifying the list at that point. This can be achieved by adding a `private Optional<LazyList<T>> alreadyComputed` field to your definition of `LazyList` and arranging for the method `tail` to consult and update it appropriately. The pure functional language Haskell arranges that all its data structures are properly lazy in this latter sense. Read one of the many articles on Haskell if you're interested.

Our guideline is to remember that lazy data structures can be a useful weapon in your programming armory. Use them when they make an application easier to program. Rewrite them in more traditional style only if they cause unacceptable inefficiency.

Now let's turn to another feature of almost all functional programming languages but one that's lacking from Java: pattern matching.

14.4 Pattern matching

There's one other important aspect to what's generally regarded as functional programming, and that's (structural) *pattern matching* (not to be confused with pattern matching and regex). Recall that chapter 1 ended by observing that mathematics can write definitions such as

```
f(0) = 1
f(n) = n*f(n-1) otherwise
```

whereas in Java, you have to write an `if-then-else` or a `switch` statement. As data types become more complex, the amount of code (and clutter) needed to process them increases. Using pattern matching can reduce this clutter.

To illustrate, let's take a tree structure that you'd like to traverse. Consider a simple arithmetic language consisting of numbers and binary operations:

```
class Expr { ... }
class Number extends Expr { int val; ... }
class BinOp extends Expr { String opname; Expr left, right; ... }
```

Say you're asked to write a method to simplify some expressions. For example, 5 + 0 can be simplified to 5. Using our domain, `new BinOp("+", new Number(5), new Number(0))` could be simplified to `Number(5)`. You might traverse an `Expr` structure as follows:

```
Expr simplifyExpression(Expr expr) {
    if (expr instanceof BinOp
          && ((BinOp)expr).opname.equals("+"))
          && ((BinOp)expr).right instanceof Number
          && ... // it's all getting very clumsy
          && ... ) {
```

```
            return (Binop)expr.left;
        }
        ...
}
```

You can see that this rapidly gets very ugly!

14.4.1 Visitor design pattern

Another way to unwrap the data type in Java is to make use of the *visitor design pattern.* In essence, you can create a separate class that encapsulates an algorithm to "visit" a specific data type.

How does it work? The visitor class needs to take as input a specific instance of the data type. It can then access all its members. Here's an example of how this works. First, you add the method `accept` to `BinOp`, which takes `SimplifyExprVisitor` as argument and passes itself to it (you also add a similar method for `Number`):

```
class BinOp extends Expr{
    ...
    public Expr accept(SimplifyExprVisitor v){
        return v.visit(this);
    }
}
```

The `SimplifyExprVisitor` can now access a `BinOp` object and unwrap it:

```
public class SimplifyExprVisitor {
    ...
    public Expr visit(BinOp e){
        if("+".equals(e.opname) && e.right instanceof Number && …){
            return e.left;
        }
        return e;
    }
}
```

14.4.2 Pattern matching to the rescue

There's a simpler solution using a feature called pattern matching. It's not available in Java, so we're going to use small examples from the Scala programming language to exemplify pattern matching. It will give you an idea of what could be possible in Java if pattern matching were supported.

Given data type `Expr` representing arithmetic expressions, in the Scala programming language (we use it because its syntax is the closest to Java), you can write the following code to decompose an expression:

```
def simplifyExpression(expr: Expr): Expr = expr match {
    case BinOp("+", e, Number(0)) => e    // Adding zero
    case BinOp("*", e, Number(1)) => e    // Multiplying by one
    case BinOp("/", e, Number(1)) => e    // Dividing by one
    case _ => expr                        // Can't simplify expr
}
```

This use of pattern matching gives an extremely concise and expressive way to manipulate many tree-like data structures. It's typically useful when building compilers or engines for processing business rules. Note that the Scala syntax

```
Expression match { case Pattern => Expression ... }
```

is very similar to the Java syntax

```
switch (Expression) { case Constant : Statement ... }
```

with Scala's wildcard `case` playing the role of `default:` in Java. The main visible syntactic difference is that Scala is expression-oriented whereas Java is more statement-oriented, but the main expressiveness difference for the programmer is that Java patterns in `case` labels are restricted to a couple of primitive types, enumerations, a few special classes that wrap certain primitive types, and `Strings`. One of the biggest practical advantages of using languages with pattern matching is that you can avoid using big chains of `switch` or `if-then-else` statements interleaved with field-selection operations.

Here it's clear that Scala's pattern matching wins on ease of expressiveness over Java, and you can only look forward to a future Java allowing more expressive `switch` statements. We make a concrete proposal for this in chapter 16.

In the meantime, let's see how Java 8 lambdas can provide an alternative way of achieving pattern-matching-like code in Java. We describe this technique purely so you can see another interesting application of lambdas.

FAKING PATTERN MATCHING IN JAVA

First, let's consider just how rich Scala's pattern-matching `match` expression form is. For example, the case

```
def simplifyExpression(expr: Expr): Expr = expr match {
    case BinOp("+", e, Number(0)) => e
    ...
```

means "check that `expr` is a `BinOp`, extract its three components (`opname, left, right`), and then pattern-match these components—the first against the `String +`, the second against the variable `e` (which always matches), and then the third against the pattern `Number(0)`." In other words, the pattern matching in Scala (and many other functional languages) is *multilevel*. Our simulation of pattern matching using Java 8's lambdas will give only single-level pattern matching; in the preceding example this would mean cases such as `BinOp(op, l, r)` or `Number(n)` but not `BinOp("+", e, Number(0))`.

First, we make a slightly surprising observation. Now that you have lambdas, you could in principle never use `if-then-else` in your code. You could replace code such as `condition ? e1 : e2` with a method call:

```
myIf(condition, () ->  e1, () ->  e2);
```

Somewhere, perhaps in a library, you'd have a definition (generic in type `T`):

```
static <T> T myIf(boolean b, Supplier<T> truecase, Supplier<T> falsecase) {
    return b ? truecase.get() : falsecase.get();
}
```

The type `T` plays the role of result type of the conditional expression. In principle, similar tricks can be done with `if-then-else`.

Of course, in normal code this would just make your code more obscure because `if-then-else` perfectly captures this idiom. But we've noted that Java's `switch` and `if-then-else` don't capture the idiom of pattern matching, and it turns out that lambdas can simply encode (single-level) pattern matching—and rather more neatly than the chains of `if-then-else`.

Returning to pattern-matching values of class `Expr`, which has two subclasses, `BinOp` and `Number`, you can define a method `patternMatchExpr` (again generic in `T`, the result type of the pattern match):

```
interface TriFunction<S, T, U, R>{
    R apply(S s, T t, U u);
}
static <T> T patternMatchExpr(
                        Expr e,
                        TriFunction<String, Expr, Expr, T> binopcase,
                        Function<Integer, T> numcase,
                        Supplier<T> defaultcase) {
    return
     (e instanceof BinOp) ?
       binopcase.apply(((BinOp)e).opname, ((BinOp)e).left,
                                          ((BinOp)e).right) :
     (e instanceof Number) ?
       numcase.apply(((Number)e).val) :
       defaultcase.get();
}
```

The result is that the method call

```
patternMatchExpr(e, (op, l, r) -> {return binopcode;},
                    (n) -> {return numcode;},
                    () -> {return defaultcode;});
```

will determine whether `e` is a `BinOp` (and if so run `binopcode`, which has access to the fields of the `BinOp` via identifiers `op`, `l`, `r`), or whether it is a `Number` (and if so run `numcode`, which has access to the value `n`). The method even makes provision for `defaultcode`, which would be executed if someone later created a tree node that was neither a `BinOp` nor a `Number`.

The following listing shows how to start using `patternMatchExpr` by simplifying addition and multiplication expressions.

Listing 14.1 Implementing pattern matching to simplify an expression

```
public static Expr simplify(Expr e) {
    TriFunction<String, Expr, Expr, Expr> binopcase =      <-- Deals with a BinOp expression
        (opname, left, right) -> {
            if ("+".equals(opname)) {                      <-- Deals with the addition case
                if (left instanceof Number && ((Number) left).val == 0) {
                    return right;
                }
```

```
            if (right instanceof Number && ((Number) right).val == 0) {
                return left;
            }
        }
        if ("*".equals(opname)) {
            if (left instanceof Number && ((Number) left).val == 1) {
                return right;
            }
            if (right instanceof Number && ((Number) right).val == 1) {
                return left;
            }
        }
        return new BinOp(opname, left, right);
    };
    Function<Integer, Expr> numcase = val -> new Number(val);
    Supplier<Expr> defaultcase = () -> new Number(0);

    return patternMatchExpr(e, binopcase, numcase, defaultcase);
}
```

Deals with the multiplication case

Deals with a `Number`

A default case if the user provides an `Expr` that's not recognized

Applies pattern matching

You can now call the `simplify` method as follows:

```
Expr e = new BinOp("+", new Number(5), new Number(0));
Expr match = simplify(e);
System.out.println(match);
```

Prints 5

You've seen a lot of information so far: higher-order functions, currying, persistent data structures, lazy lists, and pattern matching! We now look at certain subtleties, which we've deferred until the end to avoid overcomplicating the text.

14.5 Miscellany

In this section we explore two subtleties of being functional and of having referential transparency; one concerns efficiency and the other concerns returning the same result. These are interesting issues, but we place them here because they're subtleties concerning side effects rather than conceptually central. We also explore the idea of combinators—methods or functions that take two or more functions and return another function; this idea has inspired many of the additions to the Java 8 API.

14.5.1 Caching or memoization

Suppose you have a side-effect-free method `computeNumberOfNodes(Range)` that calculates the number of nodes inside a given range in a network with a tree-like topology. Let's assume the network never changes (that is, the structure is immutable), but calling the method `computeNumberOfNodes` is expensive to calculate because the structure needs to be traversed recursively. You may want to calculate the results over and over again. If you have referential transparency, there's a clever way of avoiding this additional overhead. One standard solution to this issue is *memoization*—adding a cache (for example, a `HashMap`) to the method as a wrapper—when the wrapper is called. It first consults the cache to see if the (argument, result) pair is already in the cache; if so, it can return the stored result immediately; otherwise, you call `computeNumberOfNodes`, but before returning from the wrapper you store the new (argument, result) pair in the cache. Strictly speaking, this is a nonpurely functional solution because it mutates a data structure shared by multiple callers, but the wrapped version of the code is referentially transparent.

In practice this would work as follows:

```
final Map<Range,Integer> numberOfNodes = new HashMap<>();
Integer computeNumberOfNodesUsingCache(Range range) {
    Integer result = numberOfNodes.get(range);
    if (result != null){
        return result;
    }
    result = computeNumberOfNodes(range);
    numberOfNodes.put(range, result);
    return result;
}
```

NOTE Java 8 enhances the `Map` interface with a method `computeIfAbsent` for such use cases. We mention it in appendix B. But for your information you could use the method `computeIfAbsent` as follows to write clearer code:

```
Integer computeNumberOfNodesUsingCache(Range range) {
    return numberOfNodes.computeIfAbsent(range,
                                        this::computeNumberOfNodes);
}
```

It's clear that the method `computeNumberOfNodesUsingCache` is referentially transparent (assuming the method `computeNumberOfNodes` is also referentially transparent). But the fact that `numberOfNodes` is mutable shared state, and that `HashMap` isn't `synchronized`,[2] means that this code isn't thread-safe. Even using (lock-protected) `Hashtable` or (concurrent-without-locking) `ConcurrentHashMap` instead of `HashMap` may not give the expected performance if there are parallel calls to `numberOfNodes` from multiple cores, because there's a race condition between your finding that `range` isn't in the `map` and inserting the (argument, result) pair back into the `map`. This means multiple processes might compute the same value to add to the `map`.

Perhaps the best thing to take away from this struggle is that mixing mutable state with concurrency is trickier than you'd imagine, and functional-style programming avoids it entirely, except for low-level performance hacks such as caching. A second thing is that apart from implementing tricks like caching, if you code in functional style, then you never need to care whether or not another functional-style method you call is synchronized, because you *know* it has no shared mutable state.

[2] This is one of those places where bugs breed. It's so easy to use `HashMap` here and to forget the fact that the Java manual notes that it's not thread-safe (or to simply not care because our program is currently single-threaded).

14.5.2 What does "return the same object" mean?

Let's consider again the binary tree example from section 14.2.3. In figure 14.4, variable `t` points to an existing `Tree`, and the figure shows the effect of calling `fupdate("Will", 26, t)` to produce a new `Tree`, which we'll assume is assigned to variable `t2`. The figure makes it clear that `t`, and all the data structures reachable from it, is not mutated. Now suppose you perform a textually identical call in the additional assignment:

```
t3 = fupdate("Will", 26, t);
```

Now `t3` will point to three more newly created nodes, containing the same data as those in `t2`. The question is this: "Is `fupdate` referentially transparent?" *Referentially transparent* means "equal arguments (the case here) imply equal results." The problem is that `t2` and `t3` are different references and therefore `(t2 == t3)` is `false`, so it looks as if you'll have to conclude that `fupdate` isn't referentially transparent. But when using persistent data structures that aren't to be modified, there's logically no difference between `t2` and `t3`.

We can debate this point at length, but the simplest adage is that functional-style programming generally uses `equals` to compare structured values rather than `==` (reference equality) because data isn't modified, and under this model `fupdate` *is* referentially transparent.

14.5.3 Combinators

In functional programming it's common and natural to write a higher-order function (perhaps written as a method) that accepts, say, two functions and produces another function somehow combining these functions. The term *combinator* is generally used for this idea. Much of the new Java 8 API is inspired by this idea; for example, `thenCombine` in the `CompletableFuture` class. This method takes two `CompletableFutures` and a `BiFunction` to produce another `CompletableFuture`.

Although a detailed discussion of combinators in functional programming is beyond the scope of this book, it's worth looking at a couple of special cases to give the flavor of how operations that take and return functions are a very common and natural functional programming construct. The following method encodes the idea of *function composition*:

```
static <A,B,C> Function<A,C> compose(Function<B,C> g, Function<A,B> f) {
    return x -> g.apply(f.apply(x));
}
```

It takes functions `f` and `g` as arguments and returns a function whose effect is to do `f` first and then `g`. You can then use this to define an operation, which captures internal iteration as a combinator. Let's look at the case where you wish to take data and apply function `f` to it repeatedly, say *n* times, as in a loop. Your operation, let's call it `repeat`, takes a function, `f`, saying what happens in one iteration and returning a function that says what happens in *n* iterations. A call such as

```
repeat(3, (Integer x) -> 2*x);
```

will give `x ->(2*(2*(2*x)))` or `x -> 8*x`.

You can test it by writing

```
System.out.println(repeat(3, (Integer x) -> 2*x).apply(10));
```

which prints 80.

The method `repeat` can be coded as follows (note the special case of a zero-trip loop):

```
static <A> Function<A,A> repeat(int n, Function<A,A> f) {
    return n==0 ? x -> x
                : compose(f, repeat(n-1, f));
}
```

Return the "do-nothing" identity function if `n` is zero.

Otherwise do `f`, repeated `n-1` times, followed by doing it once more.

Variants of this idea can model richer notions of iteration, including having a functional model of mutable state passed between iterations. But it's now time to move on; this chapter's role is to give a summary of functional programming as the basis behind Java 8. There are many excellent books exploring functional programming in greater depth.

14.6 Summary

Following are the key concepts you should take away from this chapter:

- First-class functions are functions that can be passed as arguments, returned as results, and stored in data structures.
- A higher-order function is a function that takes at least one or more functions as input or returns another function. Typical higher-order functions in Java include `comparing`, `andThen`, and `compose`.
- Currying is a technique that lets you modularize functions and reuse code.
- A persistent data structure preserves the previous version of itself when it's modified. As a result, it can prevent unnecessary defensive copying.
- Streams in Java can't be self-defined.
- A lazy list is a more expressive version of a Java stream. A lazy list lets you produce elements of the list on demand by using a supplier that can create more of the data structure.
- Pattern matching is a functional feature that lets you unwrap data types. It can be seen as generalizing Java's `switch` statement.
- Referential transparency allows computations to be cached.
- Combinators are a functional idea that combines two or more functions or other data structures.

15 Blending OOP and FP: comparing Java 8 and Scala

This chapter covers

- An introduction to Scala
- How Java 8 relates to Scala and vice versa
- How functions in Scala compare to Java 8
- Classes and traits

Scala is a programming language that mixes object-oriented and functional programming. It's often seen as an alternative language to Java for programmers who want functional features in a statically typed programming language that runs on the JVM while keeping a Java feel. Scala introduces many more features compared to Java: a more sophisticated type system, type inference, pattern matching (as presented in section 14.4), constructs to simply define domain specific languages, and so on. In addition, you can access all Java libraries within Scala code.

You may be wondering why we have a chapter about Scala in a Java 8 book. This book has been largely centered on adopting functional-style programming in Java. Scala, just like Java 8, supports the concepts of functional-style processing of collections (that is, stream-like operations), first-class functions, and default methods. But Scala pushes these ideas further: it provides a larger set of features around these ideas compared to Java 8. We believe you may find it interesting to compare

Scala with the approach taken by Java 8 and see Java 8's limitations. This chapter aims to shed light on this matter to appease your curiosity.

Keep in mind that the purpose of this chapter is not to teach you how to write idiomatic Scala code or everything about Scala. There are many features such as pattern matching, for comprehensions and implicits supported in Scala but not in Java, that we won't discuss. Rather, this chapter focuses on comparing the new Java 8 features to what Scala provides, so you have an idea of the bigger picture. For example, you'll find that you can write more concise and readable code in Scala compared to Java.

This chapter starts with an introduction to Scala: how to write simple programs and working with collections. Next, we discuss functions in Scala: first-class functions, closures, and currying. Finally, we look at classes in Scala and a feature called *traits*: Scala's take on interfaces and default methods.

15.1 Introduction to Scala

This section briefly introduces basic Scala features so you can get a feel for simple Scala programs. We start with a slightly modified "Hello world" example written in an imperative style and a functional style. We then look at some data structures that Scala supports—`List`, `Set`, `Map`, `Stream`, `Tuple`, and `Option`—and compare them to Java 8. Finally, we present *traits*, Scala's replacement for Java's interfaces, which also support inheritance of methods at object-instantiation time.

15.1.1 Hello beer

Let's look at a simple example so you get a feel for Scala's syntax and features and how they compare to Java. To change a bit from the classic "Hello world" example, let's bring in some beer. You want to print the following output on the screen:

```
Hello 2 bottles of beer
Hello 3 bottles of beer
Hello 4 bottles of beer
Hello 5 bottles of beer
Hello 6 bottles of beer
```

IMPERATIVE-STYLE SCALA

Here's how the code to print this output looks in Scala using an imperative style:

```
object Beer {
  def main(args: Array[String]){
    var n : Int = 2
    while( n <= 6 ){
      println(s"Hello ${n} bottles of beer")    <-- String interpolation
      n += 1
    }
  }
}
```

Information on how to run this code can be found on the official Scala website.[1] This program looks quite similar to what you'd write in Java. It has a structure similar to Java programs: it consists of one method called `main`, which takes an array of strings as argument (type annotations follow the syntax `s : String` instead of `String s` like in Java). The `main` method doesn't return a value, and so it's not necessary to declare a return type in Scala as you'd have to do in Java using `void`.

NOTE In general, nonrecursive method declarations in Scala don't need an explicit return type because Scala can infer it for you.

Before we look at the body of the `main` method, we need to discuss the `object` declaration. After all, in Java you have to declare the method `main` within a class. The declaration `object` introduces a singleton object: it declares a class `Beer` and instantiates it at the same time. Only one instance is ever created. This is the first example of a classical design pattern (the singleton design pattern) implemented as a language feature—free to use out of the box! In addition, you can view methods within an `object` declaration as being declared as static; this is why the signature of the `main` method isn't explicitly declared as `static`.

Let's now look at the body of `main`. It also looks similar to Java, but statements don't need to end with a semicolon (it's optional). The body consists of a `while` loop, which increments a mutable variable, `n`. For each new value of `n` you print a string on the screen using the predefined method `println`. The `println` line showcases another feature available in Scala: string interpolation. *String interpolation* allows you to embed variables and expressions directly in string literals. In the previous code you can use the variable `n` directly in the string literal `s"Hello ${n} bottles of beer"`. Prepending the string with the interpolator `s` provides that magic. Normally in Java you'd have to do an explicit concatenation such as `"Hello " + n + " bottles of beer"`.

FUNCTIONAL-STYLE SCALA

But what can Scala really offer after all our talk about functional-style programming throughout this book? The previous code can be written in a more functional-style form as follows in Java 8:

```
public class Foo {
    public static void main(String[] args) {
        IntStream.rangeClosed(2, 6)
                 .forEach(n -> System.out.println("Hello " + n +
                                                  " bottles of beer"));
    }
}
```

[1] See http://www.scala-lang.org/documentation/getting-started.html.

Here's how it looks in Scala:

```
object Beer {
  def main(args: Array[String]){
    2 to 6 foreach { n => println(s"Hello ${n} bottles of beer") }
  }
}
```

It looks similar to the Java code but is less verbose. First, you can create a range using the expression `2 to 6`. Here's something cool: `2` is an object of type `Int`. In Scala *everything* is an object; there's no concept of primitive types like in Java. This makes Scala a complete object-oriented language. An `Int` object in Scala supports a method named `to`, which takes as argument another `Int` and returns a range. So you could have written `2.to(6)` instead. But methods that take one argument can be written in an infix form. Next, `foreach` (with a lowercase `e`) is similar to `forEach` in Java 8 (with an uppercase `E`). It's a method available on a range (here you use the infix notation again), and it takes a lambda expression as argument to apply on each element. The lambda expression syntax is similar to Java 8 but the arrow is `=>` instead of `->`.[2] The previous code is functional: you're not mutating a variable as you did in our earlier example using a `while` loop.

15.1.2 Basic data structures: List, Set, Map, Tuple, Stream, Option

Feeling good after a couple of beers to quench your thirst? Most real programs need to manipulate and store data, so let's now look at how you can manipulate collections in Scala and how that compares to Java 8.

CREATING COLLECTIONS

Creating collections in Scala is simple, thanks to its emphasis on conciseness. To exemplify, here's how to create a `Map`:

```
val authorsToAge = Map("Raoul" -> 23, "Mario" -> 40, "Alan" -> 53)
```

Several things are new with this line of code. First, it's pretty awesome that you can create a `Map` and associate a key to a value directly, using the syntax `->`. There's no need to add elements manually like in Java:

```
Map<String, Integer> authorsToAge = new HashMap<>();
authorsToAge.put("Raoul", 23);
authorsToAge.put("Mario", 40);
authorsToAge.put("Alan", 53);
```

There are discussions to add similar syntactic sugar in future versions of Java, but it's not available in Java 8.[3] The second new thing is that you can choose not to annotate the type of the variable `authorsToAge`. You could have explicitly written `val authorsToAge : Map[String, Int]`, but Scala can infer the type of the variable for you. (Note

---

[2] Note that in Scala the terminology "anonymous functions" or "closures" (interchangeable) is used to refer to what Java 8 calls lambda expressions.

[3] See http://openjdk.java.net/jeps/186.

that the code is still statically checked! All variables have a given type at compile time.) We'll come back to this feature later in the chapter. Third, you use the `val` keyword instead of `var`. What's the difference? The keyword `val` means that the variable is read-only and can't be reassigned to (just like `final` in Java). The `var` keyword means the variable is read-write.

What about other collections? You can create a `List` (a singly linked list) or a `Set` (no duplicates) as easily:

```
val authors = List("Raoul", "Mario", "Alan")
val numbers = Set(1, 1, 2, 3, 5, 8)
```

The `authors` variable will have three elements and the `numbers` variable will have five elements.

IMMUTABLE VS. MUTABLE

One important property to keep in mind is that the collections created previously are *immutable* by default. This means they can't be changed after they're created. This is useful because you know that accessing the collection at any point in your program will always yield a collection with the same elements.

So how can you update an immutable collection in Scala? To come back to the terminology used in the previous chapter, such collections in Scala are said to be *persistent*: updating a collection produces a new collection that shares as much as possible with its previous version, which persists without being affected by changes like we showed in figures 14.3 and 14.4. As a consequence of this property, your code will have fewer *implicit data dependences*: there's less confusion about which location in your code updates a collection (or any other shared data structure) and at what point in time.

Let's look at an example to demonstrate this idea. Let's add an element to a `Set`:

```
val numbers = Set(2, 5, 3);
val newNumbers = numbers + 8      <-- Here + is a method that will add 8 to the
                                      Set, creating a new Set object as a result.
println(newNumbers)               <-- (2, 5, 3, 8)
println(numbers)                  <-- (2, 5, 3)
```

In this example, the set of numbers isn't modified. Instead, a new `Set` is created with an additional element.

Note that Scala doesn't force you to use immutable collections—it just makes it easy to adopt immutability in your code. There are also mutable versions available in the package `scala.collection.mutable`.

Unmodifiable vs. immutable

Java provides several ways to create *unmodifiable* collections. In the following code the variable `newNumbers` is a read-only view of the set `numbers`:

```
Set<Integer> numbers = new HashSet<>();
Set<Integer> newNumbers = Collections.unmodifiableSet(numbers);
```

(continued)

This means you won't be able to add new elements through the `newNumbers` variable. But an unmodifiable collection is just a wrapper over a modifiable collection. This means that you could still add elements by accessing the `numbers` variable!

By contrast, *immutable* collections guarantee that nothing can change the collection, regardless of how many variables are pointing to it.

We explained in chapter 14 how you could create a persistent data structure: an immutable data structure that preserves the previous version of itself when modified. Any modifications always produce a new updated structure.

WORKING WITH COLLECTIONS

Now that you've seen how to create collections, you need to know what you can do with them. It turns out that collections in Scala support operations similar to what the Streams API provides. For instance, you'll recognize `filter` and `map` in the following example and as illustrated in figure 15.1:

```
val fileLines = Source.fromFile("data.txt").getLines.toList()
val linesLongUpper
  = fileLines.filter(l => l.length() > 10)
             .map(l => l.toUpperCase())
```

Don't worry about the first line; it basically transforms a file into a list of strings consisting of the lines in the file (similar to what `Files.readAllLines` provides in Java 8). The second line creates a pipeline of two operations:

- A `filter` operation that selects only the lines that have a length greater than 10
- A `map` operation that transforms these long lines to uppercase

This code can be also written as follows:

```
val linesLongUpper
  = fileLines filter (_.length() > 10) map(_.toUpperCase())
```

You use the infix notation as well as the underscore (`_`), which is a placeholder that's positionally matched to any arguments. In this case you can read `_.length()` as `l => l.length()`. In the functions passed to `filter` and `map`, the underscore is bound to the *line* parameter that is to be processed.

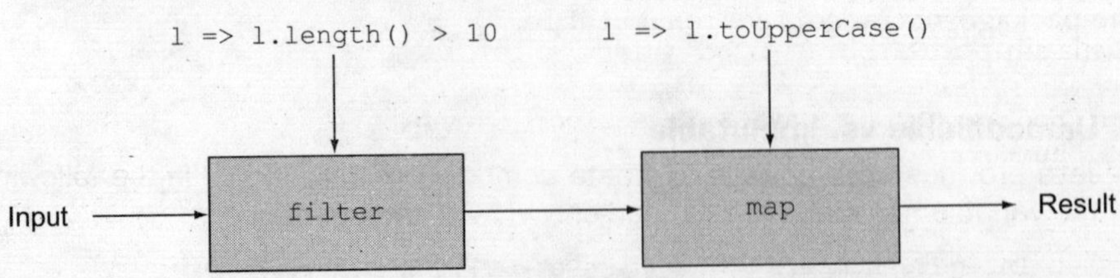

Figure 15.1 Stream-like operations with Scala's `List`

There are many more useful operations available in Scala's collection API. We recommend taking a look at the Scala documentation to get an idea.[4] Note that it's slightly richer than what the Streams API provides (for example, there's support for zipping operations, which let you combine elements of two lists), so you'll definitely gain a few programming idioms by checking it out. These idioms may also make it into the Streams API in future versions of Java.

Finally, remember that in Java 8 you could ask for a pipeline to be executed in parallel by calling `parallel` on a `Stream`. Scala has a similar trick; you only need to use the method `par`:

```
val linesLongUpper
  = fileLines.par filter (_.length() > 10) map(_.toUpperCase())
```

TUPLES

Let's now look at another feature that's often painfully verbose in Java: *tuples*. You may want to use tuples to group people by their name and their phone number (here simple pairs) without declaring an ad hoc new class and instantiate an object for it: ("Raoul", "+ 44 007007007"), ("Alan", "+44 003133700"), and so on.

Unfortunately, Java doesn't provide support for tuples. So you have to create your own data structure. Here's a simple `Pair` class:

```
public class Pair<X, Y> {
    public final X x;
    public final Y y;
    public Pair(X x, Y y){
        this.x = x;
        this.y = y;
    }
}
```

And of course you need to instantiate pairs explicitly:

```
Pair<String, String> raoul = new Pair<>("Raoul", "+ 44 007007007");
Pair<String, String> alan = new Pair<>("Alan", "+44 003133700");
```

Okay, but how about triplets? How about arbitrary-sized tuples? It becomes really tedious and ultimately will affect the readability and maintenance of your programs.

Scala provides *tuple literals*, which means you can create tuples through simple syntactic sugar—just the normal mathematical notation:

```
val raoul = ("Raoul", "+ 44 887007007")
val alan = ("Alan", "+44 883133700")
```

Scala supports arbitrary-sized[5] tuples, so the following are all possible:

```
val book = (2014, "Java 8 in Action", "Manning")    <-- A tuple of type (Int, String, String)
val numbers = (42, 1337, 0, 3, 14)    <-- A tuple of type (Int, Int, Int, Int, Int)
```

[4] A list of notable and other packages can be found at www.scala-lang.org/api/current/#package.

[5] Tuples have a limitation of 23 elements maximum.

You can access the elements of the tuples by their positions using the accessors `_1`, `_2` (starting at 1), for example:

```
println(book._1)          <-- Prints 2014
println(numbers._4)       <-- Prints 3
```

Isn't that much nicer than what you'd have to write in Java? The good news is that there are discussions about introducing tuple literals in future versions of Java (see chapter 16 for more discussion of this).

STREAM

The collections we described so far, `List`, `Set`, `Map`, and `Tuple`, are all evaluated *eagerly* (that is, immediately). Of course by now you know that streams in Java 8 are evaluated on demand (that is, lazily). You saw in chapter 5 that because of this property streams can represent an infinite sequence without overflowing the memory.

Scala provides a corresponding lazily evaluated data structure called `Stream` too! But `Streams` in Scala provide more features than those in Java. `Streams` in Scala remember values that were computed so previous elements can be accessed. In addition, `Streams` are indexed so elements can be accessed by an index just like a list. Note that the trade-off for these additional properties is that `Streams` are less memory-efficient compared to Java 8's streams, because being able to refer back to previous elements means the elements need to be "remembered" (cached).

OPTION

Another data structure that you'll be familiar with is `Option`. It's Scala's version of Java 8's `Optional`, which we discussed in chapter 10. We argued that you should use `Optional` when possible to design better APIs, in which just by reading the signature of a method users can tell whether or not they can expect an optional value. It should be used instead of `null` when possible to prevent `null` pointer exceptions.

You saw in chapter 10 that you could use `Optional` to return the insurance's name of a person if their age is greater than a minimum age, as follows:

```
public String getCarInsuranceName(Optional<Person> person, int minAge) {
    return person.filter(p -> p.getAge() >= minAge)
                 .flatMap(Person::getCar)
                 .flatMap(Car::getInsurance)
                 .map(Insurance::getName)
                 .orElse("Unknown");
}
```

In Scala you can use `Option` in a way similar to `Optional`:

```
def getCarInsuranceName(person: Option[Person], minAge: Int) =
  person.filter(_.getAge() >= minAge)
        .flatMap(_.getCar)
        .flatMap(_.getInsurance)
        .map(_.getName).getOrElse("Unknown")
```

You can recognize the same structure and method names apart from `getOrElse`, which is the equivalent of `orElse` in Java 8. You see, throughout this book you've learned new concepts that can be directly applied to other programming languages! Unfortunately, `null` also exists in Scala for Java compatibility reasons and its use is highly discouraged.

> **NOTE** In the previous code you wrote `_.getCar` (without parentheses) instead of `_.getCar()` (with parentheses). In Scala parentheses aren't required when calling a method that takes no parameters.

15.2 Functions

Scala functions can be seen as a sequence of instructions that are grouped together to perform a task. They're useful to abstract behavior and are the cornerstone of functional programming.

In Java, you're familiar with *methods*: functions associated with a class. You've also seen lambda expressions, which can be considered *anonymous functions*. Scala offers a richer set of features around functions than Java does, which we look at in this section. Scala provides the following:

- *Function types*, syntactic sugar to represent the idea of Java function descriptors (that is, a notation to represent the signature of the abstract method declared in a functional interface), which we described in chapter 3
- Anonymous functions that don't have the write restrictions on nonlocal variables that Java's lambda expressions have
- Support for *currying*, which means breaking down a function that takes multiple arguments into a series of functions that take part of the arguments

15.2.1 First-class functions in Scala

Functions in Scala are *first-class values*. This means they can be passed around as parameters, returned as a result, and stored in variables, just like other values such as an `Integer` or a `String`. As we've shown you in earlier chapters, method references and lambda expressions in Java 8 can also be seen as first-class functions.

Let's look at an example of how first-class functions work in Scala. Let's say you have a list of strings representing tweets people are sending to you. You'd like to filter this list with different criteria, for example, tweets that mention the word *Java* or tweets that have a short length. You can represent these two criteria as *predicates* (functions that return a `Boolean`):

```
def isJavaMentioned(tweet: String) : Boolean = tweet.contains("Java")
def isShortTweet(tweet: String) : Boolean = tweet.length() < 20
```

In Scala you can pass these methods directly to the built-in `filter` as follows (just as you could pass them using method references in Java):

```
val tweets = List(
    "I love the new features in Java 8",
    "How's it going?",
    "An SQL query walks into a bar, sees two tables and says 'Can I join you?'"
)
```

```
tweets.filter(isJavaMentioned).foreach(println)
tweets.filter(isShortTweet).foreach(println)
```

Now let's inspect the signature of the built-in method `filter`:

```
def filter[T](p: (T) => Boolean): List[T]
```

You may wonder what the type of the parameter `p` means (here `(T) => Boolean`), because in Java you'd expect a functional interface! This is a new syntax that's not available in Java. It describes a *function type*. Here it represents a function that takes an object of type `T` and returns a `Boolean`. In Java this is encoded as a `Predicate<T>` or `Function<T, Boolean>`. This is exactly the same signature as the methods `isJavaMentioned` and `isShortTweet` so you can pass them as argument to `filter`. The Java 8 language designers decided not to introduce a similar syntax for function types in order to keep the language consistent with previous versions. (Introducing too much new syntax in a new version of the language is seen as too much additional cognitive overhead.)

15.2.2 Anonymous functions and closures

Scala also supports the concept of *anonymous functions*. They have a syntax similar to lambda expressions. In the following example you can assign to a variable named `isLongTweet` an anonymous function that checks whether a given tweet is long:

```
val isLongTweet : String => Boolean            <-- A variable of function type String to Boolean
    = (tweet : String) => tweet.length() > 60  <-- An anonymous function
```

Now in Java, a lambda expression lets you create an instance of a functional interface. Scala has a similar mechanism. The previous code is syntactic sugar for declaring an anonymous class of type `scala.Function1` (a function of one parameter), which provides the implementation of the method `apply`:

```
val isLongTweet : String => Boolean
    = new Function1[String, Boolean] {
        def apply(tweet: String): Boolean = tweet.length() > 60
    }
```

Because the variable `isLongTweet` holds an object of type `Function1`, you can call the method `apply`, which can be seen as calling the function:

```
isLongTweet.apply("A very short tweet")        <-- Returns false
```

As in Java, you could do the following:

```
Function<String, Boolean> isLongTweet = (String s) -> s.length() > 60;
boolean long = isLongTweet.apply("A very short tweet");
```

To use lambda expressions, Java provides several built-in functional interfaces such as `Predicate`, `Function`, and `Consumer`. Scala provides traits (you can think of *traits* as interfaces for now until we describe them in the next section) to achieve the same thing:

Function0 (a function with 0 parameters and a return result) up to Function22 (a function with 22 parameters), which all define the method apply.

Another cool trick in Scala is that you can call the method apply using syntactic sugar that looks more like a function call:

```
isLongTweet("A very short tweet")        <-- Returns false
```

The compiler automatically converts a call f(a) into f.apply(a) and, more generally, a call f(a1, ..., an) into f.apply(a1, ..., an), if f is an object that supports the method apply (note that apply can have any number of arguments).

CLOSURES

In chapter 3 we commented on whether lambda expressions in Java constitute closures. To refresh, a *closure* is an instance of a function that can reference nonlocal variables of that function with no restrictions. But lambda expressions in Java 8 have a restriction: they can't modify the content of local variables of a method in which the lambda is defined. Those variables have to be implicitly final. It helps to think that *lambdas close over values, rather than variables.*

In contrast, anonymous functions in Scala can capture *variables* themselves, not the *values* to which the variables currently refer. For example, the following is possible in Scala:

```
def main(args: Array[String]) {
    var count = 0
    val inc = () => count+=1          <-- A closure capturing and incrementing count
    inc()
    println(count)                    <-- Prints 1
    inc()
    println(count)                    <-- Prints 2
}
```

But in Java the following will result in a compiler error because count is implicitly forced to be final:

```
public static void main(String[] args) {
    int count = 0;
    Runnable inc = () -> count+=1;     <-- Error: count must be final or effectively final
    inc.run();
    System.out.println(count);
    inc.run();
}
```

We argued in chapters 7, 13, and 14 that you should avoid mutation when possible to make your programs easier to maintain and parallelizable, so use this feature only when strictly necessary.

15.2.3 Currying

In chapter 14 we described a technique called *currying*: where a function f of two arguments (x and y, say) is seen instead as a function g of one argument, which returns a function also of one argument. This definition can be generalized to functions with multiple arguments, producing multiple functions of one argument. In other words, you can break down a function that takes multiple arguments into a series of functions that take a subpart of the arguments. Scala provides a construct to let you easily curry an existing function.

To understand what Scala brings to the table, let's first revisit an example in Java. You can define a simple method to multiply two integers:

```
static int multiply(int x, int y) {
  return x * y;
}

int r = multiply(2, 10);
```

But this definition requires all the arguments to be passed to it. You can manually break down the `multiply` method by making it return another function:

```
static Function<Integer, Integer> multiplyCurry(int x) {
    return (Integer y) -> x * y;
}
```

The function returned by `multiplyCurry` captures the value of `x` and multiplies it by its argument `y`, returning an `Integer`. This means you can use `multiplyCurry` as follows in a `map` to multiply each element by 2:

```
Stream.of(1, 3, 5, 7)
      .map(multiplyCurry(2))
      .forEach(System.out::println);
```

This will produce the result 2, 6, 10, 14. This works because `map` expects a `Function` as argument and `multiplyCurry` returns a `Function`!

Now it's a bit tedious in Java to manually split up a function to create a curried form (especially if the function has multiple arguments). Scala has a special syntax to do this automatically. You can define the normal `multiply` method as follows:

```
def multiply(x : Int, y: Int) = x * y

val r = multiply(2, 10);
```

And here is its curried form:

```
def multiplyCurry(x :Int)(y : Int) = x * y      <- Defining a curried function

val r = multiplyCurry(2)(10)                    <- Invoking a curried function
```

Using the `(x: Int)(y: Int)` syntax, the `multiplyCurry` method takes *two argument lists* of one `Int` parameter. In contrast, `multiply` takes *one list* of two `Int` parameters. What happens when you call `multiplyCurry`? The first invocation of `multiplyCurry` with a single `Int` (the parameter `x`), `multiplyCurry(2)`, returns another function that takes a parameter `y` and multiplies it with the captured value of `x` (here the value 2). We say this function is *partially applied* as explained in section 14.1.2, because not all arguments are provided. The second invocation multiplies x and y. This means you can store the first invocation to multiplyCurry inside a variable and reuse it:

```
val multiplyByTwo : Int => Int = multiplyCurry(2)
val r = multiplyByTwo(10)                          <— 20
```

In comparison with Java, in Scala you don't need to manually provide the curried form of a function as done here. Scala provides a convenient function-definition syntax to indicate that a function has multiple curried argument lists.

15.3 Classes and traits

We now look at how classes and interfaces in Java compare to Scala. These two constructs are paramount to design applications. You'll see that Scala's classes and interfaces can provide more flexibility than what Java offers.

15.3.1 Less verbosity with Scala classes

Because Scala is also a full object-oriented language, you can create classes and instantiate them to produce objects. At its most basic form, the syntax to declare and instantiate classes is similar to Java. For example, here's how to declare a Hello class:

```
class Hello {
  def sayThankYou(){
    println("Thanks for reading our book")
  }
}
val h = new Hello()
h.sayThankYou()
```

GETTERS AND SETTERS

It becomes more interesting once you have a class with fields. Have you ever come across a Java class that purely defines a list of fields, and you've had to declare a long list of getters, setters, and an appropriate constructor? What a pain! In addition, you'll often see tests for the implementation of each method. A large amount of code is typically devoted to such classes in Enterprise Java applications. Consider this simple Student class:

```
public class Student {

    private String name;
    private int id;

    public Student(String name) {
        this.name = name;
    }

    public String getName() {
        return name;
    }

    public void setName(String name) {
        this.name = name;
    }
```

```
    public int getId() {
        return id;
    }

    public void setId(int id) {
        this.id = id;
    }
}
```

You have to manually define the constructor that initializes all fields, two getters, and two setters. A simple class now has more than 20 lines of code! Several IDEs and tools can help you generate this code, but your codebase still has to deal with a large amount of additional code that's not very useful compared to real business logic.

In Scala, constructors, getters, and setters can be implicitly generated, which results in code with less verbosity:

```
class Student(var name: String, var id: Int)      // Initialize a Student object
val s = new Student("Raoul", 1)
println(s.name)                                   // Get the name, print Raoul
s.id = 1337                                       // Set the id
println(s.id)                                     // Print 1337
```

15.3.2 Scala traits vs. Java 8 interfaces

Scala has another useful feature for abstraction called *traits*. They're Scala's replacement for Java's interfaces. A trait can define both abstract methods and methods with a default implementation. Traits can also be multiple inherited just like interfaces in Java, so you can see them as similar to Java 8's interfaces that support default methods. Traits can also contain fields like an abstract class, which Java 8 interfaces don't support. Are traits just like abstract classes? No, because traits can be multiple inherited, unlike abstract classes. Java has always had multiple inheritance of types because a class can implement multiple interfaces. Now Java 8, through default methods, introduces multiple inheritance of behaviors but still doesn't allow multiple inheritance of state, something permitted by Scala traits.

To show an example of what a trait looks like in Scala, let's define a trait called `Sized` that contains one mutable field called `size` and one method called `isEmpty` with a default implementation:

```
trait Sized{
  var size : Int = 0                // A field called size
  def isEmpty() = size == 0         // A method called isEmpty with a default implementation
}
```

You can now compose it at declaration time with a class, here an `Empty` class that always has size 0:

```
class Empty extends Sized                // A class inheriting from the trait Sized
println(new Empty().isEmpty())           // Prints true
```

Interestingly, compared to Java interfaces, traits can also be *composed at object instantiation time* (but it's still a compile-time operation). For example, you can create a `Box` class and decide that one specific instance should support the operations defined by the trait `Sized`:

```
class Box
val b1 = new Box() with Sized           <-- Composing the trait at object instantiation time
println(b1.isEmpty())                   <-- Prints true
val b2 = new Box()
b2.isEmpty()                            <-- Compile error: the Box class declaration doesn't inherit from Sized
```

What happens if multiple traits are inherited declaring methods with the same signatures or fields with the same names? Scala provides restriction rules similar to those you saw with default methods in chapter 9.

15.4 Summary

Following are the key concepts you should take away from this chapter:

- Both Java 8 and Scala combine object-oriented and functional programming features into one programming language; both run on the JVM and to a large extent can interoperate.
- Scala supports collection abstractions similar to Java 8—`List`, `Set`, `Map`, `Stream`, `Option`—but also supports tuples.
- Scala provides richer features around functions than Java 8: function types, closures that have no restrictions on accessing local variables, and built-in currying forms.
- Classes in Scala can provide implicit constructors, getters, and setters.
- Scala supports traits: interfaces that can include both fields and default methods.

16 Conclusions and where next for Java

This chapter covers

- New Java 8 features and their evolutionary effect on programming style
- A few unfinished-business ideas started by Java 8
- What Java 9 and Java 10 might bring

We covered a lot of material in this book, and we hope you now feel that you're ready to start using the new Java 8 features in your own code, perhaps building on our examples and quizzes. In this chapter we review the journey of learning about Java 8 and the gentle push toward functional-style programming. In addition, we speculate on what future enhancements and great new features may be in Java's pipeline beyond Java 8.

16.1 Review of Java 8 features

A good way to help you understand Java 8 as a practical, useful language is to revisit the features in turn. Instead of simply listing them, we'd like to present them as being interlinked to help you understand them not merely as a set of features but as a high-level overview of the coherent language design that is Java 8. Our other aim in this review chapter is to emphasize how most of the new features in Java 8 are facilitating functional-style programming in Java. Remember, this isn't a capricious design choice but a conscious design strategy, centered on two trends, which we regard as climate change in the model from chapter 1:

- The increasing need to exploit the power of multicore processors now that, for silicon technology reasons, the additional transistors annually provided by Moore's law no longer translate into higher clock speeds of individual CPU cores. Put simply, making your code run faster requires parallel code.
- The increasing tendency to concisely manipulate collections of data with a declarative style for processing data, such as taking some data source, extracting all data that matches a given criterion, and applying some operation to the result—either summarizing it or making a collection of the result for further processing later. This style is associated with the use of immutable objects and collections, which are then processed to produce further immutable values.

Neither motivation is effectively supported by the traditional, object-oriented, imperative approach, centered on mutating fields and applying iterators. Mutating data on one core and reading it from another is surprisingly expensive, not to mention the need for error-prone locking; similarly when your mind-set is focused on iterating over and mutating existing objects, then the stream-like programming idiom can feel very alien. But these two trends are easily supported using ideas from functional programming, and this explains why the Java 8 center of gravity has moved a bit from what we've come to expect from Java.

Let's now review, in a big-picture unifying view, what you've learned from this book, and see how it all fits together in the new climate.

16.1.1 Behavior parameterization (lambdas and method references)

To be able to write a reusable method such as `filter`, you need to be able to specify as its argument a description of the filtering criterion. Although Java experts could achieve this in previous versions of Java (by wrapping the filtering criterion as a method inside a class and passing an instance of that class), this solution was unsuitable for general use because it was too cumbersome to write and maintain.

As you discovered in chapters 2 and 3, Java 8 provides a way, borrowed from functional programming, of passing a piece of code to a method. It conveniently provides two variants of this:

- Passing a *lambda*, a one-off piece of code such as

```
apple -> apple.getWeight() > 150
```

- Passing a *method reference*, to an existing method, as code such as `Apple::isHeavy`

These values have types such as `Function<T, R>`, `Predicate<T>`, and `BiFunction<T, U, R>` and have ways for the recipient to execute them using the methods `apply`, `test`, and so on. Of themselves, lambdas can seem rather a niche concept, but it's the way Java 8 uses them in much of the new Streams API that propels them to the center of Java.

16.1.2 Streams

The collection classes in Java, along with iterators and the `for-each` construct, have served us honorably for a long time. It would have been easy for the Java 8 designers to add methods like `filter` and `map` to collections, exploiting the lambdas mentioned previously to express database-like queries. But they didn't—instead they added a whole new Streams API, the subject of chapters 4–7—and it's worth pausing to consider why.

What's wrong with collections that requires them to be replaced or augmented with a similar but different notion of streams? We'll summarize it like this: if you have a large collection and apply three operations to it, perhaps mapping the objects in the collection to sum two of their fields, then filtering the sums satisfying some criterion, and then sorting the result, you'll make three separate traversals of the collection. The Streams API instead lazily forms these operations into a pipeline, and then does a single stream traversal performing all the operations together. This is much more efficient for large datasets, and for reasons such as memory caches, the larger the dataset the more important it is to minimize the number of traversals.

The other, no less important, reasons concern the ability to process elements in parallel, which is vital to efficiently exploit multicore CPUs. Streams, in particular the method `parallel`, allow a stream to be marked as suitable for parallel processing. Recall here that parallelism and mutable state fit badly together, so core functional concepts (side-effect-free operations and methods parameterized with lambdas and method references that permit internal iteration instead of external iteration, as discussed in chapter 4) are central to exploiting streams in parallel using `map`, `filter`, and the like.

Let's now look at how these ideas, which we introduced in terms of streams, have a direct analog in the design of `CompletableFuture`.

16.1.3 CompletableFuture

Java has provided the `Future` interface since Java 5. `Futures` are useful for exploiting multicore because they allow a task to be *spawned* onto another thread or core and allow the spawning task to continue executing along with the spawned task. When the spawning task needs the result, it can use the `get` method to wait for the `Future` to complete (produce its value).

Chapter 11 explains the Java 8 `CompletableFuture` implementation of `Future`. Again this exploits lambdas. A useful, if slightly imprecise, motto is that "`CompletableFuture` is to `Future` as `Stream` is to `Collection`." Let's compare:

- `Stream` lets you pipeline operations and provides behavior parameterization with `map`, `filter`, and the like, thus avoiding the boilerplate code you typically have to write using iterators.

- Similarly, `CompletableFuture` provides operations such as `thenCompose`, `thenCombine`, and `allOf`, which give functional-programming-style concise encodings of common design patterns involving `Futures`, and let you avoid similar imperative-style boilerplate code.

This style of operations, albeit in a simpler scenario, also applies to the Java 8 operations on `Optional`, which we now revisit.

16.1.4 Optional

The Java 8 library provides the class `Optional<T>`, which allows your code to specify that a value is either a proper value of type `T` *or is a missing value* returned by the static method `Optional.empty`. This is great for program comprehension and documentation; it provides a data type with an explicit missing value—instead of the previous error-prone use of the `null` pointer to indicate missing values, which we could never be sure was a planned missing value or an accidental `null` resulting from an earlier erroneous computation.

As chapter 10 discusses, if `Optional<T>` is used consistently, then programs should never produce `NullPointerExceptions`. Again you could see this as a one-off, unrelated to the rest of Java 8, and ask, "How does changing from one form of missing value to another help me write programs?" Closer inspection shows that the class `Optional<T>` provides `map`, `filter`, and `ifPresent`. These have similar behavior to corresponding methods in the `Streams` class and can be used to chain computations, *again in functional style,* with the tests for missing value done by the library instead of user code. This internal testing versus external testing choice is directly analogous to how the Streams library does internal iteration versus external iteration in user code.

Our final topic of this section concerns not functional-style programming but instead Java 8 support for upward-compatible library extensions driven by software-engineering desires.

16.1.5 Default methods

There are other additions to Java 8, none of which particularly affect the expressiveness of any individual program. But one thing that is helpful for library designers is the addition to allow *default methods* to be added to an interface. Prior to Java 8, interfaces defined method signatures; now they can also provide default implementations for methods that the interface designer suspects not all clients will want to provide explicitly.

This is a great new tool for library designers, because it provides them with the ability to augment an interface with a new operation, without having to require all clients (classes implementing this interface) to add code to define this method. Therefore, default methods are also relevant to users of libraries because they shield them from future interface changes. Chapter 9 explains this in more detail.

So far we've summarized the concepts of Java 8. We now turn to the thornier subject of what future enhancements and great new features may be in Java's pipeline beyond Java 8.

16.2 What's ahead for Java?

Let's look at some of these points, most of which are discussed in more detail on the JDK Enhancement Proposal website at http://openjdk.java.net/jeps/0. Here we take care to explain why seemingly sensible ideas have subtle difficulties or interaction with existing features that inhibit their direct incorporation into Java.

16.2.1 Collections

Java's development has been evolutionary rather than "big bang." There have been many great ideas added to Java, for example, arrays being replaced by collections and later augmented with the power of streams. Occasionally a new feature is so obviously better (for example, collections over arrays) that we fail to notice that some aspect of the supplanted feature hasn't been carried across. One example is initializers for containers. For example, Java arrays can be declared and initialized with syntax such as

```
Double [] a = {1.2, 3.4, 5.9};
```

which is a convenient abbreviation for

```
Double [] a = new Double[]{1.2, 3.4, 5.9};
```

Java collections (via the `Collection` interface) were introduced as a better and more uniform way of dealing with sequences of data such as that represented by arrays. But their initialization has been rather neglected. Think about how you'd initialize a `HashMap`. You'd have to write the following:

```
Map<String, Integer> map = new HashMap<>();
map.put("raoul", 23);
map.put("mario", 40);
map.put("alan", 53);
```

What you'd like to be able to say is something like

```
Map<String, Integer> map = #{"Raoul" -> 23, "Mario" -> 40, "Alan" -> 53};
```

where `#{...}` is a *collection literal*—a list of the values that are to appear in the collection. This seems uncontroversial as a feature,[1] but it's not yet part of Java.

16.2.2 Type system enhancements

We discuss two possible enhancements to Java type's system: *declaration-site variance* and *local variable type inference*.

DECLARATION-SITE VARIANCE

Java supports wildcards as a flexible mechanism to allow subtyping for generics (more generally referred to as use-site variance). This is why the following assignment is valid:

```
List<? extends Number> numbers = new ArrayList<Integer>();
```

[1] The current Java proposal is described in http://openjdk.java.net/jeps/186.

But the following assignment, omitting the `? extends`, gives a compile-time error:

```
List<Number> numbers = new ArrayList<Integer>();      <— Incompatible types
```

Many programming languages such as C# and Scala support a different variance mechanism called declaration-site variance. They allow programmers to specify variance when defining a generic class. This feature is useful for classes that are inherently variant. `Iterator`, for example, is inherently covariant and `Comparator` is inherently contravariant. You shouldn't need to think in terms of `? extends` or `? super` when you use them. This is why adding declaration-site variance to Java would be useful because these specifications instead appear at the declaration of classes. As a result, it would reduce some cognitive overhead for programmers. Note that at the time of this writing (June 2014) there's a proposal investigating declaration-site variance for Java 9.[2]

MORE TYPE INFERENCE

Originally in Java, whenever we introduced a variable or method, we gave its type at the same time. For example,

```
double convertUSDToGBP(double money) { ExchangeRate e = ...; }
```

contains three types; these give the result type of `convertUSDToGBP`, the type of its argument `money`, and the type of its local variable `e`. Over time this has been relaxed in two ways. First, you may omit type parameters of generics in an expression when the context determines them. For example,

```
Map<String, List<String>> myMap = new HashMap<String, List<String>>();
```

can be abbreviated to the following since Java 7:

```
Map<String, List<String>> myMap = new HashMap<>();
```

Second, using the same idea—propagating the type determined by context into an expression—a lambda expression such as

```
Function<Integer, Boolean> p = (Integer x) -> booleanExpression;
```

can be shortened to

```
Function<Integer, Boolean> p = x -> booleanExpression;
```

by omitting types. In both cases the compiler *infers* the omitted types.

Type inference gives a few advantages when a type consists of a single identifier, the main one being reduced editing work when replacing one type with another. But as types grow in size, generics parameterized by further generic types, then type

---

[2] See https://bugs.openjdk.java.net/browse/JDK-8043488.

inference can aid readability.[3] The Scala and C# languages permit a type in a local-variable-initialized declaration to be replaced with the keyword `var`, and the compiler fills in the appropriate type from the right side. For example, the declaration of `myMap` shown previously using Java syntax could be rendered like this:

```
var myMap = new HashMap<String, List<String>>();
```

This idea is called *local variable type inference*; you can expect similar developments in Java because they decrease clutter caused by redundant type repetition.

There's some small cause for concern, however; given a class `Car` that subclasses a class `Vehicle` and then does the declaration

```
var x = new Vehicle();
```

do you declare `x` to have type `Car` or `Vehicle`? In this case a simple explanation that the missing type is the type of the initializer (here `Vehicle`) is perfectly clear, and it can be backed up with a statement that `var` may not be used when there's no initializer.

16.2.3 Pattern matching

As we discussed in chapter 14, functional-style languages typically provide some form of pattern matching—an enhanced form of `switch`—in which you can ask, "Is this value an instance of a given class?" and, optionally, recursively ask whether its fields have certain values.

It's worth reminding you here that traditional object-oriented design discourages the use of `switch` and instead encourages patterns such as the visitor pattern where data-type-dependent control flow is done by method dispatch instead of by `switch`. This isn't the case at the other end of the programming language spectrum—in functional-style programming where pattern matching over values of data types is often the most convenient way to design a program.

Adding Scala-style pattern matching in full generality to Java seems quite a big job, but following the recent generalization to `switch` to allow `Strings`, you can imagine a more-modest syntax extension, which allows `switch` to operate on objects, using the `instanceof` syntax. Here we revisit our example from section 14.4 and assume a class `Expr`, which is subclassed into `BinOp` and `Number`:

```
switch (someExpr) {
      case (op instanceof BinOp):
         doSomething(op.opname, op.left, op.right);
      case (n instanceof Number):
         dealWithLeafNode(n.val);
      default:
         defaultAction(someExpr);
}
```

[3] Of course, it's important that type inference be done sensibly. Type inference works best when there's only one way, or one easily documentable way, to re-create the type the user has omitted. It's a source of problems if the system infers a different type from the one the user was thinking of; so a good design of type inference will give a fault when there are two different incomparable types that could be inferred instead of appearing just to pick the wrong one seemingly at random.

There are a couple of things to note. We steal from pattern matching the idea that in `case (op instanceof BinOp):`, `op` is a new local variable (of type `BinOp`), which becomes bound to the same value as `someExpr`; similarly, in the `Number` case, `n` becomes a variable of type `Number`. In the default case, no variable is bound. This proposal avoids much boilerplate code compared with using chains of `if-then-else` and casting to subtype. A traditional object-oriented designer would probably argue that such data-type dispatch code would better be expressed using visitor-style methods overridden in subtypes, but to functional-programming eyes this results in related code being scattered over several class definitions. This is a classical design dichotomy discussed in the literature under the name of the "expression problem."[4]

16.2.4 Richer forms of generics

This section discusses two limitations of Java generics and looks at a possible evolution to mitigate them.

REIFIED GENERICS

When generics were introduced in Java 5, they had to be backward-compatible with the existing JVM. To this end, the runtime representations of `ArrayList<String>` and `ArrayList<Integer>` are identical. This is called the *erasure model* of generic polymorphism. There are certain small runtime costs associated with this choice, but the most significant effect for programmers is that parameters to generic types can only be `Object`s. Suppose Java allowed, say, `ArrayList<int>`. Then you could allocate an `ArrayList` object on the heap containing a primitive value such as `int 42`, but the `ArrayList` container wouldn't contain any indicator of whether it contained an `Object` value such as a `String` or a primitive `int` value such as 42.

As some level this seems harmless—if you get a primitive 42 from an `ArrayList<int>` and a `String` object "abc" from an `ArrayList<String>`, then why should you worry that the `ArrayList` containers are indistinguishable? Unfortunately, the answer is garbage collection, because the absence of run-time type information about the contents of the `ArrayList` would leave the JVM unable to determine whether element 13 of your `ArrayList` was an `Integer` reference (to be followed and marked as "in use" by GC) or an `int` primitive value (most definitely not to be followed).

In the C# language, the runtime representations of `ArrayList<String>`, `ArrayList<Integer>`, and `ArrayList<int>` are all in principle different. But even if they are the same, sufficient type information is kept at run-time to allow, for example, garbage collection to determine whether a field is a reference or a primitive. This is called the *reified model of generic polymorphism* or, more simply, *reified generics*. The word *reification* means "making explicit something that otherwise would just be implicit."

Reified generics are clearly desirable; they enable a more full unification of primitive types and their corresponding object types—something that you'll see as problematic in

[4] For a more complete explanation, see http://en.wikipedia.org/wiki/Expression_problem.

the next sections. The main difficulty for Java is backward compatibility, both in the JVM and in existing programs that use reflection and expect generics to be erased.

ADDITIONAL SYNTACTIC FLEXIBILITY IN GENERICS FOR FUNCTION TYPES

Generics proved a wonderful feature when added to Java 5. They're also fine for expressing the type of many Java 8 lambdas and method references. You can express a one-argument function:

```
Function<Integer, Integer> square = x -> x * x;
```

If you have a two-argument function, you use the type `BiFunction<T, U, R>`, where `T` is the type of the first parameter, `U` the second, and `R` the result. But there's no `Tri-Function` unless you declare it yourself!

Similarly, you can't use `Function<T, R>` for references to methods taking zero arguments and returning result type `R`; you have to use `Supplier<R>` instead.

In essence, Java 8 lambdas have enriched what you can write, but the type system hasn't kept up with the flexibility of the code. In many functional languages, you can write, for example, the type `(Integer, Double) => String`, to represent what Java 8 calls `BiFunction<Integer, Double, String>`, along with `Integer => String` to represent `Function<Integer, String>`, and even `() => String` to represent `Supplier<String>`. You can understand `=>` as an infix version of `Function`, `BiFunction`, `Supplier`, and the like. A simple extension to Java syntax for types would allow this, resulting in more readable types analogously to what Scala provides, as discussed in chapter 15.

PRIMITIVE SPECIALIZATIONS AND GENERICS

In Java all primitive types (`int`, for example) have a corresponding object type (here `java.lang.Integer`); often we refer to these as unboxed and boxed types. Although this distinction has the laudable aim of increasing runtime efficiency, the types can become confusing. For example, why in Java 8 do we write `Predicate<Apple>` instead of `Function<Apple, Boolean>`? It turns out that an object of type `Predicate<Apple>`, when called using the method `test`, returns a primitive `boolean`.

By contrast, like all generics, a `Function` can only be parameterized by object types, which in the case of `Function<Apple, Boolean>` is the object type `Boolean`, not the primitive type `boolean`. `Predicate<Apple>` is therefore more efficient because it avoids boxing the `boolean` to make a `Boolean`. This issue has led to the creation of multiple, similar interfaces such as `LongToIntFunction` and `BooleanSupplier`, which add further conceptual overload. Another example concerns the question of the differences between `void`, which can only qualify method return types and has no values, and the object type `Void`, which has `null` as its only value—a question that regularly appears on forums. The special cases of `Function` such as `Supplier<T>`, which could be written `() => T` in the new notation proposed previously, further attest to the ramifications caused by the distinction between primitive and object types. We discussed earlier how reified generics could address many of these issues.

16.2.5 Deeper support for immutability

Some expert readers may have been a little upset when we said that Java 8 has three forms of values:

- Primitive values
- (References to) objects
- (References to) functions

At one level we're going to stick to our guns and say, "But these are the values that a method may now take as arguments and return as results." But we also wish to concede that this is a little problematic: to what extent do you return a (mathematical) *value* when you return a reference to a mutable array? A `String` or an immutable array clearly is a *value*, but the case is far less clear-cut for a mutable object or array—your method may return an array with its elements in ascending order, but some other code may change one of its elements later.

If we're really interested in functional-style programming in Java, then there needs to be linguistic support for saying "immutable value." As noted in chapter 13, the keyword `final` doesn't really achieve this—it only stops the field it qualifies from being updated; consider this:

```
final int[] arr = {1, 2, 3};
final List<T> list = new ArrayList<>();
```

The former forbids another assignment `arr = ...` but doesn't forbid `arr[1]=2`; the latter forbids assignments to `list` but doesn't forbid other methods from changing the number of elements in `list`! The keyword `final` works well for primitive values, but for references to objects, it often merely gives a false sense of security.

What we're leading up to is this: given that functional-style programming puts a strong emphasis on not mutating existing structure, there's a strong argument for a keyword such as `transitively_final`, which can qualify fields of reference type and which ensures that no modification can take place to the field *nor to any object directly or indirectly accessible via that field.*

Such types represent one intuition about values: values are immutable, and only variables (which contain values) may be mutated to contain a different immutable value. As we remarked at the head of this section, Java authors including ourselves sometimes have inconsistently talked about the possibility of a Java value being a mutable array. In the next section, we return to proper intuition and discuss the idea of a *value type*; these can only contain immutable values, even if variables of value type can still be updated, unless qualified with `final`.

16.2.6 Value types

In this section, we discuss the difference between *primitive types* and *object types,* linking into the discussion earlier about the desire for *value types,* which help you to write programs functionally, just as object types are necessary for object-oriented programming.

Many of the issues we discuss are interrelated, so there's no easy way to explain one problem in isolation. Instead we identify the problem by its various facets.

CAN'T THE COMPILER TREAT INTEGER AND INT IDENTICALLY?

Given all the implicit boxing and unboxing that Java has slowly acquired since Java 1.1, you might ask whether it's time for Java to treat, for example, `Integer` and `int` identically and to rely on the Java compiler to optimize into the best form for the JVM.

This would be a wonderful idea in principle, but let's consider the problems surrounding adding the type `Complex` to Java to see why boxing is problematic. The type `Complex`, which models so-called complex numbers having real and imaginary parts, is naturally introduced as follows:

```
class Complex {
    public final double re;
    public final double im;
    public Complex(double re, double im) {
        this.re = re;
        this.im = im;
    }
     public static Complex add(Complex a, Complex b) {
        return new Complex(a.re+b.re, a.im+b.im);
     }
}
```

But values of type `Complex` are reference types, and every operation on `Complex` needs to do an object allocation—dwarfing the cost of the two additions in `add`. What we need is a primitive-type analog of `Complex`, perhaps called `complex`.

The issue here is that we want an "unboxed object," and neither Java nor the JVM has any real support for this. Now we can return to the lament, "Oh, but surely the compiler can optimize this." Sadly, this is much harder than it appears; although there is a compiler optimization based on so-called escape analysis, which can sometimes determine that unboxing is okay, its applicability is limited by Java's assumptions on `Objects`, which have been present since Java 1.1. Consider the following puzzler:

```
double d1 = 3.14;
double d2 = d1;
Double o1 = d1;
Double o2 = d2;
Double ox = o1;
System.out.println(d1 == d2 ? "yes" : "no");
System.out.println(o1 == o2 ? "yes" : "no");
System.out.println(o1 == ox ? "yes" : "no");
```

The result is "yes", "no", "yes." An expert Java programmer would probably say, "What silly code, everyone knows you should use `equals` on the last two lines instead of `==`." But let us persist. Even though all these primitives and objects contain the immutable value 3.14 and should really be indistinguishable, the definitions of `o1` and `o2` create new objects, and the `==` operator (identity comparison) can tell them apart. Note that on primitives, the identity comparison does bitwise comparison but on objects it does reference equality. So often, we accidentally create a new distinct `Double` object, which the compiler needs to respect because the semantics of `Object`, from which `Double` inherits, require this. You've seen this discussion before, both in the earlier discussion of value types and in chapter 14, where we discussed referential transparency of methods that functionally update persistent data structures.

VALUE TYPES—NOT EVERYTHING IS A PRIMITIVE OR AN OBJECT

We suggest that the resolution of this problem is to rework the Java assumptions (1) that everything that isn't a primitive is an object and hence inherits `Object`, and (2) that all references are references to objects.

The development starts like this. There are two forms of values: those of `Object` type that have mutable fields unless forbidden with `final`, and those of identity, which may be tested with `==`. There are also *value types*, which are immutable and which don't have reference identity; primitive types are a subset of this wider notion. We could then allow user-defined value types (perhaps starting with a lowercase letter to emphasize their similarity to primitive types such as `int` and `boolean`). On value types, `==` would, by default, perform an element-by-element comparison in the same way that hardware comparison on `int` performs a bit-by-bit comparison. You can see this being overridden for floating-point comparison, which performs a somewhat more sophisticated operation. The type `Complex` would be a perfect example of a non-primitive value type; such types resemble C# *structs*.

In addition, value types can reduce storage requirements because they don't have reference identity. Figure 16.1 illustrates an array of size three, whose elements 0, 1, and 2 are light gray, white, and dark gray, respectively. The left diagram shows a typical storage requirement when `Pair` and `Complex` are `Objects` and the right shows the better layout when `Pair` and `Complex` are value types (note that we called them `pair` and `complex` in lowercase in the diagram to emphasize their similarity to primitive types). Note also that value types are also likely to give better performance, not only for data access (multiple levels of pointer indirection replaced with a single indexed-addressing instruction) but also for hardware cache utilization (due to data contiguity).

Note that because value types don't have reference identity, the compiler can then box and unbox them at its choice. If you pass a `complex` as argument from one function to another, then the compiler can naturally pass it as two separate doubles. (Returning it without boxing is trickier in the JVM, of course, because the JVM only provides method-return instructions passing values representable in a 64-bit machine register.) But if you pass a larger value type as an argument (perhaps a large immutable array), then the compiler can instead, transparently to the user, pass it as a reference once it has been boxed. Similar technology already exists in C#; quoting Microsoft:[5]

---

[5] To learn about the syntax and usage of structs and the differences between classes and structs, see http://msdn.microsoft.com/en-us/library/aa288471(v=vs.71).aspx.

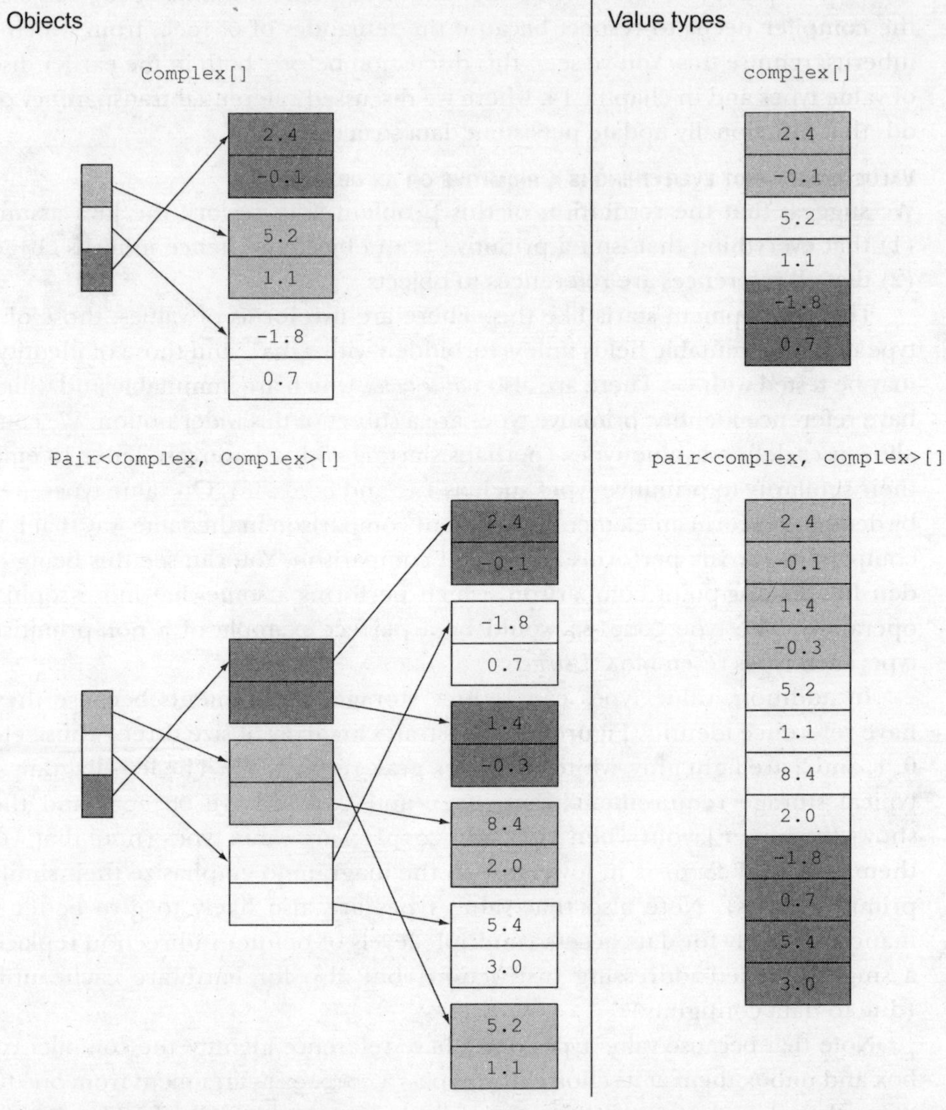

Figure 16.1 Objects vs. value types

> Structs may seem similar to classes, but there are important differences that you should be aware of. First of all, classes are [C#] reference types and structs are value types. By using structs, you can create objects [sic] that behave like the built-in [primitive] types and enjoy their benefits as well.

At the time of writing (June 2014) there's a concrete proposal for value types in Java.[6]

---

[6] John Rose, et al., "State of the Values," April 2014 Infant Edition, http://cr.openjdk.java.net/~jrose/values/values-0.html.

BOXING, GENERICS, VALUE TYPES—THE INTERDEPENDENCY PROBLEM

We'd like to have value types in Java, because functional-style programs deal with immutable values that don't have identity. We'd like to see primitive types as a special case of value types, but the erasure model of generics, which Java currently has, means that value types can't be used with generics without boxing. Object (boxed) versions (for example, `Integer`) of primitive types (for example, `int`) continue to be vital for collections and Java generics because of their erasure model, but now their inheriting `Object` (and hence reference equality) is seen as a drawback. Addressing any one of these problems means addressing them all.

16.3 The final word

This book has explored the new features added by Java 8; these represent perhaps the biggest evolution step ever taken by Java—the only comparably large evolution step was the introduction, 10 years previously, of generics in Java 5. In this chapter we also looked at pressures for further Java evolution. In conclusion, we propose the following statement:

> Java 8 is an excellent place to pause but not to stop!

We hope you've enjoyed the adventure that is Java 8, and that we've sparked your interests in exploring functional programming and in the further evolution of Java.

appendix A Miscellaneous language updates

In this appendix, we discuss three other language updates in Java 8: repeated annotations, type annotations, and generalized target-type inference. Appendix B discusses library updates in Java 8. We don't discuss JDK 8 updates such as Nashorn and Compact Profiles because they're new JVM features. This book focuses on *library* and *language* updates. We invite you to read the following links if you're interested in Nashorn and Compact Profiles: http://openjdk.java.net/projects/nashorn/ and http://openjdk.java.net/jeps/161.

A.1 Annotations

The annotation mechanism in Java 8 has been enhanced in two ways:

- You can repeat annotations.
- You can annotate any type uses.

Before we explain these updates, it's worth quickly refreshing what you could do with annotations before Java 8.

Annotations in Java are a mechanism that lets you decorate program elements with additional information (note that prior to Java 8 only declarations could be annotated). In other words, it's a form of *syntactic metadata*. For example, annotations are popular with the JUnit framework. In the following code, the method `setUp` is annotated with the annotation `@Before`, and the method `testAlgorithm` is annotated with `@Test`:

```
@Before
public void setUp(){
    this.list = new ArrayList<>();
}
```

```
@Test
public void testAlgorithm(){
    ...
    assertEquals(5, list.size());
}
```

Annotations are suitable for several use cases:

- In the context of JUnit, annotations can differentiate methods that should be run as a unit test and methods that are used for setup work.
- Annotations can be used for documentation. For instance, the `@Deprecated` annotation is used to indicate that a method should no longer be used.
- The Java compiler can also process annotations in order to detect errors, suppress warnings, or generate code.
- Annotations are popular in Java EE, where they're used to configure enterprise applications.

A.1.1 *Repeated annotations*

Previous versions of Java forbid more than one annotation of a given annotation type to be specified on a declaration. For this reason, the following code is invalid:

```
@interface Author { String name(); }
@Author(name="Raoul") @Author(name="Mario")  @Author(name="Alan")   <-- Error: duplicate annotation
class Book{ }
```

Java EE programmers often make use of an idiom to circumvent this restriction. You declare a new annotation, which contains an array of the annotation you want to repeat. It looks like this:

```
@interface Author { String name(); }
@interface Authors {
    Author[] value();
}
@Authors(
   { @Author(name="Raoul"), @Author(name="Mario") , @Author(name="Alan")}
)
class Book{}
```

The nested annotation on the `Book` class is pretty ugly. This is why Java 8 essentially removes this restriction, which tidies things a bit. You're now allowed to specify multiple annotations of the same annotation type on a declaration, provided they stipulate that the annotation is repeatable. It's not the default behavior; you have to explicitly ask for an annotation to be repeatable.

MAKING AN ANNOTATION REPEATABLE

If an annotation has been designed to be repeatable, you can just use it. But if you're providing annotations for your users, then setup is required to specify that an annotation can be repeated. There are two steps:

1. Mark the annotation as `@Repeatable`.
2. Provide a container annotation.

Here's how you can make the `@Author` annotation repeatable:

```
@Repeatable(Authors.class)
@interface Author { String name(); }
@interface Authors {
    Author[] value();
}
```

As a result, the `Book` class can be annotated with multiple `@Author` annotations:

```
@Author(name="Raoul") @Author(name="Mario")  @Author(name="Alan")
class Book{ }
```

At compile time `Book` is considered to be annotated by `@Authors({ @Author(name="Raoul"), @Author(name="Mario"), @Author(name="Alan")})`, so you can view this new mechanism as syntactic sugar around the previous idiom used by Java programmers. Annotations are still wrapped in a container to ensure behavioral compatibility with legacy reflection methods. The method `getAnnotation(Class<T> annotationClass)` in the Java API returns the annotation of type `T` for an annotated element. Which annotation should this method return if there are several annotations of type `T`?

Without diving into too much detail, the class `Class` supports a new `getAnnotationsByType` method that facilitates working with repeatable annotations. For example, you can use it as follows to print all the `Author` annotations on the `Book` class:

```
public static void main(String[] args) {
    Author[] authors = Book.class.getAnnotationsByType(Author.class);
    Arrays.asList(authors).forEach(a -> { System.out.println(a.name()); });
}
```

Retrieve an array consisting of the repeatable `Author` annotations

For this to work, both the repeatable annotation and its container must have a `RUNTIME` retention policy. More information about compatibility with legacy reflection methods can be found here: http://cr.openjdk.java.net/~abuckley/8misc.pdf.

A.1.2 Type annotations

As of Java 8, annotations can be also applied to any type uses. This includes the `new` operator, type casts, `instanceof` checks, generic type arguments, and `implements` and `throws` clauses. Here we indicate that the variable `name` of type `String` can't be `null` using a `@NonNull` annotation:

```
@NonNull String name = person.getName();
```

Similarly, you can annotate the type of the elements in a list:

```
List<@NonNull Car> cars = new ArrayList<>();
```

Why is this interesting? Annotations on types can be useful to perform program analysis. In these two examples, a tool could ensure that `getName` doesn't return `null` and that the elements of the list of cars are always non-`null`. This can help reduce unexpected errors in your code.

Java 8 doesn't provide official annotations or a tool to use them out of the box. It provides only the ability to use annotations on types. Luckily, a tool called the Checker framework exists, which defines several type annotations and lets you enhance type checking using them. If you're curious, we invite you to take a look at its tutorial: http://www.checker-framework.org. More information about where you can use annotations in your code can be found here: http://docs.oracle.com/javase/specs/jls/se8/html/jls-9.html#jls-9.7.4.

A.2 Generalized target-type inference

Java 8 enhances the inference of generic arguments. You're already familiar with type inference using context information before Java 8. For example, the method emptyList in Java is defined as follows:

```
static <T> List<T> emptyList();
```

The method emptyList is parameterized with the type parameter T. You can call it as follows to provide an explicit type to the type parameter:

```
List<Car> cars = Collections.<Car>emptyList();
```

But Java is capable of inferring the generic argument. The following is equivalent:

```
List<Car> cars = Collections.emptyList();
```

Before Java 8, this inference mechanism based on the context (that is, target typing) was limited. For example, the following wasn't possible:

```
static void cleanCars(List<Car> cars) {
}
cleanCars(Collections.emptyList());
```

You'd get the following error:

```
cleanCars (java.util.List<Car>)cannot be applied to
     (java.util.List<java.lang.Object>)
```

To fix it you'd have to provide an explicit type argument like the one we showed previously.

In Java 8 the target type includes arguments to a method, so you don't need to provide an explicit generic argument:

```
List<Car> cleanCars = dirtyCars.stream()
                                .filter(Car::isClean)
                                .collect(Collectors.toList());
```

In this code, it's exactly this enhancement that lets you write Collectors.toList() instead of Collectors.<Car>toList().

appendix B Miscellaneous library updates

This appendix reviews the main additions to the Java library.

B.1 Collections

The biggest update to the Collections API is the introduction of streams, which we discussed in chapters 4–6. There are also other updates, which we briefly review in this appendix.

B.1.1 Additional methods

The Java API designers made the most out of default methods and added several new methods to collection interfaces and classes. The new methods are listed in table B.1.

Table B.1 New methods added to collection classes and interfaces

Class/interface	New methods
`Map`	`getOrDefault, forEach, compute, computeIfAbsent, computeIfPresent, merge, putIfAbsent, remove(key, value), replace, replaceAll`
`Iterable`	`forEach, spliterator`
`Iterator`	`forEachRemaining`
`Collection`	`removeIf, stream, parallelStream`
`List`	`replaceAll, sort`
`BitSet`	`stream`

MAP

The `Map` interface is the most updated interface, with support for several new convenient methods. For example, the method `getOrDefault` can be used to replace an existing idiom that checks whether a `Map` contains a mapping for a given key. If not, you can provide a default value to return instead. Previously you would do this:

```
Map<String, Integer> carInventory = new HashMap<>();
Integer count = 0;
if(map.containsKey("Aston Martin")){
  count = map.get("Aston Martin");
}
```

You can now more simply do the following:

```
Integer count = map.getOrDefault("Aston Martin", 0);
```

Note that this works only if there's no mapping. For example, if the key is explicitly mapped to the value `null`, then no default value will be returned.

Another particularly useful method is `computeIfAbsent`, which we briefly mentioned in chapter 14 when explaining memoization. It lets you conveniently use the caching pattern. Let's say that you need to fetch and process data from different websites. In such a scenario, it's useful to cache the data, so you don't have to execute the (expensive) fetching operation multiple times:

```
public String getData(String url){
    String data = cache.get(url);
    if(data == null){                    <-- Check if the data is already cached.
        data = getData(url);
        cache.put(url, data);            <-- If not, fetch the data and then cache it in the Map for future use.
    }
    return data;
}
```

You can now write this code more concisely by using `computeIfAbsent` as follows:

```
public String getData(String url){
    return cache.computeIfAbsent(url, this::getData);
}
```

A description of all other methods can be found in the official Java API documentation.[1] Note that `ConcurrentHashMap` was also updated with additional methods. We discuss them in section B.2.

COLLECTION

The `removeIf` method can be used to remove all elements in a collection that match a predicate. Note that this is different than the `filter` method included in the Streams API. The `filter` method in the Streams API produces a new stream; it doesn't mutate the current stream or source.

---

1 See http://docs.oracle.com/javase/8/docs/api/java/util/Map.html.

List

The replaceAll method replaces each element in a List with the result of applying a given operator to it. It's similar to the map method in a stream, but it mutates the elements of the List. In contrast, the map method produces new elements.

For example, the following code will print [2, 4, 6, 8, 10] because the List is modified in place:

```
List<Integer> numbers = Arrays.asList(1, 2, 3, 4, 5);
numbers.replaceAll(x -> x * 2);
System.out.println(numbers);
```

Prints [2, 4, 6, 8, 10]

B.1.2 The Collections class

The Collections class has been around for a long time to operate on or return collections. It now includes additional methods to return unmodifiable, synchronized, checked, and empty NavigableMap and NavigableSet. In addition, it includes the method checkedQueue, which returns a view of Queue that's extended with dynamic type checking.

B.1.3 Comparator

The Comparator interface now includes default and static methods. You used the Comparator.comparing static method in chapter 3 to return a Comparator object given a function that extracts the sorting key.

New instance methods include the following:

- reversed—Returns a Comparator with the reverse ordering of the current Comparator.
- thenComparing—Returns a Comparator that uses another Comparator when two objects are equal.
- thenComparingInt, thenComparingDouble, thenComparingLong—Work like the thenComparing method but take a function specialized for primitive types (respectively, ToIntFunction, ToDoubleFunction, and ToLongFunction).

New static methods include these:

- comparingInt, comparingDouble, comparingLong—Work like the comparing method but take a function specialized for primitive types (respectively ToIntFunction, ToDoubleFunction, and ToLongFunction).
- naturalOrder—Returns a Comparator object that imposes a natural order on Comparable objects.
- nullsFirst, nullsLast—Return a Comparator object that considers null to be less than non-null or greater than non-null.
- reverseOrder–Equivalent to naturalOrder().reversed().

B.2 Concurrency

Java 8 brings several updates related to concurrency. The first is, of course, the introduction of parallel streams, which we explore in chapter 7. There's also the introduction of the `CompletableFuture` class, which you can learn about in chapter 11.

There are other noticeable updates. For example, the `Arrays` class now supports parallel operations. We discuss these operations in section B.3.

In this section, we look at updates in the `java.util.concurrent.atomic` package, which deals with atomic variables. In addition, we discuss updates to the `ConcurrentHashMap` class, which supports several new methods.

B.2.1 Atomic

The `java.util.concurrent.atomic` package offers several numeric classes, such as `AtomicInteger` and `AtomicLong` that support atomic operation on single variables. They were updated to support new methods:

- `getAndUpdate`—Atomically updates the current value with the results of applying the given function, returning the previous value.
- `updateAndGet`—Atomically updates the current value with the results of applying the given function, returning the updated value.
- `getAndAccumulate`—Atomically updates the current value with the results of applying the given function to the current and given values, returning the previous value.
- `accumulateAndGet`—Atomically updates the current value with the results of applying the given function to the current and given values, returning the updated value.

Here's how to atomically set the minimum between an observed value of 10 and an existing atomic integer:

```
int min = atomicInteger.accumulateAndGet(10, Integer::min);
```

ADDERS AND ACCUMULATORS

The Java API recommends using the new classes `LongAdder`, `LongAccumulator`, `DoubleAdder`, and `DoubleAccumulator` instead of the `Atomic` classes equivalent when multiple threads update frequently but read less frequently (for example, in the context of statistics). These classes are designed to grow dynamically to reduce thread contention.

The classes `LongAdder` and `DoubleAdder` support operations for additions, whereas `LongAccumulator` and `DoubleAccumulator` are given a function to combine values. For example, to calculate the sum of several values, you can use a `LongAdder` as follows.

Listing B.1 `LongAdder` to calculate the sum of values

```
LongAdder adder = new LongAdder();      // The initial sum value is set to 0 with the default constructor.
adder.add(10);                          // Do some addition in several different threads.
// ...
long sum = adder.sum();                 // Get the sum at some point.
```

Or you can use a LongAccumulator as follows.

Listing B.2 LongAccumulator to calculate the sum of values

```
LongAccumulator acc = new LongAccumulator(Long::sum, 0);
acc.accumulate(10);
// ...
long result = acc.get();
```

Accumulate values in several different threads.

Get the result at some point.

B.2.2 *ConcurrentHashMap*

The ConcurrentHashMap class was introduced to provide a more modern HashMap, which is concurrent friendly. ConcurrentHashMap allows concurrent add and updates that lock only certain parts of the internal data structure. Thus, read and write operations have improved performance compared to the synchronized Hashtable alternative.

PERFORMANCE

ConcurrentHashMap's internal structure was updated to improve performance. Entries of a map are typically stored in buckets accessed by the generated hashcode of the key. But if many keys return the same hashcode, performance will deteriorate because buckets are implemented as Lists with O(n) retrieval. In Java 8, when the buckets become too big, they're dynamically replaced with sorted trees, which have O(log(n)) retrieval. Note that this is possible only when the keys are Comparable (for example, String or Number classes).

STREAM-LIKE OPERATIONS

ConcurrentHashMap supports three new kinds of operations reminiscent of what you saw with streams:

- forEach—Performs a given action for each (key, value)
- reduce—Combines all (key, value) given a reduction function into a result
- search—Applies a function on each (key, value) until the function produces a non-null result

Each kind of operation supports four forms, accepting functions with keys, values, Map.Entry, and (key, value) arguments:

- Operates with keys and values (forEach, reduce, search)
- Operates with keys (forEachKey, reduceKeys, searchKeys)
- Operates with values (forEachValue, reduceValues, searchValues)
- Operates with Map.Entry objects (forEachEntry, reduceEntries, searchEntries)

Note that these operations don't lock the state of the ConcurrentHashMap. They operate on the elements as they go along. The functions supplied to these operations shouldn't depend on any ordering or on any other objects or values that may change while computation is in progress.

In addition, you need to specify a parallelism threshold for all these operations. The operations will execute sequentially if the current map size is estimated to be less than the given threshold. Using a value of `1` enables maximal parallelism using the common thread pool. Using a value of `Long.MAX_VALUE` runs the operation on a single thread.

In this example we use the method `reduceValues` to find the maximum value in the `map`:

```
ConcurrentHashMap<String, Integer> map = new ConcurrentHashMap<>();
Optional<Integer> maxValue =
    Optional.of(map.reduceValues(1, Integer::max));
```

Note that there are primitive specializations for `int`, `long`, and `double` for each `reduce` operation (for example, `reduceValuesToInt`, `reduceKeysToLong`, and so on).

COUNTING

The `ConcurrentHashMap` class provides a new method called `mappingCount`, which returns the number of mappings in the `map` as a `long`. It should be used instead of the method `size`, which returns an `int`. This is because the number of mappings may not fit in an `int`.

SET VIEWS

The `ConcurrentHashMap` class provides a new method called `keySet` that returns a view of the `ConcurrentHashMap` as a `Set` (changes to the `map` are reflected in the `Set` and vice versa). You can also create a `Set` backed by a `ConcurrentHashMap` using the new static method `newKeySet`.

B.3 Arrays

The `Arrays` class provides various static methods to manipulate arrays. It now includes four new methods (which have primitive specialized overloaded variants).

B.3.1 Using parallelSort

The `parallelSort` method sorts the specified array in parallel, using a natural order, or using an extra `Comparator` for an array of objects.

B.3.2 Using setAll and parallelSetAll

The `setAll` and `parallelSetAll` methods set all elements of the specified array, respectively sequentially or in parallel, using the provided function to compute each element. The function receives the element index and returns a value for that index. Because `parallelSetAll` is executed in parallel, the function must be side-effect free, as explained in chapters 7 and 13.

As an example, you can use the method `setAll` to produce an array with the values 0, 2, 4, 6, ...:

```
int[] evenNumbers = new int[10];
Arrays.setAll(evenNumbers, i -> i * 2);
```

B.3.3 Using parallelPrefix

The `parallelPrefix` method cumulates, in parallel, each element of the given array, using the supplied binary operator. In the next listing you produce the values 1, 2, 3, 4, 5, 6, 7, ...

Listing B.3 `parallelPrefix` cumulates in parallel elements of an array

```
int[] ones = new int[10];
Arrays.fill(ones, 1);
Arrays.parallelPrefix(ones, (a, b) -> a + b);
```

ones is now [1, 2, 3, 4, 5, 6, 7, 8, 9, 10]

B.4 Number and Math

The Java 8 API enhances the `Number` and `Math` classes with new methods.

B.4.1 Number

The new methods of the `Number` class are as follows:

- The `Short`, `Integer`, `Long`, `Float`, and `Double` classes include the `sum`, `min`, and `max` static methods. You saw these methods in conjunction with the `reduce` operation in chapter 5.
- The `Integer` and `Long` classes include the methods `compareUnsigned`, `divideUnsigned`, `remainderUnsigned`, and `toUnsignedString` to work with unsigned values.
- The `Integer` and `Long` classes also respectively include the static methods `parseUnsignedInt` and `parseUnsignedLong`, to parse strings as an unsigned `int` or `long`.
- The `Byte` and `Short` classes include the methods `toUnsignedInt` and `toUnsignedLong`, to convert the argument to an `int` or `long` by an unsigned conversion. Similarly, the `Integer` class now includes the static method `toUnsignedLong`.
- The `Double` and `Float` classes include the static method `isFinite`, to check whether the argument is a finite floating-point value.
- The `Boolean` class now includes the static methods `logicalAnd`, `logicalOr`, and `logicalXor`, to apply the and, or, and xor operations between two `boolean`s.
- The `BigInteger` class includes the methods `byteValueExact`, `shortValueExact`, `intValueExact`, and `longValueExact`, to convert this `BigInteger` to the respective primitive type. But it throws an arithmetic exception if there's a loss of information during the conversion.

B.4.2 Math

The `Math` class includes new methods that throw an arithmetic exception if the result of the operation overflows. These methods consist of `addExact`, `subtractExact`, `multiplyExact`, `incrementExact`, `decrementExact`, and `negateExact` with `int` and `long` arguments. In addition, there's a static `toIntExact` method to convert a `long` value to an `int`. Other additions include the static methods `floorMod`, `floorDiv`, and `nextDown`.

B.5 Files

Noticeable additions to the `Files` class let you produce a stream from files. We mentioned the new static method `Files.lines` in chapter 5; it lets you read a file lazily as a stream. Other useful static methods that return a stream include the following:

- `Files.list`—Produces a `Stream<Path>` consisting of entries in a given directory. The listing isn't recursive. Because the stream is consumed lazily, it's a useful method for processing potentially very large directories.
- `Files.walk`—Just like `Files.list`, it produces a `Stream<Path>` consisting of entries in a given directory. But the listing is recursive and the depth level can be configured. Note that the traversal is performed depth-first.
- `Files.find`—Produces a `Stream<Path>` from recursively traversing a directory to find entries that match a given predicate.

B.6 Reflection

We discussed several changes to the annotation mechanism in Java 8 in appendix A. The Reflection API was updated to support these changes.

Another addition to the Reflection API is that information about parameters of methods such as names and modifiers can now be accessed with the help of the new `java.lang.reflect.Parameter` class, which is referenced in the new `java.lang.reflect.Executable` class that serves as a shared superclass for the common functionality of `Method` and `Constructor`.

B.7 String

The `String` class now includes a convenient static method called `join` to—as you may guess—join strings with a delimiter! You can use it as follows:

```
String authors = String.join(", ", "Raoul", "Mario", "Alan");
System.out.println(authors);
```

Raoul, Mario, Alan

appendix C
Performing multiple operations in parallel on a stream

One of the biggest limitations of a Java 8 stream is that you can operate on it only once and get only one result while processing it. Indeed, if you try to traverse a stream for a second time, the only thing you can achieve is an exception like this:

```
java.lang.IllegalStateException: stream has already been operated upon or closed
```

Despite this, there are situations where you'd like to get several results when processing a single stream. For instance, you may want to parse a log file in a stream, as we did in section 5.7.3, but gather multiple statistics in a single step. Or, keeping with the menu data model used to explain `Stream`'s features in chapters 4–6, you may want to retrieve different information while traversing the stream of dishes.

In other words, you'd like to push a stream through more than one lambda on a single pass, and to do this you need a type of `fork` method and to apply different functions to each forked stream. Even better, it would be great if you could perform those operations in parallel, using different threads to calculate the different required results.

Unfortunately, these features aren't currently available on the stream implementation provided in Java 8, but in this appendix we'll show you a way to use a `Spliterator` and in particular its late-binding capacity, together with `BlockingQueues` and `Futures`, to implement this useful feature and make it available with a convenient API.[1]

1 The implementation presented in the rest of this appendix is based on the solution posted by Paul Sandoz in the email he sent to the lambda-dev mailing list: http://mail.openjdk.java.net/pipermail/lambda-dev/2013-November/011516.html.

C.1 Forking a stream

The first thing necessary to execute multiple operations in parallel on a stream is to create a `StreamForker` that wraps the original stream, on which you can define the different operations you want to perform. Take a look at the following listing.

Listing C.1 Defining a `StreamForker` to execute multiple operations on a stream

```
public class StreamForker<T> {

    private final Stream<T> stream;
    private final Map<Object, Function<Stream<T>, ?>> forks =
                                                    new HashMap<>();

    public StreamForker(Stream<T> stream) {
        this.stream = stream;
    }

    public StreamForker<T> fork(Object key, Function<Stream<T>, ?> f) {
        forks.put(key, f);                  // Index the function to be applied on the stream with a key.
        return this;                        // Return this to fluently invoke the fork method multiple times.
    }

    public Results getResults() {
        // To be implemented
    }
}
```

Here the `fork` method accepts two arguments:.

- A `Function`, which transforms the stream into a result of any type representing one of these operations
- A key, which will allow you to retrieve the result of that operation and accumulates these key/function pairs in an internal `Map`

The `fork` method returns the `StreamForker` itself; therefore, you can build a pipeline by forking several operations. Figure C.1 shows the main ideas behind the `StreamForker`.

Here the user defines three operations to be performed on a stream indexed by three keys. The `StreamForker` then traverses the original stream and forks it into three other streams. At this point the three operations can be applied in parallel on the forked streams, and the results of these function applications, indexed with their corresponding keys, are used to populate the resulting `Map`.

The execution of all the operations added through the `fork` method is triggered by the invocation of the method `getResults`, which returns an implementation of the `Results` interface defined as follows:

```
public static interface Results {
    public <R> R get(Object key);
}
```

This interface has only one method to which you can pass one of the key `Objects` used in one of the `fork` methods, and that method returns the result of the operation corresponding to that key.

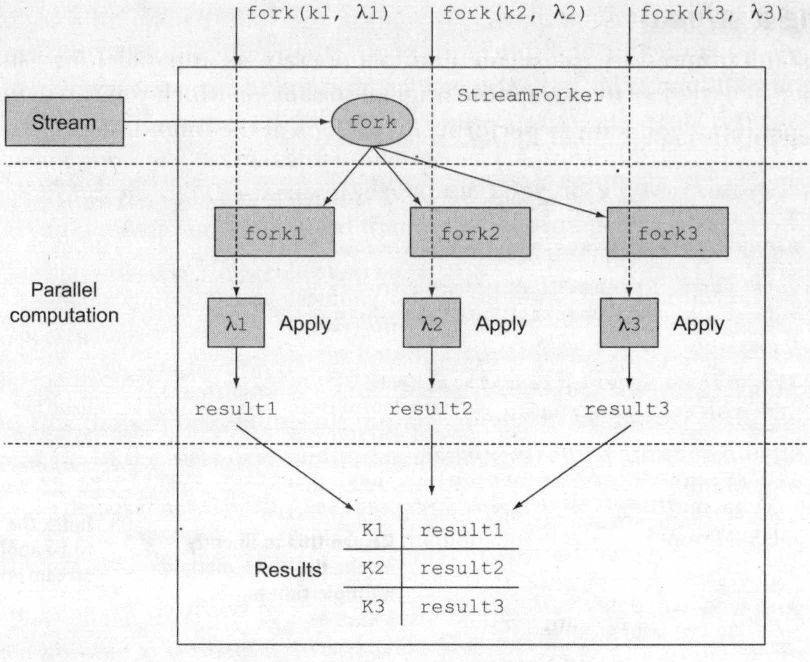

Figure C.1 The `StreamForker` in action

C.1.1 Implementing the Results interface with the ForkingStreamConsumer

The `getResults` method can be implemented as follows:

```
public Results getResults() {
    ForkingStreamConsumer<T> consumer = build();
    try {
        stream.sequential().forEach(consumer);
    } finally {
        consumer.finish();
    }
    return consumer;
}
```

The `ForkingStreamConsumer` implements both the `Results` interface defined previously and the `Consumer` interface. As you'll see when we analyze its implementation in more detail, its main task is to consume all the elements in the stream and multiplex them to a number of `BlockingQueues` equal to the number of operations submitted via the `fork` method. Note that it is ensured that the stream is sequential, because if the method `forEach` were performed on a parallel stream, its elements could be pushed to the queues out of order. The `finish` method adds special elements to those queues to signal that there are no more items to be processed. The `build` method used to create the `ForkingStreamConsumer` is shown in the next listing.

Listing C.2 The build method used to create ForkingStreamConsumer

```
private ForkingStreamConsumer<T> build() {
    List<BlockingQueue<T>> queues = new ArrayList<>();    <-- Create a list of queues, with a queue for each operation.

    Map<Object, Future<?>> actions =    <-- Map the Futures that will contain the results of the operations with the keys used to identify those operations.
            forks.entrySet().stream().reduce(
                    new HashMap<Object, Future<?>>(),
                    (map, e) -> {
                        map.put(e.getKey(),
                                getOperationResult(queues, e.getValue()));
                        return map;
                    },
                    (m1, m2) -> {
                        m1.putAll(m2);
                        return m1;
                    });

    return new ForkingStreamConsumer<>(queues, actions);
}
```

In listing C.2, you first create the `List` of `BlockingQueues` mentioned previously. Then you create a `Map`, having as keys the same keys used to identify the different operations to be executed on the stream, and having as values the `Futures` that will contain the corresponding results of these operations. The `List` of `BlockingQueues` and the `Map` of `Futures` are then passed to the constructor of the `ForkingStreamConsumer`. Each `Future` is created with this `getOperationResult` method, as shown in the next listing.

Listing C.3 Futures created with the getOperationResult method

```
private Future<?> getOperationResult(List<BlockingQueue<T>> queues,
                                     Function<Stream<T>, ?> f) {
    BlockingQueue<T> queue = new LinkedBlockingQueue<>();
    queues.add(queue);    <-- Create a queue and add it to the list of queues.
    Spliterator<T> spliterator = new BlockingQueueSpliterator<>(queue);    <-- Create a Spliterator traversing the elements in that queue.
    Stream<T> source = StreamSupport.stream(spliterator, false);    <-- Create a stream having that Spliterator as source.
    return CompletableFuture.supplyAsync( () -> f.apply(source) );    <-- Create a Future calculating asynchronously the application of the given function on that stream.
}
```

The method `getOperationResult` creates a new `BlockingQueue` and adds it to the `List` of queues. This queue is passed to a new `BlockingQueueSpliterator`, which is a late-binding `Spliterator`, reading the item to be traversed from the queue; we'll examine how it's made shortly.

You then create a sequential stream traversing this `Spliterator`, and finally you create a `Future` to calculate the result of applying the function representing one of the operations you want to perform on this stream. This `Future` is created using a static factory method of the `CompletableFuture` class that implements the `Future` interface. This is another new class introduced in Java 8, and we investigated it in detail in chapter 11.

C.1.2 Developing the ForkingStreamConsumer and the BlockingQueueSpliterator

The last two outstanding parts you need to develop are the `ForkingStreamConsumer` and `BlockingQueueSpliterator` classes we introduced previously. The first one can be implemented as follows.

Listing C.4 A `ForkingStreamConsumer` to add stream elements to multiple queues

```
static class ForkingStreamConsumer<T> implements Consumer<T>, Results {
    static final Object END_OF_STREAM = new Object();

    private final List<BlockingQueue<T>> queues;
    private final Map<Object, Future<?>> actions;

    ForkingStreamConsumer(List<BlockingQueue<T>> queues,
                          Map<Object, Future<?>> actions) {
        this.queues = queues;
        this.actions = actions;
    }

    @Override
    public void accept(T t) {
        queues.forEach(q -> q.add(t));
    }

    void finish() {
        accept((T) END_OF_STREAM);
    }

    @Override
    public <R> R get(Object key) {
        try {
            return ((Future<R>) actions.get(key)).get();
        } catch (Exception e) {
            throw new RuntimeException(e);
        }
    }
}
```

Propagates the traversed element of the stream to all the queues.

Adds one last element to the queue to signal that the stream is finished.

Returns the result of the operation indexed by the given key and waits for the completion of the `Future` calculating it.

This class implements both the `Consumer` and `Results` interfaces and holds a reference to the `List` of `BlockingQueues` and to the `Map` of `Futures` executing the different operations on the stream.

The `Consumer` interface requires an implementation for the method `accept`. Here, every time `ForkingStreamConsumer` accepts an element of the stream, it adds that element to all the `BlockingQueues`. Also, after all the elements of the original stream have been added to all queues, the `finish` method causes one last item to be added to all of them. This item, when met by `BlockingQueueSpliterators`, will make the queues understand that there are no more elements to be processed.

The `Results` interface requires an implementation for the `get` method. Here, it retrieves the `Future` that's indexed in the `Map` with the argument key and unwraps its result or waits until a result is available.

Finally, there will be a `BlockingQueueSpliterator` for each operation to be performed on the stream. Each `BlockingQueueSpliterator` will have a reference to one of the `BlockingQueues` populated by the `ForkingStreamConsumer`, and it can be implemented as shown in the following listing.

Listing C.5 A `Spliterator` reading the elements it traverses from a `BlockingQueue`

```
class BlockingQueueSpliterator<T> implements Spliterator<T> {
    private final BlockingQueue<T> q;

    BlockingQueueSpliterator(BlockingQueue<T> q) {
        this.q = q;
    }

    @Override
    public boolean tryAdvance(Consumer<? super T> action) {
        T t;
        while (true) {
            try {
                t = q.take();
                break;
            } catch (InterruptedException e) { }
        }

        if (t != ForkingStreamConsumer.END_OF_STREAM) {
            action.accept(t);
            return true;
        }

        return false;
    }

    @Override
    public Spliterator<T> trySplit() {
        return null;
    }
    @Override
    public long estimateSize() {
        return 0;
    }

    @Override
    public int characteristics() {
        return 0;
    }
}
```

In this listing a `Spliterator` is implemented, not to define the policy of how to split a stream but only to use its late-binding capability. For this reason the `trySplit` method is unimplemented.

Also, it's impossible to return any meaningful value from the `estimatedSize` method because you can't foresee how many elements can be still taken from the queue. Further, because you're not attempting any split, this estimation will be useless.

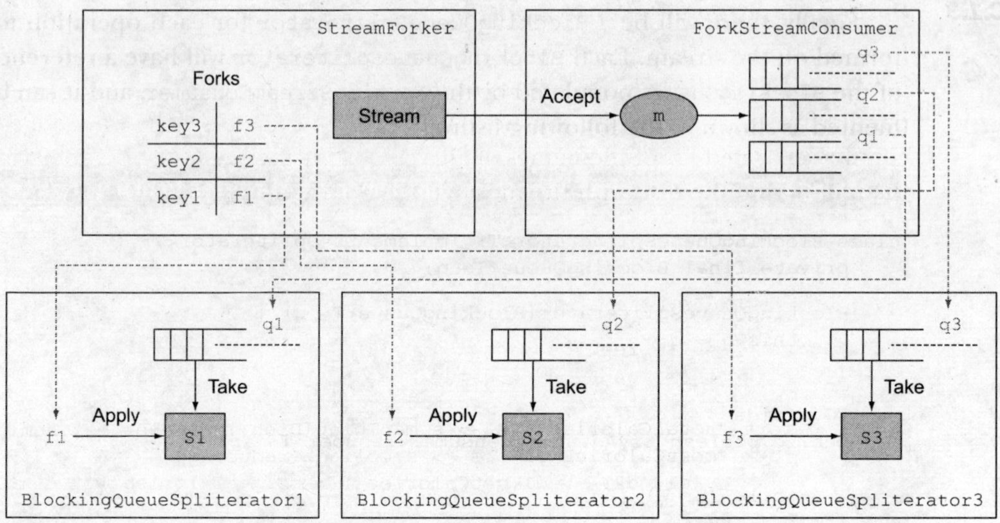

Figure C.2 The `StreamForker` building blocks

This implementation doesn't have any of the `Spliterator` characteristics we listed in table 7.2, so the `characteristic` method returns `0`.

The only method implemented here is `tryAdvance`, which waits to take from its `BlockingQueue` the elements of the original stream added to it by the `ForkingStream-Consumer`. It sends those elements to a `Consumer` that (based on how this `Spliterator` was created in the `getOperationResult` method) is the source of a further stream (on which the corresponding function, passed to one of the `fork` method invocations, has to be applied). The `tryAdvance` method returns `true`, to notify its invoker that there are other elements to be consumed, until it finds on the queue the special `Object` added by `ForkingStreamConsumer` to signal that there are no more elements to be taken from the queue. Figure C.2 shows an overview of the `StreamForker` and its building blocks.

In the figure, the `StreamForker` in the upper left has a `Map`, where each operation to be performed on the stream, defined by a function, is indexed by a key. The `ForkingStreamConsumer` on the right holds a queue for each of these operations and consumes all the elements in the original stream, multiplexing them to all the queues.

At the bottom of the figure, each queue has a `BlockingQueueSpliterator` pulling its items and acting as a source for a different stream. Finally, each of these streams, forked by the original one, is passed as argument to one of the functions, thus executing one of the operations to be performed. You now have all the components of your `StreamForker`, so it's ready to use.

C.1.3 Putting the StreamForker to work

Let's put the `StreamForker` to work on the menu data model that we defined in chapter 4, by forking the original stream of dishes to perform four different operations in parallel on it, as shown in the next listing. In particular, you want to generate a comma-separated list of the names of all available dishes, calculate the total calories of the menu, find the dish with the most calories, and group all dishes by their type.

Listing C.6 Putting the `StreamForker` to work

```
Stream<Dish> menuStream = menu.stream();

StreamForker.Results results = new StreamForker<Dish>(menuStream)
        .fork("shortMenu", s -> s.map(Dish::getName)
                                 .collect(joining(", ")))
        .fork("totalCalories", s -> s.mapToInt(Dish::getCalories).sum())
        .fork("mostCaloricDish", s -> s.collect(reducing(
                (d1, d2) -> d1.getCalories() > d2.getCalories() ? d1 : d2))
                .get())
        .fork("dishesByType", s -> s.collect(groupingBy(Dish::getType)))
        .getResults();

String shortMenu = results.get("shortMenu");
int totalCalories = results.get("totalCalories");
Dish mostCaloricDish = results.get("mostCaloricDish");
Map<Dish.Type, List<Dish>> dishesByType = results.get("dishesByType");

System.out.println("Short menu: " + shortMenu);
System.out.println("Total calories: " + totalCalories);
System.out.println("Most caloric dish: " + mostCaloricDish);
System.out.println("Dishes by type: " + dishesByType);
```

The `StreamForker` provides a convenient, fluent API to fork a stream and assign a different operation to each forked stream. These operations are expressed in terms of functions applied on the stream and can be identified by any arbitrary object; in this case we've chosen to use `Strings`. When you have no more forks to add, you can invoke `getResults` on the `StreamForker` to trigger the execution of all the defined operations and obtain `StreamForker.Results`. Because these operations are internally performed asynchronously, the `getResults` method returns immediately, without waiting for all the results to be available.

You can obtain the result of a specific operation by passing the key used to identify it to the `StreamForker.Results` interface. If in the meantime the computation of that operation completes, the `get` method will return the corresponding result; otherwise, it will block until such a result isn't available.

As expected, this piece of code generates the following output:

```
Short menu: pork, beef, chicken, french fries, rice, season fruit, pizza,
    prawns, salmon
Total calories: 4300
Most caloric dish: pork
Dishes by type: {OTHER=[french fries, rice, season fruit, pizza], MEAT=[pork,
    beef, chicken], FISH=[prawns, salmon]}
```

C.2 Performance considerations

For performance reasons you shouldn't take for granted that this approach is more efficient than traversing the stream several times. The overhead caused by the use of the blocking queues can easily outweigh the advantages of executing the different operations in parallel when the stream is made of data that's all in memory.

Conversely, accessing the stream only once could be a winning choice when this involves some expensive I/O operations, such as when the source of the stream is a huge file; so (as usual) the only meaningful rule when optimizing the performance of your application is to "Just measure it!"

This example demonstrates how it can be possible to execute multiple operations on the same stream in one shot. More importantly, we believe this proves that even when a specific feature isn't provided by the native Java API, the flexibility of lambda expressions and a bit of creativity in reusing and combining what's already available can let you implement the missing feature on your own.

appendix D
Lambdas and JVM bytecode

You may wonder how the Java compiler implements lambda expressions and how the Java virtual machine (JVM) deals with them. If you think lambda expressions can simply be translated to anonymous classes, you should read on. This appendix briefly discusses how lambda expressions are compiled, by examining the generated class files.

D.1 Anonymous classes

We showed in chapter 2 that anonymous classes can be used to declare and instantiate a class at the same time. As a result, just like lambda expressions, they can be used to provide the implementation for a functional interface.

Because a lambda expression provides the implementation for the abstract method of a functional interface, it would seem straightforward to ask the Java compiler to translate a lambda expression into an anonymous class during the compilation process. But anonymous classes have some undesirable characteristics that impact the performance of applications:

- *The compiler generates a new class file for each anonymous class.* The filename usually looks like `ClassName$1`, where `ClassName` is the name of the class in which the anonymous class appears, followed by a dollar sign and a number. The generation of many class files is undesirable, because each class file needs to be loaded and verified before being used, which impacts the startup performance of the application. If lambdas were translated to anonymous classes, you'd have one new class file for each lambda.
- *Each new anonymous class introduces a new subtype for a class or interface.* If you had a hundred different lambdas for expressing a `Comparator`, that would

mean a hundred different subtypes of Comparator. In certain situations, this can make it harder to improve runtime performance by the JVM.

D.2 Bytecode generation

A Java source file is compiled to Java bytecode by the Java compiler. The JVM can then execute the generated bytecode and run the application. Anonymous classes and lambda expressions use different bytecode instructions when they're compiled. You can inspect the bytecode and constant pool of any class file using the command

```
javap -c -v ClassName
```

Let's try to implement an instance of the Function interface using the old Java 7 syntax, as an anonymous inner class, as shown in the following listing.

Listing D.1 A Function implemented as an anonymous inner class

```
import java.util.function.Function;
public class InnerClass {
    Function<Object, String> f = new Function<Object, String>() {
        @Override
        public String apply(Object obj) {
            return obj.toString();
        }
    };
}
```

Doing this, the corresponding generated bytecode for the Function created as an anonymous inner class will be something along the lines of this:

```
 0: aload_0
 1: invokespecial #1        // Method java/lang/Object."<init>":()V
 4: aload_0
 5: new           #2        // class InnerClass$1
 8: dup
 9: aload_0
10: invokespecial #3        // Method InnerClass$1."<init>":(LInnerClass;)V
13: putfield      #4        // Field f:Ljava/util/function/Function;
16: return
```

This code shows the following:

- An object of type InnerClass$1 is instantiated using the bytecode operation new. A reference to the newly created object is pushed on the stack at the same time.
- The operation dup duplicates that reference on the stack.
- This value then gets consumed by the instruction invokespecial, which initializes the object.
- The top of the stack now still contains a reference to the object, which is stored in the f1 field of the LambdaBytecode class using the putfield instruction.

InnerClass$1 is the name generated by the compiler for the anonymous class. If you want to reassure yourself, you can inspect the InnerClass$1 class file as well, and you'll find the code for the implementation of the Function interface:

```
class InnerClass$1 implements
        java.util.function.Function<java.lang.Object, java.lang.String> {
  final InnerClass this$0;
  public java.lang.String apply(java.lang.Object);
    Code:
       0: aload_1
       1: invokevirtual #3 //Method
                              java/lang/Object.toString:()Ljava/lang/String;
       4: areturn
}
```

D.3 *InvokeDynamic to the rescue*

Now let's try to do the same using the new Java 8 syntax as a lambda expression. Inspect the generated class file of the code in the following listing.

Listing D.2 A Function implemented with a lambda expression

```
import java.util.function.Function;
public class Lambda {
    Function<Object, String> f = obj -> obj.toString();
}
```

You'll find the following bytecode instructions:

```
 0: aload_0
 1: invokespecial #1        // Method java/lang/Object."<init>":()V
 4: aload_0
 5: invokedynamic #2,  0 // InvokeDynamic
                             #0:apply:()Ljava/util/function/Function;
10: putfield      #3        // Field f:Ljava/util/function/Function;
13: return
```

We explained the drawbacks in translating a lambda expression in an anonymous inner class, and indeed you can see that the result is very different. The creation of an extra class has been replaced with an invokedynamic instruction.

The invokedynamic instruction

The bytecode instruction invokedynamic was introduced in JDK7 to support dynamically typed languages on the JVM. invokedynamic adds a further level of indirection when invoking a method, to let some logic dependent on the specific dynamic language determine the call target. The typical use for this instruction is something like the following:

```
def add(a, b) { a + b }
```

Here the types of a and b aren't known at compile time and can change from time to time. For this reason, when the JVM executes an invokedynamic for the first time,

> ***(continued)***
> it consults a bootstrap method, implementing the language-dependent logic that determines the actual method to be called. The bootstrap method returns a linked call site. There's a good chance that if the `add` method is called with two `int`s, the subsequent call will also be with two `int`s. As a result, it's not necessary to rediscover the method to be called at each invocation. The call site itself can contain the logic defining under which conditions it needs to be relinked.

In listing D.2, the features of the `invokedynamic` instruction have been used for a slightly different purpose than the one for which they were originally introduced. In fact, here it's used to delay the strategy used to translate lambda expressions in bytecode until runtime. In other words, using `invokedynamic` in this way allows deferring code generation for implementing the lambda expression until runtime. This design choice has positive consequences:

- The strategy used to translate the lambda expression body to bytecode becomes a pure implementation detail. It could also be changed dynamically, or optimized and modified in future JVM implementations, preserving the bytecode's backward compatibility.
- There's no overhead, such as additional fields or static initializer, if the lambda is never used.
- For stateless (noncapturing) lambdas it's possible to create one instance of the lambda object, cache it, and always return the same. This is a common use case, and people were used to doing this explicitly before Java 8; for example, declaring a specific `Comparator` instance in a static final variable.
- There's no additional performance cost because this translation has to be performed, and its result linked, only when the lambda is invoked for the first time. All subsequent invocations can skip this slow path and call the formerly linked implementation.

D.4 Code-generation strategies

A lambda expression is translated into bytecode by putting its body into one of a static method created at runtime. A stateless lambda, one that captures no state from its enclosing scope, like the one we defined in listing D.2, is the simplest type of lambda to be translated. In this case the compiler can generate a method having the same signature of the lambda expression, so the result of this translation process can be logically seen as follows:

```
public class Lambda {
    Function<Object, String> f = [dynamic invocation of lambda$1]

    static String lambda$1(Object obj) {
        return obj.toString();
    }
}
```

The case of a lambda expression capturing final (or effectively final) local variables or fields, as in the following example, is a bit more complex:

```
public class Lambda {
    String header = "This is a ";
    Function<Object, String> f = obj -> header + obj.toString();
}
```

In this case the signature of the generated method can't be the same as the lambda expression, because it's necessary to add extra arguments to carry the additional state of the enclosed context. The simplest solution to achieve this is to prepend the arguments of the lambda expression with an additional argument for each of the captured variables, so the method generated to implement the former lambda expression will be something like this:

```
public class Lambda {
    String header = "This is a ";
    Function<Object, String> f = [dynamic invocation of lambda$1]

    static String lambda$1(String header, Object obj) {
        return obj -> header + obj.toString();
    }
}
```

More information about the translation process for lambda expressions can be found here: http://cr.openjdk.java.net/~briangoetz/lambda/lambda-translation.html.

index